Property

T. W. Mares
114 East Whidby
Port Angeles Wash
98362

THE BATTLE OF SICILY

THE BATTLE OF SICILY

Samuel W. Mitcham, Jr.

Friedrich von Stauffenberg

ORION BOOKS • NEW YORK

Copyright © 1991 by Samuel W. Mitcham, Jr.,
and the estate of Friedrich von Stauffenberg

Published by Orion Books,
a division of Crown Publishers, Inc., 201 East 50th Street,
New York, New York 10022.
Member of the Crown Publishing Group.

ORION and colophon are trademarks of Crown Publishers, Inc.

Manufactured in the United States of America

Library of Congress Cataloging-in-Publication Data

Mitcham, Samuel W.
    Battle of Sicily / Samuel W. Mitcham, Jr., and
    Friedrich von Stauffenberg.—1st ed.
        p.   cm.
Includes bibliographical references and index.
1. World War, 1939–1945—Campaigns—Italy—Sicily. 2. Sicily
(Italy)—History—1870–1945. I. Stauffenberg, Friedrich von.
II. Title.
D763.S5M58   1991
940.54'2158—dc20   90-25168
                                                                    CIP

ISBN 0-517-57525-6
Book Design by Shari deMiskey
10 9 8 7 6 5 4 3 2 1
First Edition

CONTENTS

Maps

Maps

Tables

Acknowledgments

First of all, I would like to acknowledge the fine support provided by the Institute for Military History at the Army War College, Carlisle Barracks, Pennsylvania, which provided me with many of the unpublished documents used in this book, as well as access to its outstanding library and photograph collections. Thanks also go to the staffs of the United States National Archives, the Bundesarchiv, the Imperial War Museum, and to the department of history and the library of the United States Military Academy at West Point.

Thanks also go to Barbara Roberts and Valerie Newcomb, the interlibrary loan librarians for Huie Library, Henderson State University, Arkadelphia, Arkansas. Appreciation is extended to Professor Paula Lemming of Henderson's foreign language department for helping to translate difficult passages from German to English and helping to draft correspondence. The support of Drs. Charles Dunn, Joe T. Clark, and Gene Mueller of Henderson is also gratefully acknowledged. Finally, saving the best for last, thanks go to Donna Mitcham, a woman with the patience of a saint, for assisting in innumerable ways and for proofreading the various versions of this manuscript for what must have seemed like a million times.

S.W.M.

Introduction

THE ALLIED INVASION OF SICILY CONTINUES TO PROVOKE INTEREST IN the United States almost fifty years after it was fought. There are a number of reasons that this operation captures our imagination, including the heroics and histrionics of George Patton; the fact that it was our first amphibious invasion of the mainland of Europe and our first landing against German opposition; and because the American army came of age on the beaches and barren hillsides of Sicily, proving for the first in its own eyes and the eyes of the world that it was equal to the British army and worthy to be its full partner. The stain of Kasserine Pass was wiped out at Gela, Palermo, and especially Messina. Many Americans think that the German army took a severe beating in Sicily, and, when General Patton won the race for Messina, he permanently established the reputation of the U.S. Army as a force to be reckoned with.

Although Friedrich von Stauffenberg and I agree on a number of these points, we do not believe the German army was as badly damaged as Allied propagandists of the time indicated. Unfortunately, their lead has been followed by a number of historians. Our book takes a more balanced approach to this topic. We also take an opposing view on the subject of the race for Messina. This "race" (and I am uncomfortable calling it that) was not between Patton and Montgomery; rather, it was a three-party affair, and it was won by General Hans Valentin Hube, commander of the XIVth Panzer Corps. For thirty-eight days his weak forces held off two full Allied armies. Their peak strength totaled well in excess of 400,000 men; Hube never commanded more than 65,000 Germans. In the end he pulled off a masterful evacuation and escaped to the mainland of Italy with his entire command—despite unreliable allies, the fact that his rear was constantly exposed to enemy amphibious landings, and the fact that the Allies had complete supremacy of the air and sea and a six-to-one superiority on the ground. While Hube was accomplishing all this, Hitler was capturing Italy, a process that was incomplete when Hube finished evacuating Sicily but had gone so far by then that it was irreversible.

The purpose of this book is to tell the story of the Battle of Sicily primarily from the point of view of the Axis military commanders. Allied actions are normally covered only insofar as they affected the Axis situation or influenced Axis military reactions. Primary among these Allied actions was the decision to invade Sicily in the first place—a strategic move which we hold to be fundamentally flawed. A more proper target would have been northwestern France or (if the landings *had* to come in the Mediterranean) the shores of Sardinia, which was less well defended and exposed more of Italy to a subsequent invasion. The Sicilian landings doomed the Allies to a prolonged battle of attrition up the bloody Italian peninsula—hardly a brilliant stroke of military genius.

This study of Axis military operations in Sicily has two major and interrelated subthemes. First, it provides a look at the deterioration of the Axis at the military level. Second, it gives the reader insight into a number of fascinating characters who are virtually unknown to most English speakers. The German commander Hube, for example, had only one arm; the other had been blown off at Verdun in World War I. When the German army reorganized in 1919, it could keep only four thousand officers under the terms of the harsh Treaty of Versailles. Hube was the only handicapped officer retained. He proved to be a good choice. Not afraid of Hitler (or anyone else), he refused to obey a Fuehrer order that he fly out of the doomed fortress of Stalingrad, stating that he had ordered his men to fight to the last round and now he was going to show them how to do it! He had to be taken out at gunpoint by SS men. General Fries was also handicapped. He had lost both an arm and a leg at Rzhev in 1942, less than a year before he led the 29th Panzer Grenadier Division against Patton in Sicily. Even more fascinating was Ernst-Guenther Baade, a colorful Afrika Korps veteran who went into battle wearing a Scottish kilt and carrying a double-edged broadsword.

In addition to giving me the opportunity to study these fascinating characters and this interesting campaign in depth, *The Battle of Sicily* afforded me the opportunity to work closely with a distinguished gentleman, Friedrich von Stauffenberg, who was also a good personal friend. He was the first cousin of Colonel Count Claus von Stauffenberg, the officer who wounded Hitler during the nearly successful attempt on the dictator's life. Friedrich's father was also an aristocrat and a German General Staff officer. His son had extensive contacts with the men of the old *Panzerwaffe*, a topic that held his interest until the end. Unfortunately, he died of a prolonged illness before this book could be completed. It is dedicated to his memory and to his granddaughter, Clarissa Friedelinde Meeks. Von, you will be sorely missed.

SAMUEL W. MITCHAM, JR.

Arkadelphia, Arkansas

THE BATTLE OF SICILY

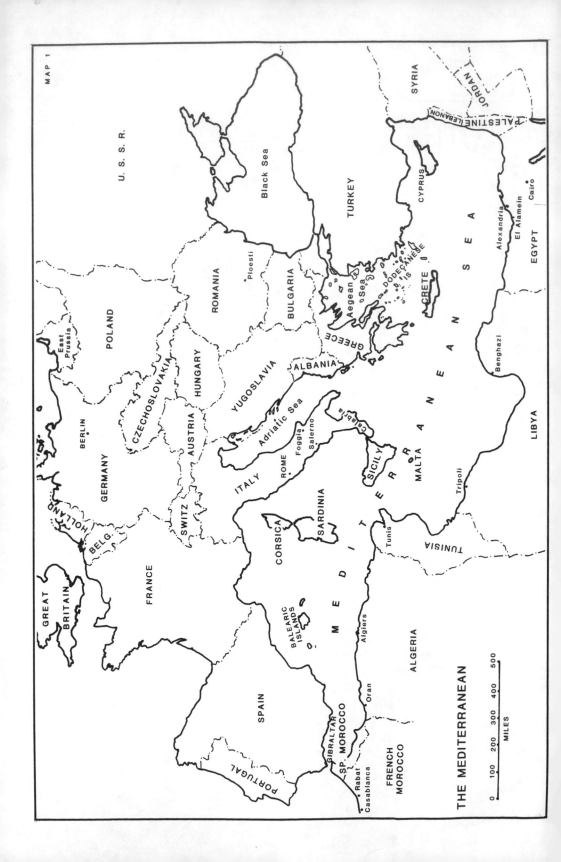

MAP 1

THE MEDITERRANEAN

0   100   200   300   400   500

MILES

✧ 1 ✧

THE GREAT BLUNDER

FIELD MARSHALL ERWIN ROMMEL, THE FAMOUS DESERT FOX, WAS AN angry man on November 24, 1942, exactly as he had been almost continuously since October 24. On that day he had cut short a stay at a hospital near Vienna and returned to North Africa to find his Panzer Army Afrika on the verge of collapse and under heavy attack at El Alamein by General Sir Bernard Law Montgomery's British 8th Army. Rommel put up a valiant defense, but the odds against him were overwhelming: Monty had 195,000 men, 1,029 tanks, 908 guns, 1,403 antitank guns, and 750 aircraft. Rommel had about half as many in each category, but too many of his Italian units were ill-equipped, prone to panic, and unwilling to fight for a corrupt and incompetent dictatorship in Rome. Rommel faced Monty with only 50,000 Germans, equipped with 211 panzers, 200 guns, 444 antitank guns, and 275 aircraft. Perhaps even more important, his supply lines across the Mediterranean were all but cut by the Royal Air Force and Royal Navy. For two weeks Rommel dashed from point to point, counterattacking here, defending there—using all his tactical genius to reimpose a stalemate on the British, despite his own steadily diminishing resources. Finally, on the afternoon of November 2, the dam broke. The last thirty-five tanks of the elite 8th Panzer Regiment—one of the two armored regiments of the Afrika Korps—launched a desperate counterattack against four hundred British tanks that were on the verge of breaking through. It was wiped out. Every single panzer was destroyed. Colonel Willy Teege, the regimental commander, died with his men. That night Rommel ordered a general retreat, which was delayed twenty-four hours by a senseless order from

1

Hitler—a delay that cost Rommel the bulk of the Italian XXth Motorized Corps. Finally, rather than sacrifice his entire army, the Desert Fox ordered a general retreat on his own initiative on the afternoon of November 4—against the direct orders of the Fuehrer. It was covered by a dozen worn, battered panzers—all that was left of the one-mighty Afrika Korps. From that point on all roads led backward for Panzer Army Afrika and its commander.

With Rommel's star on the wane at Fuehrer Headquarters, the stock of Field Marshall Albert Kesselring was on the rise. Kesselring, who was simultaneously commander in chief, South (Oberbefehlshaber Sued, or OB South) and commander in chief of the 2nd Air Fleet, was a well-mannered product of sophisticated society. He was born in Marktsheet, Bavaria, on November 20, 1885. The son of a professor, he was soundly educated at the Latin School of Bayreuth. He joined the 2nd Bavarian Foot Artillery Regiment as a *Fahnenjunker* (officer-cadet) in 1904 and received his commission in 1906. An associate of Prince Rupprecht's, he served on the Bavarian General Staff in World War I and as adjutant of an artillery regiment. He was transferred to the Luftwaffe (somewhat against his will) in 1933. Although he had distinguished himself as an air fleet commander in Poland, France, the Low Countries, and Russia, he had not directed ground forces since 1932–1933, when he commanded the 4th Artillery Regiment at Dresden. Since December 1941 he had been the senior German officer in the Mediterranean sector. He was also an incurable optimist, whether the situation called for optimism or not. On November 8 approximately 110 Allied troop and cargo ships, supported by 200 warships, desposited 112,000 American and British soldiers at Casablanca, Oran, and Algiers in French North Africa.[1] The French put up a perfunctory resistance, which ceased entirely on November 11. Rommel was now caught between two fires. Hitler, however, ordered Kesselring to transport as many troops from southern Europe to Tunis as rapidly as possible in order to establish a bridgehead in Tunisia. (Eventually these forces were designated 5th Panzer Army, under Colonel General Hans-Juergen "Dieter" von Arnim. See Appendix 1 for a table of comparative ranks.) Far from objecting to this hair-raising piece of strategic stupidity, Kesselring became one of its major advocates. Eventually this operation would cost the Axis almost 250,000 men—half of them German.

Erwin Rommel had other ideas. He could not see the wisdom of stripping the defense of southern Europe and sending irreplaceable men into a bridgehead with no depth across a sea over which the enemy had naval and aerial superiority. Instead, he advocated abandoning North Africa altogether and retiring to a defensible position in northern Italy. As early as November 11 he signaled requests to Kesselring and Marshal Ugo Cavallero, chief of the High Command of the Italian Armed Forces (Commando Supremo), asking them to come to his headquarters to discuss withdrawing the remnants of Panzer Army Afrika to Europe. Neither marshal considered it necessary to discuss these matters with Rommel, and the Desert Fox was too busy trying to get the survivors of El Alamein out of Egypt to visit them, so he dispatched Lieutenant Dr. Alfred Berndt to Germany to present his case directly to Hitler.

Doctor Berndt was no ordinary lieutenant. A former high-ranking official in the propaganda ministry, he was Rommel's de facto public relations officer, and a very effective one at that. He was also an influential Nazi who was respected by Hitler and most of his cronies.[2] This time, however, his mission was a failure. Hitler received him in Munich on November 12 and curtly gave him a message for Rommel: leave Tunisia out of your calculations and act upon the assumption that the bridgehead would be held. There would be no evacuation of Africa. Hitler also promised to send him everything he needed to rebuild his scattered forces, but, given the demands of Tunisia and the Eastern Front, Rommel knew how empty a promise this was. His already low spirits sank lower each day.

Despite his deepening depression and ill health (he fainted several times that week), Rommel conducted a masterful retreat from El Alamein to Mersa el Brega, more than eight hundred miles away. Aided by Montgomery's lack of aggression, he escaped the vastly superior 8th Army despite a lack of supplies and absolute Allied control of the sea and air. In the meantime, Rommel's temper grew worse and worse. Kesselring failed to keep his promise to fly in 250 tons of supplies a day and was delivering only about 60 tons a day. Despite these shortages, Rommel was able to install his men safely behind the Mersa el Brega line virtually without loss. Nevertheless, the veteran panzer army was crippled. This was the situation on November 24, when Marshals

Cavallero and Kesselring finally deigned to come to Libya. Their meeting with Rommel took place near the marble arch called Arco dei Fileini, on the Cyrenaica-Tripolitania border, and it was stormy.

During the three-hour conference Rommel bluntly described the situation to the overly optimistic Kesselring, Cavallero, and Italian Marshal Ettore Bastico, Rommel's nominal superior in North Africa. His army's German elements were reduced to the fighting strength of one weak division, Rommel said, and his three remaining Italian divisions were useless. He had only 35 tanks and 57 antitank guns, while Montgomery had more than 420 tanks and 300 armored cars, 400 guns, and 550 antitank guns, plus complete command of the air. Rommel demanded fifty 75-mm antitank guns, fifty Panzer Mark IV (PzKw IV) special tanks, and seventy-eight large-caliber guns, plus at least four thousand tons of fuel and four thousand tons of ammunition. Furthermore, Rommel declared, he must have them within ten days or he would be forced to retreat to Tripolitania. He broached the subject of evacuation, but here "I came up against the solid opposition of Kesselring and Cavallero," Rommel recorded later. It was clear to the Desert Fox that they "had not come with any intention of learning from events and thus forming a rational judgment; they believed the fault lay with us and thought they could improve our fighting spirit with bombastic and magniloquent phrases. Me, they regarded as a pessimist of the first order. . . ."[3] The meeting ended without any agreements.

Two days later Rommel received new orders—a consequence of the Arco dei Fileini meeting. Giving orders through Marshal Bastico, Mussolini reiterated his demand that the Mersa el Brega line be held. He even ordered Rommel to attack the British. Furthermore, Rommel was not to retreat any farther without Bastico's permission. Naturally, this order infuriated the Desert Fox. On an impulse he boarded a Heinkel and flew to Fuehrer Headquarters in East Prussia for a personal audience with Adolf Hitler. He felt sure that he could convince the dictator of the folly of the current strategy once Hitler knew all the facts.

Rommel's airplane landed at three P.M. He was met by Field Marshal Wilhelm Keitel, commander in chief of the Armed Forces High Command (Oberkommando des Wehrmacht, or OKW); General of Artillery Alfred Jodl, chief of operations at OKW; and Major General Rudolf Schmundt, chief of the army personnel office. Schmundt was friendly, as usual; however, Keitel and Jodl were "extremely wary and reserved."[4] Rommel ignored this warning sign. At five P.M. he was ushered into the Fuehrer's presence.

Adolf Hitler was in a foul mood. In Russia, General Friedrich Paulus's 6th Army had been surrounded at Stalingrad, and Hitler was feverishly planning a rescue operation and an emergency airlift. The last thing he wanted to hear was a gloomy report from the commander of a momentarily quiet, secondary front. "There was a noticeable chill in the air from the outset," Rommel recalled later.[5] Hitler greeted the Desert Fox rudely: "How dare you leave your theater of command without my permission?"[6]

Again Rommel ignored the warning signs and launched into a carefully prepared speech, describing the depleted state of his forces and the failure of the Italian supply system on which his army depended. Unfortunately, he came too quickly to the point, stating that the situation in North Africa was hopeless and that the abandonment of the region should be accepted as long-term strategic policy.

Hitler exploded. For the first time Rommel was treated to one of his famous scenes. The supreme war lord even went so far as to suggest that the men of the Afrika Korps had thrown their weapons away in their haste to escape from the British.

Unlike Keitel, Field Marshal Rommel was not accustomed to being addressed in this manner. He interrupted the Fuehrer's tirade and declared, bluntly and loudly: "Africa cannot be held! The only thing left for us is to try and transport as many Germans out of Africa as we can."[7]

At that point Hitler *really* exploded. He called Rommel a defeatist and accused his men of being cowards. Generals who had made this sort of suggestion in Russia had been shot, he bellowed. He would not yet do that to Rommel, he declared, but the field marshal had better be careful. Not intimidated, Erwin Rommel again tried to bring the discussion back to the Mediterranean—to explain the causes for his defeat at El Alamein and the reasons why North Africa should be abandoned. Continually interrupted by Reichsmarschall Hermann Goering, commander in chief of the Luftwaffe, the conquerer of Tobruk tried to press home his arguments. At one point the Fuehrer banged his fist on the table and screamed: "Withdraw from Africa!?! Never!" Turning to Keitel, he asked the OKW chieftain what arms they had at Naples.

Six thousand rifles, Keitel replied.

"Send them over at once," Hitler ordered, as if he had just solved all Rommel's problems.

Not to be fobbed off with six thousand rifles, Rommel asked, "Of what use would they be, Mein Fuehrer?" In spite of Hitler's violent and unreasonable attitude, he continued to evaluate the situation in North Africa logically and concluded that it simply could not be held. "Let me withdraw the panzer army to Italy so that it can defend the Continent against Eisenhower's anticipated invasion."

"I no longer want to hear such rubbish from your lips," Hitler replied, his voice ice-cold. "North Africa will be defended as Stalingrad will. Eisenhower's invading army will be defeated at the Italian front door and not in the Sicilian parlor." Rommel tried to continue, but Hitler cut him off again. "North Africa will be defended and not evacuated. That is an order, Herr Generalfeldmarschall!" Again out of control, Hitler raved on and on about the Eastern Front in the winter of 1941–1942 and how only his hold-at-all-costs order had saved the army. Now he expected his orders to be ruthlessly obeyed in Africa as well.

Rommel interrupted to ask whether it was better to lose Tripoli or the Afrika Korps.

The Afrika Krops did not matter, Hitler replied. It would have to fight to the bitter end.

Rommel, now scarlet with rage at Hitler's tantrum, invited Hitler or some members of his entourage to come to Africa and show them how to do it.

"Go!" Hitler screamed, completely unglued. "I have other things to do than to talk to you!"

Rommel saluted, turned on his heel, and walked out. Although Hitler immediately ran after him to apologize for his behavior, the damage was done.[8] Rommel was disillusioned with Hitler, and Hitler was fed up with Rommel. And the great strategic decision had been made. "Europe is being defended at Tunis," Hitler declared.[9] Any organized evacuation was forbidden. Even worse than this, Hitler insisted on reinforcing Tunisia with everything he could lay his hands on. Initially he sent in the Headquarters, XCth Corps (General of Panzer Troops Walter Nehring), with little more than the 5th Parachute Regiment and the 11th Parachute

Engineer Battalion, but these units were soon reinforced with the veteran 10th Panzer Division, the Barenthin Glider Regiment, the Italian Superga Division (also known as the 1st Assault and Landing Division) from Italy, and the 50th Special Brigade from Tripoli. Later, on December 18, General Nehring, a veteran panzer leader and the former commander of the Afrika Korps, was relieved of his command for being what Berndt and Goebbels called an "outspoken pessimist"[10] (i.e., he agreed with Rommel on the issue of holding Tunisia). His headquarters was upgraded and redesignated 5th Panzer Army, and he was replaced by General von Arnim. Still the units were rushed across: a newly formed "Tiger" tank detachment (the 501st), the ad hoc Division von Manteuffel, Kampfgruppe (Battle Group) Schmid of the elite Hermann Goering Panzer Division, and the 999th and 334th Infantry divisions—all fresh units at or near strength. Altogether, Arnim alone had more than a hundred thousand men. Not only this, but Rommel's battered army was reinforced and the Luftwaffe contributed new formations as well—fighter wings, bomber groups, torpedo squadrons. Hitler virtually stripped his southern flank to reinforce Tunisia, a very risky procedure considering the tenuousness of his supply lines. Yet thanks to the Fuehrer's orders, more men and equipment were arriving every day.

In January 1943 Rommel abandoned Tripoli (as he predicted he would be forced to do), and his Panzer Army Afrika entered the Tunisian bridgehead. It included two veteran German panzer divisions, two light divisions, and a German parchute brigade. It also included two Italian armored divisions, two Italian motorized divisions, four Italian infantry ("semi-motorized") divisions, and the elite Folgore Parachute Division. Later other Italian divisions were added. No doubt about it: the panzer army controlled a formidable array of forces—on paper. Unfortunately, all of its units were under strength, and many of them were in remnants. Equally important was the fact that most of its tanks and heavy equipment lay burned out at El Alamein, around Tobruk, on the Gazala Line, at Knightsbridge, Halfaya Pass, Mersa Matruh, Fuka, Benghazi, Agedabia, or any of a dozen other battlefields on the Western Desert. Despite these losses, the *Panzertruppen* turned on their tormentors again in January and February 1943 and distinguished themselves once more, notably against the green U.S. IInd Corps in a local victory at Kasserine Pass. However, fate was against them, and Erwin Rommel (now commander in chief [C-in-C] of Army Group Afrika) knew it. His supplies had to be transported across the Mediterranean by the Italian Navy and merchant marine, and this the Italians could not do. Desperate, the Desert Fox decided to make one more appeal to Adolf Hitler.

The Rommel-Hitler meeting took place at the Fuehrer's secret headquarters in southern Russia on March 10, 1943. During this private and relatively calm discussion, the field marshal offered an unprecedented personal guarantee to successfully defend "our southern European flank" with troops evacuated from Tunisia and reequipped in Italy. Instead, Hitler relieved him of his command. The next day he decorated Rommel with the Oak Leaves, Swords, and Diamonds of the Knight's Cross—just about the highest decoration Nazi Germany had to offer—and sent him off to Semmering in the Austrian Alps for long-overdue medical treatment. Dieter von Arnim succeeded him in command of Army Group Afrika.

The end in Tunisia came quickly after Rommel's departure. Before he left, he and von Arnim had calculated that they would need at least 150,000 tons of supplies per month to hold the bridgehead. The Italian High Command (Commando Supremo) arbitrarily reduced this figure to 120,000 tons (or, rather, to 80,000 tons, since its calculations assumed that up to one third of the tonnage bound for North Africa would be sunk). Unfortunately, the Italian Navy was not able to reach even this modest goal, largely because Kesselring's 2nd Air Fleet was absolutely ineffective in its attempts to protect merchant shipping, or to defeat the U.S. and Royal Air Forces, or to check the Royal Navy. In March von Arnim received only 29,000 tons of supplies, and in April this figure dwindled to 23,000 tons. Shipping losses during this period totaled 41.5 percent of the ships dispatched. In the first week of May Arnim received only two thousand tons. He said later that even without the pressure of the Allied armies, he would have had to capitulate by July 1 because he could no longer feed his soldiers.

Arnim did not have to wait. The Allies began their final offensive on May 6. Many of the panzers of the Afrika Korps sputtered into their last battle propelled by low-grade Tunisian wine. Both Tunis and Bizerte fell on the afternoon of May 7, and mass surrenders began. Colonel General von Arnim was captured on May 12, along with the last remnants of the Afrika Korps. The last resistance ended during the afternoon of May 13. About 240,000 Axis prisoners were taken, including 130,000 Germans. It was a disaster of the first magnitude. The German civilians called it "Tunisgrad."

As if this catastrophe were not enough, Hitler and Mussolini had compounded it by stripping their southern flank of combat units in order to reinforce a lost cause in Tunisia. With Army Group Afrika gone, there was almost nothing left with which to defend their southern flank. Sicily, for example, had only one ad hoc German division and a few marginal Italian formations, and Sardinia had even fewer units. Now Hitler, the Duce, Kesselring, OKW, Comando Supremo, and a host of lesser headquarters were preoccupied with two questions: Where would the Allies strike next, and when?

✧ 2 ✧

UNEASY ALLIES

LIKE THEIR AXIS COUNTERPARTS, THE ALLIED LEADERS HAD A GREAT strategic debate in late 1942. Basically, Allied military planning centered around two schools of thought. The first, which might be labeled the direct approach, was advocated by the Chief of Staff of the United States Army, General George C. Marshall, and his supporters. It called for an invasion of northwestern Europe *in 1943.* The brilliant Marshall had opposed the Allied landings in French North Africa and had made it clear that he considered the entire Mediterranean theater of operations a sideshow that was dangerous because it might distract the Allies from their primary objective. The second school of thought, whose principal architect was General Sir Alan Brooke (later Viscount Alanbrooke), chief of the Imperial General Staff, called for a peripheral (or Mediterranean) strategy of attacking the Germans at points of opportunity, where they were weakest. According to this school, the next step, after North Africa was cleared, should be an invasion of Sicily—a move calculated to knock Italy out of the war. Since this plan was in almost diametric opposition to Marshall's, the top Allied military and political leaders converged on Casablanca in January 1943, where they met in a summit conference to iron out their differences.

Casablanca was the last major strategic conference completely dominated by the British. General Marshall had made the mistake of divulging too much information to his friend Field Marshal Sir John Dill, chief of the British joint staff mission to Washington. According to Brigadier General (later General) Albert C. Wedemeyer, Marshall's chief of war plans, Dill "got extremely close to Marshall and provided the British chiefs and the P.M. with information on Marshall's thinking which Marshall shouldn't have given him." Wedemeyer was convinced that Dill had "sold Marshall short" at Casablanca.[1] The British leadership, agreeing with Brooke, tore Marshall's cross-channel attack plans to pieces, using the information supplied by Dill. "They swarmed down upon us like locusts," General Wedemeyer recalled. "From a worm's eye viewpoint it was apparent that we were confronted by generations and generations of experience in committee work, in diplomacy, and in rationalizing points of view. They had us on the defensive practically all the time."[2]

Marshall, seeing that he had been outmaneuvered, capitulated and, on January 17, agreed to limited operations in Mediterranean Europe following the fall of Tunisia. After further debate, the conferees picked their specific target: Sicily, as recommended by Brooke. Lord Mountbatten and Admiral Andrew B. Cunningham, the gifted commander of the British Mediterranean Fleet, among others, thought Sardinia a more appropriate target, but they were overruled.

The Combined Chiefs of Staff conferred with Churchill and Roosevelt on the evening of January 18, and the next day the decision to invade Sicily was made. Three days later the chiefs decided to launch the invasion on July 10, between moonset at 12:31 A.M. and first light at 4:39 A.M. This timing would give the paratroopers some moonlight to jump by, but the moon would set by the time of the landings, giving as little light as possible to the Italian coastal defense gunners. Later, in his desire to prevent the Germans from reinforcing Sicily and to take advantage of the opportunity for rapid exploitation of the victory in Tunisia, Marshall would urge that the invasion date be moved up to June. He was again unsuccessful, and on April 10 the Combined Chiefs of Staff finalized the date of the invasion as July 10,[3] giving Kesselring another badly needed month to prepare the Axis defenses, but this is getting ahead of our story.

The high command for the invasion was set on January 23. Once again the British domination of the Casablanca Conference was clearly in evidence. General Eisenhower was confirmed as commander in chief of the Allied Expeditionary Force, but he was, in effect, chairman of a committee arrangement based on the British system. All three of his service chiefs were British: Admiral Sir Andrew B. Cunningham, naval commander in chief, Mediterranean; Air Chief Marshal Arthur Tedder, commander in chief, Allied Mediterranean Air Forces; and General Sir Harold Alexander, commander in chief of the 15th Army Group and Ike's deputy C-in-C. Alexander and Headquarters, 15th Army Group, would actually be responsible for overall command of the ground battle.

When the Casablanca Conference adjourned, the principal strategic decisions had been made, and the invasion of Sicily entered the operational planning phase. It had been decided that two major commands would participate in the invasion: the British 8th Army under General Sir Bernard Law Montgomery and the U.S. Ist Armored Corps (later the U.S. 7th Army), whose commander was Lieutenant General George S. Patton, Jr. Both were to be subordinate to Sir Harold Alexander, commander of the 15th Army Group.

Although he had had a very successful military career to date, Alexander had little concept of how to plan operations at the army group level and above and had few ideas of his own. He was far too easily influenced by subordinates who had stronger personalities than he, and this was especially true in the case of Bernard Montgomery. Of Alexander, D'Este wrote:

> He was also one of the most intellectually lazy men ever to hold high command; he loathed detail and paperwork and was never comfortable articulating strategy or in outlining guidance to his staff. As a result, planning at 15th Army Group was chaotic and his staff found it almost impossible to obtain guidance or decisions; Alexander never seemed to know what he wanted.[4]

As the war progressed, even the senior British commanders developed serious doubts about Alex's ability. Cunningham, the First Sea Lord after the death of Pound, described him as "totally unfit for the job" as Allied supreme commander in Italy, and Montgomery wrote that Alexander had a "limited brain" and could not "make up his mind and give quick decisions; he cannot snap out clear and concise orders. . . . The higher art of war is beyond him. . . . And so Alexander has acquired a false reputation as a great commander in the field, and as a great strategist."[5]

During the planning of the Sicilian campaign, Alexander did indeed seem to be out of his depth. Unfortunately, the man he selected as the chief of his Sicilian planning staff (Force 141) was also in over his head, so the planning floundered. The staff produced eight separate plans, all flawed except—arguably—the last.

Plan "Husky 8" called for Patton's army to land on the northwestern coast of Sicily, near Palermo. Montgomery's forces would land near Syracuse, and both would then advance along the coasts toward the strategic objective of the campaign: Messina, the key to the island.

Husky 8 was approved by everyone except Montgomery. This forceful personality, fresh from his victories over the Desert Fox, virtually overruled his superiors and insisted that Patton come ashore at Gela, on the southern coast. Instead of racing for Messina, the Americans would now be charged with protecting Monty's left flank, while the British 8th Army drove on the city. However, much to Patton's disgust, both Eisenhower and Alexander abandoned their previous support for Husky 8 and endorsed Montgomery's plan, which received final approval on May 2. When Alexander told him about the decision and, somewhat embarrassed, asked him if he was satisfied with it, Patton clicked his heels, saluted, and said, "General, I don't plan—I only obey orders." Privately, however, he was furious. "This is what you get when your Commander-in-Chief [Eisenhower] ceases to be an American and becomes an Ally," he fumed to his staff. However, now that the order had been given, Patton loyally accepted the new scheme despite his personal reservations. When Admiral Cunningham tried to persuade Patton to protest the new plan, Patton said, "No, Goddamnit, I've been in this Army thirty years and when my superior gives me an order I say 'Yes, Sir!' and then do my Goddamndest to carry it out."[6]

That was the end of the operational debate. Montgomery had had his way, although he left hard feelings in his wake—a pregnant beginning to the Allied reentry into Europe. As a footnote, Sir Andrew Cunningham went to his grave convinced that Plan 8 should have been executed, as did Patton and many others.

The ham-fisted and time-consuming planning effort represented a defensive victory for the Germans at a time when they had nothing with which to defend Sicily. Since the plan did not receive final approval until May 13, it could not be executed until July 10. B. H. Liddell Hart wrote:

> These delays in the planning were more regrettable since only one of the ten divisions to lead the invasion of Sicily was engaged in the final stages of the North African campaign, and seven of them were fresh entries. A landing in Sicily soon after the Axis collapse in Africa would have found the island almost naked of defense.[7]

As we shall see, the Germans reacted quickly to resolve this situation.

THE DETERIORATING AXIS

IF THE ALLIES HAD A DIFFICULT TIME WORKING TOGETHER, THE situation was even worse on the other side of the Mediterranean. The Rome-Berlin Axis was never much more than a personal alliance between their two dictators, Mussolini and Hitler. In fact, the two peoples had been historic enemies. "The Dark Ages began when the savage vigour of the Germans broke up the system of Mediterranean civilization which the Romans had established," Elizabeth Wiskemann wrote. A "tradition of conflict between Italy and Germany lingered on ever after through the centuries."[1]

This tradition was initially continued by the Fascist regime of Benito Mussolini, which seized power in Rome in October 1922. The turning point in Italo-German relations took place on October 3, 1935, when Italy invaded Ethiopia. Within a week, with only three dissenting votes, both the council and the assembly of the League of Nations branded Italy the aggressor and voted financial and economic sanctions against it. Nazi Germany, which was not a member of the League, ignored the sanctions and helped Italy weather the crisis. "Britain, by her hostile but indecisive sanctions policy, pitched him [Mussolini] right across the Rhine to Hitler," Telford Taylor wrote later.[2] The alliance was formalized in October 1936, when Count Galeazzo Ciano, Italy's new thirty-four-year-old foreign minister and the son-in-law of Mussolini, visited Hitler at Berchtesgaden and established the basis for Italian-German cooperation. Ciano and German Foreign Minister Baron Konstantion von Neurath signed a secret protocol that outlined the two nations' common foreign policy in Berlin on October 21.

The Italian alliance did not exactly fill Germany's enemies with dread. During the Sudetenland crisis, for example, French Minister of Colonies Georges Mandel predicted that in case of war, "Germany will be beaten in six months without Mussolini; in three months with Mussolini."[3] Eight months later, in April 1939, Winston Churchill echoed these sentiments when he remarked, "There is a school of British strategists who hold that in a world struggle with Nazidom it would be a positive advantage to have Italy as an enemy."[4] The reason for this contempt was the poor performance of the Italian "volunteers" in the Spanish Civil War and the absolutely miserable state of unpreparedness into which the Italian armed forces had deteriorated. The Wehrmacht, of course, knew all this, but had no influence on Hitler's foreign policy.

Hitler invaded Poland on September 1, 1939, and Britain and France declared war on Nazi Germany two days later. Realizing the pitiful state of his armed forces—he was simultaneously minister of war, air, and navy—Mussolini refused to enter the conflict. Italy sat on the sidelines until the summer of 1940. Then, when it appeared that Germany had already won the war, Mussolini decided to enter the conflict on Hitler's side, even though only 20 percent of his divisions were at war strength and more than 70 percent of his armored divisions did not have a single tank. Nevertheless, Mussolini thought he could launch an attack, lose a few hundred men, and then sit at the peace table as a full partner and expand his empire even farther for a very cheap price. One is reminded of the words Otto von Bismarck uttered six decades before: Italy "has a large appetite but very poor teeth."[5] It was the beginning of the end for Fascist Italy.

Despite the objections of the senior Italian generals, Mussolini's divisions launched an offensive against French Alpine forces in mixed rain and snow on June 18, 1940. It bogged down immediately. Within a few days the Italian General Staff asked that the German panzer units advancing down the Rhone valley be diverted eastward to help the Italians break out of the mountains. When France surrendered on June 25, the Italian war effort had accomplished virtually nothing; nevertheless, Mussolini was upset that he received very little new territory when the peace terms were signed.

"The sole significance for Germany of the active entrance of Italy into the war in the summer of 1940 was a heavy burden,"

Colonel General Heinrich von Vietinghoff commented later, adding:

> Hitler kept the faith with Mussolini as he did with almost no other human being, to the ruin of both men and of their two peoples. To help him, to support him . . . [Hitler] plunged into the African and Balkan adventures, without following any big over-all plan. Blinded by Mussolini's unquestionably considerable success in the domestic political field, he did not see—and *did not want* to see—how war-weary the Italian people were after the Abyssinian War, how little value his [Mussolini's] armed forces had, how incompletely equipped they were with all modern means.[6]

The Italian alliance caused Adolf Hitler nothing but trouble. Mussolini invaded Greece from Italian-occupied Albania on October 28, 1940. He expected a quick and easy victory, but, on November 8, the Greeks counterattacked, and from that point on the initiative lay with the Greeks. Naturally, the Italian commander was made the scapegoat and sacked, but this did nothing to stop the Greek advance. By November 14 the Italians had been pushed back to their jump-off points, and on November 22 the Greeks overran Koritsa (Korce), the forward base of the Italian air force. By December 4 some 28,000 Italian soldiers had been captured, along with enough arms to equip two divisions.

Greece and Albania were not the only places where Italian forces were in trouble in 1940. On December 9 British Lieutenant General Sir Richard O'Connor's Western Desert Force, consisting of 31,000 men, attacked the Italians in Egypt. The Italian 10th Army disintegrated as the British, Australians, and Indians pushed it out of Egypt and pursued the survivors across Libya, finally threatening Tripoli itself. By the time the British pursuit ended on February 8, 1941, O'Connor had captured 130,000 men, 1,300 guns, and 400 tanks. The Western Desert Force had suffered only two thousand casualties. "The police in Tel Aviv gave us a better fight than this," one Australian remarked contemptuously.[7]

In mid-December 1940, with his forces in serious trouble on all active fronts, Mussolini was finally forced to swallow his pride and ask the Germans for help. Hitler immediately dispatched the Xth Air Corps to Sicily and southern Italy, along with an air transport wing to operate between Italy and Albania. When this proved insufficient, he sent Rommel and the Afrika Korps to Libya and invaded Greece and Yugoslavia on April 6, 1941. By April 30 the Western Desert Force, which was redesignated 8th Army, had been pushed back into Egypt and the British had been expelled from southern Europe.

After the fall of Athens, Hitler turned his attention to the east and invaded Russia on June 22, 1941. He never consulted Mussolini about the venture, other than to ask him—in a letter dated June 21—what forces he could contribute to the effort. Despite the objections of Commando Supremo (the Italian supreme command and the counterpart to OKW), the Duce initially dispatched an expeditionary corps of four divisions under the command of General Giovanni Messe. Later, in the spring of 1942, this corps was expanded into an army (the 8th) under the command of Marshal Italo Gariboldi. By the time of the Battle of Stalingrad, Italy had ten divisions in Russia.

The Russian campaign marked a turning point in Mussolini's relationship with his own people. The army almost unanimously opposed the venture, as did the soldiers who served there. Also, the ill-equipped 8th Army was badly outclassed by the resurgent Red Army, which attacked it in overwhelming numbers in the winter of 1942–1943. The Italian 8th Army was slaughtered; 75 percent of its men were lost, and Italian morale and Mussolini's popularity plummeted.

Then came Operation Torch, the Allied invasion of French North Africa. The first German troops landed in Tunis on November 11. Two days later, contrary to the wishes of the German high command, the first Italian troops followed them. The reason was simple: Mussolini was not going to allow himself to be excluded from a territory to which Italy had claims. As a result, some of Italy's best divisions would be lost when the Tunisian bridgehead collapsed in May 1943. Meanwhile, Mussolini took his first hesitant steps toward freeing himself from Hitler. Ironically, in doing so he further weakened his own control over the military. On February 1, 1943, following the fall of Tripoli, he dismissed Marshal Count Ugo Cavellero, the pro-German chief of Commando Supremo, and replaced him with Generale d'Armata Vittorio Ambrosio, a man who was thoroughly anti-German and who later joined the conspiracy to overthrow the dictator. Mussolini instructed the general to bring home Italy's divisions from Russia and the Balkans and to stand up to the Germans.

Meanwhile, Mussolini took steps to keep his own position secure. On February 6, 1943, at the time of the fall of Stalingrad, he dismissed most of his cabinet (dubbed the "Ciano cabinet") and replaced it with men who he thought were more loyal to him personally. He seems to have seen clearly that the Axis could not extricate itself from its increasingly hopeless military position as long as the German army bled itself white in Russia; consequently, on March 6 and 23, he wrote letters to Hitler urging that a separate peace be negotiated with the Soviet Union. Hitler, however, refused to consider it, so the Axis continued down the road to disaster. Meanwhile, in April 1943, Mussolini took further steps to consolidate his eroding power in the face of growing dissent at home. Acting on the advice of Heinrich Himmler, he appointed Carlo Scorza secretary of the Fascist party. Described as "an ambitious thug,"[8] Scorza sent groups of Fascist hoodlums into the streets to harass and intimidate the general population. Unlike in past years, however, the opposition and the citizenry struck back, and some of the Blackshirts were themselves beaten up or murdered in the night. Scorza's efforts to rejuvenate the party were unsuccessful. Defeatism was already too widely spread. Unrest grew. Representatives of the pre-Fascist political parties began to meet cautiously. On May 1 several labor unions marched in May Day parades despite official police bans, and unauthorized demonstrations were held. Mussolini was obviously losing control of the situation. He was now opposed by the royalist Officers' Corps, the anti-Fascist political parties, the labor unions, and a growing number of dissident Fascists.

The collapse of the Tunisian bridgehead in May came as a severe shock to the Italian population. "The loss of their last colony was a heavy blow to the Italian people," Kesselring's chief of staff recalled, "for it meant that all the energy and sacrifice which had been expended over half a century in building up the colonial territories had been in vain. So vanished for many Italians the hope of a better future."[9]

"They were tired of a war which had been unpopular from the beginning," German Major General Burkhart Mueller-Hillebrand wrote later, "and yearned for peace at any price. . . . [After Tunisia] Mussolini's prestige was shattered."[10]

On May 15, three days after Axis resistance in North Africa ended, King Victor Emmanuel III sent several discouraging memoranda to Mussolini, concluding that Italy must "consider very seriously the possibility" of severing her fate from that of Nazi Germany.[11] Mussolini, however, ignored these suggestions. And the war went on.

By the end of May 1943 Italy was, as Garland and Smyth wrote, "in the tragic and ridiculous position of being unable either to make war or to make peace."[12] Economically Italy was a vassal of the Reich, being heavily dependent on Germany or German-occupied territories for coal, iron, oil, rubber, and other essential commodities. Its industrial production was inadequate for modern warfare, and its war equipment was hopelessly inferior to that of the Russians and the Western Allies, especially in regard to tanks and airplanes. Of the 2 million men in the Italian armed forces at the end of 1942, about 1,200,000 were serving in foreign areas, including Russia, North Africa, southern France, Croatia, Slovenia, Greece, Dalmatia, Montenegro, and the islands of the Aegean Sea. Also, its best trained and equipped divisions were serving abroad. The worst units were at home and in the Balkans. Marshal Badoglio recalled "artillery divisions manning the coastal defences without artillery, with very few arms and with no transport."[13] The morale of these units was rock bottom, of course, although Italian morale was generally bad everywhere. General of Infantry Dr. Edmund von Gleise-Horstenau, commander of the German forces in Croatia, grumbled to a friend that he had never seen anything like the Italian 2nd Army. "The officers live by smuggling Jews, the NCO's smuggle arms, tobacco and salt, and the soldiers simply steal. They leave the mountains to the partisans." He also complained that the 2nd Army would not fight for twenty-four hours, but his reports never got beyond Keitel (i.e., to Hitler) unless they were "optimistic and seasoned with coarse jokes."[14] The Italian Air Force was in equally bad straits, and the Italian Navy, while still formidable on paper, had remained so only by religiously avoiding battle with the Royal Navy (except for the submarine service, which performed always with courage and sometimes with incredible bravery).

With his own army ill-equipped, ill-trained, and demoralized, one would think Mussolini would have welcomed German aid, especially after the collapse of Tunisia. However, the Duce, ignorant of the state of his own forces and influenced by Ambrosio, wanted to defend Italy with Italian forces alone and was in no hurry to accept German units. As he had told Marshal Badoglio some time before, "If they get a footing in the country we shall never be rid of them."[15] In early May 1943 Hitler offered to send Mussolini five mobile divisions with modern equipment. He then sent to Rome the commander in chief of the navy, Grand Admiral Karl Doenitz, to get Mussolini's answer, find out what the Italians were doing, and do all he could to strengthen the Axis resistance. Doenitz arrived on May 12 and met with Mussolini at 11:30 A.M. on May 13. He found him "well, optimistic, composed, very frank, sincere, and amicable." Doenitz reported back to Hitler:

> The Duce stated that he is confident about the future. The only result of British air raids on Italy will be that the people will learn to hate the British, which has not always been the case. This helps in carrying on the war. If there is one Italian who hates the British, it is he himself. He is happy that his people are now learning the meaning of the word hate as well. He answered the Fuehrer's offer of five divisions by stating he wants only three of them. This refusal came as a surprise to the C-in-C, Navy. The Duce explains that he had asked that these three divisions should include six armored battalions with 300 tanks. . . .[16]

In turning down his offer, Mussolini upset Hitler, who immediately became suspicious of Italy's desire to remain in the war—especially in view of the fact that Mussolini had requested additional German aid a few weeks before and Hitler had, in principle, agreed to provide it.[17] The Fuehrer's suspicions were no doubt heightened when Ambrosio ordered the withdrawal of the remnants of the Italian army from Russia and began withdrawing units from southern France and the Balkans. On May 19 OKW issued a report recommending a buildup of German forces, at least in northern Italy. The next day Hitler held a Fuehrer Conference on Italy, with Rommel, Keitel, and Warlimont present, among others. During the discussions Rommel—angling for a new command—fanned Hitler's fears, pointing out that the Italians might defect to the Allies and cut the Brenner Pass, putting the few German forces in Italy in a hopeless position. Hitler commented that it would be good to have Rommel in authority in Italy if it did try to defect, but he refrained from giving the Desert Fox a new assignment. Two days later, on May 22, OKW issued Plan "Alarich": a contingency plan to be implemented if Mussolini's government collapsed. It called for the formation of an army group of thirteen to fourteen divisions under Field Marshal Rommel to rapidly assemble and occupy all of Italy. Six or seven of these divisions were to be mobile units hurriedly withdrawn from the Eastern Front. Later, when the political situation temporarily stabilized, the number of divisions earmarked for Alarich was reduced to eight, taken from Germany or OB West (the commander in chief, Western Front).

Meanwhile, on May 22, General of Infantry Enno von Rintelen, the chief OKW liaison officer in Italy and the military attaché to Rome since 1936, obtained a firm commitment from the Italians to accept four German divisions: a panzer grenadier division (eventually designated the 15th), to be reconstituted in Sicily by June 1; a panzer grenadier division (later designated the 90th), to be created by the expansion of the German brigade on Sardinia; the Hermann Goering Panzer Division, much of which had been destroyed in Tunisia, to be reconstituted on the mainland; and the 16th Panzer Division, to be reconstituted in France and then sent to Italy. The Italians also agreed to accept Headquarters, XIVth Panzer Corps, led by General of Panzer Troops Hans Valentin Hube, to prepare the German troops for combat. Only two questions remained: Where would this combat take place, and when?

✧ 4 ✧

THE DEFENDERS

FIELD MARSHAL ALBERT KESSELRING, THE COMMANDER IN CHIEF, South (OB South), began analyzing the situation in southern Europe in the spring of 1943 with an eye to where the Allies would strike next if Army Group Afrika were destroyed. In April he sent an appreciation to OKW, stating that the enemy "would gain more from an operation against Sardinia and Corsica if the Allied objective were the speedy capture of Rome." Kesselring also concluded that the capture of Corsica would facilitate an offensive against southern France.[1]

Gradually, however, as he and his staff studied the problem and the Anglo-American behavior, Kesselring reached a different point of view. Noting their limited training in amphibious operations (Operation Torch he dismissed as "a peacetime exercise") and the great importance they attached to powerful air cover, Kesselring concluded that the Allies would choose a target within range of their short-range fighters. This limitation made Sicily the most likely victim and ruled out southern France, northern Italy, and the Balkans. Although he considered it unlikely, Kesselring did not altogether rule out an invasion of Sardinia and Corsica, or so he says in his memoirs. Lieutenant General Fridolin von Senger und Etterlin, who was in Rome in June and met with Kesselring several times before the landings, had a slightly different recollection. "Field Marshal Kesselring also expected a landing on Sardinia just as much as Sicily," he wrote in 1947. "He feared the landing on Sardinia because he had only weak forces there, whereas he believed he had sufficient troops on the mainland. . . ."[2]

In early May 1943 Kesselring brought up the subject with Mussolini, who believed that the Allies would invade southern

France next. This was mostly wishful thinking on his part. The diplomatic OB South soon convinced him that Sicily and Sardinia were the most likely targets, and in fact, the Italian dictator was so thoroughly convinced that he gave Admiral Doenitz quite a lecture on the subject when they met on May 13. The Duce told Doenitz that Sicily was in greater danger than Sardinia was and supported his contention "by referring to the British press, which had repeatedly stated that a free route through the Mediterranean would mean a gain of 2,000,000 tons of cargo space for the Allies."[3]

Most of the members of Commando Supremo picked Sardinia as the most likely target, and with some excellent reasons. First, it was a stepping-stone to southern France. Second, Allied air forces based in Sardinia and Corsica (which would not be held if Sardinia fell) could bomb the entire Italian mainland and southern Germany as well. Third, Sardinia was the gateway to the Po River valley, Italy's most important agricultural and industrial region. Finally, the capture of Sardinia would effectively bottle up the Italian Navy in the Tyrrhenian Sea. Capturing Sicily, they pointed out, would not put the Allies within escorted bomber range of the important industrial targets in the Po River valley or southern Germany; nor would it serve as a springboard for an invasion of central or northern Italy. In other words, Sicily was not seen as an important enough target to warrant an invasion of the magnitude that the Anglo-Americans were preparing.

Most of the Axis military experts seemed to agree with Commando Supremo. Luftwaffe Field Marshal Baron Wolfram von Richthofen picked Sardinia, as did the paratrooper expert General Kurt Student. Marshal Badoglio, although retired, was considered an expert on Italian military geography and was still consulted by members of the Italian high command. He also expected the landings to occur in Sardinia and later denounced Husky as "a severe strategic mistake." Supermarina, the General Staff of the Italian Navy, also anticipated operations to be directed against Sardinia, as did Admiral Doenitz and the High Command of the German Navy (Oberkommando der Kriegsmarine, or OKL). Agreement was far from unanimous, however. Generale d'Armata Alfredo Guzzoni, the former undersecretary of war, expressed as early as 1942 the opinion that the Allies would be wise to attack Calabria, the mainland of southwestern Italy (i.e., the "toe" of the Italian "boot"). This move, he said, would cut off and trap all the

Axis forces in Sicily. His views were later shared by German Major General Eberhard Rodt, who commanded the 15th Panzer Grenadier Division in Sicily. Adolf Hitler and OKW had another theory altogether. They thought that the eastern Mediterranean was more greatly threatened than was the west or the center and anticipated an invasion of Greece or the Balkans.

The Fuehrer made his choice for several reasons. First of all, the Balkans were more important to the German war effort than Italy was. The Third Reich got 60 percent of its bauxite, 24 percent of its antimony, 21 percent of its copper, more than half its oil, and all its chromium from Balkan sources. Second, a German reaction to an invasion of Greece or the Balkans would be more difficult than would be the case in Italy. In Greece, all Axis reinforcements and supplies would have to be shipped over a single rail line of limited capacity, running for 1,300 kilometers (more than 800 miles) through an area vulnerable to air and partisan attack. Italy, on the other hand, had an extensive and functioning network of communications, well laid out to counter any Allied move. Politically, Hitler feared the repercussions a Balkans invasion might have on neutral Turkey and his southeastern allies, Hungary and Romania. Finally, the German dictator suspected that the Allies wanted to seize the Balkans quickly, to forestall a Soviet occupation of the region. What finally convinced the Fuehrer that the landings would come against Greece and Sardinia, however, was "the man who never was."

Operation Mincemeat was a brilliant deception plan hatched in the fertile minds of Lieutenant Commander Ewen Montagu of British naval intelligence and Flight Lieutenant Charles Cholmondeley, an air ministry intelligence officer. Under this plan, the body of Major William Martin of the Royal marines was released by a British submarine in the Gulf of Cadiz so that the currents would wash it ashore near Huelva, Spain. Martin, an official messenger, had apparently drowned after his airplane had crashed into the sea. Still handcuffed to his wrist was a briefcase, which the Spaniards opened. Inside were top-secret documents from London directing General Sir H. Maitland "Jumbo" Wilson, commander in chief, Middle East, to veil his invasion of Greece by simulating an attack on the Dodecanese Islands. The Spanish, as Montagu predicted they would, handed copies of the documents over to German secret agents. Soon they were in the hands of Admiral Wilhelm

Canaris, chief of the Abwehr (German military intelligence), who gave translated copies to Adolf Hitler.

Major William Martin never existed. Like the top-secret documents, his identity was fake. The man in the Royal marine uniform was actually a British civilian who had died of pneumonia, the symptoms of which resemble drowning. His body had been packed in dry ice for the submarine journey to the gulf.

Hitler fell for Mincemeat hook, line, and sinker. On May 14 he expressed the belief that "the discovered Anglo-Saxon order confirms the assumption that the planned attacks will be directed mainly against Sardinia and the Peloponnesus."[4] As a result, during the summer of 1943 many reinforcements were sent to Greece and southeastern Europe. The remnants of several divisions destroyed at Stalingrad were sent to the Balkans to rebuild, as were newly forming SS combat units. Before the end of May, OKW sent the 1st Panzer Division to Greece, despite the bitter objections of Colonel General Heinz Guderian, the inspector of panzer troops, who rated the 1st as Germany's strongest reserve. By July 7 there were thirteen German divisions in the Balkans. OB South had only six at its disposal—less than half as many.

Sicily (Map 2) is shaped like an isosceles triangle. Its long sides—the north and south—are about 175 miles long, and its base—the east coast—is 120 miles long. It has an area of about 10,000 square miles (about the size of Vermont) and lies 90 miles from Cape Bon, Tunisia, 120 miles from Malta, and only 2 miles off Calabria on the Italian mainland, from which it is separated by the Straits of Messina. Militarily it has been important since antiquity. Its invaders included Sicans, Sicels, Phoenicians, Greeks, Carthaginians, Romans, Vandals, Byzantines, Arabs, Saracens, Normans, Spaniards, Austrians, and Italians. Earlier in World War II it had been, in effect, a giant aircraft carrier that the Xth and later the IInd Air Corps had used to pound Malta. Now at least some of the Allies wanted to use it as a stepping-stone to Italy and the mainland, but it was a pretty rough rock. On the northeast side lies Mount Etna, a conical volcano that exceeds ten thousand feet in elevation, is twenty miles in diameter, and is never entirely dormant. It is surrounded by the Caronie Mountains, which are the highest and most rugged on the island. Mountains hug the northern coast and are generally quite high. They gradually slope down from the north to the southern part of the island, with periodically steep inclines, which would prevent the rapid advance of tanks. Only to the south does the island become open and suitable for armored vehicles. Unfortunately, this shallow gradient also extends out into the sea. The water is shallow, and most of the harbors, including Sciacca, Porto Empedocle, and Licata, are artificial. Syracuse is a natural harbor, but it has a fairly limited capacity (about a thousand tons per day in 1943) and had not been important since the days of the Roman flat-bottom boats. The best harbors in 1943 were Messina (with a port capacity of 4,000 to 5,000 tons per day), Palermo (2,500 tons), and Catania (1,800 tons).

The interior of Sicily is barren, uneven, and unstable. The rocks are mainly soft sandstone that erodes easily, producing slopes that are steep and subject to frequent landslides. As a consequence, the towns of the interior are perched on lofty hills and form natural fortresses. The roads are rarely straight or level and are frequently tortuous. In 1943 many of them were also unpaved. Travel off the road is often impossible for anything except mules and infantrymen.

There are only three areas of reasonably level ground on the entire island, and they were very important in 1943 because the terrain dictated that the airfield be constructed here. The most important was the Catania-Gerbini cluster on the Catania plain, about midway up the east coast. Within supporting distance lay the southeastern concentration, behind Gela and the southern coast, which included the Comiso, Biscari, and Ponte Olivo airfields. The third and least important cluster was located on the narrow coastal plain on the western tip of the island. It included Castelvetrano and Trapani and was used to cover Palermo, the Sicilian capital.

The climate of Sicily in the summer is typically Mediterranean: hot and dry. July is normally the driest month of the year, and 1943 was no exception. The Canadian Official History reported that "July is not included among the months recommended for tourist travel in the island, an omission which the men of the 1st Division, sweltering on sun-baked hills and in the fiery valleys of the interior and choked by the dust which the combination of heat and drought engendered, could heartily endorse."[5]

The people of Sicily are as impoverished as their soil. The population of the island in 1943 was 4 million, but only 10 percent

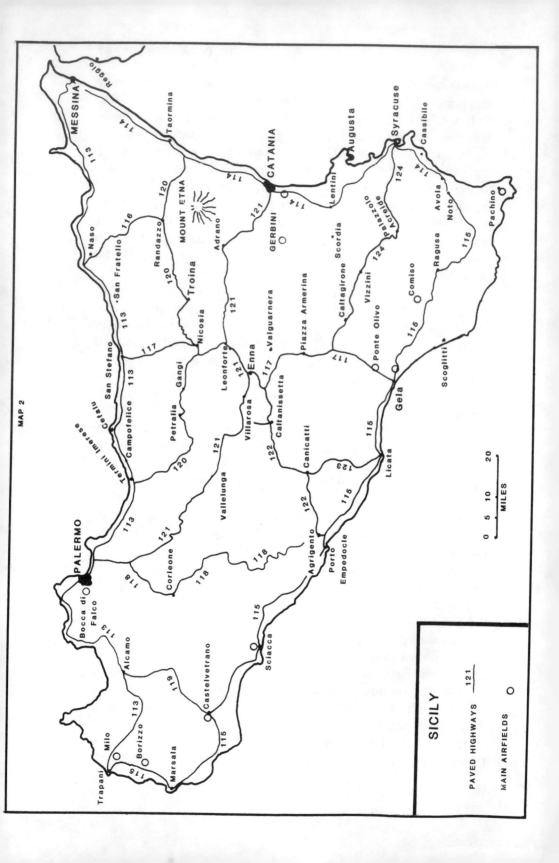

MAP 2

SICILY

PAVED HIGHWAYS ____121

MAIN AIRFIELDS ○

0 5 10 20
MILES

lived in the cities. Agriculture was the dominant occupation, and in spite of the poor quality of the soil, 90 percent of the island was cultivated. In fact, deforestation, overcultivation, absentee owner- ship, and poor farming practices accounted for much of the island's severe poverty. Sicily was the wheat granary for the Roman Empire, but in modern times the thin soils of the steep slopes had been eroded to the point that yields were very, very low. Now the main crops were citrus fruits, vines, olives, and almonds. The people lived under the discreditable system of land tenure called *latifunda*, which dated back to feudal times. Sicilian peasants worked long hours under harsh conditions their entire lives for a landlord they might never see. They were poor, ignorant, illiter- ate, and politically apathetic. The intolerant and opinionated General Patton, for one, did not like them. He once told his staff that he could not understand how Arabs could share their hovels with animals; in Sicily, he added that he could not understand how animals could live with Sicilians in their yards. Of course, that was before he saw Polish Jews, Patton snickered later.[6]

Despite Patton's contempt for them, the plight and mood of the Sicilians were militarily important in 1943, because they manned the coastal defense positions and were thus the first line of defense against an Allied invasion. Dr. Goebbels was convinced that the Italians would fight very bravely in defense of their own soil, although Admiral Wilhelm Canaris, chief of the Abwehr, doubted it. For once the head of the German military intelligence branch was right.

There had always been a gap between the Sicilians and the Italians, and it had grown during the war. The Sicilians felt that the government in Rome had never had any interest in them, except as cannon fodder. Allied bombing made things worse. Sicily first became a target during the Tunisian campaign when the Allies attempted to disrupt the flow of supplies to North Africa. The coastal cities, naturally enough, were the targets, especially Cata- nia and Messina whose residents fled into the interior, largely because the Fascists had not constructed air-raid shelters. Rural housing was soon at a premium, and hundreds of families were forced to live in huts and caves in the black lava fields around Mount Etna. Morale was naturally very low, and Mussolini did not help any when he referred to Sicilians as "decadent people." In another speech, this one on June 24, 1943, from the balcony of

Rome's Palazzo Venezia, Mussolini stated that the heroic Italians would defeat any Allied attack "on our mainland."[7] This unfortunate remark had a very bad effect on Sicilian morale. Was Mussolini writing them off? Fear and defeatism spread like wildfire and were accelerated by a very effective Allied propaganda campaign. Conditions soon reached the point where the Germans were concerned that the Sicilians might actively aid the invaders. To prevent this, Wehrmacht officers countered with scare tactics, telling terrible tales to frighten the uneducated and unsophisticated peasants into at least remaining neutral. One German officer told the residents of the inland town of Vittoria, "American paratroopers are cutthroats. You had better beware of them if they should land. All of the paratroopers are former convicts of the worst type—murderers, rapists and thugs. They were released from prison to join the paratroopers."[8]

Such speeches convinced many Sicilian civilians. They would spend D-Day hiding their wives and daughters rather than helping the Anglo-Americans.

Had the morale of the Sicilian people and the long, unbroken string of Italian defeats affected the morale of the Italian 6th Army? The answer was—of course! Private Alberto Testaecca, a gunner in an artillery unit near Syracuse, commented later about morale and how he was supplied:

> [W]e in the Army saw very little of anything. We only saw poverty, hunger, discomfort and dirt. Always hunger . . . there was no order; there was no discipline. We soldiers had to go into the villages to scrounge bread from the civilians, whilst the civilians came to the Army camps with the same aspirations. But they were disappointed. They must have seen us with toes sticking out of our boots. Our horses could hardly stand. . . .[9]

To prepare the island for defense, Commando Supremo named Generale di Corpo Mario Roatta commander of the Italian 6th Army in February 1943. Despite Hitler's charge three months later that he was "the Fouche of the Fascist revolution, a completely characterless spy," Roatta did, in fact, work hard to put the island on a wartime footing.[10] When he arrived, the 6th Army had only partial control over the territorial antiaircraft defenses (manned by the Fascist militia headquartered in Palermo) and no control over the militia ground units, the navy, or the air force. To implement his will, Roatta had to coordinate with seven military and nine civilian agencies. Roatta, one of Italy's most intelligent generals, knew his way around the corridors of power in Rome. He obtained a decree from Commando Supremo making him Armed Forces Commander, Sicily—and giving him control of all agencies and armed forces on the island, except the three Naval Fortress Areas *(Piazza Militare Marittima)* of Messina-Reggio, Augusta-Syracuse, and Trapani, under Rear Admiral Pietro Barone, Vice Admiral Priamo Leonardi, and Vice Admiral Giuseppe Manfredi, respectively.[11] The handful of torpedo boat units under Captain Mimbelli also remained independent of Roatta.[12]

As soon as he gained control of them, General Roatta set both civilian and service personnel to work on an obstacle and fortifications network extending up to fifteen miles behind the beaches. He also assigned each military unit to a specific defensive sector. But, despite having achieved a limited unity of command, there was much Roatta could not do because of inadequate resources. Much of the matériel and equipment earmarked for the 6th Army was diverted to North Africa and lost. Roatta, for example, requested 160,000 tons of cement a month to construct fixed defenses, but only 7,000 tons a month was sent, and much of that went to the navy and air force. As a result, few antitank traps could be constructed.

Roatta's construction program, through no fault of his own, was a failure. He could not even supply his men with the basic necessities—such as food. On May 13 a naval conference chaired by Admiral Arturo Riccardi, chief of *Supermarina,* was held in Rome. The report on Sicily stated that Allied air bombardments had cut off the coastal traffic by which Sicily was supplied. Only forty small vessels were still available to supply the island, and bread and other provisions were in short supply, for the wheat grown in Sicily was suitable only for pasta. The island produced plenty of bad wine but not much bread or meat.

When Prince Umberto, the army group commander, toured Sicily during Easter, he was appalled. He saw troops just lying about, in dirty uniforms, with equipment (that was bad enough to begin with) poorly maintained and generally neglected. Despite the fact that his staff car had two pennants on it, very few soldiers bothered to salute. Umberto's visit resulted in several court-martials but no fundamental change in the situation. Many of the troops still had rifles made in 1915. Many still were barefoot, and others considered themselves lucky to have sandals. The shortage of boots was so serious that training had to be curtailed in order to save on footwear. There were huge quantities of boots available in 6th Army's warehouses, but they were all of surplus overly large sizes, useless for most of the men. In Catalina, a few miles away, there were several warehouses full of boots of the more normal sizes, but they could not be issued because the officials in Rome would not authorize it.

In the latter part of May, Roatta gave a speech during which he made a remark that was interpreted as a slight on Sicilian patriotism. With the gap between Sicilians and Italians already too wide, Commando Supremo kicked Roatta upstairs. He was appointed Chief of the General Staff of the Army and on May 30 was succeeded in command of the 6th Army by sixty-six-year-old General d'Armata Alfredo Guzzoni.

Guzzoni seems an odd choice for this command. Born in Mantua on April 12, 1877, he graduated from the military academy at Modena (Italy's best) at the age of eighteen and was commissioned second lieutenant. In 1911, as a captain, he fought in the Italo-Turkish War. He saw more combat duty in World War I before he was named Chief of the Operations Office of the Italian Supreme Command. He held a number of posts in the interwar years, including Commandant of Modena, before he was named Vice Governor of Eritrea in 1935. An experienced veteran, he commanded a corps in Albania in 1939 and an army in southern France in 1940, and then served as Undersecretary for War and Assistant Chief of the General Staff of the Army. Although he was one of the regime's most competent generals, he was not an awe-inspiring personality. Physically rather small and heavy-set, he was known as a political soldier (like most Italian generals) and as an ambitious "operator."[13] In addition, he was sixty-six years old in 1943, had been retired for two years (since May 1941), had never even been to Sicily before, and had never showed the slightest interest in the place. His chief of staff, Colonel Emilo Faldella (soon to be Generale di Brigata), was young and capable, but was also new to Sicily and had never even met Guzzoni, much less served under him—a rare occurrence in the Fascist army.[14] Nevertheless, they made an effective team.

When Guzzoni first inspected his new command, he was shocked. His coastal battalions were under strength, overaged, badly equipped, and spread hopelessly thin. In some cases a single battalion had to cover twenty-five miles of shoreline. The 6th Army averaged only one antitank gun for every five miles of coastline, and its guns were outdated and of low caliber—no match for those of the Royal or American navies. In addition, Guzzoni needed 8,000 tons of supplies per day to meet civilian and military requirements but was receiving only 1,500 to 2,000 tons per day.

Guzzoni found that the only places on the island that were really prepared for defense were the Naval Fortress Areas of Trapani, Messina-Reggio, and Syracuse-Augusta. These areas had large-caliber coastal defense batteries, antiaircraft and mobile artillery batteries, torpedo boat units, special units, and "everything conducive to a vigorous defense," Guzzoni said later.[15] Unfortunately, most of the naval guns were old, were of short range, and were manned by undependable reservists, and the anti-aircraft guns were chronically short of ammunition. Still, the Naval Fortress Areas were in much better shape than was the rest of the island. Catania and Palermo were similarly equipped but much weaker.

General Guzzoni found his four mobile divisions in much worse condition. The Aosta (28th) and the Napoli (54th) Infantry divisions were poorly trained and operating at reduced levels of strength and equipment. The Assietta (26th) Division was also low in men and equipment, although its training and morale were better.[16] Only the Livorno (4th) Assault and Landing Division, which had recently been moved from Rome to Sicily, was fairly well trained, two-thirds motorized, and equipped with a fair number of light tanks. Like the other "mobile" divisions, however, it was very short in artillery ammunition, communications equipment, fuel, and other vital areas of supply.

If the Italian mobile units were in poor condition, the six coastal defense divisions were almost at the point of disintegration, especially in predominantly Sicilian units. Most of the officers took Sundays off to be with their families, who were usually not authorized to be there in the first place. The 206th Coastal Defense Division, for example, had a total armament of 215 submachine guns, 474 machine guns, 65 guns in batteries, and 46 "isolated" guns. According to General Faldella, this establishment gave the division two automatic rifles and three machine guns per kilometer, with two pieces of artillery every three kilometers. The division also had an average of only about thirty-six men per mile of frontage.

What kind of men formed the ranks of this unit? The records of the 206th Coastal Defense Division show that morale was "almost unbelievably low." Many of the officers assigned to the unit had not been on active duty since they had been lieutenants in World War I. When he inspected them, Prince Umberto court-martialed several for "complete ignorance" of even the most basic elements of military etiquette and training.[17] "The Chief of the General Staff, General Roatta, stated quite openly that these units were not to be relied on," General Westphal recalled.[18] They had neglected every aspect of training and discipline. No continuous system of coastal defense existed. Minefields, obstacles, antitank ditches, fortifications, and even trenches were lacking altogether or were widely separated, badly sited, and beyond the fire support of the other badly sited positions. The few defensive posts ("strong points") lacked garrisons, weapons, troop shelters, overhead cover, and camouflage. There was almost no defense in depth, other than a few roadblocks. Martin Blumenson noted, "An inland blocking line behind the coastal fortifications, supposed to be a strong barrier, consisted of a carefully traced, colored-pencil mark on a map."[19]

Major General Achille d'Havet was sent to Sicily to straighten out this notoriously bad unit, but there was little he could do other than send back reports stating that some of his soldiers could not fix bayonets because they were afraid of cutting themselves with their own weapons.

The 206th Division was not an isolated case in Sicily in 1943; in fact, it was typical. Even if it had been the exception to the rule, however, it would still have been significant, because it occupied the sector from Gela to Syracuse—where the British 8th and most of the U.S. 7th armies would land on July 10.

Although sixty-six years of age, General Alberto Guzzoni was still very energetic. Breuer called him a "vigorous and competent tactician."[20] Although he did not possess the dynamic personality of a Patton or a Montgomery, he threw himself into his task, habitually working seventeen-hour days to prepare the island for defense. He did not despair but instead resolved to do what he could; he also counted on his two German divisions to put backbone in the Italian units and teeth in the defense of Sicily.

Colonel Bogislaw von Bonin had served on Rommel's staff and was the Ia (operations officer) of the 5th Panzer Army during its last battles in North Africa. He was recalled by OB South and flew out of the ever-diminishing pocket on May 8, making him one of the last officers to leave Tunisia. When he arrived in Rome, he was named chief of a special staff *(Einsatzstab)* charged with organizing two German motorized divisions: one in Sicily and one in southern Italy. At that time, von Bonin recalled, "there was not one battle-worthy formation of the German Army in Italy, including the islands."[21]

Only one German divisional-level headquarters existed in Sicily at the time: the ad hoc Division Kommando Colonel Baade (Division Command Colonel Baade), which had been formed in April to control the march (replacement) battalions bound for Africa. The evolution of this division is an excellent example of the effective but improvised manner in which the Germans could organize units in a crisis. During the first week in May, when it became obvious that Army Group Afrika could not hold out, Baade stopped sending troops to Tunisia and organized Panzer Grenadier Regiment Palermo (Ist, IInd, IIIrd, and IVth battalions) from the 46th, 47th, 48th, 50th, and 56th March battalions.[22] This was the only German ground unit ready to offer even token resistance when Colonel General von Arnim surrendered.

"At the time of the capitulation of Tunis the outlook in Sicily, as everywhere, was very black," Kesselring recalled later. "I counted on the enemy's following up his victory, if not immediately, at least after the shortest possible breather. . . . Every day the enemy gave us was a day gained, however, and gradually a striking force was organized."[23]

Colonels von Bonin and Ernst-Guenther Baade reacted quickly to take advantage of the Allied generosity. There were thirty thousand Germans on the island, including flak troops, Luftwaffe, naval, and supply and support personnel. The replacements, army supply and support troops, and some of the flak units were incorporated into Baade's command, which was redesignated *Division Sizilien* (Division Sicily) on May 14. Under their direction, new subordinate units were formed within the emerging division, including Regiment Ens (two battalions); Regiment Koerner (the three battalions of the former Panzer Grenadier Regiment Palermo); and Regiment Fullriede (three battalions), which absorbed the 63rd, 65th, and 67th March battalions. Later these units became the 1st, 2nd, and 3rd Sicily Grenadier regiments and then the 104th, 115th, and 129th Panzer Grenadier regiments, respectively.

Baade's artillery was grouped into four battalions under HQ, Artillery Regiment Sicily (later Headquarters, 33rd Motorized Artillery Regiment). The elements of this unit came from odds and ends scattered all over the place. The staff came from the 190th Artillery Regiment, a unit that was largely destroyed in Tunisia but was re-forming at Naples; the Ist Battalion was the former Ist Battalion, Hermann Goering Panzer Artillery Regiment (a Luftwaffe unit absorbed by the army); the IInd Battalion was the former 557th Heavy Artillery Battalion; and the IVth Battalion was formerly the II/53rd Artillery Regiment, a recently rebuilt "Stalingrad" unit given to the division by OB South. Only the IIIrd Battalion was created from scratch. The Ist Battalion was equipped with heavy guns, the IInd had three batteries of 170-mm cannon, the IIIrd had two light batteries and one mortar battery, and the IVth had three light batteries. The new regiment was commanded by Major Theodor Simon, a reserve officer.

In addition, Division Sicily included Panzer Grenadier Battalion Reggio (formerly the 69th March Battalion); Flak Battalion Sicily (formerly Flak Battalion Neapel and later the redesignated 315th Flak Battalion, with 1st, 2nd, and 4th companies); Division Unit 33, which eventually became the 999th Signal Battalion; and the 215th Panzer Battalion, which was assigned to the division from OB South.[24]

The men of the new division were a varied lot. Most of the members of the 129th Panzer Grenadier Regiment, for example, had fought with panzer units on the Eastern Front. Most of the men of the 104th Panzer Grenadier were tough survivors of the Afrika Korps, many now returning to duty after having recovered from wounds. Although there were more than the optimum number of green replacements, there were plenty of hardened, experienced NCOs to keep them alive while they learned the ropes. They blended together well. During most of the Battle of Sicily they formed the hard center of the Axis line—the rock on which everything else was built. And their officers were also capable, experienced veterans.

The original divisional commander, Colonel Ernst-Guenther Baade, was colorful, idiosyncratic, and one of the mavericks of the German army. In the field, for example, he wore a black beret with a tartan plaid ribbon, with a huge claymore (a double-edged broadsword formerly used by Scottish Highlanders) at his side instead of the traditional Luger.

Baade was born at Falkenhagen on August 20, 1897, the son of a Brandenburg landowner. As a child he developed a lifelong love for horses. Young Baade volunteered for service when World War I began and was commissioned *Leutnant* in the 6th Dragoon Regiment in 1916. Discharged in 1920, he farmed his own estate in Holstein, where he bred horses, but later rejoined the army. Before the invasion of Poland he and his wife earned a reputation as international horse-show jumpers. He also became fluent in English and French, which enabled him to talk to the British on their own radio nets in World War II.

Ernst-Guenther Baade was a major commanding the 17th Reconnaissance Battalion (a cavalry unit) when World War II broke out. After fighting in Poland and France, he transferred to the motorized branch and, in April 1942, as a lieutenant colonel, was named commander of the 115th Motorized Infantry Regiment of the 15th Panzer Division, which was then serving with the Afrika Korps in Libya.

Baade was a gentleman who believed in chivalry. He was also personally brave and professionally competent; hence, he had no problems in the Afrika Korps, despite his peculiarities. He played a leading role in the capture of Bir Hacheim and won the Knight's Cross for his part in the capture of Tobruk, later adding the Oak Leaves. Before World War II was over he would win the Swords as well, making him one of the most decorated soldiers of the war. In the meantime he led patrols wearing a kilt and radioed cease-fires to enemy artillery units that tried to interfere with his raids.[25] Once, after a captured British engineer guided him safely through a minefield, Baade let the man go as a reward. His unpredictable actions caused anger and irritation at OKW but did not seem to ruffle Rommel or, later, Hube or von Senger. The daring colonel was sent to Sicily to expedite supplies in the latter part of 1942.

For secondary commanders, the new division was exceedingly fortunate. Lieutenant Colonel Karl Ens of the 104th Panzer Grenadier had risen to regimental command in the Afrika Korps before he was seriously wounded. Colonel Theodor Koerner of the 115th was a veteran engineer officer, while Lieutenant Colonel Fritz Fullriede of the 129th Panzer Grenadier had distinguished himself as leader of the 961st (Penal) Grenadier Regiment in Tunisia from December 1942 to early April 1943, when he was wounded at Fondouk al-Aovareb and evacuated back to the hospital at Messina. All but Koerner held the Knight's Cross of the Iron Cross.

Colonel Baade was replaced as divisional commander by Major General Eberhard Rodt on June 9, 1943.[26] However, Baade's adventures in Sicily were far from over, as we shall see.

Rodt was born in Munich on December 4, 1895, and, like Baade, entered the army as a volunteer when World War I broke out. Also like Baade, he joined the cavalry; he was commissioned second lieutenant in the 2nd Bavarian Regiment of Uhlans in 1915 and served throughout the war. Here, however, the similarities ended, for Rodt's career had not been nearly as unusual or successful as Baade's.

Eberhard Rodt remained in the service with the Reichswehr in the interwar years and was promoted slowly. As a major he assumed command of Ist Battalion, 18th Cavalry Regiment on October 1, 1936, and was promoted to lieutenant colonel in 1938. He assumed command of the 7th Cavalry Regiment when the war started and led it in the Polish campaign. He was transferred to the panzer branch shortly thereafter.

Lieutenant Colonel Rodt led the 25th Reconnaissance Battalion, 25th Motorized Division, in France during the Six Weeks' Campaign of 1940. In October he was promoted to colonel and transferred to the staff of the 2nd Panzer Division. It was in October 1941, with the division deep in Russia, when Rodt took over command of the division's panzer grenadier brigade, which consisted of two motorized infantry regiments, plus a motorcycle battalion and a reconnaissance battalion. He led this unit to within ten miles of Moscow, and elements of his command got Nazi Germany's only glimpse of the Kremlin before they were thrown back.

After fighting in the Russian winter offensive, during which his unit suffered heavy losses, Rodt was transferred to the command of the 22nd Panzer Grenadier Brigade of the 22nd Panzer Division on February 1, 1942. The new unit had been resting in France and had been hurriedly sent to Russia to contain Soviet counterattacks on the Kerch peninsula in the Crimea, where Rodt first commanded them. In these battles the 22nd performed badly and was pulled out of the line and sent to Kharkov to regroup. It is difficult to say what part Rodt had in this fiasco, but it is safe to say that he did not distinguish himself.

The 22nd Panzer was not again committed to heavy fighting prior to November 1, 1942, when Rodt assumed command of the division. Having been placed in reserve amid the inclement weather of the Donets, Rodt's tankers had used hay and straw to insulate their panzers against the freezing precipitation. Unfortunately, the mice of the area also made themselves at home and made meals off the insulation of the tanks' wiring.

On November 19 the Soviets launched a massive offensive and crushed the Romanian 3rd Army. The only unit that could prevent the encirclement of Friedrich Paulus's 6th Army in Stalingrad was Lieutenant General Ferdinand Heim's XXXXVIIIth Panzer Corps, which had only one German division: Rodt's 22nd Panzer. (The only other division in Heim's corps was the Romanian 1st Armored, whose tanks were so light that they were nearly useless against the Russians.) Unfortunately, most of Rodt's tanks could not move or quickly broke down because of electrical failure. The division was slaughtered; only remnants escaped across the Don.

General Heim was relieved of his command, court-martialed, and thrown into prison for his failure. Rodt retained his position until early February 1943, when the battered and unlucky 22nd Panzer Division was disbanded. Rodt, most of his staff, and his surviving soldiers were sent to Italy to rest and recuperate. This is where Rodt was when he received his promotion to major general on March 1. When Tunisia collapsed, the men of the former 22nd Panzer were incorporated into Fullriede's 129th Panzer Grenadier Regiment. They were soon followed to Sicily by Rodt and his staff officers.[27]

On June 29 Division Sicily was redesignated 15th Panzer Grenadier Division, named after the 15th Panzer, one of the two divisions of the Afrika Korps. All of its subordinate regiments also bore old Panzer Army Afrika numbers, as did the 90th Panzer Grenadier Division, then being formed under Major General Carl-Hans Lungershausen (under the general direction of Colonel von Bonin) in Sardinia.

In the meantime, on June 1, Kesselring and General von Rintelen, the German military attaché, met with Ambrosio and persuaded him to accept a second German division in Sicily: the Hermann Goering unit.

During its career, the "H.G." unit probably had more names than any other unit in the Wehrmacht. At various times it was called Police Detachment z.b.V. Wecke (z.b.V. means "for special purposes"), State Police Group Wecke, z.b.V., State Police Group General Goering, Regiment General Goering, Division Hermann Goering, the Hermann Goering Panzer Division, the Hermann Goering Parachute Panzer Division, and the Hermann Goering Parachute Panzer Corps (with the 1st H.G. Parachute Panzer and the 2nd H.G. Parachute Panzer Grenadier divisions).[28] Appendix 2 shows the evolution and titles of the division and provides exact dates. The "parachute" designation, incidentally, was an honorary one.

The Goering unit began in early 1933, when Prussian Minister of the Interior Hermann Goering controlled most of the German police. Originally it was a 414-man police unit under the command of Major Wecke, who was eventually hanged as a war criminal in Prague in 1945. In 1935, after Hitler reintroduced conscription in Germany, it was incorporated into the Luftwaffe as a regiment. During this period it controlled Germany's first, embryonic parachute battalion, the 1st Jaeger, but lost its airborne units in early 1938. Gradually the "General Goering" evolved into a flak regiment.[29]

Entry qualifications for this unit were very stiff. Enlistment terms were for twelve years. Members had to be "Aryan," eighteen to twenty-five years old, at least 1.68 meters tall, unmarried, Nazi, and in excellent physical condition. Membership had its advantages, however, not the least of which were the superb barracks at Berlin-Reinickendorf. Designed and built under Goering's personal supervision, they included every possible comfort and convenience.

The regiment took part in the occupation of Austria, the Sudetenland, and Czechoslovakia, and minor elements of the

General Goering fought in Poland and Norway. The unit first distinguished itself, however, in the French campaign, where, as part of Panzer Group Kleist, it advanced to the English Channel and helped force the evacuation of Dunkirk. Its heavy 88-mm guns proved particularly effective against French tanks in Mormal Forest.

After France the General Goering was transferred to Romania to guard the vital Ploesti oil fields, but it did not really come into its own until Hitler invaded Russia on June 22, 1941. By October the Goering Regiment had destroyed 161 Soviet aircraft, 324 tanks, 45 bunkers, 167 artillery pieces, and 530 machine guns, and had taken 11,000 prisoners. For this incredible record of accomplishment Colonel Paul Conrath, the regimental commander, and three of his officers were awarded the Knight's Cross. Reichsmarschall Hermann Goering was so impressed with "his" unit's performance that in early 1942, he ordered it expanded into a brigade. Hardly had this expansion begun when he decided to convert it into a division despite its lack of joint training. To make up for this deficiency, Goering drafted men from the air force, including five thousand paratroopers from various units, all of whom had fought in Russia and Crete. Goering also acquired the services of Wilhelm Schmalz, an army colonel who had won the Knight's Cross while commanding a motorized rifle battalion in France. Schmalz became the commander of the 2nd Hermann Goering Grenadier Regiment and the principal adviser and instructor for the division.

The new Hermann Goering Division was not completely formed in November 1942, when most of it was committed to action in Tunisia as ad hoc Kampfgruppe Hermann Goering (Battle Group Hermann Goering), Luftwaffe Major General Josef Schmid commanding. When Tunisia fell, the H.G. Division lost four grenadier battalions, two flak battalions, a panzer battalion, most of the reconnaissance unit, part of the engineer battalion, and the signal and medical battalions. Nevertheless, since elements of the division were already in Italy, awaiting transport to Tunisia, it was decided to rebuild the division as a panzer unit in Italy and later in Sicily.

On June 20 Kesselring began sending the H.G. across the Straits of Messina, a process that was completed on July 1,[30] although new recruits and replacements continued to arrive until Sicily was evacuated. The new division was to include all the units shown in Table 1. However, time prevented this ambitious reorganization, and the division was far from completely ready when the Allies struck. The Headquarters, 2nd Hermann Goering Panzer Grenadier Regiment, for example, was apparently used to form the panzer grenadier brigade headquarters, and a new 2nd Panzer Grenadier Regiment had not yet been completely formed. By July the Hermann Goering Panzer Regiment had only about thirty-five PzKw III tanks and about the same number of PzKw IV's—well under half of its planned establishment.

The PzKw III (or Mark III) was the former main battle tank of the German Army, but now it was old and becoming outdated. It mounted a long-barreled 50-mm gun or, in a few cases, a short-barreled low-velocity 75-mm gun as opposed to the 76-mm gun of the American Sherman tank, which was generally superior to it, except in range. The PzKw IV's, on the other hand, mounted a 75-mm long-barreled main battle gun and were about equal to the Shermans in combat. The PzKw III's and IV's weighed about 24.5

T A B L E   1

ORDER OF BATTLE, HERMANN GOERING PANZER DIVISION
July 1943

Division Commander: Lieutenant General Paul Conrath
Chief of Staff: Lieutenant Colonel Bergengruen

Hermann Goering Panzer Grenadier Brigade *(Panzergrenadierbrigade Hermann Goering z.b.V.)* (Brigade Schmalz): Colonel Schmalz

   1st Hermann Goering Panzer Grenadier Regiment
   2nd Hermann Goering Panzer Grenadier Regiment
   1st and 2nd Hermann Goering Field battalions *(Feldsatzbataillons)* (later redesignated IIIrd Battalion, 1st H.G. Panzer Grenadier Regiment, and IIIrd Battalion, 2nd H.G. Panzer Grenadier Regiment)

(1st) Hermann Goering Panzer Regiment: (two panzer battalions and one assault gun battalion)

Hermann Goering Flak Regiment (two battalions)

Hermann Goering Panzer Artillery Regiment: (three, later four, battalions, plus a mixed battalion of heavy field howitzers and cannon, plus one observation battery and one rocket launcher battery) and 26 tons, respectively. For Sicily, the 2nd Company of the army's 504th Heavy Panzer Battalion (2/504th) was attached to the 1st Hermann Goering Panzer Grenadier Regiment. This unit was equipped with seventeen PzKw VI Tiger I tanks—monsters that weighed 56 tons and mounted deadly 88-mm guns. They were more than a match for any Allied tank—when they ran. The Tiger, however, was a new tank in 1943 and was undergoing more than its share of teething problems.

The Hermann Goering was also short of infantry. Although it was supposed to have two panzer grenadier regiments, it had enough men for only about two full battalions, although it employed three under-strength battalions in the first days of the Battle of Sicily. The division also lacked about a third of its artillery establishment, its flak regiment was under strength, and it had only about half its supply and support units, although the attachment of

---

Hermann Goering Engineer Battalion

Hermann Goering Panzer Reconnaissance Battalion

Hermann Goering Panzer Signal Battalion

Hermann Goering Supply Battalion

Hermann Goering Maintenance Battalion

Hermann Goering Bakery Company

Hermann Goering Butcher Company

Hermann Goering Medical Battalion

Attached units:

    2nd Company, 504th Heavy Panzer Battalion (Tiger tanks)
    923rd Fortress Battalion
    3rd Parachute Regiment
    4th Parachute Regiment
    Elements of the 1st Parachute Artillery Regiment
    1st Parachute Signal Battalion (–)
    1st Parachute Engineer Battalion (–)

SOURCES: Bender and Petersen, *Herman Goering,* p. 28; Tessin, *Verbaende und Truppen,* vol. 13, p. 130; vol. 14, pp. 117, 120.

the ad hoc army Construction Battalion Messina helped alleviate this problem, at least to a degree.

In short, the Hermann Goering Panzer Division was inferior to the 15th Panzer Grenadier Division in combat strength in July 1943. It was also inferior to its army counterpart in leadership. Perhaps this was the worst deficiency the Hermann Goering Panzer Division had in 1943. Except for Schmalz, the subordinate commanders of the H.G. were markedly inferior to Ens, Koerner, Fullriede, and the others. The commander of the Hermann Goering Panzer Regiment, for example, was a former bomber pilot who had been grounded because he had a nervous condition. Why he was given command of a panzer regiment is anyone's guess, but many of his peers were air force officers who were equally unqualified to direct a ground battle.

The 15th Panzer Grenadier also had a better divisional commander than did the Hermann Goering. Although General Rodt had not been a success as a divisional commander in Russia, he was to be—ironically enough—a very successful defensive tactician against the Western Allies. Usually this worked the other way around. Luftwaffe General Paul Conrath was another matter.

Paul Conrath was born on November 21, 1896, but details about his early life are sketchy. He began his military career as an artillery second lieutenant on the Western Front in 1914 and served as a police officer in Berlin from 1920 to 1935, when he transferred to the Luftwaffe as a major of flak artillery. In 1937 he became a battalion commander in the Regiment General Goering and, the following year, became adjutant to Goering himself. Cashing in on this influential contact, Conrath assumed command of his old regiment and, as we have seen, distinguished himself on the Russian Front in 1941. However, commanding a motorized flak regiment against Russians and leading an under-strength panzer division in counterattacks against people like Patton, Montgomery, and Terry Allen were two entirely different things. Kesselring and General von Senger both noted that Conrath had "too little experience in handling modern, combined arms."[31] He nevertheless retained the backing and support of Reichsmarschall Goering and received a promotion to lieutenant general on July 1, 1943—ten days before the Allies landed.[32]

✦ 5 ✦

PANTELLERIA, THE PLAN
AND THE AIR BATTLES

WHILE THE GERMANS HASTILY ORGANIZED THEIR TWO DIVISIONS, General Dwight D. Eisenhower turned his attention to the island of Pantelleria and the small Pelagian group, which also includes Lampedusa, Lampione, and Linosa. Fifty-three air miles from Cape Granitola, Sicily, Pantelleria posed a potentially serious threat to Husky. No surprise invasion could be launched because of the German Freya radar stations on the island and on Lampedusa. The airfield at Pantelleria could also threaten the Sicilian shipping lanes, and the islands were known refueling points for U-boats and torpedo boats operating in the central Mediterranean.

The problem was that Pantelleria was reputed to be very strong. It was a small island, roughly elliptical in shape, 5 by 8 miles, with a total area of 42.5 square miles. About twelve thousand civilians lived there. The island's coastline was irregular, featuring steep cliffs and a notable absence of beaches. There was only one feasible landing area, at the town and harbor of Porto di Pantelleria, on the northwest end of the island. Even there only light draft vessels could be accommodated. Tricky offshore currents and high surf further complicated the problem.

The interior of the island was also easily defensible. The terrain was hilly and extended to an elevation of 2,743 feet. The soil was largely composed of lava, pumice, and volcanic ash, much of it incapable of supporting heavy vehicles, much less tanks. Hundreds of high, thick stone walls, which divided the arable land into fields, afforded excellent defensive positions, as did the island's houses. Made of stone and/or plaster, they could easily be turned into miniature fortresses.

Mussolini had begun turning this naturally defensible island into

45

a real fortress in the mid-1920s and had declared it off-limits to foreigners in 1926; therefore, military intelligence about the island was incomplete. It was known, however, that the Italians had constructed a five-thousand-foot runway on the northern end that could handle four-engine bombers. On the southeastern side there was a huge underground hangar, about 1,100 feet long, complete with an electric light plant, water supplies, and repair facilities. This complex could protect and sustain at least eighty fighter aircraft.

Allied photo reconnaissance revealed that Pantelleria had more than a hundred gun emplacements, some hewn from solid rock, supplemented by pillboxes, machine gun nests, and other strong points. It was defended by at least ten thousand men. Mussolini boasted that it was impregnable. Fascist propaganda called it the "Gibraltar of the central Mediterranean." Had the defenders been Waffen SS men, Eisenhower would no doubt have bypassed the island and accepted the risk to Husky.

But the defenders were not SS men. They were Italians, drawn from diverse elements of the armed forces and members of the Brigade Pantelleria of Guzzoni's 6th Army.[1] None of them had been battle-tested, nor were they conditioned to aerial and naval bombardments. They were, in fact, isolated, with little hope of relief. Their morale was thought to be poor, judging from the performance of the Pantelleria-based aviation units that had fought in the Tunisian campaign. Eisenhower recalled that "Admiral Cunningham, in particular, agreed with me that the place could be taken at slight cost. We based our conviction upon the assumption that most Italians had had a stomachful of fighting and were looking for any good excuse to quit."[2]

Eisenhower decided to take Pantelleria by means of an air bombardment that would be "sort of a laboratory experiment to determine the effect of concentrated heavy bombing on a defended coastline." On May 9 he ordered Air Chief Marshal Tedder "to concentrate everything" against the island,[3] including the heavy and medium bombers of the RAF, Middle East, if necessary.

After a few minor air raids, the real offensive began on May 18. Simultaneously, the Royal Navy instituted a naval blockade aimed at completely isolating the island. Between May 29 and June 4 only three small vessels reached Porto di Pantelleria and found the facilities severely damaged. By June 1 the town itself was "practically destroyed," according to the U.S. Official History, and the port was "in ruins."[4] The airfield had been neutralized, the electric power plant had been knocked out, there were water shortages on the island, and garrison morale was plummeting. Italian antiaircraft fire was described as "weak and inaccurate."[5]

Between May 18 and June 6 the Allied air forces flew 1,700 sorties and dropped more than nine hundred tons of bombs on the port and the airdrome and four hundred tons on the gun positions. Around-the-clock bombing began on June 6, growing in intensity until D-Day (June 11). In all, Allied aircraft flew 3,647 sorties against the island in June and dropped 4,844 tons of bombs.

On June 8 five British cruisers and eight destroyers directed an all-out bombardment against Porto di Pantelleria. Under the cover of this fury, three British motor torpedo boats roared across the harbor and, at a range of three hundred yards, raked the pier with their Bredas and heavy machine guns. Of the sixteen Italian shore batteries that could have returned fire, only five did so—and three of these fired only "occasionally."[6] The other two did not hit anything, and one of them was silenced by the warships.

The naval task force demanded that the island surrender, but the island commander, Vice Admiral Gino Pavasi, signaled Rome that he was not even going to bother to respond. Two days later he ignored a second ultimatum, signaling Mussolini, "Despite everything, Pantelleria will continue to resist." This message went out over the island's last operational radio.[7] Many of the troops, who were overage local militia, had already deserted.

The night of June 10–11 saw an all-out, continuous air assault— an obvious prelude to the final attack. Admiral Pavasi began to lose his nerve. He reported to Rome that Allied bombers had plunged the island into "a hurricane of fire and smoke," adding ominously: "the situation is desperate, all possibilities of effective resistance have been exhausted."[8]

At about nine A.M. Pavasi gave the order to surrender at eleven A.M. Word did not reach the Allied assault commander, however. At ten A.M., in perfect weather, the men of British Major General W. E. Clutterbuck's 1st Infantry Division lowered their boats and, half an hour later, started toward the shore, eight miles away. The first assault craft hit the beach in the harbor area at 11:55 A.M. and entered Porto di Pantelleria, which had been without food or water for three days. A few Italians fired small arms at them but did not hit anybody. By 12:20 P.M. the town was secure, and by 5:30 P.M. it was all over. Admiral Pavasi signed the formal surrender in the underground hangar at 5:35 P.M. By the end of the day the British 1st Infantry had rounded up more than eleven thousand prisoners and had seized eighty-four aircraft. Their casualties consisted of one soldier who had been severely bitten by a local jackass.

Casualties on both sides were surprisingly low. Over the island itself, Allied air units had lost four aircraft shot down, ten missing, and sixteen damaged. Italian losses were also low. POW statements indicated that most gun crews had not remained at their posts but instead had fled into the relatively safe hills. Fewer than two hundred Italians had been killed, and no more than two hundred had been wounded. The Allies had gained a fighter base within range of Sicily at very little cost.

Even as Admiral Pavasi was signing the surrender of Pantelleria, the Allied air forces were blasting the nearby island of Lampedusa, which was defended by a garrison of 4,300 men, two tank platoons, and thirty-three coastal and antiaircraft guns. As was the case at Pantelleria, the defenders were older, inexperienced militiamen, but they gave a somewhat better account of themselves than had those at the main island. At least they did not run away.

The battle began shortly after noon, when twenty-six B-26's attacked the town and port of Lampedusa throughout the afternoon. B-25's, A-20's, and A-36's from the Tactical Air Force bombed the town and nearby gun emplacements, and the British Wellingtons continued the attack that night. Italian antiaircraft fire was described as "inadequate but fairly accurate."[9]

Before midnight a British naval task force of four light cruisers and six destroyers opened up on installations on the island. The next day, June 12, the aerial bombardment increased in intensity, and, by late afternoon, 270 tons of bombs had been dropped on the defenders. One third of the batteries were knocked out, but the rest kept firing.

Seeing that he could not keep up this unequal struggle for long, the island commander urgently requested air support. Rome signaled back: "We are convinced that you will inflict the greatest possible damage on the enemy. Long live Italy!"[10]

Clearly abandoned, feeling betrayed, and convinced that he had done his duty, the commander ordered the white flags raised. Elements of the 2nd Coldstream Guards Battalion, which had been waiting offshore, came in and took charge of the prisoners and some three thousand civilians. Air base command personnel arrived shortly after the Coldstream Guards, and Lampedusa airfield would be serviceable by June 20. Meanwhile Linosa surrendered without a fight on June 13, and Lampione was found to be undefended. The entire Pelagian Island group was now in Allied hands.

Field Marshal Kesselring called the fall of Pantelleria and Lampedusa "a particularly dismal chapter in the Italian record" that removed the last doubts in his mind as to where the invasion would occur.[11] A startled OKW changed its position slightly. Although it still expected the invasion in Greece and Sardinia, it now considered an invasion of Sicily more possible than it had before. Pantelleria also exposed the true state of Italian morale for all the world to see and made the Italian High Command more amenable to German help. The day after Pantelleria fell Kesselring persuaded Commando Supremo, Ambrosio, and OKW to allow the Hermann Goering Panzer Division to move to Sicily.[12]

The Italian attitude was, in fact, changing, and new German units began to enter Italy at Mussolini's invitation. These included the 3rd and 29th Panzer Grenadier and 26th Panzer divisions, as well as the Headquarters of the LXXVIth Panzer Corps. Simultaneously, Hans Hube's XIVth Panzer Corps was ordered to cooperate with the Italian 7th Army against a possible invasion of southern Italy.[13]

The arrival of these troops indicated that the opportunity that had opened for the Allies after the fall of Tunisia was rapidly passing, if it had not passed already. The Axis southern flank, although not particularly strong, was no longer stripped of defenders.

If the Italians were willing to accept German divisions, they still wanted to limit German command prerogatives; therefore, they refused to allow a German corps headquarters to set foot in Sicily. Even so, there was a great need for a German liaison staff to deal with a whole variety of command and logistical problems and to coordinate activities between the 6th Army and its German components. The man who filled this post needed to be both a competent and experienced panzer commander and a diplomat. Such a man was Fridolin von Senger und Etterlin, a devout Catholic and a highly cultured officer known for his suave urbanity.

Senger was born at Waldshut, Baden, on September 4, 1892. He served a compulsory one-year term in the artillery in 1910 and then attended Freiberg University and became a Rhodes scholar at St. John's College, Oxford, until the outbreak of World War I. Recalled to active duty, he spent the war as an artillery officer on the Western Front. During the war he was granted regular officer status, was promoted to first lieutenant, and was selected for the four-thousand-man Officers' Corps when the Reichswehr was created in 1920. He spent most of the Weimar era with his regiment, the 18th Cavalry, at Stuttgart. In 1938, as a lieutenant colonel, he was named commander of the 3rd Cavalry Regiment at Goettingen. He was promoted to full colonel in March 1939 and, when the war broke out, was named commander of the 22nd Cavalry Regiment.

In February 1940 Major General Baron Wolfram von Waldenfels died of a stroke, and Colonel von Senger moved up to command the 2nd Cavalry Brigade, only to have his beloved horses phased out in favor of trucks, half-tracks, and motorcycles. It was called "Motorized Brigade von Senger" during the French campaign, where it did very well, especially in supporting Major General Erwin Rommel's 7th Panzer Division in the battles of the Channel ports in early June.

Recognizing Senger's agile intellect, the army next assigned him to the Italian-French Armistice Commission in Turin. Although technically only an observer, the shrewd colonel was able to influence the Italians' opinions and simultaneously made numerous friends among the Italians during his two-year tenure. Meanwhile, on September 1, 1941, he was promoted to major general.

Senger fulfilled his role in Turin so well that the Army High Command would not approve his requests for field service until the Franco-Italian Treaty was about to be ratified. It was October 10, 1942, before he assumed his new post: commander of the 17th Panzer Division.[14] Among the new staff officers was his own son, the future Doctor Ferdinand von Senger, who would become a noted author and expert on armored warfare.

When Stalingrad was surrounded, the 17th Panzer was rushed from its relatively quiet sector opposite Moscow to the Don River area, where it took part in the fruitless attempt to rescue the German 6th Army. By then von Senger was becoming more and more disillusioned about the Nazi party and its leader; still, he proved to be an excellent panzer commander, covering the rear of General Hermann Hoth's 4th Panzer Army against repeated Soviet attacks all the way back to the Donets during the first months of 1943. For this achievement he was awarded the Knight's Cross for gallantry. In June, however, he was recalled from the field and summoned to Fuehrer Headquarters.[15]

Adolf Hitler received Major General von Senger at the Obersalzberg on June 22, 1943. Also present were Keitel and Warlimont. "Hitler's orders were vague," Senger recalled, but he was surprised by the Fuehrer's knowledge of numerous details. Hitler discussed at length the possibility of defending Sicily even without Italian help with the two German divisions and the thirty thousand other men currently stationed there with antiaircraft units, the Luftwaffe ground organization, supply formations, and other units. He "was counting on Italy's defection in the near future" as a result of the intrigues of the royal court, social circles, the royalist General Staff, and others, Senger wrote later. Hitler also commented that "because they failed to cross over to Sicily immediately after their landing in North Africa, [the Allies] had already lost the Battle of the Mediterranean."[16]

After this rambling monologue ended, von Senger ate breakfast alone with Warlimont in the latter's apartment. Warlimont appraised the situation more realistically than Hitler had. He told the veteran cavalryman that in case of an invasion, his mission would be best carried out by transferring the majority of the German troops in Sicily to the mainland. He also commented on the improbability of salvaging most of the equipment.

After the general situation conference, Senger spoke with Keitel alone. "He had received reports about the local Sicilian conditions from General Hube," Senger remembered, "and apparently considered a successful defense as hopeless as did General Warlimont." The OKW chieftain also considered it impossible to keep the weak German forces together as a closed unit for use as a mobile reserve, because of the nature of the mountain roads and Allied air superiority.[17]

After leaving Hitler's headquarters in Obersalzberg, Senger met with Kesselring in Rome, where he found the optimism of the

Luftwaffe field marshal in stark contrast to the realism of Warlimont and Keitel. Later, in an unpublished manuscript, Senger wrote, "Many officers fighting in Africa (including Colonel von Bonin) charged that Kesselring held far too optimistic views of the situation, as a result of which the influence of Rommel, who had better opportunities for a correct appraisal, had been unduly restricted. I found these charges confirmed to the extent that Kesselring obviously considered the possibility of successfully defending Sicily with far too much optimism."[18]

The next day Kesselring escorted von Senger to Sicily to install him in his new post. This June 26 meeting at the 6th Army Headquarters at Enna, in the center of the island, was far more than a mere social call, however. Key German and Italian unit commanders on the island were also summoned to discuss the tactical plans for repelling the Allied invasion. Colonel Schmalz was present, as were Rodt, Conrath, and others. Schmalz later recalled with envy the impeccably dressed Italian officers and their luxurious headquarters.

The atmosphere of the conference was cool from the outset. Guzzoni was pessimistic about the general situation, and Kesselring was optimistic, as usual. General Guzzoni expected the Allies to attack in the middle of July and was dubious about the outcome of the battle. Tactically he had already assigned the western half of the island to Generale di Corpo Mario Arisio's XIIth Corps, which had the Assietta and Aosta divisions, three and a half coastal divisions, and the reinforced 104th Panzer Grenadier Regiment (Lieutenant Colonel Ens) from the 15th Panzer Grenadier Division. These German troops had been sent to the western end of Sicily at Kesselring's insistence in early June.

Guzzoni assigned Generale di Corpo Carlo Rossi's XVIth Corps the task of defending eastern Sicily with the Napoli Division and two coastal defense divisions. He placed the Hermann Goering Panzer Division and the bulk of the 15th Panzer Grenadier Division in reserve in southeast Sicily, under the XVIth Corps. Livorno— the best of the Italian divisions—he also posted in southeastern Sicily, but in 6th Army reserve so that he could personally decide the time and place of the main Italian counterattack. Guzzoni said that he expected the Allies to land in southeastern Sicily. According to his plan, the Italians would conduct a delaying action until the Germans and the Livorno could launch a concentrated counterattack where it had the greatest chance of success and throw the Allies back into the sea. Colonel Schmalz, who distrusted Italians in general and Guzzoni in particular, did not think Guzzoni wanted to defend the coast at all.

Up until this point Field Marshal Kesselring had not made a single misstep since the fall of Tunisia. He had correctly sized up the Allied intentions and taken appropriate countermeasures, both on his Sicilian front and in his rear. Now, however, he committed what proved to be one of the greatest tactical blunders of the campaign. He wanted to send the 15th Panzer Grenadier to the western end of the island (in the Caltanissetta-Enna and Salemi areas) to guard against an attack against Palermo, while the Hermann Goering Division, part of which was still en route to Sicily, assembled at Caltagirone in the southeast. Another regimental group of the 15th Panzer Grenadier would be assigned to the Catania sector on the east coast, under Brigade Schmalz. In other words, Kesselring wanted to scatter the 15th Panzer Grenadiers—the best division in Sicily—all over the island.

Albert Kesselring was a forceful, convincing man. General Guzzoni was a competent tactician but not what one would call a strong personality; rather, he "was always conciliatory and prepared to moderate differences." Senger recalled, "With regard to the employment of German forces, Guzzoni was entirely willing, even against his own better knowledge, to adapt himself to Kesselring's wishes, since he realized that the German divisions were the backbone of his defense."[19]

Coupled with Hitler's strategic ineptitude, Kesselring's decision robbed the 6th Army of its only chance to repel the invasion. This eventually doomed the entire campaign to failure.

Like Guzzoni, Rodt considered this decision wrong and opposed it because of its lack of concentration. Also like Guzzoni, Rodt's objections were listened to politely and then overruled by Kesselring. Linklater, the British official historian, commented that this "nervous dispersion made it impossible for them to launch an early concentrated assault against any part of the invading forces."[20] Montgomery later agreed with Guzzoni and Rodt, when he expressed the opinion that the Germans had dissipated their strength.[21]

Major General von Senger also objected to the plan. Like Kesselring, he feared a landing in western Sicily, which might cut off both German divisions in southeastern Sicily (i.e., Husky 8). Senger opposed the plan not because of its dissipation of strength but because of Kesselring's *choice* of divisions to dissipate. He pointed out that the 15th Panzer Grenadier was familiar with the local conditions, terrain, and population. They had a well-organized reconnaissance system along the coast, greater combat strength, and a more experienced divisional commander who had General Staff training. "By way of contrast," he noted later in a Foreign Military Study for the U.S. Army,

> the Hermann Goering Division was characterized by internal and external weaknesses to a considerable degree. To begin with, this division did not control any substantial infantry strength at all, for it had only two battalions, in addition to the armored personnel carrier battalion. No information could be obtained as to whether other battalions were in the process of activation or en route. Although the division had an armored regiment of its own, the "Tiger" tank company, which was stationed as GHQ troops on the island, had for some time been attached for tactical and logistical purposes to the 15th Panzer Grenadier Division—another reason for leaving this division here in eastern Sicily. Even more dangerous were the division's internal weaknesses, about which the superior commanders had no accurate information at this time. The division commander had, as Kesselring himself notes in this study, "too little experience in the handling of modern, combined arms." As a former police officer he apparently had not received such training as the Army would otherwise have considered necessary for this sort of mission. Of those two of his regimental commanders who held the most important combat positions [had to be relieved] . . . immediately after the beginning of action, because they were unfit to command. Similar defects were evident in other ranks. . . .
>
> In view of these circumstances it should be noted that it was a mistake to entrust the Hermann Goering Division with the more important task, namely, the defense of eastern Sicily.[22]

After agreeing to Kesselring's disastrous modification of his tactical battle plan, General Guzzoni made his final dispositions for the expected invasion (Map 3). Appendix 3 shows the detailed order of battle of the Italian 6th Army, including the composition of the mobile groups.[23] In total, Guzzoni had 230,000 Italian divisions and 30,000 German soldiers. None of the Italian divisions were considered particularly reliable by the Germans.

The Naval Fortress Areas of Messina-Reggio, Trapani, and Augusta-Syracuse remained independent of the 6th Army's control.

Meanwhile, Kesselring conducted his last briefing with his German divisional commanders prior to the invasion. "It makes no difference whether or not you get orders from the Italian Army at Enna," he told them. "You must go into immediate action against the enemy the moment you ascertain the objective of the invasion fleet."

"If you mean to go for them, Field Marshal, then I am your man," Paul Conrath replied.

"I returned home feeling pretty confident," Kesselring recalled.[24]

One thing Kesselring did not have confidence in was his own branch of the service: the Luftwaffe. It had been in continuous action since the Torch landings and before and had been badly led, badly equipped, and badly shot up. Morale in most units was at a low ebb in July 1943.

Although it was not apparent to everyone at the time, the Luftwaffe in general had been in a state of mismanagement and decline for years. The technological superiority it had enjoyed in its early campaigns was a thing of the past by early 1943. More important, it was fighting multiple enemies on multiple fronts and was being crushed by pure weight of numbers. In the Mediterranean theater in particular things were about as bad as they could be.

The demise of the Luftwaffe in the Mediterranean began during the Alamein battles but was accelerated during the Tunisian campaign. A good case study of this decline is the 77th Fighter Wing (Jagdgeschwader 77, or JG 77), under the command of Major Johannes "Macki" Steinhoff, who became commander of the West German air force in the 1970s.

JG 77 (the *Herzas*, or Ace of Hearts, wing) was one of the better units in the Fighter Branch (*Jagdwaffe*). It had served in Poland, Denmark, Norway, the Battle of Britain, Russia, over Malta, and

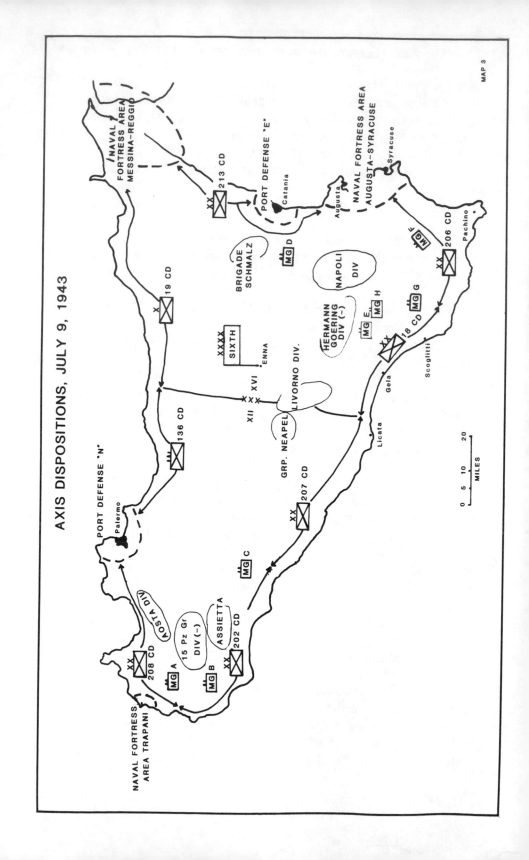

AXIS DISPOSITIONS, JULY 9, 1943

MAP 3

in Egypt and Libya, where it had flown in support of the Afrika Korps. It already had more than 1,300 aerial victories when it arrived in Tunisia in early 1943.[25] Its commander on March 23, 1943, was twenty-four-year-old Major Joachim Muencheberg, a Pomeranian.

Muencheberg was a physical fitness enthusiast and one of the best fighter pilots in the Luftwaffe. He had already scored 135 victories, 102 of them against the Western Allies, and most of them against the RAF. Hitler had personally decorated him with the Knight's Cross with Oak Leaves and Swords.

On March 23, JG 77 engaged a vastly superior force of U.S. fighters over Tunisia. Muencheberg found himself surrounded almost immediately. He maneuvered rapidly and skillfully, successfully avoiding machine gun bursts from several opponents, until he was just on the point of eluding his pursuers. Then his wing collapsed and his aircraft buried itself in the Tunisian earth, killing him instantly.

Major Steinhoff, a Saxon with more than 150 kills (mostly on the Eastern Front), was called to Berlin and offered command of JG 77 or a wing stationed in Germany. Without hesitation, the twenty-nine-year-old Steinhoff[26] chose the 77th Fighter. He was immediately sent to Italy for a pep talk from Field Marshal Kesselring. Just out of the rigors of the winter battles on the Russian Front, Steinhoff was chauffered through the luxurious Roman suburb of Frascati and into the villa that housed OB South. He was not impressed. He called Kesselring's staff officers, dressed in their white tunics, "unbelievably gorgeous creatures." He found their manner of talking down to him, as if they knew much more than he, both pompous and "downright insulting. . . . I found their foppish affectation and general superciliousness insufferable."[27]

When he was ushered into Kesselring's office, OB South told him that he must convince his people that North Africa had to be held at all costs. Steinhoff's first job, he said, was to restore the fighting spirit of his pilots, to rekindle the élan that had inspired everyone during the drive to El Alamein.

"A day or two later I had come to grips with reality," Steinhoff wrote later. An RAF pilot pumped several bullets into his radiator, and he was forced to make a belly landing south of Kairouan.[28]

By the time of the end in Tunisia, JG 77 had suffered heavy casualties and was "physically and mentally exhausted."[29] Its pilots took off for Trapani airfield in western Sicily only in intervals between attacks by Kittyhawks and Spitfires, with their mechanics stuffed inside the fuselages and with no way to escape if the aircraft were shot down into the sea. When the wing landed in Sicily it had only its airplanes, pilots, and mechanics; everything else had been lost, including signals equipment, tools, motor transport, spare parts, fuel trucks, cargo trucks, avionics equipment, typewriters, mess equipment, ammunition stocks—everything, including anyone they could not stuff into the belly of an Me-109. They had only 40 aircraft left (their establishment called for 100 to 120), and none of these could be maintained. This, then, was the type of unit with which the Luftwaffe was supposed to defend Sicily.

Kesselring turned up at the airfield on May 8, radiating confidence and optimism. He told Steinhoff that his mission now was to defend Sicily. He would try to send the wing some equipment, personnel, and new aircraft, but they were to recuperate where they were. Steinhoff's request to withdraw to Italy to rebuild his unit was denied.

Later that day Kesselring was conferring with naval officers on the upper floor of their headquarters when the harbor was struck by an air raid. Kesselring's aide was killed, the staircase was destroyed, and Kesselring had to escape by sliding down a rope to the street—and he was no longer a slim, trim second lieutenant. Both of his palms were burned and had to be wrapped in gauze and put into slings.

The next day Kesselring gave Steinhoff permission to withdraw to Bari, on the Adriatic coast of mainland Italy, to rest and rebuild his unit. This did not help much, however. For example, by the time of the invasion, the 2nd Air Fleet had furnished only one ambulance to the wing.

The plight of the Ace of Hearts wing was not unusual. From November 1942 to May 1943 the Luftwaffe lost 2,442 aircraft in the Mediterranean, 40.5 percent of its entire force structure as of November 10, 1942. The Allied air forces now outnumbered the Axis air forces by 2.5 to 1, but the Italian air force, with brave pilots but hopelessly obsolete airplanes, counted for little. The Luftwaffe alone was outnumbered at least four to one.

Sicily had become a target in February 1943, three months before the remnants of JG 77 limped into Trapani. The attacks were delivered mainly by the B-17's of the 12th U.S. Air Force and the B-24's of the 9th U.S. Air Force, with assistance from the Wellingtons of the RAF, Middle East. Their main targets were airfields and ports. On March 1 Felicita Alliata di Villafranca, who lived on her family estate not far from Palermo, wrote in her diary, "Weather always beautiful. Another punishment from God. The moonlight favors the air raids; always more frequent bombings, machine-gunnings of trains, sinkings in the Messina Straits, fire and explosions in Palermo . . . hunger . . . lack of everything."[30]

Throughout April the bombings intensified. Sicily, southern Italy, and Sardinia were bombed repeatedly in an attempt to isolate the Tunisian battlefield. Palermo was attacked eight times during the month, Messina six times, and Trapani six times. Palermo was particularly hard hit on May 12 by four hundred aircraft flying in perfect formation.

That same day Admiral Arturo Riccardi, chief of the Italian Naval General Staff, complained to Grand Admiral Doenitz that the air attacks were causing such severe damage in the Straits of Messina that it had become difficult to maintain the garrison in Sicily. Not even 130 heavy antiaircraft guns had discouraged the attackers. Fighter-bomber attacks also increased alarmingly. Railroad traffic on the island had come to a complete standstill, and Riccardi was forced to ship supplies by sea from Naples. Rear Admiral Pietro Barone, the Italian naval commander of Messina-Reggio, seemed close to despair.[31]

The debacle in Tunisia and the fall of Pantelleria brought a particularly strong reaction from OKL, the High Command of the Luftwaffe. The RAF historian noted that "the Luftwaffe headquarters staff in the Mediterranean, which had shown itself lamentably wanting in ability and energy, was strengthened by the transfer of energetic and experienced officers from Russia."[32] A new command, *Fernkampffuehrer Luftflotte 2* (Bomber Command, 2nd Air Fleet), was established under the command of Colonel Dietrich Peltz. Subordinate to the IInd Air Corps, it controlled all long-range bombers in Sicily, Italy, and southern France. Adolf Galland, the "General of Fighters" (i.e., inspector general of fighters and ground attack aircraft), was sent to Sicily to speed the arrival of pilots and aircraft and to restore the efficiency and morale of the fighter units. Most shocking of all to the Italians, Field Marshal Wolfram von Richthofen replaced Kesselring as commander in chief of the 2nd Air Fleet, although Kesselring remained as OB South.

Hitler had designated Kesselring *Oberbefehlshaber Sued* in October 1941, when he decided to move his Headquarters, 2nd Air Fleet, and the entire IInd Air Corps from the Russian Front to Italy. Hitler intended that Kesselring assume the task of directing and assuring safe passage for the military convoys bound for North Africa. When he arrived in Rome, however, the Italians balked. Marshal Cavallero told him politely but firmly that Italian honor would not allow this arrangement. He refused to allow Kesselring to command Italian air or naval units or the convoys. Although he retained the title of commander in chief, South (OB South), it was for the moment not justified. All Kesselring commanded in 1941 and 1942 was a two-corps air fleet in the Balkans and southern Italy, plus a few units in North Africa.

All this had changed by 1943, of course. Kesselring was rapidly acquiring ground forces and was well on his way to becoming a real C-in-C, South. Hitler now apparently thought, probably correctly, that the jobs of OB South and C-in-C, 2nd Air Fleet had grown too big for one man and that a shake-up in the Mediterranean theater was necessary. Goering's jealousy of Kesselring—who was mentioned by some as the Reichsmarschall's possible successor—might have played a role. In any case, the appointment of von Richthofen was an unfortunate one.

Wolfram von Richthofen was an arrogant, demanding prima donna. The nephew of the famous Red Baron, Wolfram had joined his uncle Manfred's wing in 1918, after spending the first three years of World War I as a cavalry officer on the Eastern Front. After Manfred was killed, Wolfram flew under the command of his successors, the last of whom was Captain Hermann Goering. When World War I ended, Wolfram, who had eight confirmed "kills," returned to school and earned an advanced degree in engineering. In the Reichswehr years he served in the secret air force and spent considerable time in Italy, studying under Marshal Italo Balbo, the Italian aviation innovator. After the Nazis took power, Richthofen came into his own, serving as chief of staff and later as commander of the Condor Legion in Spain, where he pioneered the close air support techniques that helped make the blitzkrieg so successful in the early years of World War II. He was also a pioneer and early advocate of terror bombing, a technique he had also learned in Spain. He firebombed Warsaw in 1939, plastered Belgrade and Leningrad in 1941, and all but leveled Stalingrad in 1942. He had led the Stuka-heavy VIIIth Air Corps in Poland and France, over Britain, and in Yugoslavia, Greece, Crete, and Russia. He had defeated the British Mediterranean Fleet in 1941 and had distinguished himself as commander in chief of the 4th Air Fleet in the Stalingrad campaign, for which he was awarded his marshal's baton. Now he had come to save the Mediterranean for the Third Reich.

Richthofen had worked well with Kesselring when the former's VIIIth Air Corps was part of the latter's air fleet on the Western Front in 1940 and in Russia in 1941. Now, however, Richthofen was determined to act independently. He decided that the invasion would come against Sardinia and, despite all of Kesselring's re-monstrations, moved the bulk of his fighters there. From mid-May until July 10, 1943, the number of aircraft in Sicily actually declined from 415 to 175 in spite of the fact that the Mediterranean was receiving 40 percent of all German aircraft production—mainly Me-109 and FW-190 single-engine fighters. Table 2 shows the Luftwaffe's dispositions by sector from May 14 to July 10.

There was no respite for Sicily. Catania was now an almost deserted city. As a result of Fascist inefficiency and lack of organization, many of the streets remained blocked with debris from bombing attacks. Electricity and water supplies were intermittent, the sewage system was entirely disrupted, the already sparse food supply became more irregular, and there were not enough air raid shelters. It was the same in all the other cities. In Syracuse many of the remaining inhabitants lived in the ancient Christian catacombs of Saint Giovanni, where they found an occasional skull.

Meanwhile, in mid-June, the Air Commander Sicily (*Flieger-fuehrer Sizilien*), Lieutenant General Theodore Osterkamp, was relieved of his command by Goering's special plenipotentiary, General Galland, and was replaced by Lieutenant General Alfred Mahncke, another veteran of the Russian Front. Osterkamp was a fifty-one-year-old fighter pilot who still flew operational missions with men half his age. Born in Dueren in the Rhineland in 1892, he had led the 2nd Naval Fighter Squadron (*Marinejagdstaffel 2*) in

TABLE 2

LUFTWAFFE DISPOSITIONS IN THE MEDITERRANEAN
BY SECTOR
MAY 14–JULY 10, 1943

Sector	14 May 1943	1 June 1943	14 June 1943	3 July 1943	10 July 1943
Sardinia	80	80	115	175	115
Sicily	415	275	315	290	175
Central and southern Italy	200	360	290	345	460
Southern France and northwestern Italy	—	80	80	165	135
Greece and Crete	125	185	220	305	265
Totals	820	980	1,020	1,280	1,150

SOURCE: March, p. 258.

Flanders in World War I, where he shot down thirty-two enemy airplanes and won the coveted *Pour la Merite* (the Blue Max). In 1919–1920 he fought with the anti-Communist Iron Division in Russia against the Bolsheviks. After joining the Luftwaffe, he served as commandant of the 1st Fighter School (1935–1939), and in November 1939 he organized and was the first commander of the 51st Fighter Wing, which was to register more than eight thousand kills during the war. Osterkamp accounted for six of the kills himself during the French campaign and the Battle of Britain, where he was commander of fighter units in Kesselring's 2nd Air Fleet. Later sent to Italy, he was called Onkel Theo (Uncle Theo) by his men, who had a great affection for him.[33] Galland's move did nothing to improve morale or the military situation in Sicily. Kesselring was quite unhappy about this decision and later commented, "Unfortunately, at this very inopportune moment our leading fighter-pilot, General Osterkamp, was relieved by the German ace fighter-pilot, General Galland. There was nothing to be done about it. With Osterkamp's departure we lost the benefit of his invaluable local experience."[34]

Galland himself raced from airfield to airfield, trying to inspire the pilots and accomplishing nothing, as he admits in his memoirs.

Alternately commanding from west and east Sicily, I instigated almost anything that was still justifiable. But we could really do nothing about the overwhelming Anglo-American superiority. Our pilots were exhausted to a terrifying degree. . . . Our ports in Sicily, our bases, the supply and repair stations in the south of Italy, all were subjected to the Anglo-American hail of bombs. Bari, the assembly station for the aircraft replacements from home, was hard hit several times. Hundreds of new fighter aircraft were lost.[35]

The morale of Luftwaffe fighter pilots in the Mediterranean declined precipitately from the latter half of May through early July, a period during which they fought no fewer than twenty-one major air battles against vastly superior enemy forces. Goering recognized what was happening but not the cause. He brought great pressure on 2nd Air Fleet to get better results. One order is particularly astonishing. It read:

Together with the fighter pilots in France, Norway and Russia, I can only regard you with contempt. I want an immediate improvement in fighting spirit. If this improvement is not forthcoming, flying personnel from the commander down must expect to be remanded to the ranks and transferred to the Eastern Front to serve on the ground.

On June 25 the Reichsmarschall went one step further. He issued an order demanding that one pilot from each fighter group in the 2nd Air Fleet be court-martialed for cowardice in the face of the enemy. Several outraged group commanders, their Knight's Crosses dangling from their necks, intervened for their pilots and turned themselves in for trial, forcing Galland to quietly sweep the matter under the rug. It had done nothing to improve morale, however.

Steinhoff and the other wing and group commanders knew that the men were exhausted and had been driven almost beyond hope. Of his pilots, Steinhoff wrote in his diary on July 5, "I had long been aware that they had ceased taking unnecessary risks. . . . Now they only went for the easy kills—the solitary flier, the inexperienced pilot who had broken away from his formation, the crippled straggler. . . . But now we were tired, worn out and dispirited."[36]

With their opposition deteriorating, the American twin-engine, twin-boomed P-38 Lightnings, which had been escorting bombers, began attacking ground targets in southern Sicily if they did not encounter enemy fighters in their escort duties. Trains were favorite targets, but so were trucks, wagons, and troop units. German soldiers already dreaded the appearance of the Lightnings, and the "German glance"—a fugitive look over the shoulder for enemy airplanes—arrived in Europe.

Despite their newfound caution, the fighter wings in Sicily were being crushed by sheer weight of numbers. German industry was producing 847 fighters per month, while the Anglo-Americans were manufacturing more than twice as many; in fact, they were producing four-engine bombers at a rate nearly twice that for German *fighters* (1,024 per month for the United States, 405 for Britain). Russian aircraft production figures are not included here because of their notorious unreliability, but the Soviet contribution tilted the balance even further against Germany.

With the odds shifting against the Axis, the demand on OKL for fighter pilots increased dramatically. OKL responded by rushing replacements through the Me-109 transition schools far too quickly. In 1940, novice pilots received seventy-five hours in the single-engine fighter before being sent to operational units. This was reduced to 50 hours in 1942 and 25 hours in 1943, as opposed to 75 for their British and 125 for their American counterparts. The new Allied aviators also got twice as much flight time in basic flight school as did the new German pilots. As a result, during the air battles for Sicily, the new German pilots were clearly inferior to their Anglo-American opponents.

Despite all this, the German aviators took off day after day, despite mounting losses, and were soon exhausted. They had reason to be worn out and demoralized. They were facing four thousand Allied aircraft, and they were fighting for their own bases. Nineteen major Axis airfields were bombed in June alone, as well as twelve newly constructed fields of lesser importance. Messina, the principal line of supply from the mainland to Sicily, was also a major target. In June it was attacked several times by

Flying Fortresses during daylight hours and by RAF Wellingtons at night. From June 12 to July 2 the U.S. North African Air Force alone raided it eleven separate times, dropping 829 tons of bombs. On June 25 four U.S. B-17 bomber groups pounded the ferries to Italy, railroad yards, docks, warehouse areas, and other targets. More than three hundred tons of bombs were dropped on Messina alone, while complementary raids were launched against Reggio and San Giovanni, across the straits on the mainland. The OKW War Diary recorded: "Heavy damage to private dwellings, public buildings, barracks and other military objectives. Fuel stores in flames, ammunition dumps blown up. Rail link between Palermo and Catania cut. Casualties reported to date: 62 dead, 75 injured."[37]

Field Marshal von Richthofen tried to turn the tables on the Allies by bombing their airfields and invasion ports, but he was hamstrung by his own bomber wings (*Kampfgeschwadern* or KG), which were notoriously poor. Of the 250 to 300 bombers in the 2nd Air Fleet, only an average of 55 percent were serviceable on any given day, and because of the shortage of trained crews, only half of these could be used at any one time. These were generally incapable of finding their targets or even finding their way back to base. On the average, only twenty-five to thirty German bombers reached the target area per mission, and losses were disproportionately high—10 to 15 percent per mission—often as a result of faulty navigation (i.e., because the navigator could not find his way back home).[38] Results, of course, were negligible. From April 1 to July 9, only nine Allied ships were sunk by Axis aircraft.

On June 22, Richthofen and Italian General Rino Corso Fougier, the head of Superaereo, the High Command of the Italian Air Force, agreed in principle to retire most of their bombers to continental airfields; Richthofen, however, wanted to launch one more major blow at Allied shipping. More than a hundred Ju-88's, FW-190 fighter-bombers, and Italian CANT.Z-1007's struck an eastbound convoy off Cap Bon. Six Axis aircraft were shot down by the British Coastal Air Command, which was responsible for convoy cover. No ships were sunk and no Allied aircraft were shot down. Shortly thereafter, all but a handful of the Italian torpedo bombers and four-engine bombers and the twin-engine German bombers were withdrawn to bases at Pisa and Perugia, leaving virtually nothing but fighter aircraft (i.e., defensive aircraft) in Sicily and southern Sardinia.[39]

The Allies began their final, all-out air offensive during the last half of June, especially from July 1 on. Their objectives were to eliminate the Axis air forces and communications centers; to isolate Sicily from the mainland by sinking the Messina ferries; to neutralize the railroads in Sicily and southern Italy, in order to cut 6th Army's supply lines and make it impossible to reinforce the island; and to further lower Axis (especially Italian) morale.

JG 53 (the "Ace of Spades" wing) was one of the main targets. Based at Comiso, a former Italian air force base, it was attacked numerous times in June, and particularly heavily on June 26. All its hangars and many of its aircraft were destroyed. During the following week almost every major airfield and communications center was hit, many of them several times. During the night of July 2–3 the Northwest African Air Force (NAAF) dropped 1,520 tons of bombs on the Gerbini-Catania fields alone. The Foggia airdrome on the Adriatic coast of Italy and the fields in southern Sardinia were also bombed.

The Allied bombers attacked each airfield often, as they had learned from experience that spasmodic raids caused only temporary damage. On some occasions Allied heavy bombers would attack one or two airfields in a sector, and when the German or Italian fighters diverted to an undamaged field, the Allies would follow with a concentrated blow against them. As the Luftwaffe increased its dispersion by using satellite strips, the Anglo-Americans countered with mass strafing and fighter-bomber attacks. "A follow-up with fragmentation bombs added measurably to the effectiveness," a U.S. Air Force report stated. Against the hangars the Americans used 500-pound GP (general-purpose) bombs; against the more primitive satellite fields they used 100-pound demolition and 20-pound fragmentation (antipersonnel) bombs in 120-pound clusters.[40] They were very effective. On July 5, for example, a raid on the Gerbini complex destroyed about fifty of the fifty-four aircraft present, according to Johannes Steinhoff. He recalled: "A bomb carpet is a terrible weapon. . . . Particularly effective were the smaller bombs which the enemy released by the thousand. They made only shallow craters and the fragments, projected outwards at high velocity and close to the ground, shredded the outer skins of our aircraft as though they were made of paper."[41]

An FW-190 fighter-bomber group was pretty much destroyed at Gerbini, as was I/JG 77 and an Me-109 group from both the 51st and 53rd fighter wings. It was a major blow to the Luftwaffe. Richthofen's fighter-bomber concentration in Sardinia was also attacked. Serviceability here declined from 55 to 35 percent, mainly because of fragmentation and GP bombs. As a result, the Luftwaffe forces available to reinforce Sicily were weakened, and German bombers found it difficult to use the Sardinian airfields as forward landing grounds. In Sicily, according to Generale di Brigata Emilio Faldella, about two hundred Italian airplanes were destroyed on the ground and only seven in the air. About one hundred German airplanes were destroyed on the ground and in the air during the week of July 3–10, although exact figures are not available. Among the German dead were second Lieutenant Herbert Broennle of I/JG 53, a man with fifty-seven victories, killed in action on July 4; and First Lieutenant Hans Roehring of III/JG 53, seventy-five victories, killed on July 7.[42]

On July 9, the day before the landings, the Allied air forces had approximately 4,900 operational aircraft, divided among 146 American and 113.5 British squadrons. That day they launched twenty-one major raids against airfields and other targets from Sciacca to Taormina. The Luftwaffe Headquarters at Taormina as well as the nearby Church of San Domenico, were destroyed, leaving forty-five dead. Gerbini and seven of its twelve satellite fields were now unusable, as was Comiso, Catania, and Bocca di Falco. Palermo, Trapani, Cagliari, Messina, and others were attacked and suffered varying degrees of damage. Castelvetrano had to be abandoned, and several other fields were only usable in emergencies. Only Sciacca and Trapani/Milo were fully operational on July 10. The Luftwaffe had only about fifty operational airplanes left on the island as the Allied invasion fleet began its final approach to Sicily.[43]

Despite the fact that the Luftwaffe had been largely neutralized and the Italian railroad targets were attacked as far north as the Brenner Pass, the Allied air forces were less successful than they hoped in isolating the battlefield. Throughout June men and equipment poured into Sicily, including the entire Hermann Goering

Panzer Division and smaller units. Even though the Messina ferries were attacked many times and at least four were sunk, the Germans continued to ferry four hundred railroad cars per day across the straits by using Siebel ferries, naval barges, fishing boats, and the ferrying equipment of the Army's 771st Engineer Landing Battalion. Railroad damage was repaired quickly, using Italian railroad and construction units. "In conclusion," read an after-action report of Luftwaffe Major General Conrad Seibt, the supply and logistics expert with OB South, "it may be stated that by the beginning of July, adequate supplies for a three-month period had been stockpiled, as ordered, despite numerous difficulties."[44]

Logistically at least, the German units on Sicily and part of the Italian 6th Army were prepared for the Allied invasion of July 10, 1943.

✧ 6 ✧

THE ALLIES APPROACH

THE FINAL HUSKY PLAN DIVIDED THE ASSAULT FORCES INTO AN
Eastern Task Force and a Western Task Force. The Western
Naval Task Force, which would land Patton's 7th Army, included
580 ships and beaching craft (vessels that came up on their own
bottoms) and 1,124 shipborne landing craft. The Eastern Naval
Task Force controlled 795 ships and beaching craft and 715 shipborne landing craft. Each navy provided gunfire support for troops
of its own nation, but the Royal Navy also provided two covering
forces for the entire operation.

A total of 2,590 naval vessels would be used in the initial assault
alone. They would bring ashore 115,000 British Empire and
66,000 American soldiers, 14,000 vehicles, 600 tanks, and 1,800
guns. It would be the largest amphibious operation in history up
until that time.

The Husky plan called for airborne landings by elements of two
divisions, followed by eight simultaneous seaborne assaults by
seven divisions and several independent ranger and commando
formations, to be made along approximately a hundred miles of
coastline between Cape Murro di Porco (just below Syracuse)
around the southeastern tip of Sicily, as far west as Licata. The
plan reflected Alexander's low estimation of the American combat
capabilities, a view he shared with Montgomery. (Alexander had
been overall ground commander in Tunisia and had been de-
pressed by the American performance at Kasserine Pass; he had
mistaken inexperience and local incompetence for national military
ineptitude.) In any event, the assault was British-heavy, and all of
the major ports were in the British zone.

Eighth Army planned to come ashore on beaches fronting the

Gulf of Noto, just south of Syracuse, on both sides of the south-eastern tip of Sicily. The plan called for Montgomery to take the ports of Syracuse, Augusta, and Catania quickly. Patton's 7th Army was to land to the west, along seventy miles of beach on the Gulf of Gela, with only the minor ports of Licata and Gela available. Even after the initial assaults, Patton would have to rely on the open beaches for resupply and maintenance.

Specifically, 8th Army's D-Day objectives were Pachino Airfield and the important road and railroad communications centers of Novo, Avola, Cassibile, and Ponte Grande. These were to be taken in order to form a firm base for the attack through Syracuse and Augusta and to open up the road leading north to Catania and Messina, the strategic objective of the campaign.

On Montgomery's right (northern) flank, the 1st Air Landing Brigade was to capture the vital Ponte Grande Bridge on the edge of Syracuse Bay a few hours before the landings. Then Lieutenant General Sir Miles Dempsey's XIIIth Corps was to land on a two-division front. On the north, the British 5th Infantry Division was to land in the vicinity of Cassibile, while the British 50th (Northumbrian) Infantry Division was to land on its left, attack inland, and capture Avola. Lieutenant General Sir Oliver Leese's XXXth Corps formed the southern prong of Monty's attack. The 231st Independent (Malta) Brigade was to land on the east coast just north of Pachino. The 51st Highland Division was to land on the southernmost tip of the Pachino peninsula, while the Canadian 1st Infantry Division was to land on the southwest part of the peninsula at Costa Dell'Ambra. The 40th and 41st Royal Marine Commandos were to land on the left flank of the Canadians, on the extreme left flank of the British 8th Army.

The initial objectives of the U.S. 7th Army were the ports of Gela and Licata and the towns and airfields of Ponte Olivo, Comiso, and Biscari. The 45th Infantry Division was to land on the American right flank and was then to advance inland and capture the airfield at Comiso. The 1st Infantry Division, reinforced with the 1st and 4th Ranger battalions, was to capture Gela and push inland to Ponte Olivo.

The Allied extreme left flank was the responsibility of Major General Lucian K. Truscott's U.S. 3rd Infantry Division, which was directly subordinate to 7th Army. Its D-Day objectives were the small port and airfield at Licata. Counting attachments, Truscott's division numbered 45,000 men.

The American assault landings were code-named (left to right) Joss, Dime, and Cent, while those of the British were called Bark West, Bark South, Bark East, Acid South, and Acid East. The 7th Army had the 2nd Armored Division (minus CCA) in floating reserve, while the U.S. 9th Infantry Division was in army group reserve. Montgomery's reserve unit was the British 78th Infantry Division, which, like the U.S. 9th, was still in North Africa. Table 3 shows the order of battle of the 15th Army Group on D-Day, and Appendix 4 gives a more detailed breakdown of Allied forces.

T A B L E 3

ORDER OF BATTLE, 15th ARMY GROUP,
July 10, 1943

15th Army Group: General Sir Harold Alexander
  British 8th Army: General Sir Bernard L. Montgomery
    XIIIth Corps: Lt. Gen. Sir Miles Dempsey
      5th Inf. Div.: Maj. Gen. G. C. Bucknall
      50th Inf. Div.: Maj. Gen. S. C. Kirkman
    XXXth Corps: Lt. Gen. Sir Oliver Leese
      231st (Malta) Bde: Brigadier Roy Urquhart
      51st Inf. Div.: Maj. Gen. Douglas Wimberley
    1st Can. Inf. Div: Maj. Gen. Guy Simonds
    1st British Airborne Div.: Maj. Gen. G. F. Hopkinson
    40th and 41st Commandos: Brigadier R. E. Laycock
    In reserve (Africa):
      78th Inf. Div.: Maj. Gen. Vivian Evelegh

  U.S. 7th Army: Lt. Gen. George S. Patton, Jr.
    IInd Corps: Maj. Gen. Omar N. Bradley
      45th Inf. Div.: Maj. Gen. Troy H. Middleton
      1st Inf. Div.: Maj. Gen. Terry Allen
    3rd Inf. Div.: Maj. Gen. Lucian K. Truscott, Jr.
    82nd Airborne Div.: Maj. Gen. Matthew B. Ridgway
    Floating reserve:
      2nd Armored Div.: Maj. Gen. Hugh J. Gaffey*

  Army Group Floating Reserve:
    U.S. 9th Inf. Div.: Maj. Gen. Manton S. Eddy

*Excluding Combat Command (CCA), which was attached to the U.S. 3rd Infantry Division.

Perhaps the most controversial part of the final Husky plan was the parachute/glider attacks. The first airborne assault (Husky One) was to take place just before midnight on July 9. The 505th Regimental Combat Team (RCT) of the U.S. 82nd Airborne Division was to seize the high ground called Piano Lupo (about seven miles northeast of Gela), disrupt enemy communications north and northeast of the landing beaches, conduct ambushes against targets of opportunity, create havoc in the enemy's rear, and generally make a nuisance of itself. The only reason that the entire U.S. 82nd Airborne Division was not dropped was that the Americans lacked the transport aircraft to move it all at once.

Simultaneously with the initial American drop, the gliders of British Colonel George Chatterton's Glider Pilots' Regiment were to crash-land their Horsa and Waco gliders near Syracuse, depositing Brigadier Philip H. W. "Pip" Hicks's 1st Air Landing Brigade near enough to seize and hold the vital Ponte Grande Bridge, allowing the British main assault force to cross the Anapo River and seize Syracuse quickly. The 1st Air Landing assault was code-named Ladbroke.

A second American night drop (Husky Two) was scheduled for July 10–11, when Colonel Reuben H. Tucker's 504th RCT (minus one battalion) plus divisional support troops would jump into zones west of Gela, an area already secured by Gavin's 505th—or so the plan said. The third regiment of the 82nd Airborne, the 325th Glider Infantry, was not scheduled to be used in Sicily. It was immobilized because all available gliders had been turned over to the British.

The final airborne drop (Operation Fustian) was to occur on the night of July 13–14. Brigadier Gerald Lathbury's British 1st Parachute Brigade was to seize the key Primosole Bridge over the Simeto River, paving the way for Monty's advance into the Catania plain.

All of these drops were to take place at night because the Allies were not sure that the Luftwaffe had been neutralized. A night drop would help protect the slow, unarmed C-47 transports (called Goony Birds) and would aid in the tactical surprise. Colonel Chatterton objected to the plan, pointing out that his pilots had had minimal training in the Horsa gliders and none at all in the American Wacos and that they would have to crash-land at night, under enemy fire, in unfamiliar terrain. All of this, he felt, exceeded the capabilities of his relatively inexperienced men. His objections were overruled. The operation went ahead as planned, despite the risks.

On July 4 Axis long-range aerial reconnaissance aircraft spotted twenty-five merchant ships off Cape Serrat, and Axis intelligence reported that about one hundred enemy vessels were approaching the Mediterranean via the Straits of Gibraltar. In Sicily, General Guzzoni was nervous about these reports. He met with his chief of staff, Colonel Faldella, and General von Senger und Etterlin at 6th Army Headquarters in Enna. Senger expressed the belief that the Allies were preparing simultaneous attacks against Sardinia, Greece, and Sicily but conceded that a lone attack against Sicily might be imminent. Noting increased Allied convoy activity in North Africa, the increasingly powerful aerial offensive against Sicily, and the number of heavy warships in the central Mediterranean, Guzzoni put 6th Army on full alert. He had acted prematurely. The Allied invasion did not get under way until the following day and would not reach Sicily until five days after that. Guzzoni was already on his guard, but, in a sense, he was like the little boy who cried wolf. The already disillusioned coastal gunners had to endure yet another in a long series of what they considered to be senseless alerts. And again nothing happened. On Sicily, alerts were beginning to lose their meaning.

And where was the Italian Navy while Admiral Cunningham was assembling his huge invasion armada? The startling answer is that most of it was in port, doing nothing, while the fate of Fascist Italy was being decided.

When Mussolini declared war on France and the United Kingdom on June 10, 1940, Italy had an impressive and unusually fast fleet—on paper. During World War II, however, it almost never left port. On November 11, 1940, twenty obsolete Royal Navy Swordfish biplanes, equipped as torpedo bombers, took off from the aircraft carrier *Illustrious,* attacked the Italian naval base at Taranto, and inflicted heavy damage on the battleships *Littorio, Duilio,* and *Conte di Cavour.* At the cost of two biplanes shot down, the British had crippled almost half of the Italian fleet and inflicted a severe inferiority complex on the rest, effectively neutralizing it for the rest of the war. The Royal Navy had convinced the Italian Supermarina that it would be foolishly suicidal to venture out of port, and most of it never did.

The Italian Navy had brief moments in 1941 and 1942 when it might have accomplished something against a Royal Navy weakened by the Luftwaffe and/or U-boat attacks or diverted to threats elsewhere. Instead, it pled a fuel oil shortage and technical problems, and the surface ships remained in port. Grand Admiral Erich Raeder, commander in chief of the German Navy from 1939 to 1943, periodically sent a few U-boats to the Mediterranean to help the Italians, but never many. On January 30, 1943, Raeder was retired by Hitler and replaced by Admiral Karl Doenitz, until then commander of the U-boat branch.

The new Grand Admiral's attitude toward the Mediterranean was similar to that of his predecessor. He agreed to send a few more U-boats to the region for nuisance and harassment purposes but persuaded Hitler not to send any more. He correctly pointed out that submarines could not halt an invasion (as the U.S. Navy had discovered in the Philippines in 1941–1942) and claimed (also correctly) that he had no more U-boats to spare, having lost forty-one in the Atlantic in May alone. Besides, Admiral Doenitz was exasperated by the Italian Navy. "It would be better for the Italian ships to get into a fight even at the risk of heavy losses, rather than to fall into the hands of the enemy without a fight," he told Hitler.[1] As a result of Doenitz's strategy, the Germans had only six submarines in the vicinity of Sicily when the Allied invasion fleet sailed and eleven others in the eastern and western Mediterranean, which could be quickly diverted to Sicilian waters. Small as this effort was, it equaled the Italians' contribution of sixteen submarines.[2]

None of these statements are meant to imply that Doenitz's strategy was not perfectly correct or reasonable, because it was. The Mediterranean was a secondary theater for the navy, and he treated it as such. He did, however, make positive contributions to the Axis cause in Sicily, even if he refused to waste any of his limited combat resources on it.

First of all, Doenitz appointed a former minesweeper officer, Vice Admiral Friedrich Ruge, as German Naval Commander, Italy. Doenitz correctly guessed that the sophisticated and diplomatic Ruge would smooth relations between the navy, Supermarina, and OB South, end the squabbling, and put the energy of the few

German naval forces in Italy to work in the area Doenitz considered most important: supplying the islands of Sicily, Sardinia, and Corsica.[3]

Doenitz visited Rome from May 12 to May 15 and told Admiral Riccardi that he considered Sicily the most likely target of the invasion. A defeat at sea would not be decisive to them, he said, but if the supply system failed—as it had in Tunisia—then the islands could not be held. "We must therefore use every available means to get as much matériel to the islands as possible. Even small vessels will have to be used for shallow harbors and open bays. We can worry about distribution later on." Doenitz preached the same sermon to General Ambrosio the next day. He recommended that a large number of loading and unloading points be established on both the mainland and Sicily, "since adequate air cover can never be expected. This calls for improvisation, such as collecting small craft and using them as lighters. . . ." Doenitz even suggested that submarines and cruisers be used, if necessary, in a supply role.

Ambrosio objected to this suggestion, saying that he felt submarines and cruisers should fight. Doenitz replied that the Italian Navy had "already ceased fighting. When the serious need for transport is compared with what may be gained by engaging the enemy, the former takes precedence."[4]

Later that day the Grand Admiral met with the representative of the German Transportation Ministry (BVM), Senatssyndikus Essen, who was involved with efforts to help Organization Todt improve many small harbors in the region and construct 150 unloading points. Doenitz backed these efforts and saw to it that convoys of small auxiliary vessels, landing craft, and ferries would be available for transporting men, equipment, and supplies to Sicily.

To help supply the island, Doenitz assigned the 2nd Landing Division under Commander Baron Gustav von Liebenstein, who directed the landing craft of the 2nd, 4th, and later the 10th Landing flotillas. The Grand Admiral also dispatched the Headquarters, 7th Naval Security Division (Commander Bergelt), to the sector to take charge of the minesweepers, transport escort vessels, and antisubmarine vessels.

Against Liebenstein's small, unescorted vessels, the Allied bombers were trying to shoot gnats with cannons. Naturally enough, they simply left them alone most of the time. As a result, the ground units in Sicily were always at least adequately supplied. Doenitz's vessels would pay even larger dividends later, when the time came to evacuate the island.

Other than ferrying supplies, the Axis navies had almost no successes and suffered some costly failures against the Allies. On April 10 the photographic reconnaissance wing of the Northwest African Air Force discovered several large Italian warships "smugly anchored behind nets in Maddalena Bay, Sardinia." Shortly afterward, twenty-four B-17's bombed and sank the cruiser *Trieste* from an altitude of 19,000 feet. At the same time, thirty-six more B-17's damaged the cruiser *Gorizia* so badly that it was forced to proceed to La Spezia, where it was attacked by the RAF. And that was the end of the surface battle as far as the capital ships were concerned. No place within range of the Allied bombers was considered safe, and soon there were no harbors that qualified, even for the smaller vessels. By June 1943, Italian Rear Admiral Pietro Barone, the commander of Naval Fortress Area Messina-Reggio, wrote, "There no longer existed a harbor or naval base in Sicily where ships great or small could remain in safety."[5]

The German Navy was also heading in the other direction. As a result of the "Major William Martin" incident, most of the German E-boats (motor torpedo boats called S-boats by the Germans) were transferred to the Peloponnesus. The one squadron left at Porto Empedocle on the southern coast was transferred to Trapani on the western tip (where it was useless) just days before the invasion. The E-boats at Salerno and Palermo were transferred to Messina, as were the Italian MAS (light torpedo) boats formerly stationed at Trapani. The few German U-boats in the area sank a few of the invasion fleet's vessels, including two American LSTs (landing ship, tank). The Italian Navy did not even do that. On July 8, Supermarina proposed deploying all available submarines in the Straits of Sicily to resist the landings, but Vice Admiral Sansonnetti and Commander Kreisch, the Captain of U-boats, Italy, declined to do so because they did not know the positions of their own minefields! As a result, the High Command of the Italian Navy decided to employ all submarines south of Sicily *after* the invasion began in hopes of breaking up supply convoys. Naturally they accomplished nothing.[6]

The only action the Italian Navy saw prior to the landings occurred during the night of July 9–10. At 7:30 P.M. Supermarina ordered all Italian boats at Porto Empedocle to move to Augusta. En route, these boats (including torpedo boats) discovered the western convoy of the Allied invasion, which was carrying the U.S. 3rd Infantry Division. Rather than attacking, they turned around and headed for Trapani, alleging a "violent enemy reaction."[7] Neither side had suffered any casualties.

As the Allied invasion vessels prepared to sail from their North African ports, Axis reconnaissance aircraft reported on July 5 that the number of hospital ships in North Africa had increased from two to sixteen. Guzzoni took this as further proof that an invasion was imminent. Another intelligence report reached Rome that day, apparently from an agent in Libya. It at last informed Italian intelligence that Montgomery's missing 8th Army Headquarters had been located between southern Tunisia and Tripoli. The Allies had taken the precaution of temporarily renumbering it 12th Army, but the pro-Italian spy had not been deceived. His (or her) report convinced Italian military intelligence that an invasion of Sicily was imminent. Apparently it also convinced Mussolini, who signaled Guzzoni the next night, "You are to defend Sicily at all costs."[8] At 12:45 P.M. on July 7, the deputy chief of staff telephoned the 6th Army commander and told him that he could expect an attack very shortly.

The following day, July 8, General Guzzoni ordered the southern shore ports of Licata, Porto Empedocle, and Sciacca prepared for demolition. Commando Supremo issued similar orders for Trapani and Marsala.

Hitler still would not believe that Sicily was the target of the invasion. On July 9, at a Fuehrer Conference, he and General Jodl agreed that Greece was a more likely objective than Italy and that any landings on Sicily or on the Italian boot would be just stepping-stones to the Balkans. For this reason they had placed sixty thousand troops on the island of Crete alone. The Balkans obsession continued to dominate Hitler's mind even though, in reality, the region had never entered into Allied strategic planning. Meanwhile, Allied ships pressed on closer and closer to Sicily.

At 3:20 A.M. Luftwaffe spotters located a convoy of seventy to ninety vessels about twenty miles south of Pantelleria, proceeding in an easterly direction at high speed. When he received this message later that morning, Guzzoni concluded that the invasion was not far off.

At 1:30 P.M. OKW received reports of 150 to 180 ships in five convoys, including warships and landing craft, heading north. This report would not reach Hitler for several hours, however. Meanwhile, an aide handed Kesselring an urgent message, apparently from Richthofen, reporting that Luftwaffe aircraft had spotted a powerful invasion fleet in the Mediterranean. Its destination was still unknown. Kesselring promptly alerted all German forces from Greece and the Balkans to Sardinia. He warned his staff that the long-awaited invasion might be at hand.[9]

At 4:30 P.M. OB South finally received aerial reconnassaince reports confirming that the convoys were steering toward Sicily and concluding that their destinations were the southern and eastern coasts of the islands. Kesselring's staff immediately passed this information along and at 4:40 P.M. recorded that "all troops in Sicily had been alerted."[10]

But had they been?

Guzzoni received reports of additional convoys at 6:10 P.M., and by 6:30 P.M. reconnaissance aircraft had reported six convoys heading toward Cape Passero and Gela Bay. More sighting reports came in as the night wore on. At seven P.M. Guzzoni ordered a partial alert, and at ten P.M. the entire Italian 6th Army was ordered to go to full alert.[11]

Meanwhile, a *tramontana* was blowing. The Italian counterpart of the French mistral, the *tramontana* is an unseasonably hard, cold wind that swiftly whipped the sea into what Majdalany called "a flurry of white-capped waves." There was some question on both sides as to whether or not landings were possible in such seas. The Admirality in London signaled Admiral Cunningham and asked him what he intended to do. "Weather not favorable, but operations proceeding," the fleet commander signaled back.[12]

At the same time, ten P.M., Guzzoni's orders reached Generale di Divisione d'Havet's headquarters in southeastern Sicily. The general consulted his naval advisers, who assured him that the weather was too rough and the seas too high for a landing. D'Havet no doubt concluded that Guzzoni was just being nervous again. He went to bed. As a result, the alert was largely ignored in the vital southeastern sector. Many officers went to sleep at their

Above: Motorcycle troops of the Hermann Goering Panzer Division. After fighting in Sicily, these troops fought in Italy, Russia, and Poland. They ended the war fighting Soviet forces in East Prussia. (Bundesarchiv, Kolbenz)

Right: Field Marshal Albert Kesselring (center), the Commander-in-Chief, South, speaks with Reichsmarschall Hermann Goering (left) on the day Kesselring received the Diamonds to his Knight's Cross. As OB South, Kesselring played a pivotal role in the campaign in Sicily. (U.S. National Archives Photo 242-HLB-234-3)

Above: **General Sir Harold Alexander *(right),* Commander of the 15th Army Group, receives a report from a subordinate while an American lieutenant colonel looks on. Alexander was criticized by Montgomery and others for a lack of decisive leadership during the Sicilian campaign. (U.S. National Archives Photo 80-G-58431)**

Left: **Generals Montgomery *(left)* and Patton exchange insincerities at Palermo, July 28, 1943. (U.S. National Archives Photo 111-SC-180655)**

Top right: A rare photo of General Hans Valentin Hube, the commander of the XIV Panzer Corps, who, with only four divisions, successfully tied down two Allied armies for more than a month and then escaped with nearly his whole command intact. (Imperial War Museum)

Top left: Major General Walter Fries, commander of the 29th Panzer Grenadier Division. Despite having lost an arm and a leg on the Russian Front, the tough Fries did an excellent job in opposing Patton's drive on Messina, during which his division constituted the main delaying force. (Bundesarchiv, Kolbenz)

Bottom: Major General Eberhard Rodt, commander of the 15th Panzer Grenadier Division. During the Battle of Sicily, his division formed the dependable center of the German line and inflicted heavy casualties on the U.S. 1st Infantry Division at Troina. (Bundesarchiv, Kolbenz)

Above: In this photo the photographer, looking from Enna toward Gela, shows the difficult nature of the terrain over which Patton's 7th Army and Montgomery's 8th had to advance, and why Hube was able to conduct a successful delaying action. (U.S. Army War College Photo)

Below: The results of a chance meeting on the road to Palermo: Italian dead and dying lie in and beside the road while U.S. army medics dress the wounds of an American lieutenant. The Italian truck was surprised by the American patrol and hit "friendly" mines while trying to escape. (U.S. Army War College Photo)

Above: An army mule, coming ashore reluctantly at Licata, Sicily, in the zone of the U.S. 3rd Infantry Division. Due to the terrain, these mules became an important part of the invasion. (U.S. Army War College Photo)

Below: American artillerymen tow their 155-mm gun over a dirt road in the rough terrain of Sicily, July 1943. In Sicily, the terrain favored the defenders to such an extent that it robbed the Allies of their superior mobility and often deprived them of supporting artillery for some periods of time. (U.S. Army War College Photo)

Above: **Members of the U.S. 82nd Airborne Division killed by German tanks in the sector of the U.S. 45th Infantry Division. This photo was taken on July 13, when the paratroopers had been dead about two days. (U.S. National Archives Photo 111-SC-183823)**

Right: **Major General James M. Gavin, 1944. As a colonel in July 1943, Gavin commanded the 505th Parachute Infantry Regiment of the 82nd Airborne Division during the invasion of Sicily. The drop of the 505th was so scattered that Gavin was not sure for several hours that he had actually landed in Sicily. (U.S. National Archives Photo 286-MP-NETH-2374)**

Top: Sicilian refugees returning home, near the town of Parvo, July 17, 1943. (U.S. Army War College Photo)

Bottom: An American Sherman tank, part of the U.S. 2nd Armored Division, enters Palermo on July 22, 1943. Note the proliferation of white flags in the area as the Sicilian civilians hasten to surrender and get out of Mussolini's unpopular war. (U.S. National Archives Photo 111-SC-179709)

Above: **Generale di Brigata Giuseppe Molinero, the commandant of Palermo, and his captor, Major General Geoffrey Keyes, the deputy commander of the U.S. 7th Army, July 22, 1943. (U.S. National Archives Photo 111-SC-180126)**

Below: **Italian prisoners of war talking with an American private of Italian descent. This photo was taken outside of Gela on July 11, 1943—the second day of the invasion. (U.S. National Archives Photo 111-SC-181029)**

regular times, and the lethargic coastal units, wearied by weeks of false alarms, relaxed their vigil instead of increasing it.

Meanwhile, Allied air forces bombed the headquarters of the Livorno Division at Caltanisetta and the Napoli Division HQ at Palazzolo Acreide. Syracuse and Catania were also hit, and the Italian naval headquarters and HQ, Port Defense E were seriously damaged. Then Syracuse, Catania, Taormina, Trapani, and Augusta were bombarded by Allied warships, firing at long range with their big guns. Most of the sleepy coastal defense gunners, however, knew nothing of this; the sound of the bombs, shells, and explosions was drowned out by the *tramontana*.[13]

On July 9 General Dwight D. Eisenhower was settling into his new advanced headquarters on Malta, where he occupied a guest room provided by General Lord Gort, the island commander. Ike became increasingly concerned as the favorable weather of the morning gave way to heavy, gusting winds. They would have a particularly devastating effect on the paratroopers, Eisenhower knew, and yet if the airborne drops were not made, the entire operation might fail. Summoning up all of his courage, as he would do in the Normandy invasion the following year, Eisenhower decided not to abort the jumps. The order was given to proceed with scheduled operations in spite of the high winds. The first lift of C-47's, loaded with paratroopers, took off at 10:10 P.M. and was followed one hour later by the second lift.[14] The invasion of Sicily had begun.

Far away in East Prussia, another entirely different group of paratroopers was set in motion by Adolf Hitler. Having finally read the OKW report of 1:30 P.M., Hitler decided that the invasion just might be aimed at Sicily, after all. At ten P.M. the Fuehrer ordered that the German 1st Parachute Division (1st, 3rd, and 4th Parachute regiments) be alerted for possible immediate transfer from France to Sicily, via airdrop if necessary.[15] This order came very late, insofar as the German defense of Sicily was concerned; but, as late as it was, it did not come too late.

Shortly after midnight on July 10 the *tramontana* subsided somewhat, and the first vague reports of Allied parachute landings reached the Italian 6th Army. Guzzoni knew at once that the invasion had begun. He declared a state of emergency and exhorted soldiers and civilians alike to join together and repel the landings. More realistically, at 1:45 A.M. he ordered his corps commanders to expect landings all along the southern and eastern coasts.[16]

Even now, however, the Italian 206th Coastal Defense Division was sleeping peacefully. Undisturbed by its headquarters, it was blissfully unaware that it was about to be hit by the largest amphibious landing in the history of the world.

The handful of German naval technicians at the search radar stations were not asleep on the night of July 9–10, but they might have thought they were dreaming. Their screens were going wild, lit up with hundreds of blips. Surely, they decided, there could not be that many ships out there. After some discussion they concluded that their equipment must be malfunctioning. They decided not to report their discovery until morning.[17]

✦ 7 ✦

D-DAY

IN 415 B.C. ALCIBIADES SAID, "IF SYRACUSE FALLS, ALL SICILY FALLS also, and Italy immediately afterwards."[1] Although it had lost much of its military significance since the Peloponnesian Wars, Syracuse was still an important Sicilian port and the initial objective of the invasion. According to the final Husky plan, the "Red Devils" of the British 1st Air Landing Brigade were to seize the Ponte Grande bridge, which crossed the Anapo River one and a half miles southwest of Syracuse, and hold it until relieved by elements of the British 5th Infantry Division, part of Montgomery's main landing operation. Six Horsa gliders, each carrying twenty-eight men, were supposed to land almost on top of the vital stone bridge, capture it, remove the demolition charges, and await relief. In the meantime, 137 Waco gliders, each carrying thirteen men, would land in several zones one and a half to three miles from the bridge and rush to Ponte to reinforce their comrades. That was the plan, anyway.

At sunset on July 9 the Red Devils boarded their gliders at six airfields in the vicinity of Kairouan, Tunisia. At six P.M. the 147 tow planes began to take off, each with a loaded glider behind it. One hundred nine of these airplaines were C-47's (called Dakotas by the British), which were flown by the inexperienced pilots of the U.S. 51st Troop Carrier Wing. All 147 gliders had British pilots from the Glider Pilot Regiment, but these men had only five hours' training time in the American Wacos. Many had not advanced beyond the first solo stage when they arrived in North Africa three weeks before the operation began. Troop Carrier Command therefore had only three weeks to train them in navigation and night flying. It simply could not be done. In addition, because of the *tramontana,* the winds aloft were blowing at forty miles per hours: too much for the inexperienced pilots.[2]

The assault elements of the 1st Air Landing Brigade included 2,075 men, seven jeeps, six pieces of artillery, and ten 3-inch mortars. The air formations were joined at 10:20 P.M., and the flight to Sicily began. They encountered strong winds, poor visibility, communications failures, and flak at several points. Most of the formations broke up to avoid Italian searchlights. Some pilots climbed and others descended, while some banked left and others banked right. One Horsa, loaded with bangalore torpedoes, was hit by an antiaircraft (AA) shell and exploded, throwing debris everywhere. Half of the intercoms failed, preventing the two pilots from giving the order to release. Some glider pilots did not await the order to release but cut loose on their own—too soon. Others released on order, only to find that the order had been given too soon. Ten gliders were not released at all for one reason or another. The entire operation was a mess. At least 65 Wacos plunged into the sea, including that of Colonel Chatterton, who was saved from drowning by a Red Devil, but at least 252 other men were drowned. Fifty-nine gliders were scattered over twenty-five miles of land between Cape Passero and Cape Murro di Porco. Only 12 gliders landed in the general vicinity of the landing zone—12 out of 147.

Through this massive confusion flew Staff Sergeant D. P. Galpin in Glider Number 133, a British Horsa carrying a platoon of South Staffordshire troops under Lieutenant Louis Withers. Galpin was either an excellent pilot, or very lucky, or both. He alone landed in the designated area, only two hundred yards south of the Ponte Grande bridge. Withers, realizing that he could not count on help, decided to attack the key position with the troops at hand. He swam the river with half his men, and on a prearranged signal, the platoon attacked the bridge from the north and the south. After a brief firefight the Italians (part of the 120th Coastal Infantry Regiment) abandoned the pillbox on the north side and melted into the darkness while Withers and his men ripped out the demolition charges and threw them into the water. Then they waited for help.

Ponte Grande bridge was in the zone of Naval Fortress Area Augusta-Syracuse, one of the most heavily fortified strongpoints in southern Europe. It included the two ancient cities and twenty-four coastal defense batteries, five antiparatrooper/glider batteries, hundreds of machine guns, and several mobile combat groups, any one of which could have recaptured the bridge. Lieutenant Withers and his twenty-seven men were in a dangerously exposed position as July 9 faded imperceptibly into July 10—D-Day.

Meanwhile, on the La Maddalena peninsula, about 150 British glidermen attacked and captured the Cape Murro di Porco radio station. They had acted quickly, but not quickly enough. Before the Red Devils broke through the door, the radio broadcast the news of the glider landing. Among those who received the warning was General Carlo Rossi, the commander of the XVIth Corps. Rossi immediately gave orders for four combat groups to rush to the critical bridge and recapture it. Any one of the four could have done the job, but they never got the order. Hundreds of Red Devils, accidentally scattered all over the island, had cut the telephone wires on which the corps commander depended. Italian communications were disrupted to the point where General Rossi could not launch a major counterattack. Meanwhile, scattered groups of glidermen made their way to Ponte Grande; by 6:30 A.M. on July 10, eighty-seven British soldiers were holding the bridge.[3]

Meanwhile, from south of Syracuse to Licata, thirteen infantry battalions of the Italian 206th and 207th Coastal Defense divisions and the 18th Coastal Defense Brigade, supported by a handful of artillery batteries, faced one of the largest amphibious assaults of the war. Map 4 shows the detailed dispositions of the coastal defense battalions, and Map 5 shows the Allied landings and their dispositions for D-Day.

About seven miles south of Ponte Grande, at 2:45 A.M., the British infantry division began to land on the coast of Sicily. Opposition was light. The coastal town of Cassibile fell about eight A.M., and the few Italian guns that fired on Acid North were quickly silenced by the destroyer Eskimo. The forty-nine landing craft assigned to the division were capable of putting seven hundred men per hour on the beaches, so the buildup proceeded slowly but steadily. There was some confusion on the beachhead, but no more than was normal in an amphibious operation; nevertheless, it was three P.M. before the division, spearheaded by the 2nd Royal Scots Fusiliers, was ready to move off its beachhead and advance on the Ponte Grande bridge and Syracuse.[4]

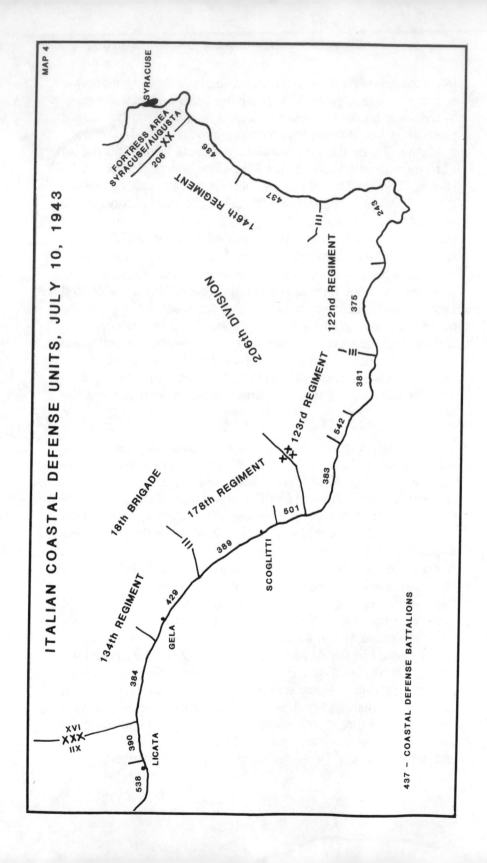

ITALIAN COASTAL DEFENSE UNITS, JULY 10, 1943

MAP 4

FORTRESS AREA
SYRACUSE/AUGUSTA

SYRACUSE

206

436

146th REGIMENT

437

243

206th DIVISION

122nd REGIMENT

375

381

123rd REGIMENT

542

383

18th BRIGADE

178th REGIMENT

501

SCOGLITTI

389

134th REGIMENT

429

GELA

384

390

LICATA

XVI
XII

538

437 — COASTAL DEFENSE BATTALIONS

As the British landings and buildups proceeded with minimal interference from the 206th Coastal Defense Division, the Italians at Syracuse slowly began to react against the small band of men at the Ponte Grande bridge. They were seriously handicapped by the fact that the commander of the Syracuse garrison was killed at the very beginning of the battle, but gradually the Italians rallied. Two companies of sailors attacked first but were beaten back. Gradually they were reinforced as the Italians shelled the bridge with mortars and, finally, field guns. The Italian 385th Coastal Battalion joined the battle, and at about 11:30 A.M., the 1st Battalion of the Italian 75th (Napoli) Infantry Regiment came up, and the fighting . became desperate. (This unit had been placed at the disposal of the Syracuse garrison commander by General Rossi, who was acting on the orders of General Guzzoni.) Early in the afternoon the Italians struck at the bridge from three sides. The Red Devils held on, but by 2:45 P.M. there were only fifteen unwounded defenders, although several of the wounded continued to fight. Finally, at 3:30 P.M., the end came when the ammunition ran out. A small group on the south side of the bridge escaped, but the wounded had to be abandoned to the clemency of the enemy. The few unwounded or lightly wounded survivors on the north side threw their weapons into the Anapo River and surrendered. The Italian commander then sent the thirteen or so prisoners back to Syracuse, but en route the guards were ambushed by another group of Red Devils, and the defenders of Ponte Grande were free again.

Back at the Anapo, the Italians feverishly tried to rewire the bridge for demolition, but they did not have time to finish the job. At 4:15 P.M the 2nd Battalion, Royal Scots Fusiliers arrived, attacked, and recaptured the bridge.[5] The road to Syracuse was open.

The 1st Air Landing Brigade, having accomplished its mission, albeit with unsatisfactorily high losses, was withdrawn from the battle and embarked for Africa on July 13. During Operation Ladbroke it had lost 313 killed (252 of them drowned) and 174 wounded or missing, for a high casualty rate of 23.5 percent. The glider pilots lost an additional fourteen killed and eighty-seven wounded or missing.

In the meantime, the British 8th Army stormed ashore south of

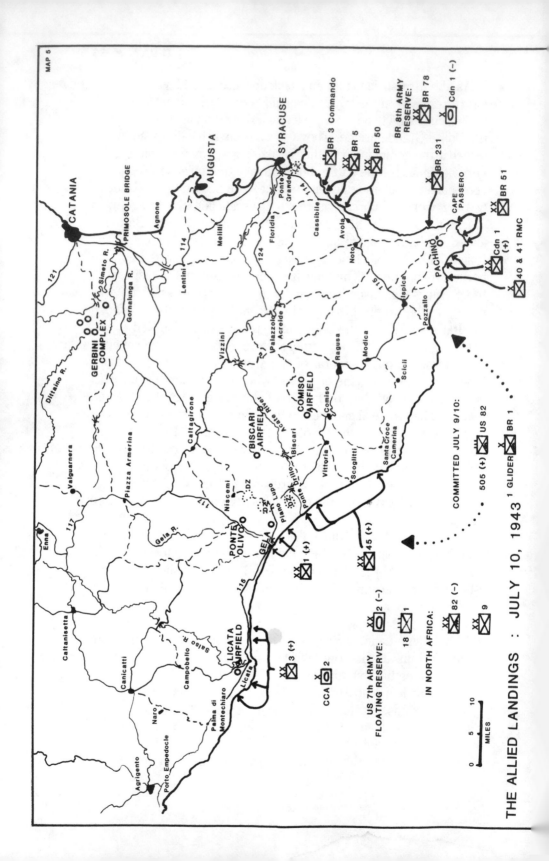

MAP 5

THE ALLIED LANDINGS : JULY 10, 1943

Syracuse against light resistance. Major General Sidney C. Kirkman's 50th Infantry Division suffered considerably from rough seas and landed about an hour late. Frequently men and/or equipment were deposited at the wrong place, and there was more than a little confusion. By nightfall the Northumbrians had only nine guns ashore. Nevertheless, by eight A.M. all of the Italian batteries in the sector had been silenced, and the main divisional objective, the town of Avola, population 22,000, fell at ten A.M.

Lieutenant General Sir Oliver Leese's XXXth Corps landed on the "Bark" beaches south of Avola. His northern flank was covered by the 231st Independent Brigade—also known as the Malta Brigade—which did everything about as well as it could be done on D-Day. It landed at Marzamemi right on time and achieved a tactical surprise so complete that the assault troops found the entire crew of an Italian 75-mm fieldpiece, concealed in a shed fifty yards behind the beach, fast asleep. The soldiers manning one battery of five coastal defense guns did wake up in time to lay down a barrage two hundred yards off the beach, but they did not hit anything and were quickly silenced by a pair of Dutch gunboats. By noon the brigade had reached the road running north of Pachino, its final objective of the day. It then began pushing on toward Palazzolo Acreide and Vizzini.

To the south, Major General Douglas Wimberley expected little resistance when his 51st (Highland) Infantry Division landed. Just before D-Day, an aerial photograph revealed a party of local women bathing on one of his main assault beaches. General Wimberley was right. His men waded ashore on three separate beaches between 2:45 and 4:30 A.M. Things went so smoothly that the LCTs (landing craft, tank) had all the tanks and antitank guns ashore by daylight.

The Pachino peninsula is arid, flat, and almost treeless: good terrain for deploying troops. The Italians, who demonstrated no will to resist, were quickly disarmed and hurried back to the beaches for transport to North Africa. As they advanced, the Highlander infantrymen soon got rid of their heavy packs by dumping them into a remarkable variety of brightly painted Sicilian carts, dilapidated autos, or the backs of "liberated" mules and donkeys. The advance assumed almost a comic-opera quality. At seven A.M. the division took what Morison called "the poor little town" of Pachino,[6] and by nine A.M. they had linked up with the

Canadians, having accomplished all their main objectives for D-Day.

On Wimberley's left flank the 1st Canadian Infantry Division experienced more difficulty in landing than Monty's other divisions had, owing to the fact that they landed on the southern shore of Sicily, where sea conditions just offshore were worse. They were about two hours late getting ashore but quickly made up for lost time and were soon advancing inland toward their most important D-Day objective: the Pachino Airfield, located a mile west of the town and three miles from the Canadian beaches. In an emergency this field was capable of handling sixty to eighty fighter aircraft, so Montgomery, Cunningham, and Tedder all wanted it seized quickly.

Resistance was very light as the Canadians advanced inland. They found that the horse-drawn Italian 54th Artillery Regiment of the Napoli Division had virtually melted away, its men having deserted before the Canadians arrived. At seven A.M. they attacked Maucini, a village one mile inland and two miles from the airfield, and took a dozen prisoners. Then a Canadian sergeant fired a single warning shot over an Italian battery north of the village. The entire strongpoint garrison of three officers and thirty-five men left their dug-in positions with their hands up and surrendered.

The Italians at the Pachino Airfield put up an equally determined resistance. One soldier fired one shot in defense, but he missed. The Canadians returned fire and killed one Italian. Then a dozen Italians threw up their hands and surrendered one of the most important airfields in southern Europe. A nearby howitzer battery was found deserted.

About noon there was a brief firefight when a company of Canadians attacked an Italian position north of the airfield. Two Canadians were killed and two wounded before an Italian garrison of 130 men surrendered. The defenders' weapons had included a battery of four 6-inch guns.

Only on the Canadian left, in the zone of Brigadier R. E. Laycock's Special Service Brigade, did the Italians show any aggressive spirit. Here the Blackshirt unit of the 206th Coastal Defense Division launched a counterattack, supported by heavy mortar and antitank fire. The fanatical Fascists halted the lightly armed Commandos and threatened to separate them from the

Canadian 2nd Brigade. Fortunately for the invaders, there was a Canadian heavy mortar unit nearby. It bombarded the Italians with what Laycock called "devastating accuracy." The Blackshirt attack collapsed as quickly as it had begun. The Commandos pursued, capturing the Italian horse-drawn artillery and a large quantity of ammunition. It was the only counterattack in the Canadian sector all day long. By nightfall the Canadians were several miles inland. They had taken 650 prisoners, including 20 Luftwaffe support personnel. Their losses for the day were seven killed and twenty-three wounded.

The following day the 40th and 41st Royal Marine Commandos of Laycock's brigade, having carried out their mission of covering the Canadian left, were withdrawn into army reserve. They had lost six men killed and nineteen wounded.[7]

As important as the advances of the Canadians, the Commandos, the Highlanders, and the Northumbrians were, they were all of secondary importance to that of the 5th Infantry Division, which had the primary mission of the 8th Army: to seize and hold the all-important port of Syracuse. After retaking Ponte Grande at 4:15 P.M., the division's vanguard was only about two miles from the city. Here it halted, reorganized, and awaited reinforcements for the final attack.

Meanwhile, an ugly chain reaction began in Vice Admiral Primo Leonardi's Naval Fortress Area Syracuse-Augusta, when a small German antiaircraft detachment withdrew to the north, apparently to join Brigade Schmalz. This had a demoralizing effect on the Italians, who soon panicked and were seized with a positively frenzied orgy of destruction. Despite the absence of a direct threat, they blew up fixed positions, gun emplacements, fuel tanks, and ammunition stockpiles. Hundreds of sailors and soldiers deserted. The crew of an armored train at Targia (on the line between Augusta and Syracuse) blew up its four 120-mm guns and numerous smaller weapons, claiming they had to because they had no water for the locomotives.

Naval Fortress Area Syracuse-Augusta was the most massively fortified defensive position in all of Sicily. To defend the two ancient cities and twenty miles of coast, it had at least twenty-three coastal defense batteries (four of them of 6-inch caliber), five antiparatrooper batteries, dozens of reinforced bunkers, miles of barbed wire, mobile assault troops, minefields, armored trains, armored cars, and hundreds of machine guns. Yet when the vanguard of the 5th Infantry Division marched into Syracuse on the evening of July 10, they found it abandoned and the port undamaged. In their haste to escape, the Italians had even neglected to destroy the harbor installations. The city was quickly occupied and the British 5th continued its advance northward on a two-brigade front. They took Floridia from the disintegrating Napoli Division that evening, and the pursuit continued. It was not halted until after nightfall, when the Britishers ran into Brigade Schmalz, which had hurriedly come down from Catania to oppose the landing forces. Schmalz's men had hurriedly dug in on good defensive positions at Priolo, midway between Syracuse and Augusta, and stopped the British vanguards in their tracks. Later that night, after being shelled by British naval gunfire, Colonel Schmalz retired to his next delaying position at Melilli, with the Napoli Division on his right flank and the fortress of Augusta on his left. Knowing that he could not halt the British with his meager forces, Schmalz had already decided to conduct a delaying action all the way back to the Simeto River, south of Catania. He hoped that by then reinforcements would arrive that would enable him to hold this line and keep the British armor from reaching the Catanian plain; otherwise, there was a distinct danger that nobody could stop Montgomery before he reached Messina and bottled up the entire garrison of Sicily.

No one was more surprised at the ease of Montgomery's D-Day victory than General Montgomery himself. On July 9, the very eve of the landings, he had written in his diary, "I am under no illusions as to the stern fight that lies ahead." He did not believe that the U.S. and Royal air forces had established air supremacy over the invasion area. He was sure that the Luftwaffe and its Italian allies were "holding back and not fighting, obviously according to orders." He expected a bitter battle on July 10, with the Italians stiffly defending their home soil, supported by a valiant and undefeated Luftwaffe.[8] Instead, he encountered weak resistance and enjoyed complete aerial superiority in the British sector. The Italian coastal defense troops deserted or surrendered in droves, and the overly dispersed Napoli Division did little better. According to one British author, the Italians "stampeded to the safety of our prisoner-of-war cages on the beach in such terrific disorder that our troops faced greater danger from being trampled upon than from bullets."[9]

How did Montgomery explain his miscalculation? With three words: "I was wrong." He went on to state that the Allied air forces had definitely won the air battle before the invasion took place, and he even sat down and wrote a letter of appreciation to his personal enemy, Air Chief Marshal Tedder.[10] This, however, could not correct a mistake Monty had made based on his over-estimation of Axis ground and aerial resistance. He had made his initial forces combat-heavy, loaded with infantry, tanks, guns, and heavy weapons. The assault troops lacked vehicles, fuel, and the logistics and support units necessary to sustain the momentum of an advance, and it would take a long time to remedy the situation. At the moment all that stood between Montgomery and Messina were a few demoralized Italian units and one well-led German battle group that amounted to little more than a reinforced panzer grenadier regiment. But the British pursuit could only go at infantry speed. Would it be fast enough? This question was uppermost in the mind of Wilhelm Schmalz as he deployed his troops at Melilli. It did not concern General Guzzoni, however. Why not? Because, as incredible as it may seem, no one had bothered to inform him that Syracuse had fallen and that his left flank was on the verge of collapse. It must be recalled that Naval Fortress Area Syracuse-Augusta was under the command of Vice Admiral Leonardi, who was not subordinate to Guzzoni's 6th Army Headquarters at Enna. Leonardi had not informed Guzzoni that his command was disintegrating. And why not? Because Leonardi did not know it himself! He remained secure in the comfortable isolation of his headquarters at Melilli and did not learn that Syracuse had fallen until the following morning.

Later, when General Guzzoni learned what had really happened at Syracuse, he recommended that Leonardi be court-martialed immediately. Fortunately for Leonardi, the decision on Guzzoni's recommendation had to come from Rome. Months later, after Mussolini had been deposed and reinstated, the Fascists held a trial and sentenced Leonardi to death in absentia. By this time the lucky admiral was behind Allied lines.

Ironically, after the war, when anything that smacked of anti-Fascist behavior made an Italian a hero, the new government in

Rome revoked the death sentence and awarded Leonardi a Silver Medal for gallantry in the defense of Syracuse and Augusta!

Meanwhile, blissfully unaware that the situation on the eastern flank had placed his entire army on the edge of disaster, General Guzzoni was even now preparing to commit his mobile reserves to a counterattack at Gela, 50 air miles away—or more than 100 miles away using the narrow, tortuous Sicilian roads.

And how had the Americans made out on D-Day?

Husky One, the American airborne jump launched on the night of July 9–10, suffered from the same problems as the British glider attack and some others besides. The U.S. 52nd Troop Carrier Wing, which was to drop them, was also inexperienced in night formation flying. It was expected to fly a long, circuitous route to reach the drop zone in order to avoid flying over the Allied fleets. It was also expected to fly the entire mission at an altitude of two hundred feet to avoid enemy radio directional finders. With gusting winds of forty miles per hour, these factors combined to present the young American aviators with navigational problems that were beyond their capabilities.

The paratroopers of Colonel James M. Gavin's 505th Regimental Combat Team were supposed to land near Farello to capture the high ground and road junctions six miles north and northeast of Gela, positions that commanded the exits from the beaches over which the U.S. 1st Infanty Division would storm ashore. However, when they bailed out around midnight, the "All-Americans" were scattered from Niscemi to areas east of Santa Croce Camerina. At least twenty-three planeloads landed in the British sector; some came to earth south of Syracuse, more than fifty miles from their assigned zones. Jumping from altitudes as low as three hundred feet, a great many of the men were shaken or dazed, and there were quite a few broken bones and sprained ankles. Almost everyone was disoriented. Colonel Gavin, for example, was not sure what country he was in for several hours.

Despite their dispersion, the well-trained warriors did not panic. They knew that something like that could happen, and they knew what they were supposed to do. Breuer wrote:

Finding themselves alone or in tiny packets on parachuting into Sicily, the All-Americans promptly realized the corporation had dissolved, so they went into business for themselves. Spontaneously, small raiding parties led by junior officers and noncoms stalked through the dark countryside, creating fear and confusion among German and Italian soldiers and commanders. In a manner reminiscent of Indian warfare tactics of America's Old West, these stealthy raiders, many wearing war paint and with their heads shaved, lay in wait in the darkness along roads, then ambushed Axis couriers and officers taking urgent orders to German and Italian command posts.[11]

Not knowing where the paratroopers had landed or in what strength demoralized the Italians and Germans. Their uncertainty was heightened by other U.S. aircraft, which dropped hundreds of paratroop dummies to deceive the enemy further. The confusion was so great that the aides to General Guzzoni estimated that the Allies had landed three or four airborne divisions, numbering some fifty thousand men. Some Italian commanders and units panicked and withdrew up to ten miles during the night. By dawn Radio Rome was broadcasting that five, perhaps ten, American airborne divisions, numbering 60,000 to 120,000 men, had landed in Sicily. The actual number was 3,405.

Some parachute elements did land roughly where they were supposed to, although in smaller numbers than anticipated. Lieutenant Colonel Arthur "Hard Nose" Gorham, commander of the 1st Battalion of the 505th RCT, for example, took "Objective Y," where the roads from Vittoria and Caltagirone (by way of Niscemi) met. Located in the Piano Lupo hills, this important road junction was guarded by a series of pillboxes, which the Italians promptly abandoned. In the darkness, as more and more paratroopers came in alone or in small groups, Colonel Gorham awaited the Germans or the relief columns of the U.S. 1st Infantry Division, whichever came first.

As the American paratroopers clashed with the Italians and Germans in the darkness, Admiral Hewitt's Western Task Force made its final maneuvers prior to the landings. It had already broken into three parts for the actual assaults: Task Force 86 (Rear Admiral Richard L. Conolly) would deposit the U.S. 3rd Infantry Division on the Joss beaches, Task Force 81 (Rear Admiral John L. Hall) would unload Terry Allen's 1st Infantry

Division on the Dime beaches, and Rear Admiral Alan G. Kirk's Task Force 85 would land Troy H. Middleton's 45th on the Cent beaches.

Like their British counterparts, these American naval task forces were equipped with a large assortment of landing craft, as outlined in Table 4. One of the most valuable naval vessels in Sicily, however, was the DUKW (pronounced "duck"), an amphibious vehicle of almost legendary reputation and versatility. With a speed of 50 mph on land and 5.4 mph on water and a range of 240 miles on land and 50 miles on water, it was used to transport ammunition and supplies from Liberty ships to units on shore and then return with the wounded and prisoners. Some naval officers later averred that the invasion might not have been successful without the DUKW.

It was good that the Americans had such excellent equipment, because they needed it. Weather conditions were still poor, the seas were high, and the beaches were terrible. In fact, the entire U.S. zone of operations bordered on abysmal for this type of

T A B L E   4

ALLIED LANDING CRAFT USED IN HUSKY

LCA = landing craft, assault (35 men)
LCF = landing craft, flak (500 tons)
LCG = landing craft, gun (500 tons)
LCI = landing craft, infantry (200 men; 250 tons)
LCM = landing craft, medium (30-ton troop transporter)
LCP = landing craft, personnel (9 tons)
LCS = landing craft, support
LCT = landing craft tank (300 to 350 tons) (also known as LVT)
LSI(L) = landing ship, infantry (large) (used to carry LCAs)
LSI(M) = landing ship, infantry (medium)
LSI(S) = landing ship, infantry (small)
LST = landing ship, tank (2,000 tons)
LSH = landing ship, headquarters (with special communications equipment)

SOURCES: Pack, *Husky*, pp. 44–45; Blumenson, *Sicily*, p. 44.

operation. In this area three rivers (the Salso, Gela, and Acate) empty into the Gulf of Gela, flowing through three flat and reasonably fertile coastal plains on which the towns of Licata, Gela, and Scoglitti are situated. Around these plains was a scalloped mountain wall from which closely built hilltop towns looked down on the plains, valleys, and beaches. These towns made excellent defensive positions, while the plains were ideal terrain for a counterattack, especially just after an amphibious landing, when the enemy is most vulnerable.

The beaches themselves were numerous, but their gradients were far too gradual (hence no major ports) and were fronted by "false beaches." A false beach is a sandbar with enough water over it to float LCPs or LCIs but not the heavier and critical LSTs, which carried most of the U.S. armor, artillery, and heavy equipment. Between the false beaches and the real beaches lay "runnels": miniature lagoons deep enough to drown a tank or vehicle. Gaps can always exist in false beaches, but there were few of them off the southern Sicilian coast, and the techniques used to detect them today did not exist in 1943. Therefore, the U.S. Navy was going to have to construct pontoon causeways from the LSTs in the deeper water across the false beaches and runnels to the landing beaches. All this, of course, was going to require time and was going to expose the causeways and LSTs to air attack. Also, the infantry on the beachhead would be vulnerable to counterattack until a sufficient number of LSTs had been unloaded to give it strength. The entire proposition was pretty risky, but neither Admiral Hewitt nor General Patton had any choice. They watched anxiously as the first American landing craft prepared to "hit the beaches" at 2:45 A.M. on July 10.

The plan called for the 45th Infantry Division (the Thunderbirds) to land in two groups of beaches located on either side of the tiny fishing village of Scoglitti. The Cent landings, however, were fouled up from the beginning. Because of the rough weather, the main assault landing was postponed an hour, but it was too late to get the word to the scout boats and the landing craft that already were in the water. As a result, the initial landings were piecemeal affairs, and the confusion increased as the day wore on. All Cent beaches faced a westerly wind, and the surf was very heavy. These factors, combined with a southeasterly current, carried several boat waves south of their objectives. The confusion was greatest on Middleton's left flank, in the zone of Colonel Forest E. Cookson's 180th RCT, perhaps because the landing craft carrying the colonel and his entire staff landed miles to the north, in the zone of the 1st Infantry Division. Other elements of the 180th landed miles to the south, on unscheduled beaches. The confusion was total, and the leaderless 180th was completely disorganized.

The rest of the division was not in much better condition. Heavy surf, lack of definite landmarks, strong lateral currents, and inexperienced boat crews combined to paint a thoroughly disorganized picture. Landing craft losses were very high, especially among the LCPs, many of which were broached. By midmorning 150 to 200 craft were stranded or swamped on offshore bars and on the landing beaches. Salvage parties were overwhelmed. The next day, when General Bradley landed at Scoglitti with a few members of his staff, he saw what he called "a dismal sight": more than two hundred assault craft "wallowed in the surf after having burned out their engines in crossing the runnels while coming ashore. Bulldozers churned through the soft sand, dragging pallets of supply from the water's edge to be piled in dumps behind the grassy dunes."[12]

Even when an LCT or LCG arrived at the correct beach, it did little good because the sand dunes behind the beach were too soft for heavy equipment. As a result, the beaches became more and more congested and more and more confused. Despite all efforts, Admiral Kirk found beach unloading still "completely blocked" as late as the morning of July 12. It was not a good start for the Thunderbirds of the 45th Infantry Division.

The artillerymen of the Italian howitzer battery at Cape Camerina must have looked upon this scene with amazement. They could have easily inflicted heavy casualties on the Americans if they had had ammunition, but they did not. Their guns were captured French pieces, and their artillery ammunition was Italian and would not fit. So they left for home, as did most of the other coastal gunners of the 206th Coastal Defense Division.

Meanwhile, despite the confusion on the beaches, Colonel C. M. Ankcorn got elements of his 157th RCT moving inland on the morning of D-Day. Advancing quickly, he captured his first objective, the town of Santa Croce Camerina, at about noon. It was not much of a battle because there were no Germans in this sector and the Italians (the 501st Coastal Defense Battalion) were putting up only perfunctory resistance. As the Americans approached the town, white flags began to appear. Five hundred Italians surrendered and others took to the hills. Ankcorn was joined in the village by a battalion-sized contingent of U.S. paratroopers, who had earlier captured the nearby village of Marina di Ragusa and frightened the defenders of Cape Scaramia (the Italian 383rd Coastal Defense Battalion, on the extreme right wing of the 206th Coastal Defense Division) into surrender or retreat.

About two hours later, at two P.M., the 1st Battalion of the 179th RCT finally captured Scoglitti from the rapidly disintegrating 389th Coastal Defense Battalion of Colonel Sebastianello's 178th Coastal Defense Regiment. Here a fisherman's cove offered a good landing place for one LCT at a time. A hard road led out of Scoglitti to the dirty little city of Vittoria (population 36,000), about six miles inland. Vittoria was also in American hands by late afternoon, and by nightfall Middleton had pushed his center and his right flank about seven miles inland, with Colonel Robert B. Hutchins's 179th pushing on toward Comiso Airfield against crumbling opposition from the 18th Coastal Defense Brigade of the 206th Division. There was a hole on Middleton's left, however, because the 180th RCT was still scattered over about twelve miles of beaches. Also, the Thunderbirds' beachhead lacked armor, artillery, and depth.

Coming ashore in the center of the American line was Major General Terry Allen's 1st Infantry Division, perhaps the most independent unit in the U.S. Army. Led by the hard-drinking, hard-charging Allen, it had a reputation as a fighting unit, and it did not seem to matter to its men or its commander whether it was fighting Germans, Italians, British, or other members of the U.S. Army. Known as the Big Red One from the patch its men wore on their left sleeves, it was a law unto itself and was highly contemptuous of anyone who was not a Big Red One. It had made itself particularly famous for a drunken spree in Algeria, during which it wrecked a large number of bars in Oran and hospitalized numerous soldiers who happened to be wearing the wrong patch. Despite its undisciplined attitude, the 1st Infantry Division had excelled in Tunisia, and General Patton steadfastly insisted on having it in the center of his line, instead of the 36th Infantry

Division, as originally proposed by Eisenhower. George S. Patton had a great deal of confidence in the Big Red One, but less in its commander.

The main objectives of the 1st Infantry Division on D-Day were the port of Gela and the Ponte Olivo Airfield. The second objective was to be taken in conjunction with the 82nd Airborne Division.

Gela, formerly known as Terranova di Sicilia, was one of the oldest Greek sites in Sicily and one of the dirtiest. Surrounded by vineyards and wheat fields on three sides, it was located on a plateau about 150 feet above the Mediterranean. Gela was characterized by unattractive chalk-gray buildings, dirty alleys, wash hanging from iron balconies, rubbish, and litter. It did not even have a harbor, only a long steel pier, built by the Italian government, extending well out into the sea, which made it militarily important. A winding road up the cliff connected the pier with the town. As insufficient as Gela was compared to Syracuse or Augusta, this little city was in the center of the American zone and, in a sense, was the focal point of the U.S. 7th Army. In fact, Patton had assigned a special force (attached to the 1st Infantry Division) to take it.

Force X was commanded by Lieutenant Colonel William O. Darby, the "father" of the Rangers, the American counterpart of the British Commandos. It included the tough, elite 1st and 4th Ranger battalions, two engineer battalions, and three companies of large 4.2-inch mortars. Not that the Americans expected heavy resistance. The landing beach (Beach Red) was not mined, as the aerial photos indicated; in fact, it was covered with fishing boats, which would not be there if it were mined. Also, the defenders were part of the Italian 18th Coastal Defense Brigade, and this gave the Rangers further cause for confidence.

The Ranger landing got started about an hour late, and it was a much tougher fight than they initially expected. First of all, the fishing boats on Beach Red turned out to be old hulks that had been lying there for some time. The beach was heavily mined and covered by pillboxes. One platoon, which landed in a cross fire between two pillboxes, was practically annihilated. The remainder of the company, led by the wounded first sergeant, captured the pillboxes, and the Rangers gradually fought their way up the slope toward Gela.

The Italian opposition was much more spirited than expected.

This sector was defended by Major Rubellino's 429th Coastal Battalion, which, unlike most of the coastal defense units, was not disposed to run or surrender.[13] Even though one of Rubellino's companies had been wiped out by paratroopers during the night, the Americans had to fight for every trench and pillbox. Although the Italians were not as well trained or disciplined as the elite Rangers, they fought courageously for four hours before being overwhelmed. The 429th suffered 45 percent combat casualties, including 5 officers killed and 4 wounded and 185 enlisted men killed or wounded. The Rangers took two hundred prisoners when the garrison finally surrendered at about eight A.M. Even then the victory was somewhat empty. Per Guzzoni's orders, the steel pier—the main reason for attacking Gela in the first place—had been destroyed by Italian demolition squads while the Rangers' landing craft were approaching the beach.

Elsewhere in the 1st Division's zone, opposition was much lighter. To the east of Gela, in the division's center, Colonel John W. Bowen's 26th Regimental Combat Team landed virtually without opposition. Bowen even sent a battalion westward across the Gela River to help the Rangers subdue the 429th when the town of Gela did not surrender as quickly as anticipated. He sent another battalion inland to seize the high ground overlooking the Ponte Olivo Airfield. To Bowen's east, the 16th RCT established a beachhead and drove inland toward Piano Lupo and the planned linkup with Gavin's paratroopers. What little resistance that was offered was quickly silenced by U.S. naval gunfire or by the infantry. Soon the Italians were surrendering in bunches. One U.S. naval officer recalled that the Italian prisoners he transported back to Algiers on July 10 were "the happiest crowd you ever saw. Those who could speak English even joked with their G.I. guards, saying 'We're going to Brooklyn—you poor guys have to stay in Sicily!'"[14]

By midmorning on D-Day, Terry Allen's division was pushing cautiously inland against light and crumbling opposition toward its linkup with the American paratroopers. Allen was not overly concerned that he did not yet have many tanks, vehicles, or heavy guns on shore, that his bridgehead lacked depth, or that, because of bad weather and poor navigation, there was only one LST with a pontoon causeway in the entire Dime sector. After all, he was facing only the remnants of the 18th Coastal Defense Brigade and was screened from a major counterattack by a reinforced regiment of paratroopers.

Or so he thought. General Allen was unaware of how badly astray the parachute drop had gone. The high ground to his north was, in reality, only lightly held by a few hundred badly organized paratroopers who were virtually without heavy weapons of any kind. He was also unaware that in the hills beyond lay the Hermann Goering Panzer Division.

Meanwhile, the left flank of the entire invasion was the responsibility of Major General Lucian K. Truscott, Jr., probably the best American divisional commander in the European theater of operations at that time. He felt very strongly that the marching ability of contemporary American infantry units was distinctly inferior to that of General T. J. "Stonewall" Jackson's "Foot Cavalry," which had so confounded its opponents in the American Civil War. When he assumed command of the mediocre 3rd Infantry Division in April 1943, he instituted a program of discipline and rigorous physical training, insisting that the standard march rate of his division would be 4 miles an hour instead of the 2.5 mph adhered to by the rest of the army. In a short period of time the 3rd Infantry improved remarkably, and in Sicily Truscott's division was later rated as the best trained and disciplined of the 7th Army's units.

Truscott's main D-Day objective was the small city of Licata, a center of sulfur manufacture and export that had a small artificial harbor. His assault suffered from the same problems as the other American landings, but none of this materially affected the landings of the 3rd Infantry Division. The mobile units of the Italian XIIth Corps—Aosta, Assietta, and the 15th Panzer Grenadier Division—were too far west to interfere, and all the invaders faced was the 390th Coastal Defense Battalion (of the 207th Coastal Defense Division), supported by the 145th Coastal Artillery Battalion. Both of these units were demoralized and panicky, and they surrendered as quickly as possible at every opportunity. The only potentially serious threat to the Joss force attack was a four-cannon Italian railroad battery at Licata, but it was quickly destroyed by a series of naval salvos, as were a pair of searchlights.

Near Licata, a band of American infantrymen walked into a hastily abandoned command post (CP) whose occupants had fled without firing a shot. Michael Chinigo, an American war correspondent accompanying the squad, had just entered the CP when the telephone rang. Chinigo, who spoke fluent Italian, picked it up and said, *"Chi c'e?"* (Who's there?). An Italian general answered and wanted to know whether or not the Americans were landing.

"Of course not," Chinigo replied.

"Fine," the general replied, and hung up. He never did bother to ask who he was talking to or why he had received such an unmilitary greeting.

By 11:30 A.M. Licata was firmly in American hands and the 3rd Infantry had lost fewer than one hundred men. Salvage parties had already partially cleared the harbor, and shortly after noon Truscott and his staff came ashore and set up headquarters at Palazzo La Lumia. About that time the 538th Coastal Defense Battalion, which had been deployed as a tactical reserve, launched a counterattack, but it was quickly defeated, and the Americans continued to advance against token resistance. By nightfall, all of Truscott's initial objectives had been taken, and on his right the 30th RCT was advancing down the coastal road (Highway 115) and was near the place where it was supposed to link up with IInd Corps. In the rear, Brigadier General Maurice Rose's Combat Command A (CCA) of the 2nd Armored Division was off-loading from its landing craft. It had been a very satisfactory day for Truscott and his men. True, Arisio's XIIth Corps was already moving in units to halt the further westward advance of the 7th RCT toward Palma di Montechiaro, but Italian resistance did not figure to stiffen too much. The U.S. 3rd Infantry Division had already taken three thousand prisoners.[15]

As the American infantry struggled forward, the navy struggled against the elements, false beaches, disrupted timetables, and the Luftwaffe.

With their 4,300 aircraft, the Allied air superiority over the beaches should never have been in question; yet, after having done a magnificent job of defeating the Luftwaffe and the Italian Royal Air Force, the Allied air forces did an absolutely miserable job of protecting the American convoys and beachheads and supporting the ground troops during the critical first three days of the invasion. Admiral King reported later that there were no fighter patrols over the landing zones, no fighter protection for his naval artillery spotter planes, and no bombers or fighter-bombers on call. "The air battle was separate and foreign, apparently unconcerned about the situation in the CENT area," he said later.[16]

It was almost as if the air forces were fighting their own war. Allied tactical air forces were under the command of Air Marshal Sir Arthur Coningham, a friend of Tedder but a man who had little use for either Montgomery or Patton. Coningham's HQ, NATAF (Northwest African Tactical Air Forces), was indifferent and even hostile to requests for air support from ground units and routinely turned down even the most justifiable requests for aerial reconnaissance. This attitude brought Coningham into conflict with U.S. Colonel Lawrence P. Hickey, an advocate of close air support. Hickey's XIIth Support Command was charged with the task of providing direct support for Patton's army in Sicily, so Hickey chose to collocate his headquarters with Patton's. Coningham viewed this tactically sensible decision as a sign of weakness and a surrender of air force prerogatives to a ground force commander. He soon replaced Hickey with Major General Edwin House, but control of operational assignments was retained by NATAF. On D-Day, Allied aircraft roamed far to the Axis rear, bombing Sicilian roads, Gerbini, Trapani/Milo, and Sciacca but not the positions just in front of the invading infantry. Nor were the rapidly advancing Mobile Group E, Brigade Schmalz, or the Hermann Goering Panzer Division seriously attacked. "You can get your Navy planes to do anything you want, but we can't get the Air Force to do a Goddamn thing!" General Patton complained to Admiral Hewitt just before the landings.[17] "Because Allied air-surface coordination was almost nonexistent," Wallace wrote, "the German pilots enjoyed a kind of field day, in spite of their inferiority in numbers."[18]

From their often damaged airports and primitive satellite fields, Axis pilots flew 150 to 200 sorties—a very respectable number considering their handicaps. JG 77, for example, was low in ammunition and only had enough coolant and hydraulic fluid to last two days. It had lost contact with the Air Commander, Sicily and with the IInd Air Corps but continued to attack Allied bomber formations and to fly reconnaissance missions in the invasion area, "even though we did not know to whom we were to report the results," the commander noted. Captain Freyberg's Ist Group even managed to shoot down six bombers but lost four of the sixteen

Me-109's that were engaged. Among those killed was Freyberg himself, a holder of the Knight's Cross.[19]

The Luftwaffe also attacked the beaches, the landing craft, and the more or less stationary convoys, causing relatively minor damage but adding immeasurably to the nervousness and confusion of the invaders. All morning Axis air commanders, including Baron von Richthofen, sent aircraft from Italy to Sardinia to refuel, and from there to Sicily to attack the invading convoys. It did little good. The damaged Sardinian airfields could not handle many planes, and the Axis bombers that did attack usually missed everything except the Mediterranean Sea. The U.S. Navy's Official History described the aim of the Axis bombers as "very inaccurate," which was very fortunate, since the convoys had almost no air protection until July 12.[20] The navy sent up several SOCs (Seagull scout observation float planes) to direct naval gunfire for the ground forces, but because they had no fighter protection, most of them were shot down or run off by Messerschmitts. Fortunately, the sole surviving SOC from the light cruiser *Savannah* managed to direct naval gunfire on Mobile Group E and played a significant role in the ground battle before it was jumped by a pair of Messerschmitts. This Seagull, piloted by Lieutenant C. G. Lewis, managed to escape by flying out to sea. Had the SOCs been properly protected by Allied air force fighters, Axis casualties would have been much more severe and their counterattacks would not have been as dangerous as they turned out to be.

Perhaps the Luftwaffe's greatest contribution on D-Day was its disruption of LST operations. Both Allen's and Middleton's divisions desperately needed tanks, vehicles, and heavy guns, but there were few places in the American zone where such things could be landed; therefore, they had to depend on LSTs with pontoon causeways. Unfortunately, there were only two available in the Gela zone, and one of these was destroyed by a Messerschmitt, along with twenty-one men. As night fell, only one pontoon causeway was operational in the entire Dime force area and only three LSTs had been unloaded. By dawn on D + 1 (July 11), the American beachheads would still lack artillery, tanks, heavy weapons, and depth. Bradley's IInd Corps would still be very vulnerable to a counterattack on the second day of the invasion, and Paul Conrath's Hermann Goering Panzer Division would still have a fairly good chance of pushing them off the island.

And what about General Guzzoni? What had he done to counter the Allied invasion? What about the confident General Conrath, who had pledged to throw the Allies back into the sea?

Based on the information he had, the sixty-six-year-old commander of the Italian 6th Army acted prudently, wisely, and swiftly on July 10. By one A.M. on D-Day he had already sent orders to all German and Italian formations to go into action. On his orders, the piers at Gela and Licata were blown up, and at 1:30 A.M. he ordered Generale di Corpo Carlo Rossi to expect landings in the Gela-Agrigento area.

By four A.M.—an hour and fifteen minutes after the invasion had touched ground—Guzzoni realized that there were so many landings that he could not possibly counter them all. He considered Syracuse safe, however, because of the presence of Generale di Divisione Count Giulio Cesare Gotti-Porcinari's Napoli Division and Admiral Leonardi's fortress defense troops and the nearness of Colonel Schmalz's Kampfgruppe at Catania. Correctly guessing that there would be no landing at or north of Catania, Guzzoni ordered Schmalz to reinforce Porcinari and Leonardi. He also decided to counterattack against Gela with the Livorno and Hermann Goering divisions. He took Livorno out of army reserve, gave it to Rossi's XVIth Corps, and ordered it to coordinate its attacks with that of the Luftwaffe panzer division. He also attached two previously independent units—Mobile Groups E and H—to the XVIth Corps for the counterattack. Map 6 shows the Axis counterattacks of July 10.

Meanwhile, shortly before ten P.M. on July 9, Lieutenant General Paul Conrath received word at his headquarters at Caltagirone that an Allied landing in southeast Sicily was imminent. He at once divided his division into two combat groups and ordered them to get ready to jump off for the beaches at Gela and Scoglitti. Their objective would be to push the invaders back into the sea. His division was certainly positioned for such a counterattack, as several important roads ran through Caltagirone. However, by occupying this central position, Conrath had also placed his men about twenty-seven miles from Scoglitti and twenty-five miles from Gela. He had also badly underestimated the time it would take him to reach these objectives. Also, despite Kesselring's orders, he wanted his plan approved by 6th Army before he moved, and communications between Enna and his divisional headquarters had been cut—no doubt by some wayward American paratrooper. It was early in the morning of July 10 before Conrath reached General von Senger und Etterlin via the independent German commo network. Conrath outlined his plan to Senger, who approved it at once and said that he would notify Guzzoni. Conrath promised to jump off without further delay. But it was four A.M. before his two combat groups moved out in column formation. Using three separate roads, they headed for their assembly areas south of Biscari and Niscemi, from where they planned to form up in battle formation and strike. They had been alerted six hours before, and more than four hours before the Allies landed. Now the enemy had been ashore for more than an hour, and they were still twenty-five miles from the beaches. The road march was very difficult. The roads were poor, and soon it was daylight. The three columns became targets for a few Allied air strikes and for ambushes and obstacles put up by small groups of tough American paratroopers. At nine A.M.—five hours after they started—Paul Conrath's men were still struggling toward their assembly areas.

General Rossi acted more quickly. Leaving Conrath to attack the American right, he ordered Captain Giuseppe Granieri's Mobile Group E from Niscemi to divide into two columns. One column was to advance to Piano Lupo, oust the paratroopers from the high ground there, and then attack along Highway 115, striking Gela from the northeast. The second column was to advance along Highway 117, past Ponte Olivo Airfield, and hit Gela from the north. Meanwhile, Generale di Divisione Domenico Chirieleison's Livorno Division would advance down the secondary road from Butera to attack the port city from the northwest.

This was not a particularly good plan. The troops were dispersed, and communications between Livorno and Mobile Group E were lacking. Sixteenth Corps itself was suffering communications problems. It had lost contact with many of its subordinate units and had no way of knowing what the Germans were doing. The attack did have an objective, however, and even if it did lack concentration, it was at least striking an enemy that had just

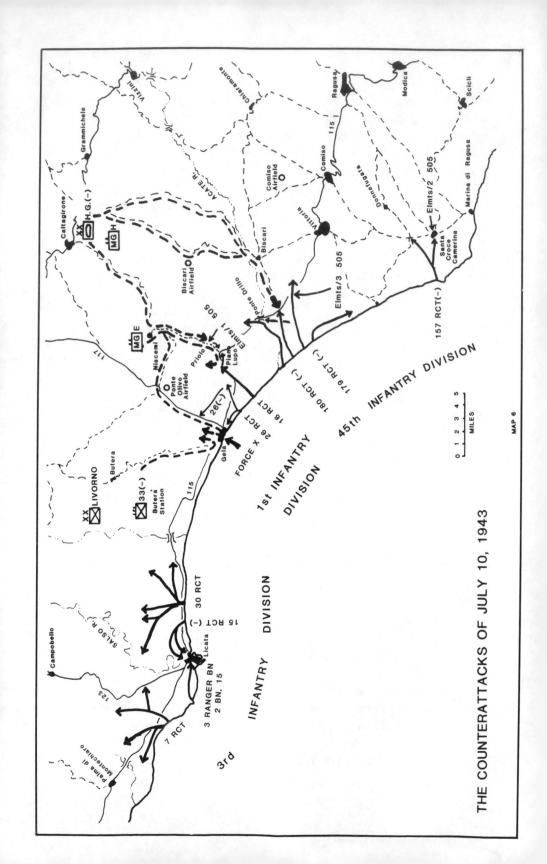

THE COUNTERATTACKS OF JULY 10, 1943

0 1 2 3 4 5
MILES

MAP 6

landed; therefore, the opposition would be as disorganized as it would ever be. Also, the Americans might well be short of armor and heavy weapons, and some of them might still be seasick. This opportunity might never present itself again, so the Italian tanks rolled forward.

Mobile Group E was a battalion-sized task force with about four companies of motorized infantry, a company of 47-mm antitank guns, a troop of motorcyclists, and two armored companies. The tank units were equipped with about thirty Renault-35 tanks, which the Germans had handed over to Italy after France surrendered in 1940. They weighed only ten tons and were armed with 37-mm guns. In addition, the mobile group had sixteen three-ton "baby" tanks and some World War I Fiats, which were even smaller. They were certainly no match for Sherman tanks—but the Shermans were still offshore on LSTs in the Gulf of Gela.

The left-hand column of Mobile Group E moved out in column formation in trucks, followed by tanks, some artillery pieces, and a few armored cars. It proceeded to Casa del Priolo, about one and a half miles north of the Americans' Objective Y, the junction of the Niscemi Road and Highway 115. It did not realize that it was riding into an ambush.

Earlier that morning, Lieutenant Colonel Gorham, the commander of the 1st Battalion, 505th Parachute Infantry Regiment, had seized the bleak hill mass called Piano Lupo and assembled a force of less than a hundred men. Most of Gavin's combat team was supposed to land here, but Gorham did not seem concerned. He would play the cards that were dealt him.

Hard Nose Gorham was tough, resourceful, heroic, and self-reliant. Strangely enough, he was only twenty-eight years old and had graduated from West Point only five years before. From the scattered equipment drops, his men had already recovered two 60-mm mortars with fifty shells and three machine guns with six thousand rounds of ammunition. Also, prior to dawn, some of his men had overrun an Italian strongpoint (a thick-walled stone farmhouse). They had killed fifteen Italians and captured forty more, along with twenty machine guns and nearly 500,000 rounds of ammunition. This represented a major victory for the lightly armed paratroopers. Gorham quickly distributed the weapons among his men. Then he set up an ambush on the Niscemi Road and waited for something to shoot.

At this point the left column of Mobile Group E appeared. Gorham immediately opened up on the trucks, which contained two companies of Italian infantry. For some reason the group commander did not send in his tanks, and in open ground many of the surprised infantrymen were slaughtered. The killing continued until the Italians brought up a single artillery piece and set it up just out of rifle range of the American position. As the shells began to land, Gorham fell back toward Piano Lupo. The Italians also raced for the hills and got there first. The paratroopers engaged them anyway.

At the same time, coming up from the beach, the 16th RCT had overcome light resistance and was advancing up the coastal road (Highway 115) toward its scheduled linkup with the 505th at Piano Lupo. They arrived at 8:42 A.M. to find a desperate battle in progress. The Italians were just about to commit their armor when the 16th arrived. They immediately attacked the Italians and called for fire support from the navy. The destroyer *Jeffers* answered with nineteen salvos from her 5-inch guns. The Italian infantry quickly "went to ground" at Piano Lupo and never advanced beyond the relative safety of the hills. The twenty tanks, however, passed through the infantry and pushed the 16th RCT back a mile or so, when the tanks were again brought under a devastating fire by the big guns of the American warships. Two tanks were knocked out, others were hit, and without infantry support, the rest broke off the engagement and retired into the hills northeast of Gela. At eleven A.M. the 16th RCT rejoined the paratroopers and helped them clear the Italian infantry out of Piano Lupo.

Meanwhile, the Rangers and engineers north of Gela spotted the right-hand column of Mobile Group E, about twenty-five tanks, advancing onto the open plain. They were perfect targets for Allied fighter-bombers, but none appeared despite the frantic calls from the ground troops. The air force had laid down strict requirements that all requests for air support had to be made at least twelve hours in advance! Fortunately, the navy was more flexible. The U.S. destroyer *Shubrick* bombarded the Italian tanks as heavily as possible, her fire directed by an efficient shore fire-control party. Three tanks were blown apart, and the rest slowed. Then nine or ten speeded up and at 10:30 A.M. broke through the American perimeter at Gela.

Unsupported by infantry, the Italian tankers were obviously

unsure of what they were supposed to do. The heterogeneous groups of Rangers, infantrymen, and combat engineers fought them from the rooftops and alleyways with bazookas, dynamite, rocket launchers, hand grenades, and one 37-mm antitank gun. The Italian tanks could not elevate their guns to deal with the Rangers, and their casualties were mounting. Several tanks were damaged and two were knocked out in the twenty-minute battle. Then, at 10:50 A.M., all of the surviving Italian tanks but one retreated, harassed all the way back to the hills by naval gunfire. The lone tank that was left behind surrendered.

Shortly after the tanks fled, the 3rd Battalion of the 33rd (Livorno) Infantry Regiment marched across the plain and attacked Gela from the west. They marched forward in almost a parade-ground formation, closely packed, showing great courage but absolutely no tactical skill. Carlo D'Este noted that the advance was "reminiscent of nineteenth-century warfare" and was a "sad illustration of the ineptitude of the Italian Army."[21] Had they advanced when the tanks of Mobile Group E entered Gela, Force X would have been in serious trouble. Now, however, the Italian infantrymen were like sheep for the slaughter. The Rangers opened up on them with mortars, captured artillery, rifles, and machine guns. Rank after rank went down. It was butchery. Soon the survivors fled, leaving behind a field covered with dead and wounded. Even now, Paul Conrath's columns had not reached their assembly areas.

The Italian attacks had done surprisingly well against the Americans, as uncoordinated as they were. Had the Hermann Goering Panzer Division been on hand, there is little doubt that a sizable part of the U.S. 7th Army would have been thrown back into the sea. Yet it was two P.M. before the division's right-hand column reached its assembly areas south of Niscemi.

The H.G. Division was badly tailored for this counterattack. Its right-hand column—*Kampfgruppe Rechts* (Battle Group Right)—consisted of the panzer regiment with a recon company attached, the artillery regiment with two heavy battalions, and the engineer battalion, minus one company. *Kampfgruppe Links* (Battle Group Left), going into action twelve to fifteen miles away, consisted of the panzer grenadier regiment (two battalions), a two-battery artillery battalion, and the Tiger company.[22] In this organizational arrangement Conrath had clearly violated the principles of combined arms operations. His tanks were without adequate infantry support, and his infantry regiment had very few tanks, especially as many of the Tigers were suffering from problems in their steering mechanisms. In addition, many of his green troops were inadequately trained for ground warfare and were panicky because of the numerous small ambushes by American paratroopers. Besides all this, Kampfgruppe Rechts attacked across the same ground over which Mobile Group E had already advanced; therefore, the Americans were ready to bring previously registered naval gunfire down on the newest threat. Nevertheless, the advance began at two P.M.

Kampfgruppe Rechts got nowhere. It was halted near Priolo by U.S. Navy 5- and 6-inch guns, while in the battle group's rear Gorham's men and elements of the 16th RCT engaged the reconnaissance company and the under-strength engineer detachment, which was fighting as infantry. The panzer regimental commander, Colonel Urban (the bomber pilot with the nervous disorder), fell back quickly. General Conrath, who was personally accompanying this battle group, relieved Urban of his command and personally took charge of the task force. His efforts at getting the attack back on track were unsuccessful, however.

Farther east, Kampfgruppe Links was supposed to attack the left flank of the U.S. 45th Infantry Division, smash it, and then turn northwest, cross the Acate River, and take Piano Lupo in the rear. Had they attacked in the morning, they would have met light resistance, for this was the area left bare when the initial 180th Regimental Combat Team's landings miscarried. By now, however, the 1st and 3rd battalions of the regiment had landed, had plugged the gap, and were organized and in position in dense olive groves north of the coastal road. Conrath, however, had no idea where his infantry-heavy battle group was, because it had lost contact with divisional headquarters some time before.

Kampfgruppe Links was quickly halted by a relatively small force consisting of the 1st Battalion, the 180th RCT, a handful of itinerant paratroopers, and one battery of artillery. Although well suited for infantry in the defense, the dense olive groves restricted the movements of the Tigers. In addition, many of the junior officers and NCOs in the Luftwaffe panzer grenadier regiment were not up to their tasks. To make matters worse, some of the Tigers broke down, blocking the others and shutting down the

armored advance. Throughout the entire battle one of the Kampfgruppe's two infantry battalions remained uncommitted, mainly
because the task force had no overall leadership. At two P.M. the
commander of Kampfgruppe Links pushed too far forward and was
pinned down by a group of American riflemen. For a critical hour
he was unable to even lift his head, much less command his troops.
By 3:30 P.M. the battle group's attack had been brought to a halt.

Earlier, Paul Conrath had sent his chief of staff, Lieutenant
Colonel Hellmut Bergengruen, to find out what was happening on
the left flank. At about four P.M. communications were finally
reestablished with division headquarters, and Bergengruen issued
his report. Furious when he learned what had happened, General
Conrath relieved the leader of the panzer grenadier regiment of his
command, replacing him with Colonel Bergengruen, and after
considerable exhortation, persuaded him to try again.[23] This time
Kampfgruppe Links began to gain ground. With the remaining
Tigers leading and the infantry right behind, it overran the 1st
Battalion and took most of its men prisoner, including its commander. The few survivors streamed south, where they ran into
the 3rd Battalion, which halted the initial attack only four miles
from the 45th Division's beaches and right behind the Big Red
One. It seemed for a moment that the 3rd might suffer the same
fate as its sister battalion; then, for some unexplained reason,
the Germans panicked and fled wildly to the rear, unpursued by
the surprised Americans, who had not been getting the best of the
battle. The Luftwaffe/panzer officers could not stop them until just
south of Biscari.

Recognizing a fait accompli, Conrath called off the battle at four
P.M. He decided to try again the next day despite the objections of
General Guzzoni, who wanted the counterattack continued on
D-Day if at all possible.[24]

Why the Hermann Goering Division's counterattack of July 10
failed and how much the American airborne assault contributed to
the success of the Husky landings have been subjects of con-
troversy ever since the battle took place. General Eisenhower
commented that the losses in both the American and British glider
units were "inexcusably high," but they nevertheless made a
significant contribution to the Allied success in both army sectors.
He did, however, express skepticism about using large-scale air-

borne drops in the future.[25] Some people, such as General Gavin, seem to claim that the U.S. paratroopers saved the 7th Army.[26] General Kurt Student, then commander of the German parachute corps and the "father" of the German airborne branch, claimed later that the American paratroopers had prevented the Hermann Goering Division from pushing the 7th Army back into the sea.[27] However, several of the German commanders who fought in Sicily disagreed with Student. General of Panzer Troops (then Major General) Walter Fries concluded that the American paratroopers were ineffective in Sicily,[28] while Colonel Bergengruen said that the paratroopers caused confusion among the Italians but did not affect German operations.[29] General von Senger disagreed, stating that the Hermann Goering failed to throw the enemy back into the sea "due to the fact that the parachutists had been dropped in its attack zone, and although they were nowhere committed in compact units, they were able to cause considerable trouble." He also placed part of the blame on the difficult terrain, the command system of the division, and its lack of tradition with respect to ground warfare.[30] General Patton would have agreed with him on the last point. "The German troops have not fought as well as those we destroyed in Tunisia," he wrote. "They have shown gallantry, but bad judgment."[31] Kesselring, while conceding that the American paratroopers caused heavy casualties and "extraordinary delay" in the movement of the H.G. Division,[32] placed the blame for the failure of the German counterattack squarely on the doorstep of Lieutenant General Conrath.[33]

In our view, it seems quite likely that Kesselring was right. An aggressive panzer commander of the stamp of Rommel, Hube, or Guderian would probably have blown through the lightly armed paratroopers, who, despite their unquestionable bravery, would not have been able to prevent a properly led German armored division from reaching the sea. Of course Kesselring must shoulder much of the blame himself, for it was he who sent away the more capable Rodt and the better prepared 15th Panzer Grenadier Division and thus indirectly left the ineffective Conrath in charge of the counterattack in the first place.

During the night of July 10–11 the Axis commanders sorted out their various commands and made plans for the next day's battle. All the major commanders—Kesselring, Guzzoni, von Senger,

Rossi, and Conrath—planned to resume the counterattacks and throw the Americans back into the sea.

Lieutenant General Paul Conrath spent much of the evening touring his command, relieving commanders, issuing severe reprimands, and threatening to have people shot for cowardice. He reorganized the Hermann Goering Division into three columns by splitting Kampfgruppe Rechts in two and then ordered them to be ready to counterattack at daybreak on July 11.

Farther north, at Enna, General Guzzoni was also making plans and issuing orders. Even now he had not been informed that Syracuse had fallen to the British. Rumors to that effect had reached his HQ, but he dismissed them as gross exaggerations.

Guzzoni was concerned about his right flank, where Truscott's 3rd Infantry had penetrated up to fourteen miles inland and would soon be in a position to threaten Enna, the geographic center of Sicily and the site of the 6th Army's Headquarters. The loss of Enna would also give the Americans control of the road network through the mountains and isolate the Axis forces in the west. To prevent this, Guzzoni committed the 177th Bersaglieri Regiment under Colonel Venturi into the gap between Livorno's right flank and the 207th Coastal Defense Division's disintegrating left. He ordered Venturi to prepare to attack toward Licata from the north, while the 207th was to form a special battle group to attack from the west. Guzzoni also ordered the Italian 162nd Artillery Battalion, a self-propelled unit in army reserve, to move from the northern coast to blocking positions in the Canicatti area—a move that was completed on July 11.

While all this was going on, a debate raged over what to do with the 15th Panzer Grenadier Division. By midmorning on July 10 Guzzoni was satisfied that there would be no landings west of Licata. He wanted to move the division from western Sicily to the area east of Enna in the Caltanisetta–Barrafranca–Piazza Armerina sector. He consulted with von Senger, who agreed, and at noon Guzzoni issued the order. It apparently never reached General Rodt, however. Whether this particular communications failure was caused by bad staff work at 6th Army or XIIth Corps Headquarters, by the interference of American paratroopers, or by the fact that Rodt's new HQ at San Marguerita was not yet fully functioning is not clear. In any event, Kesselring objected to the move. At 6:21 P.M. he radioed the 6th Army from Rome and warned against the complete evacuation of western Sicily by German forces. This time, however, Guzzoni insisted that his decision regarding the 15th Panzer Grenadier be implemented. After an exchange of messages, Kesselring reluctantly gave in. Unfortunately, because of the time lost in this long-distance debate and assorted communications problems, the division had acted on its own initiative by the time the decision was made.

Major General Eberhard Rodt did not receive a single definite order all day long on July 10. He did, however, receive disconcerting reports on the rapid progress of the U.S. 3rd Infantry Division and the disintegration of the left flank of the 207th Coastal Defense Division. At this rate, Rodt knew, the Americans would soon be threatening his headquarters. Since there were no reports of landings on the northern coast or in the west, Rodt deployed most of his division against Truscott's likely lines of advance.[34] He sent Combat Group Ens (Lieutenant Colonel Ens's own 104th Panzer Grenadier Regiment, reinforced with an engineer company, a flak company, an antitank platoon, and the IInd Battalion, 33rd Artillery Battalion, equipped with heavy 170-mm guns) from Salemi to positions northwest of Butera to screen his eastern flank. At the same time he sent Group Fullriede from San Marquerita toward the hills north of Licata, where it was to engage the American 15th RCT. Group Fullriede consisted of the IInd and IIIrd battalions of the 129th Panzer Grenadier Regiment, reinforced with the Ist and IIIrd battalions, 33rd Artillery Regiment (medium howitzer units), an engineer company, and a flak company, all under the command of Lieutenant Colonel Fritz Fullriede. (Because of transportation problems, the I/129th had not moved from the Comiso sector on July 10, where it was engaged against American paratroopers. It later joined Group Schmalz before returning to its parent division.) Colonel Geisler's ad hoc Group Neapal (one infantry battalion, the 115th Panzer Reconnaissance Battalion, and Captain Huettig's Mortar Unit Sicily) was ordered to cover Rodt's relatively weak center, between the two combat groups.[35]

General Aristo, commander of the Italian XIIth Corps, made his own plans and command arrangements for defending western Sicily during the night of July 10–11. He created a new formation, *Ragruppamiento* (Tactical Group) Schreiber, under the command of Generale di Brigata Otto Schreiber, who was replaced as commander of the 207th Coastal Defense Division by Colonel Augusto de Laurentiis, formerly of Port Defense "N" (Palermo). Tactical Group Schreiber included Tactical Group Venturi (the 177th Bersaglieri Regiment and the 526th Bersaglieri Battalion); the 1st Machine Gun Company; one ad hoc artillery battalion formed from the remnants of the 161st and 163rd battalions of the 10th Artillery Regiment; the IIIrd Battalion of the 30th (Assietta) Infantry Regiment reinforced with remnants of the 6th (Assietta) Infantry Regiment; the 157th Artillery Regiment (Self-Propelled); the 19th "Centuaro" Artillery Battalion; a battalion of the 22nd Artillery Regiment; and Tactical Group Campobello di Licata-Ravanusa (the 17th Blackshirt Battalion and Cavalry Squadron Palermo).[36] It also included the reinforced German 129th Panzer Grenadier Regiment (Fullriede), which Aristo temporarily detached from the tactical control of the 15th Panzer Grenadier. The tactical group was deployed in a semicircle from positions southwest of Agrigento to a point south of Canicatti. Rodt was to hold the line from east of there to Mazzarino, on the right boundary of the Livorno Division. Twelfth Corps' line would be a thin one at best, manned largely by poorly motivated Italian units, not all of which would reach their assigned positions by daybreak on July 11; however, it was the best General Aristo could do under the circumstances.

Aristo's arrangements placed the 15th Panzer Grenadier Division considerably farther west than 6th Army intended, but they did at least offer the Italians the hope of holding western Sicily. When Guzzoni learned about these dispositions on July 11, he apparently acquiesced to them, at least for the time being.[37] By that time he had many other things on his mind.

As the night wore on, Generale di Corpo Carlo Rossi summoned Generale di Divisione Domenico Chirieleison and Lieutenant General Paul Conrath to his headquarters at Enna. He ordered them to launch a concerted attack on Gela at six A.M. The Germans were to converge on the city from the northeast in three columns while the Italians converged on it from the northwest, also in three columns. This time Rossi wanted a coordinated attack. When he returned to his headquarters early on the morning of July 11, Conrath found orders from Kesselring instructing him to skirt to the west of the American positions at Piano Lupo and drive onto the Gela plain, north of the city. From there the panzers would be on flat terrain, ideal for maneuvering.

Conrath's final plan only partially resembled Kesselring's idea. Kampfgruppe Links, with the Tigers and the infantry, was to attack from its positions south of Biscari, cut the coastal road, pivot ninety degrees, and recapture the Ponte Dirillo Bridge over the Acate. Simultaneously, in the division's center, the Ist Battalion/H.G. Panzer Regiment, reinforced with miscellaneous engineer and flak units, was to attack down the Niscemi Road to Piano Lupo, eliminating Gorham's men and the 16th RCT. On the division's far right flank the IInd Battalion/H.G. Panzer Regiment (reinforced) was to attack from the vicinity of Ponte Olivo Airfield onto the Gela plain.

At three A.M. on July 11—three hours before the attack was to begin—General Guzzoni learned from Fridolin von Senger that the rumors he had dismissed were true: Syracuse had definitely fallen. This news shook Guzzoni. Concerned by the need to prevent the British from getting onto the Catania plain, from which Messina would be threatened, he gave orders modifying his counterattack. As soon as the Hermann Goering's counterattack showed any sign of success, he instructed Rossi and Conrath, the Germans were to be diverted eastward to roll up Patton's right flank and threaten the rear of the British 8th Army, thus taking the pressure off Catania; simultaneously, Livorno was to take Gela and then strike westward toward Licata, against the U.S. 3rd Infantry Division. Fifteenth Panzer Grenadier Division would support Livorno when it turned west. In other words, the converging attack was to transform itself midstream into a divergent one. This was not Guzzoni's best idea. First, however, the Big Red One had to be destroyed, along with the various airborne bands and the Ranger battalions at Gela.

✧ 8 ✧

COUNTERATTACK AND RETREAT

ACCORDING TO GENERAL ROSSI'S PLAN, CONRATH WAS SUPPOSED TO attack at six A.M. In fact, he was not ready until 6:15 A.M., and even then he had been unable to make contact with Chirieleison's Livorno Headquarters by either radio or telephone. Deciding that he could wait no longer, and hoping that the Italians would launch their attacks simultaneously with his as previously arranged, he gave the order to advance. All three of the Hermann Goering columns surged forward.

On the Livorno's left flank lay Colonel Carlo Martini's battle group, which had been built around what was left of Mobile Group E, Lieutenant Colonel Ugo Leonardi's IIIrd Battalion of Martini's own 34th (Livorno) Infantry Regiment, and the Ist Battalion of Colonel Adamo Telo's 28th Artillery Battalion. Seeing the German panzer battalion move out from Ponte Olivo Airfield, Colonel Leonardi headed for Gela with his battalion, quickly followed by the rest of Martini's battle group. By 6:30 A.M. the other two Italian columns had also moved into the attack (Map 7). It would, many of the attackers knew, be decisive in the outcome of the Battle of Sicily, if not in the entire Italian war. In a sense, this offensive would be the Pickett's Charge of the Axis. If it failed, defeat was inevitable.

Overhead the skies were clear of Allied aircraft; they had been grounded on Malta and Pantelleria by fog. Meanwhile, a dozen Italian bombers pounded Gela, while offshore German aircraft attacked American naval vessels. Initially everything seemed to be going according to plan. By seven A.M. the Livorno's central

117

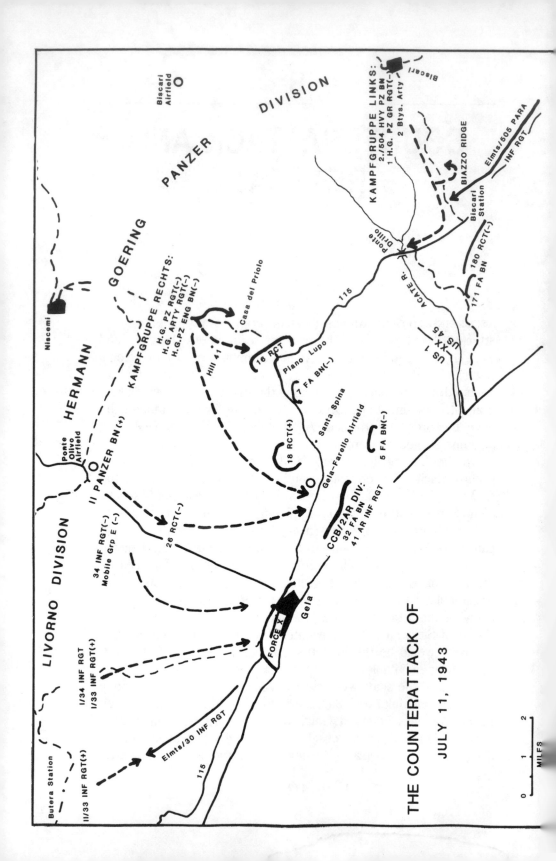

THE COUNTERATTACK OF
JULY 11, 1943

KAMPFGRUPPE LINKS:
2./504 HVY PZ BN
1 H.G. PZ GR RGT(−)
2 Btys. Arty

Biscari

Elmts/505 PARA
INF RGT

BIAZZO RIDGE

Biscari
Station

180 RCT(−)

171 FA BN

ACATE R−

US 45
XX
US 1

Ponte Dirillo

PANZER   DIVISION

Biscari
Airfield

GOERING

HERMANN

Niscemi

KAMPFGRUPPE RECHTS:
H.G. PZ RGT(−)
H.G. ARTY RGT(−)
H.G.PZ ENG BN(−)

Casa del Priolo

Hill 41

16 RCT

115

Plano Lupo

7 FA BN(−)

Santa Spina

5 FA BN(−)

18 RCT(+)

Gela−Farello Airfield

Ponte
Olivo
Airfield

II PANZER BN (+)

34 INF RGT(−)
Mobile Grp E (−)

26 RCT(−)

LIVORNO DIVISION

CCB/2 AR DIV:
32 FA BN
41 AR INF RGT

FORCE X

Gela

I/34 INF RGT
I/33 INF RGT(+)

Butera Station

II/33 INF RGT(+)

Elmts/30 INF RGT

115

0   1   2
MILES

column (the Ist Battalion/33rd Infantry Regiment and the I/34th Infantry Regiment, reinforced by a mortar battalion and the III/28th Artillery Regiment under Colonel Mario Mona of the 34th Infantry) had reached the western outskirts of Gela, while Martini's group was fighting the Rangers in the streets of the town. Only the right-hand column (the IIIrd Battalion/33rd Infantry Regiment, the II/34th Infantry, the II/28th Artillery Regiment, and the 109th Artillery Battalion) had been halted by a company-sized patrol of the 30th RCT, which had been dispatched by Truscott to make contact with the Rangers at Gela. It met the Italians about 2 miles southeast of Butera Station (and 4.5 miles north of Gela) and stopped them cold.[1]

Meanwhile, the Italian columns broke through the American main line of resistance and reached the outskirts of Gela, where they were halted by the Rangers, who were well supported by the attached 4.2-inch mortars. "Kill every one of the Goddamn bastards!" General Patton roared at the local Ranger commander as the Italians pushed across the plain toward the Ranger command post. About half the attackers were killed or wounded, mostly by the fifteen 6-inch guns of the light cruiser *Savannah*. It fired five hundred deadly rounds from its heavy guns into the Livorno ranks and broke the back of their attacks. Around 8:30 A.M., after two hours of courageous fighting, the Italians finally fell back. Livorno's equipment was simply unable to stand up to the American artillery and naval pounding. The Rangers followed quickly and took about four hundred stunned and dazed prisoners. U.S. Army Captain James B. Lyle, who had directed the naval gunfire with such deadly precision, followed the Ranger advance. "There were human bodies hanging from the trees," he recalled later.

Livorno and the Rangers were not the only units to suffer heavy casualties on July 11. In fact, the entire sector from Gela to south of Biscari was a sea of smoke, blood, and confusion. On the German right flank the sixty medium tanks of the reinforced IInd Battalion of the Hermann Goering Panzer Regiment overran a battalion of the 26th Infantry Regiment and rapidly pushed back the center of the Big Red One. The 26th was especially hard-pressed because all of its antitank guns had gone down with a sunken LST. Meanwhile, on the left, the infantry-heavy Kampfgruppe Links broke through the front of what was left of the 180th

RCT. Spearheaded by several Tigers, it drove the Americans back to Biazzo Ridge, cut the coastal highway, penetrated a regimental command post, and reached positions only a little more than two miles from the beaches.

The key position was still the Piano Lupo hill mass, in the center of the Hermann Goering's front. General Conrath himself led the central column—the reinforced Ist Battalion of the H.G. Panzer Regiment—down the Niscemi Road toward the first American position: Hill 41.

Hill 41 had been taken at dawn on July 11 by Hard Nose Gorham against light opposition from a German outpost. Almost immediately his paratroopers and the accompanying 2nd Battalion, 16th RCT spotted Conrath's column going into the attack with twenty-one medium panzers, well supported by the Hermann Goering Artillery Regiment. Most of the men of the 2nd Battalion were recent replacements, in battle for the first time, and a reinforced panzer battalion in the attack was too much for them. More than half of them broke and ran away. The rest fought as fiercely as did the paratroopers. Many Americans were crushed to death in their foxholes. Two tanks were knocked out by bazooka fire, but the panzertruppen overran the hill and pursued the Americans south, toward the junction of the Niscemi Road and the coastal highway.

By 9:30 A.M. the Americans were being pushed back everywhere. General Patton was at Gela, personally cheering on the army and naval engineers, who were working feverishly to repair the demolished pier so they could land Patton's tanks. General Bradley also went up front. He drove from his CP, the former headquarters of the Italian *carabinieri* (police) at Scoglitti, along the coastal road, through the zone of the 45th Infantry Division, only minutes before the highway was cut by the panzer grenadiers. He found Terry Allen at Gela. By now the IInd Panzer Battalion was pushing back the left flank of the 16th RCT and elements of the Ist Panzer Battalion had looped southwest of Piano Lupo and were nearing Santa Spina on the coastal road, only two thousand yards from the shoreline. "It's the Hermann Goering Division!" the disheveled and nearly exhausted divisional commander reported. "They've Goddamned near broken through to the beach. We're having a hell of a fight, but we can hold 'em!" he assured his corps commander.

Even as they spoke, the U.S. 7th Army formed its final defensive positions on the sand dunes south of the coastal road, on the very edge of the invasion beaches. Here the 32nd Field Artillery Battalion, coming ashore in DUKW, moved directly into firing positions, where they were protected by the 41st Armored Infantry Regiment and the 18th RCT from Patton's floating reserve. Then Shermans were put ashore as well, but they immediately stalled in the soft sand. The final American positions would have to be held with guns and cannon—not tanks.

Meanwhile, casualties mounted in the Hermann Goering Panzer Division. The *Savannah* put dozens of rounds from its heavy guns into the IInd Panzer Battalion, while the destroyer *Glennon* shelled the Niscemi Road with 193 rounds from its 5-inch guns. At 10:30 A.M., as the IInd Panzer Battalion pushed to within two miles of Gela, the cruiser *Boise* fired thirty-eight rounds of 6-inch shells into the German tanks. The IInd Panzer, however, pushed on toward the beaches despite the shelling.

The battle east of Gela reached its crisis point around eleven A.M. By now it was a real free-for-all, and the U.S. Navy could no longer intervene: the Germans and Americans were too intermingled in close combat for the big guns.[2]

The U.S. 16th Infantry was pretty well cut up. Only two of its nine antitank guns were still in operation, and the panzers had broken through its front in several places. Lieutenant Colonel Joseph Crawford had saved the remnants of his 2nd Battalion by withdrawing it to terrain unsuitable for tanks, so it had been bypassed and was effectively out of the battle. Colonel Gorham's surviving paratroopers continued to hold their positions in the hills, but the Ist Panzer Battalion had broken through the All-Americans in several places and was now well south of Piano Lupo, ready to add its weight to the final attack. Most of the survivors of the 16th RCT retreated into the sand dunes under the protective guns of the 32nd Field Artillery.

Conrath thought that he had won the battle. His men had pushed to within two thousand yards of the beach and raked supply dumps and landing craft with their guns. "Pressure by the Hermann Goering Division has forced the enemy to reembark temporarily," he signaled 6th Army HQ.

At Enna, General Guzzoni was also elated. His signals staff had intercepted a message, presumably from George Patton, instructing the 1st Infantry Division to prepare to reembark. Elements of Kampfgruppe Links had reached Ponte Dirillo, and the way was paved to roll up the American right flank now that the Big Red One was being pushed into the sea. After a brief consultation with General von Senger, Guzzoni instructed General Rossi to put the revised plan into effect that afternoon. The Germans were to wheel eastward toward Vittoria, roll up the U.S. 45th Infantry Division, and push on through the night to Palazzolo Acreide and Syracuse.

The order was premature. Patton had never ordered the 1st Infantry Division to prepare to reembark. The mystery of the interception has never been solved, but apparently it was a matter of a mistranslation by an Italian staff officer. Paul Conrath never reached the beaches, although he got very close.

The German attack was finally halted just in front of the American final defensive positions by the guns of the 32nd Field Artillery Battalion, the 16th Cannon Company, the heavier weapons of the 18th RCT and the 41st Armored Infantry Regiment, and four Shermans that the tankers and shore parties had finally managed to get off the beaches and onto the fringe of the coastal plain. Ten panzers were knocked out, and others were hit. The Luftwaffe tankers halted and then slowly began to retreat. This put a little distance between them and the Americans, so the *Boise* instantly opened up on them with her 6-inch guns. The retreat became faster and more confused, and although it never degenerated into a rout, Conrath was unable to get the attack going again. The Americans did not pursue, so at two P.M. the Luftwaffe ground commander called off the battle and fell back toward his original positions. American opposition had been too determined; Patton now had too many guns, antitank weapons, and infantry units on shore, and there were altogether too many naval warships off shore to eject the 7th Army. Also, the Hermann Goering Division had suffered too many casualties.

It is not possible to state exactly how many panzers the Hermann Goering Division lost during its counterattacks of July 10 and 11, but its tank strength on July 9 stood at ninety, excluding the seventeen Tigers of 2/504 Heavy Panzer Battalion. On July 14 it had forty-five operational PzKw III's and IV's. Fourteen of the Tigers had been knocked out on July 11, although four of these had been repaired and were operational three days later. How many of the other models were knocked out on July 10 and 11 but were later repaired and returned to combat is not known, but there were a few. The total number of panzers destroyed, then, must have been ten Tigers and thirty to forty Mark III's and IV's, for a total of forty to fifty tanks completely destroyed. It is safe to state that the H.G. Panzer Regiment lost at least a third of its tank strength on July 11 and that about half of its tanks were at least seriously damaged. Thirty officers and six hundred men were also lost. Small wonder Conrath called off the battle.

Kampfgruppe Links was not in a position to call off its battle so easily. It had attacked Biazzo Ridge with 750 grenadiers, its Tigers, and a panzer artillery battalion at nine A.M., fighting against a handful of misdropped American paratroopers and small elements of the 180th RCT. Unfortunately for them, Colonel James M. Gavin was only half a mile to the southeast at the time, marching along the coastal road from Vitorria to Gela with about 250 paratroopers. He immediately rushed to the sound of the guns and threw his men into a counterattack. From that point on Biazzo Ridge drew American units like a magnet. Both sides suffered heavy casualties, but Middleton, whose headquarters was only three miles away, sent in everything he could spare: bazookas, 81-mm mortars, 75-mm howitzers, a 155-mm battery, half a dozen Shermans, and several half-tracks towing antitank guns. Even so, the German battle group should have overrun the American positions. "They had more than enough capabilities to wipe us off the ridge," Major (later Colonel) Benjamin H. Vandervoort recalled. "Either their mission was to defend or their commander was lousy."[3]

Once again the men of the 1st Herman Goering Panzer Grenadier Regiment exhibited nervousness and its leadership showed confusion. Colonel Bergengruen was unable to take the ridge, and as new American units arrived, he assumed a largely defensive position. By five P.M. the ridge was firmly in American hands; Kampfgruppe Links had been driven off the field, pursued by Gavin's ad hoc combat group, which knocked out several Tigers, captured another, and captured several field guns and twelve large mortars. Gavin himself limped after his men with a mortar fragment in his leg. It was not a dangerous wound, but it was certainly a painful one.

To the west Kampfgruppe Rechts retreated to positions running generally from Casa del Priolo to the Ponte Olivo Airfield. On its right, Generale di Divisione Chirieleison fell back to the high ground to the north, where his artillery could still fire on the Gela plain. That afternoon General Guzzoni ordered that all offensive action in the XVIth Corps area be halted. The Hermann Goering Division was to withdraw to Caltagirone as soon as possible. On July 12 it was to move to Vizzini for commitment against the British, who were now recognized as the major threat. The Livorno Division was to establish a line from Mazzarino to Caltagirone to cover Conrath's withdrawal.

Unaware of these instructions, General von Senger went forward that afternoon and tried to order the division of attack eastward toward Comisco at 6:30 P.M., but his efforts came to nothing. General Conrath decided to ignore Senger and obey Guzzoni, at least partially. The former police officer had decided to withdraw. What he did not tell either Guzzoni or von Senger was that he intended to take his own sweet time about it.[4]

Meanwhile, Patton ordered his men to pursue the retreating enemy as rapidly as possible. General Bradley, commander of the U.S. IInd Corps, wanted to slow the American advance so that he could consolidate his bridgehead. Patton overruled him. He ordered the U.S. 1st Infantry Division forward and complained to Eisenhower that Bradley was insufficiently aggressive.[5]

Troy Middleton would probably have agreed with Patton. Even while the Battle of Biazzo Ridge was raging on his left flank, the commander of the 45th Thunderbird Division was not distracted from one of his main missions: the capture of the Comiso Airfield. He sent the 157th and 179th Infantry regiments forward to take it in a deep pincer movement. Opposition was light, confined mainly to long-range shelling and a few machine gun bursts. The airport fell around 4:30 P.M. The Thunderbirds captured 125 Axis airplanes (of which only 20 were operational), 200,000 gallons of aviation gas, and 500 bombers. One German airplane escaped just as the Americans moved in.

A few minutes later a Ju-88 bomber flew near the field and was fired upon. The pilot landed anyway, jumped out of the cockpit, and began furiously cursing the gunners, whom he took to be Italian. The former National Guardsmen took him prisoner. Realizing that the Germans did not expect them to be ten miles inland and did not know that Comiso had fallen, the Thunderbirds let two Luftwaffe fighters land and captured them in the same manner.

Shortly thereafter, army engineers and an antiaircraft battalion sent by General Bradley occupied Comiso, and the two regimental combat teams continued inland. The 179th advanced north along a secondary road, while the 157th advanced east toward a linkup with the Canadians. One rifle company ignored the boundary line between the U.S. 7th and British 8th armies and entered the city of Ragusa (population 40,000), where it captured the mayor, the chief of police, and the town's switchboard intact. Members of the unit spent the rest of the day amusing themselves by answering telephone calls from anxious Italian garrisons that wanted to know how the battle was going on the beaches. Meanwhile, as Kampfgruppe Links withdrew, the 180th RCT on the left flank of Middleton's division passed through Colonel Gavin's lines and took Biscari about eight P.M.

On the extreme left flank of the entire invasion, Major General Lucian K. Truscott was fighting his own battle virtually in isolation—and he was experiencing virtually nothing but success.

At dawn on July 11 he attacked along the entire front with (from left to right) his 7th RCT, 15th RCT, Combat Command A (CCA), and the 30th RCT. His swift action caught Group Schreiber before it could complete its deployment, and several Italian units were quickly overwhelmed. One infantry battalion (the 527th Bersaglieri) was reduced to about one hundred men, while the remnants of two artillery groups escaped with only ten guns between them. The heaviest fighting of the day took place at Palma di Montechiaro, which fell at about one P.M. The surviving Italians fled along Highway 115, closely pursued by the 7th RCT. Meanwhile, CCA pressed forward against light resistance, which consisted mainly of snipers. It was just outside Naro at six A.M., where it was met by two civilians, the mayor and his son. They told CCA that the town was not occupied. Naro was the first town in Europe to be captured by elements of the 2nd Armored Division.

Shortly afterward, eighteen B-26 bombers partially destroyed the town. "The attack resulted from the Air Corps' refusal to permit direct air-ground communications and its refusal to recognize the fluidity of a battlefield situation," the 2nd Armored Division's historian wrote later. "This was not the first time, nor would it be the last, that American troops suffered because of the uncoordinated efforts of the Air Corps and ground troops."[6] During the first week of the invasion CCA alone lost fourteen vehicles and seventy-five men to "friendly" air attacks.

Two miles northeast of Naro CCA ran into the 35th Bersaglieri Battalion of the 10th Bersaglieri Regiment, which had moved up from Agrigento that morning. Because of the rough terrain, the American armored and reconnaissance units had to halt and call for infantry support. The advance began again at four P.M. against stiffening opposition. The Italians withdrew at nightfall, but CCA halted four miles south of Cancatti.

In the meantime, the 15th RCT attacked along Highway 123 from Favarotta (seven miles north of Licata) toward Campobello. It was opposed by Group Venturi (Colonel Venturi's reinforced 177th Bersaglieri Regiment), which was moving down the highway to attack Licata. A fierce battle began about 4:45 A.M. and lasted four hours, during which U.S. artillery fired more than 1,500 rounds on Italian positions. Group Venturi was mauled. After a successful American infantry attack, it fell back to Campobello, having lost three artillery pieces and half its automatic weapons. Generale di Divisione Enrico Francisci, Guzzoni's chief liaison officer with the Fascist Militia, was among the casualties, as was Colonel Venturi. Despite his wounds, however Venturi remained in command.[7]

Colonel Fullriede's reinforced 129th Panzer Grenadier Regiment was also defeated. Much to Fullriede's surprise, the Americans, supported by tanks, bypassed his right (western) flank and wheeled behind it in the direction of the Canicatti-Serradifalco Highway—his main escape route. Fullriede lost several men and a large number of vehicles before he extricated his regiment, disengaged, and fell back to positions northeast of Canicatti.[8]

As soon as Ottorino Schreiber learned that Venturi and Fullriede had been defeated, he ordered Group Neapel to Campobello. All thought of offensive action was forgotten. The German 115th Reconnaissance Battalion under Captain Poth delayed the Americans and covered the withdrawal of Group Venturi, which fell back to Case San Silvestro. Group Neapal followed at about four P.M., leaving the town to the enemy.

Meanwhile, on Truscott's far right flank, the 30th RCT covered fourteen miles against light resistance, took Riesi, and made contact with the 1st Infantry Division. The U.S. 3rd Infantry Division had ballooned out of its original bridgehead and had advanced up to fourteen miles, occupying positions in a broad semicircle roughly along the line Palma di Montechiaro–Naro–Campobello–Riesi. As night fell Truscott was looking upon Caltanissetta and Enna as his next objectives.

During the night General Aristo tried valiantly to organize a defense against Truscott's expanding torrent. He ordered several units to converge on the Canicatti-Serradifalco sector, including the IIIrd Battalion of the 30th (Assietta) Infantry Regiment, the II/6th (Aosta) Infantry Regiment, and the 233rd and 19th "Centauro" Artillery battalions, with their 75-mm and 105-mm guns, respectively. The only question was, would the short night of the Sicilian summer afford them time to arrive before the next American attack, or would they be caught on the roads in daylight and be decimated by the increasingly ubiquitous fighter-bombers?

If July 11 was a day of success and victory for the 3rd Infantry Division, it was a day of disaster for the U.S. 82nd Airborne Division.

That morning General Patton ordered the reinforcement of the 1st Infantry Division by an airborne drop behind Allied lines near Gela, as specified in the original Husky Two plan. The force to be dropped was Colonel Reuben Tucker's 504th Regimental Combat Team, which included the two battalions of the 504th Parachute Infantry Regiment, the 376th Parachute Field Artillery Battalion, and engineer, medical, and signal troops—2,304 men in all. At 8:45 A.M. Patton issued a top-priority message to his subordinate commanders, instructing them to notify their men, especially their antiaircraft battalions, to expect the drop at about 11:30 P.M. that night. However, not all of them got the word.

July 11 was a cloudless night—typical of the Mediterranean in summer—with a bright first-quarter moon. The antiaircraft gunners on ship and shore were nervous, and with good reason. The Luftwaffe had been back again—and again and again. Despite their superiority in numbers, the U.S. Air Corps neglected to protect the beaches; the Luftwaffe, however, visited them frequently.

U.S. transports were strafed all day, and, at 3:40 P.M., the ammunition ship *Robert Rowan* suffered a direct hit and was blown apart in a spectacular explosion during an attack on American shipping by sixteen FW-200 and He-111 bombers escorted by eight fighters. At 7:30 P.M. the U.S. 1st Infantry Division reported that it had been under dive-bomber attack for more than two hours. Later, beginning at about 9:50 P.M., there was a major air attack against the 7th Army beaches, and the transports were forced to weigh anchor and disperse. In all, Axis aircraft flew an estimated 475 sorties against the Allied beachheads on July 11, most of them against the U.S. 7th Army and the naval forces supporting it. Nevertheless, the antiaircraft gunners did not fire as the C-47 transports approached the beaches at 10:15 P.M.

Only they were not C-47's. They were Ju-88's from Bomber Command, 2nd Air Fleet, sent by Colonel Dietrich Peltz to pound the beaches and naval convoys in the fourth major raid of the day. The attack lasted nearly an hour. One dive-bomber missed the destroyer *Murphy* by only a hundred yards. Pandemonium broke out as the harbor at Gela, the ships, the landing facilities, and the invasion beaches were bombed and strafed. Then the Nazi war birds disappeared to the north. The gunners relaxed, but only for a few minutes. Then they heard the sounds of the engines again. Another Luftwaffe formation appeared, this time very low. The first few aircraft were not fired on, but soon the sky was bright with tracers; American gunners fired shell after shell and round after round, knocking Ju-88 after Ju-88 from the sky.

Only they were not Ju-88's. They were C-47's, carrying Colonel Tucker's paratroopers.

Survivors of the airborne units later testified that the first serial of American paratroopers bailed out over Farello airfield without incident. Then an unknown machine gunner opened fire, followed by another and then another. The C-47's, flying only seven hundred feet above the deck, were easy targets. The U.S. Official History recorded that "it seemed as though every Allied AA gun in the beachhead and offshore was blasting planes out of the sky. The slow-flying, majestic columns of aircraft were like sitting ducks."[9] Many paratroopers deliberately bailed out prematurely, electing to take their chances on the ground. Several of these were mistaken for German parachutists and were shot to death in their harnesses by IInd Corps' infantrymen. Some of the aircraft were hit and forced to ditch into the sea, where the American destroyers riddled the helpless airplanes with heavy machine gun bullets. Seeing the inferno, several pilots turned sharply and dropped their loads in the less dangerous British sector. Several other pilots, at the end of the formation, simply refused to enter the cauldron. They turned around and flew back to Tunisia with the bellies of their C-47's still full of paratroopers. Perhaps they were the wisest of all.

Colonel Tucker was more fortunate than most. The C-47 in which he was flying had more than a thousand bullet and flak holes through its fuselage, but it still managed to reach the drop zone at Farello. On the morning of the next day he formed up 400 All-Americans near Gela—400 out of 2,304. By late afternoon the total had risen to 555. Stragglers continued to come in for days.

As a result of this disaster, all future planned airborne and gliderborne operations were canceled, including the one in which the division's heavy equipment was to be brought over by glider. The subsequent preliminary investigation revealed that 23 C-47's out of 144 had been destroyed, but only 6 went down before the paratroopers could jump out. Another 37 planes were badly damaged, although others were hit. Troop Carrier Command lost 60 pilots and crewmen killed and 30 others wounded. The 82nd Airborne Division eventually reported that the 504th RCT lost 81 dead, 132 wounded, and 16 missing, for a total of 229 casualties during the tragedy. The 376th Parachute Field Artillery Battalion, which was aboard some of the last aircraft, suffered particularly high casualties. Among the dead was Brigadier General Charles L. Keerans, Jr., the assistant divisional commander.

General Eisenhower quickly fired off an angry cable to Patton and demanded a full investigation of the incident, but the exact cause of the catastrophe was never pinpointed. It was never determined who fired first or even whether army, Navy, or merchant marine gunners had initiated the disaster. Air Chief Marshal Tedder's report probably came closer to the truth than any other, because he did not attempt to apportion blame but rather concluded that Husky Two had been fundamentally flawed to begin with, since it required the pilots to fly over thirty-five miles of an active combat zone full of inexperienced troops, in an area which the Luftwaffe was still operating. "Even if it was physically possible for all the troops and ships to be duly warned, which is doubtful," Tedder wrote, "any fire opened either by mistake or against enemy aircraft would almost certainly be supported by all troops within range—AA firing at night is infectious and control almost impossible.[10]

With the dawn of July 12, the Battle of Sicily entered a new phase in the American zone. The U.S. Navy, aided by army engineers, had had two days to overcome the false beaches and find good landing points for their LSTs, LCTs, etc. By the start of the third day of the battle, Patton had enough tanks, artillery, supplies, and heavy equipment to go over to the offensive on all sectors. The 7th Army advanced rapidly all along the line, except in the Niscemi Road–Piano Lupo sector, where General Conrath had decided to conduct his own private war. An hour before dawn Lieutenant Colonel Crawford of the 2nd Battalion, 16th RCT, accompanied by about a company of migrant paratroopers, advanced and captured Hill 41 in the Piano Lupo sector from an H.G. outpost, even though Crawford was seriously wounded by a German machine gun bullet during the attack. With incredible pigheadedness, General Conrath decided to take it back. Just when the Hermann Goering Panzer Division was badly needed to prevent Montgomery from overwhelming Group Schmalz and pushing on to Messina, thus bagging the whole 6th Italian Army, Conrath ignored his orders and attacked Hill 41 even though it no longer had the slightest military significance.

For whatever reason, the Battle of Hill 41 resumed at seven A.M. Before long a battalion of the 1st Infantry Division and part of the 505th RCT (all now operating under Colonel Gorham) were surrounded by the Luftwaffe panzertruppen. By this point, however, the Big Red One had its artillery ashore and the Hermann Goerings were pounded by 155-mm guns. The first German attack was halted within seventy-five yards of the American positions. Lieutenant Colonel Arthur "Hard Nose" Gorham was up front with his men, as usual, when a panzer approached. Gorham grabbed a rocket launcher and aimed it at the tank, but this time the Germans fired first—with their main battle gun. The American airborne branch lost one of its most promising officers.

Disaster faced the defenders of Hill 41 all along the line, but at the last possible moment Shermans from Combat Command B of the 2nd Armored Division arrived and attacked the Luftwaffe tankers from the rear. A prolonged tank battle ensued, but Hill 41 was saved. The battle was not over, however. Elements of the Hermann Goering Division made three more frontal assaults against the hill. All were poorly coordinated and lacked sufficient infantry support, and all were easily repulsed. That day Conrath issued a bitter order to his troops, stating that he had seen men "running to the rear hysterically crying because they had heard the detonation of a single shot. . . ." Once again he threatened severe measures, including death sentences.[11]

Elsewhere, the remnants of Livorno withdrew to the north. During the night what was left of Colonel Mona's group was surrounded, and most of it was forced to surrender. Colonel Mona himself escaped, along with a few remnants, although he was wounded in the breakout.

Colonel Leonardi was also in serious trouble. At 10:30 P.M. on July 11 the pursuing Americans attacked and almost surrounded his battalion, and Colonel Martini saved it only by committing his last reserves. At two A.M., however, the Americans were attacking again, and there were no more reserves. At dawn Leonardi surrendered his decimated battalion, along with the remnants of Mobile Group E. Livorno had, by now, lost more than half of its men and most of its combat units.[12] Shortly afterward, at about 8:45 A.M., the 26th RCT advanced up Highway 117 and captured the important Ponte Olivo Airfield from remnants of the Livorno Division. The Italians had retreated so rapidly that glasses of wine were found filled but abandoned on the tables in the Officers' Mess. By ten A.M. the 26th had advanced five miles inland, taking the high ground to the north. Meanwhile, the Headquarters of the Livorno Division had been located, and the U.S. forward observers called on H.M.S. *Abercrombie* to bombard it with its long-range guns, but Captain G. V. B. Faulkner regretfully replied that the target was out of range. Faulkner then had an ingenious idea. He flooded his port bilges and almost ran his ship aground but finally got sufficient elevation to fire. The *Abercrombie* scored several hits on the Italian divisional headquarters, and Captain Faulkner was awarded the U.S. Silver Star for his daring and gallant action.

Also in the zone of the 1st Division, Colonel Darby's 1st and 4th Ranger battalions broached a minefield near Butera and captured the hilltop town and a demoralized Livorno rear guard of about three hundred men. Two Rangers were slightly wounded.

On the American right, the advance of Middleton's 45th Infantry Division slowed as it met increasing numbers of Germans in the rough terrain north of the Comiso airfield. Nevertheless, it pushed back elements of the 1st Hermann Goering Panzer Grenadier Regiment and made contact with the 1st Canadian Infantry Division at Ragusa. The U.S. 7th and British 8th armies had linked up.

On Patton's left flank General Truscott was pushing forward, as usual. He was greatly aided by the American fighter-bombers, which ranged far to the rear and smashed Schreiber's reinforcements before they could reach the front lines. When the III/30th (Assietta) Regiment reached Serradifalco at seven A.M., for example, it had already lost thirty of its trucks and 20 percent of its combat effectives to Allied air attacks. Arriving later, the II/6th (Aosta) was down to 7 officers and 100 men, while the 28th Anti-Tank Company of the Aosta Division had only three guns and 57 men left out of a normal contingent of 228 men and eight guns. The 233rd "Centauro" Artillery Battalion of the Assietta Division arrived with only six guns, while the 19th Centauro could muster only four. Schreiber immediately reorganized his reinforcements into two weak infantry battalions and three artillery units, with a total strength of thirteen guns—far less than the number General Aristo had sent him. As a result, when General Truscott launched his main attack, he split Group Schreiber in half by capturing Canicatti and cutting Highway 122 at about three P.M. Fortunately for Schreiber, Colonel Fritz Fullriede's 129th Panzer Grenadier Regiment was near at hand, holding a breaker position in the hills north of the city. As the Italians fell back toward the Serradifalco–San Cataldo line, Fullriede turned back attacks from Combat Command A and knocked out or disabled forty-three American tanks.[13] Only after nightfall did the 129th Panzer Grenadiers follow the Italians and retire toward the new line.

Karl Ens was also up with his 104th Panzer Grenadier Regiment on July 12. Earlier that day he had visited Rodt's headquarters and had been wounded during an Allied bomber attack. He nevertheless refused to turn over command of his regiment and by the end of July 12 had temporarily stopped the American 15th RCT and elements of the 30th Infantry Regiment well short of the critical road passing through Caltanisetta and Pietraperzia. Rodt, however, was still worried. Livorno, on his left flank was dissolving. At the moment it was concentrating in a cork grove near Mazzarino, licking its wounds and reorganizing its infantry units into a provisional three-battalion regiment under Colonel Mona. Group Schreiber on Rodt's right also appeared to be disintegrating. If this process continued, Rodt would lose all contact with the Hermann Goering and could easily be isolated in western Sicily with both of his flanks exposed. The Axis front, it seemed, was on the verge of total collapse.

✧ 9 ✧

PRIMOSOLE BRIDGE

WHILE PATTON'S ARTILLERY WAS BATTLING THE PANZERS ON THE edge of the beaches and the American Rangers were fighting Italian tanks in the streets of Gela, Montgomery was rapidly advancing northward against decreasing Italian opposition. He came ashore with Lord Mountbatten on the southern end of the Pachino peninsula at seven A.M. on July 11 to find that Syracuse had been captured intact, the entire Pachino peninsula had been cleared, one thousand Italian prisoners of war were ready for shipment to Africa, and an airstrip was already operational. At Syracuse not even the cranes and quay facilities had been damaged. Montgomery immediately went from being pessimistic to being overly optimistic. This optimism would have a profound effect on the battle in the next few days.

One man who was not optimistic was Colonel Wilhelm Schmalz. Even as he rushed his ad hoc brigade toward Syracuse on the morning of July 10, he had grave doubts about leaving Catania undefended. From the time he made contact with the British later that day, he conducted a delaying action up the eastern coastal highway (Highway 114), slowly relinquishing the villages of Priolo, Melilli, and Sortino. Monty, meanwhile, began to advance in two main directions: toward Augusta and northwest, toward Vizzini (Map 8).

Schmalz received little help from the Italians of the Napoli Division, which "melted into thin air," according to Kesselring.[1] On July 11, while Brigade Schmalz held up the British 17th Brigade at Priolo, the 13th Brigade attacked Solarino on his right flank. The Napoli commander, Generale di Divisione Giulio Porcinari, had posted two battalions of his 75th Infantry Regiment there for just such an eventuality, yet the town fell without the British suffering a single casualty. "[T]he myth that the Italians would fight with great fortitude in defence of their own country was exploded," the diarist of the 2nd Wilts Battalion recorded.[2] With his flank thus turned, Colonel Schmalz fell back toward Augusta.

As Schmalz retreated, southeastern Sicily was in an uproar. Refugee columns clogged the roads to the north. They were joined by Italian deserters, most of whom were now dressed as civilians; many deserters took to robbing, stealing, and looting from villagers and fugitives. It was a sorry spectacle. Fascist officials fled, law and order broke down, and there was anarchy in the countryside. To make matters worse, the dust often made it impossible to tell the difference between refugee columns and military formations from the air. Many fleeing civilians were strafed as a result, adding to the horror, misery, and confusion.

On the night of July 11 Schmalz decided to abandon Augusta and to withdraw by stages to Lentini. This was a tough decision, because it would widen the gap between his units and the rest of the Hermann Goering Division. The British would be in a position to advance into the eighteen-mile gap in the Axis line between Vizzini and Lentini, cutting the road between these two towns. Such a move would prevent the Hermann Goering Panzer Division from joining Group Schmalz in the defense of Lentini, which would compel yet another retreat. General Conrath's slowness and apparent lack of appreciation for the true situation had endangered Catania and, ultimately, Messina. But Schmalz had little choice except to take the chance that the British would not take full advantage of their opportunity. His orders to his brigade for July 12 were to fall back along Highway 114, which runs west of Augusta, leaving the defense of the city to the incompetent Admiral Leonardi and his rapidly disintegrating Fortress Area command.

The War Diary of the German Liaison Staff with the 6th Army is full of reports of bad news for the night of July 11–12. Shortly after midnight the Italian XVIth Corps informed 6th Army that, contrary to expectations, the main combat elements of the Hermann Goering Division would not arrive in the Caltagirone area on July 12 but rather during the night of July 13–14. This seriously upset Guzzoni's timetable and made it seem increasingly unlikely that the slow

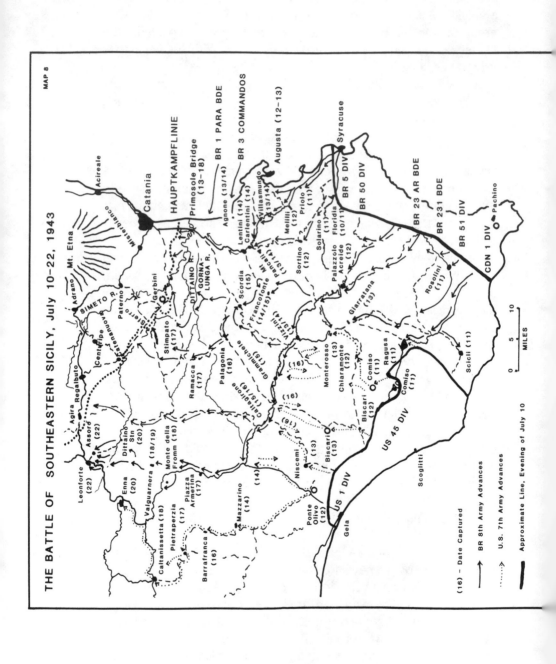

MAP 8

THE BATTLE OF SOUTHEASTERN SICILY, July 10–22, 1943

(16) – Date Captured

→ BR 8th Army Advances

⋯⋯▷ U.S. 7th Army Advances

━━━ Approximate Line, Evening of July 10

MILES

0   5   10

Conrath would be able to link up with Brigade Schmalz in time to save Catania; therefore, Messina itself was in jeopardy.

The most disturbing news, however, came in at 3:50 A.M. The Hermann Goering Division reported that its panzer grenadier regiment had been split into two groups, one of which had been cut off by the Americans and reduced to a few minor elements south of the Acate River—which meant that it would probably be destroyed. The other group was also cut off by the rapidly advancing U.S. 45th Infantry Division, but north of the river. It still had combat strength and intended to fight its way through to the Hermann Goering Panzer Regiment. In other words, it was fighting for its life and heading *west,* not east. There would be no help for Battle Group Schmalz from the Hermann Goering Division, at least in the foreseeable future. A little more than a reinforced panzer grenadier regiment was facing the entire British XIIIth Corps.

The situation was not quite as bleak for Colonel Schmalz as it appeared, however. Hitler had already authorized air-dropping the 3rd Parachute Regiment (*Fallschirmjaeger*-Regiment 3, or FJR 3) at Lentini to reinforce him, and it would be followed by most of the rest of the 1st Parachute Division. At the moment Guzzoni was mainly concerned with establishing a continuous front and containing the Allied bridgehead as far south as possible. At 9:10 A.M. he ordered the Hermann Goering Division to move into the defensive sector Caltagirone-Granmichele-Vizzini. Once there, it was to conduct a delaying action and slowly fall back to the north; it was not to counterattack. The Napoli Division was to defend in its current positions and "tenaciously hold Palazzolo Acreide in order to cover the left flank of the Hermann Goering Division." Schmalz was also ordered to hold his present positions. How he was to do so was not specified. Livorno was ordered to shift into the area between Mazzarino and San Michele di Ganzeria, to cover the right flank of the H.G. Division. The Assietta Division was instructed to move into the Bisaquino–Prizzi–Lercara area, forty kilometers (about twenty-five miles) south of Palermo, while the 15th Panzer Grenadier Division was to disengage and go into army reserve in the centrally located Pietraperzia-Valgernera area.[3]

A supplementary order to the German forces was issued by von Senger at 10:05 A.M. and transmitted at 11:25. It instructed Rodt's 15th Panzer Grenadier to cover the right flank of the

Hermann Goering, told Conrath to establish contact with the Napoli Division at Palazzolo Acreide, and stated that Group Schmalz "must hold its present line at all costs."[4]

About the same time this order was being issued, British Brigadier G. W. Richards's 23rd Armoured Brigade was advancing on Palazzolo Acreide from the southeast. It then divided into two columns and attacked the bombed-out town from the east and west simultaneously. The town fell quickly. Then Richards turned his command onto Highway 124 for the drive on Vizzini.

Meanwhile, to the east, Wilhelm Schmalz was ignoring General von Senger's already outdated instructions. He had no intention of carrying out an order to hold at all costs that would endanger the existence of his command. On the morning of July 12 his brigade, supported by a few of the more reliable remnants of Napoli, launched a "rather severe" counterattack against the British XIIIth Corps, temporarily forcing it to go over to the defensive.[5] The objective of this attack was to cover a withdrawal to good defensive positions centering on Lentini, and it worked, just as it had been diagrammed. The drawback, of course, was that Augusta was left uncovered by German forces.

Augusta lay fifteen miles up the coast from Syracuse and had a large artificial harbor. Admiral Leonardi, at last awake to the true situation in his Fortress Area, left his headquarters to direct the defense of the city personally. By the night of July 11–12 the same panic that had seized Syracuse had gripped Augusta as well, and there were few sailors and soldiers left to man the guns. That night British Rear Admiral Troubridge tried to take the port via a naval *coup de main,* but was chased out by shore guns—one of which was fired by his counterpart, Admiral Leonardi, and two members of Leonardi's staff who had replaced a crew of deserters. It was perhaps the only time in World War II in which one admiral personally fired on another. Physical bravery was not enough for Admiral Leonardi, however; most of his men were gone. At 7:30 P.M. H.M.S. *Ulster Monarch,* escorted by a destroyer and two motor gunboats, entered the harbor and landed troops, who quickly silenced the few operational batteries. The vanguard of the British 5th Infantry Division arrived later that evening and completed the conquest of the city.

Unfortunately for the British, the bulk of the 5th Infantry Division and the rest of the 8th Army were considerably farther back.

Most of the infantrymen had already marched from sixty to a hundred miles and fought several skirmishes and rearguard actions in boots that had been inundated with salt water. The thermometer reached 100 degrees every day, and the Mediterranean sun was merciless. Foot problems were common, and supply problems, caused by a shortage of vehicles, also slowed the advance.

On July 13 a battalion-sized detachment of Italians caused further delay to the British. It launched a surprise counterattack, broke through British lines, and briefly reoccupied the Italian seaplane base at Augusta. The following morning more British units came up and forced it to retire. A British port development party moved in on July 14, and the port was in full operation by July 16. The port capacity of Augusta had been reduced to only 1,600 tons of cargo per day, however, because of the heavy damage caused by Allied air bombardments.

On the morning of July 12 Field Marshal Albert Kesselring showed up at Enna to find out what was going on. During the previous three days he had received only scanty information, some of which was not true. His liaison officer, General von Senger, had only one or two radios, which he had borrowed from troop units. The range of these stations did not extend to Rome, however, and were generally used to capacity for the transmittal of orders to German units in the field. On the other hand, Kesselring had a direct telephone line to Headquarters, IInd Air Corps, on the east coast of Sicily. Although this corps no longer had any combat aircraft, it still possessed large quantities of signal equipment. "This air force corps disseminated, rather indiscriminately and without confirming their accuracy, alarming news which it had received from sundry sources," Senger recalled.[6]

Kesselring met with Guzzoni and von Senger at 9:15 A.M. and confirmed Guzzoni's dispositions. The weight of the 6th Army would shift to the left flank. The Hermann Goering Division was again ordered to aid Battle Group Schmalz and the remnants of the Napoli Division. The idea of holding Vizzini indefinitely was abandoned, and the trio agreed to let Schmalz withdraw gradually to the Lentini-Francofonte line, where it would make contact with Conrath's left flank.

The only disagreement came when the advisability of sending additional German units to Sicily was discussed. Kesselring especially wanted to bring over the 29th Panzer Grenadier Division and recover the initiative in Sicily. "His inveterately over-optimistic appraisal of a given situation undoubtedly induced him to plan the reopening of a counterattack," Senger recalled.[7] Neither Guzzoni nor Senger wanted the 29th Panzer Grenadier sent over yet, because the possibility of an Allied landing on the undefended northern coast of Sicily still existed, as did the possibility of a landing in Calabria. Either contingency might result in the isolation and eventual capture of the Axis garrison in Sicily. Kesselring let the matter drop, although he did not credit Guzzoni's pessimistic report of the battle situation. Senger's views were similar, but the field marshal dismissed them as well. He had already decided to conduct an inspection of the front in order to see for himself. Then he would ask Fuehrer Headquarters for permission to move the 29th Division to the island.

While the Axis generals talked, the Allies continued to advance on a broad front. On the morning of July 12 the Canadians ran into unusually stiff resistance at Modica. All or parts of four Canadian battalions finally stormed the place, capturing seven field guns, five medium guns, and one antitank gun, along with several hundred Italian prisoners. The reason for the tougher than normal defense was the presence of Generale di Divisione Achille d'Havet, commander of the 206th Coastal Defense Division. He was finally captured by a Canadian sergeant but asked to be allowed to surrender to a high-ranking officer. As a major escorted him out of town, much of the civilian population of Ragusa came out to boo the fat little general. He was finally taken to General Simond's headquarters, where he surrendered to the commander of the 1st Canadian Infantry Division. He was the first Axis general captured by the Canadians in World War II.

D'Havet's capture also signaled the end of the 206th Coastal Defense Division. After the fall of Modica, a platoon of infantry, supported by a troop of tanks, turned south to clear the village of Scicli, between Modica and the coast. The Edmonton Regiment's unit diary reported that "the tanks fired three shots over the town and 1,100 prisoners emerged from the hills and gave themselves up."[8] During the night large numbers of Italians were rounded up in the hills around Ragusa by the 2nd Canadian Infantry Brigade.

Other units of the 8th Army made similar progress. By nightfall the 23rd Armoured Brigade was within sight of Vizzini.

As the Allies mopped up against the Italians, the first substantial German reinforcements arrived in Sicily. The first to reach the front was the IInd Battalion of the 382nd Panzer Grenadier Regiment and the Panzer Grenadier Battalion Reggio, both of which had been part of OB South's reserve.

Colonel Wolfgang Maucke's 382nd Panzer Grenadier Regiment was a rebuilt unit. The original 382nd had been part of the 164th Light Afrika Division, which had been destroyed in Tunisia. It had absorbed the ad hoc Panzer Grenadier Regiment Neapal ("Naples" in English), which was made up of two battalions of rear-area "African" troops plus an infantry cannon company and an antitank company. Initially earmarked for the 15th Panzer Grenadier Division, it was attached to the Hermann Goering Division in this emergency. After provisionally motorizing the IInd Battalion, using Hermann Goering vehicles, Conrath sent it straight to Vizzini. The rest of the regiment was sent to Group Schmalz a day or two later.

Panzer Grenadier Battalion Reggio had been created in Italy in May 1943 from the 69th March Battalion. It was also earmarked for the 15th Panzer Grenadier Division, but had been held in reserve on the tip of the Italian boot until after the invasion began. Kesselring quickly sent it south to reinforce Colonel Schmalz. The largest and most important reinforcement Schmalz received that day, however, was Colonel Ludwig Heilmann's 3rd Parachute Regiment, a part of the 1st Parachute Division.

General Alexander later called the men of the 1st Parachute Division "the best soldiers in the world." They were commanded by Lieutenant General Richard Heidrich, a tough, blunt-jawed veteran of the Eastern Front. Like the 2nd Parachute Division, the 1st Parachute was part of Kurt Student's XIth Air Corps, the senior parachute headquarters of the Wehrmacht at that time.

By the order of the Fuehrer, the entire XIth Air Corps (thirty thousand men) was placed on full alert early on July 10. Later that morning Heidrich was summoned to Kesselring's HQ in Rome and was told that most of his division was being committed to Sicily. The insertion would take place in four drops. The first to be committed would be the 3rd Regiment (1,400 men), which would jump at seven P.M. on July 12. They would be followed by the second group, which consisted of the 1st Parachute Machine Gun Battalion and the radio company of the 1st Parachute Signal Battalion. The third group to land would consist of the 4th Parachute Regiment, the 1st Engineer Battalion, and part of the 1st Parachute Anti-Tank Battalion. The final drop would include the 1st Parachute Regiment and a battalion of the 1st Parachute Artillery Regiment.[9] (The 1st Regiment, however, was never dropped.) The divisional headquarters, however, would not be committed to the island; all of the parachute units would be attached to Brigade Schmalz.

Predictably, Heidrich did not care for this command arrangement, which probably says more about the faith Kesselring had in Schmalz than anything else. In any event, Heidrich telephoned Colonel Heilmann about midnight and ordered him to conduct an aerial reconnaissance of the drop zone the following day.

Heilmann was very worried about this jump because of Allied air superiority. During his own reconnaissance flight his pilot was forced to fly low in the Mount Etna foothills to avoid detection. Then the pilot had to set down at Catania, an airfield so pitted with fresh bomb craters that Heilmann called the landing "a work of art."[10] A drop zone was selected west of Catania, but there was barely time to call in the map coordinates before the hundred-plus He-111's carrying 1,817 paratroopers took off for Sicily.

With General von Senger and Colonel Schmalz, Field Marshal Kesselring watched the first paratroop drop on the evening of July 12. It was close to perfectly executed, with only a few minor injuries—twisted ankles and so forth. The operation continued for the next several days with success because, Kesselring observed, "the British fighters' rigid time-table gave us repeated opportunities to risk the move."[11] In fact, all the British and American air units had lunch and dinner about the same time every day. The Germans quickly learned when it was safe to conduct air operations, ferrying activities and so forth, without the risk of being bombed or strafed. Allied predictability would save the lives of many German soldiers in the days ahead.

Within minutes of landing the 3rd Parachute Regiment rendezvoused with Schmalz's trucks, and soon they and the colonel were on their way to reinforce Brigade Schmalz south of Lentini. At eight P.M. Heilmann met with Colonel Schmalz outside Lentini and received his orders: his IInd Battalion was to rush to Francofonte, where it was to help plug the gap between Group Schmalz and the rest of the Hermann Goering Division. The rest of the regiment was told to take up defensive positions between Carlentini and the sea.

General Alfredo Guzzoni was still at his desk in Enna, even though it was nearly midnight. July 12 had been one of the most tiring days of his life. Not only were most of his Italian units dissolving, but Group Schreiber was being pounded; Livorno, his best unit, was in remnants; and the gap between Brigade Schmalz and the Hermann Goering had not been narrowed. General Conrath was withdrawing his division in stages and in a very leisurely manner; several orders by the 6th Army and by General von Senger to speed up the withdrawal were treated like so much waste paper by the former police officer. Nor could he or von Senger relieve Conrath of his command, because Conrath was a favorite of Reichsmarschall Goering.

Suddenly there were explosions all around. American bombers were attacking the ancient walled city of Enna, and 6th Army Headquarters was their main target. It was reduced to a shambles, and Guzzoni was almost killed. Shaken and incoherent, he told an aide that it was too bad a bomb had not landed on him.

Because of the raid, 6th Army Headquarters was temporarily *hors de combat*. The building was virtually demolished, all signal communications except a few radios had been knocked out, and there was no choice left except to move the HQ, especially since the Americans obviously knew where it was and would undoubtedly come back. What was left of Guzzoni's staff, however, could not persuade the stunned general to leave. He kept talking about staying and sharing the fate of his men. He was finally persuaded to leave by the combined efforts of his chief of staff, Colonel Faldella, and General von Senger, but only after considerable debate.[12]

On the other side of the hill, Montgomery was as wildly optimistic as Kesselring had been earlier. He believed that he had a chance to end the campaign in a matter of days. He felt that, if the Americans could hold the German attack at Gela, Leese's XXXth

Corps would be able to cut behind them by driving inland to Enna. Thus the Axis forces in central Sicily would be trapped between the Americans and the British and would be destroyed. Following this triumph, the British corps would make a "left hook" west of Mount Etna, possibly trapping the rest of the Germans between it and Dempsey's XIIIth British Corps, which would be blitzing up the coast toward Catania and Messina.

This was not a good plan. Besides the obvious friction it would provoke by offending American sensibilities (it implied that they were good for little except covering the British left flank), it was incredibly ambitious—far too ambitious. In his enthusiasm, Montgomery had apparently lost sight of the fact that he was no longer operating in the desert, with its wide expanse of open terrain. He was now on a mountainous island which offered few routes of advance, many excellent defensive positions, and little scope for maneuver, operating against an enemy who had a talent both for combat engineering and for recovering quickly. And speed was not exactly Montgomery's strong suit, especially during the initial battles in Sicily. As late as July 14–15, Monty would have only 4,000 vehicles and 16,000 tons of supplies on the island; at the same time, Patton would have landed 7,000 vehicles and 17,000 tons of supplies,[13] and his army was, at that time, somewhat smaller than Montgomery's. On July 12 the 8th Army was considerably less maneuverable vis-à-vis Patton's forces than even this ratio suggests. The U.S. 7th Army was much better equipped at this time to be a maneuver and pursuit force than was the British 8th; yet Monty's plan would, in effect, relegate it to the bench.

On the evening of July 12 Montgomery informed Alexander that he now intended to have the XXXth Corps advance through Caltagirone, Enna, and Leonforte. He suggested that his army operate offensively to the north, in order to cut the island in two. The American army would face west and hold the ports and airfields.

Approving this plan also meant taking Highway 124 away from the Americans, turning the U.S. 45th Infantry Division around, and marching it almost all the way back to the invasion beaches. In spite of this, Alexander approved the plan and at eight P.M. on July 13 issued orders to this effect, despite the fact that elements of Middleton's Thunderbirds were within a thousand yards of the highway. The road was already within easy range of his artillery.

Now the 45th Division had to turn around, march to the rear, and reinsert itself into the battle area west of the 1st Infantry Division. This move, in effect, forced IInd Corps to halt its offensive for several days.

Weeks later, after Sicily had fallen, Patton visited Montgomery, and during their conversation, the American complained about the injustice of Alexander taking away the Vizzini-Caltagirone Highway at that time. Monty smiled and said, "George, let me give you some advice. If you get an order from Army Group that you don't like, why, just ignore it. That's what I do."[14]

Alexander's decision to rubber-stamp Monty's plan temporarily eliminated an entire U.S. corps that was flushed with victory. It also took the pressure off the Hermann Goering Division and divided Montgomery's main effort into two parts, violating the principle of mass. It shifted half of the 8th Army's effort from flat terrain (where it could use its tanks) to the mountainous interior, where armor could not be used effectively. It also meant that the pressure was shifted from a coastal sector to the interior, where the Royal Navy could not be used. Also, in the two weeks it would now require for Montgomery and Patton to reach positions north of Mount Etna, the Germans would have time to bring up and deploy about half of the 1st Parachute Division and most of the 29th Panzer Grenadier Division and to prepare for the eventual evacuation of the island.

Montgomery, of course, could foresee none of this on July 12. He figured to be in Catania on or about July 14. He might have gotten a foretaste of things to come the next day, July 13. The Highland Division and the 23rd Armoured Brigade tried to take Vizzini, which was defended by the Hermann Goering Panzer Reconnaissance Battalion and a few detachments, including the Panzer Grenadier Battalion Reggio. After Vizzini fell, Leese ordered, the Highlanders and the armored brigade were to push on to Caltagirone, which they were to capture that evening.

But the British could not even take Vizzini on July 13. By early morning Brigadier Richards's tankers were already in position to attack, but had to wait for the infantry, which was struggling forward in the hot Mediterranean sun. (Tanks attacking without infantry support, Richards knew, would be sitting ducks for the German antitank gunners.) Some of the Highland units had marched thirty-five miles in twenty-four hours, and their columns were strung out for miles. It was almost nightfall before the British could attack (with two infantry divisions and the 23rd Armoured), but they were not able to eject the reece troops and panzer grenadiers; in fact, after midnight on July 13–14 they had to deal with German counterattacks. The German battle group continued to hold the town all day long on July 14 as well, repulsing a series of uncoordinated British attacks. Finally, during the evening, General Wimberley came up to personally direct a coordinated attack on the town. This attack went forward at one A.M. on July 15 and struck thin air: Reggio and the Luftwaffe panzer reconnaissance battalion had gone.

Beginning early on July 12, General Guzzoni had sent order after order to Paul Conrath, instructing him to make contact with the right flank of the disintegrating Napoli Division. Conrath made no attempt to execute this order, because he was hard-pressed by the Americans (especially the 45th Infantry Division) and he had suffered heavy losses in tanks and men—particularly in infantry— even though the panzer grenadier battalion trapped south of the Acate had miraculously managed to elude its pursuers and reach friendly lines. There would be no further talk of counterattack after the fall of Vizzini, primarily because the Napoli Division had virtually ceased to exist.

Generale di Divisione Count Giulio Cesare Gotti-Porcinari, commander of the Napoli Infantry Division, had spent July 12 trying to rally the remnants of his shattered command. His artillery regiment was practically gone—either captured or deserted—and one of his infantry regiments had been encircled between Syracuse and Palazzolo Acreide. The rest of his units were also in pretty poor condition. On the morning of July 13, a British patrol pushed through one of the many holes in Napoli's sector and captured Gotti-Porcinari and most of his staff. That did it for Napoli. Although a few of its units were later reorganized in the rear (mainly the I/76th Infantry Regiment and the 110th Artillery Battalion), Napoli itself was attached to the Hermann Goering Division for the rest of the campaign and was finished as an independent combat force.[15]

Meanwhile, Montgomery decided to break through to Catania by means of a combined land, air, and sea assault. He was sure that one more blow would send the Germans and their reluctant allies hustling back toward Messina in full retreat. "I shall be in Catania tonight!" he boasted to U.S. Major Robert Henriques, Patton's liaison officer to his headquarters.[16]

There was little time to plan Operation Fustian, the airborne part of the assault. At seven P.M. on July 13 Brigadier Gerald Lathbury's 1st British Parachute Brigade boarded 135 C-47's and 11 Albermarles around Kairouan, Tunisia. The strength of Lathbury's drop force was 1,856 Red Devils, and their objective was to seize and hold Primosole Bridge, which crossed the Simeto River seven miles south of Catania, until they could be relieved by the advancing 8th Army. Two hours after the paratroopers jumped, eighteen other gliders were to land near the bridge with ten antitank guns and seventy-seven gliderborne artillerymen. Meanwhile, a force of British Commandos was to land a short distance to the southeast and seize the Malati Bridge over the smaller Leonardo River.

Primosole Bridge was the key. It was four hundred feet long, was built on girders, and stood about eight feet above the sluggish, brown water of the Simeto River, whose banks were bordered by thick, green reeds. North of the bridge was tree-lined countryside, dominated by olive and almond groves that offered the defenders good concealment. To the south, the terrain was so flat that it provided no cover whatsoever. Eighth Army needed to take this bridge quickly; otherwise, the Germans might rally in the excellent defensive terrain to the north and the battle for Catania could be a long one. Map 9 shows the Primosole Bridge sector, around which the campaign focused for several days.

Lathbury's plan for capturing Primosole Bridge called for the 1st Parachute Battalion (Lieutenant Colonel Alastair "Jock" Pearson) to carry out a *coup de main* by landing north and south of the bridge. Simultaneously, Lieutenant Colonel E. C. Yeldham's 3rd Parachute Battalion was to land about a thousand yards north of the bridge to establish defenses against a possible counterattack from Catania. The 2nd Battalion under Lieutenant Colonel John D. Frost was to secure the high ground to the south of the Simeto, where three small but critical hills—code-named Johnny I, II, and III—controlled access to the bridge from that direction.

What the British did not know was that Major Schmidt's 1st Parachute Machine Gun Battalion had landed at Catania in the

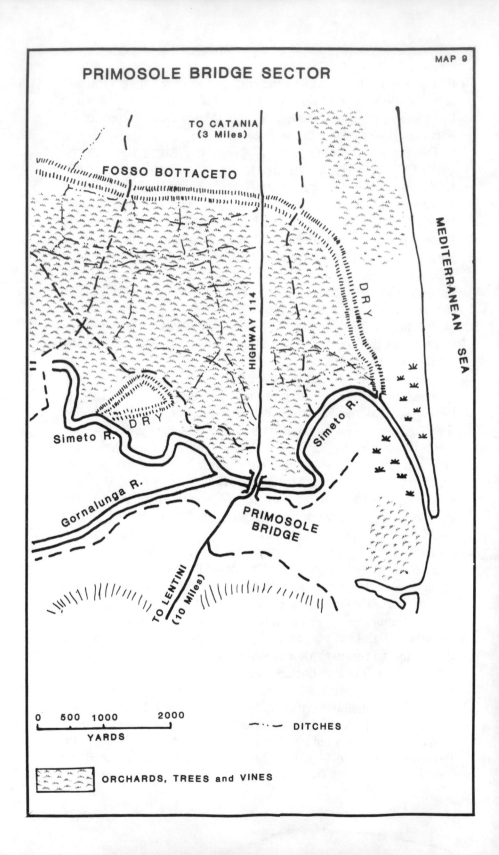

MAP 9

PRIMOSOLE BRIDGE SECTOR

TO CATANIA
(3 Miles)

FOSSO BOTTACETO

MEDITERRANEAN SEA

DRY

HIGHWAY 114

DRY

Simeto R.

Simeto R.

Gornalunga R.

PRIMOSOLE
BRIDGE

TO LENTINI
(10 Miles)

0   500   1000   2000   — · — DITCHES

YARDS

ORCHARDS, TREES and VINES

early morning, in the midst of yet another British air raid. Several German aircraft were shot down or destroyed on the ground, including two Me-321 Gigant transports. Most of the battalion's antitank weapons were destroyed.

Major Werner Schmidt, like many other officers in the Wehrmacht and SS, was a former police officer. He had been in the Linden Inspectorate of the Berlin police before joining the Hermann Goering Regiment in the early days of the Nazi regime. Since this unit was then training paratroopers, he transferred easily into the airborne arm. He was destined to win his Knight's Cross in Sicily.[17]

If the loss of part of his unit disturbed him, he did not show it. He quickly formed up his survivors and ordered them to march south, toward the Primosole Bridge, while he borrowed a jeep and drove to the Command Post of the 3rd Parachute Regiment to report to Colonel Heilmann.

"Something is bound to happen tonight," the colonel said. "The enemy will try to sneak through to the Catania Plain, and to do it, he'll send in more troops—either by sea or by air. If he manages to land them in our rear and dig in, then we're cut off for sure. So your battalion will remain south of Catania. Hold the bridge over the Simeto."[18]

Heilmann had divined Lathbury's plan perfectly. As a result of this order, the German gunners dug in two thousand yards south of the Primosole Bridge, on the edge of an orange grove on the west side of Highway 114—well within machine gun range of the main British drop zones.

As Schmidt's machine gunners dug in, the first Allied troop carriers took off from Kairouan, heading for Primosole Bridge. Most of the flights, however, drifted far off course, and one flew over an Allied naval convoy just southeast of Cape Passero, on the southeastern tip of Sicily. The sailors immediately opened up with a deadly flak barrage, and two C-47's quickly went down in flames. Two others, taking evasive action, collided and plunged into the sea together, killing everyone on board. Many Red Devils were killed or wounded inside airplanes that managed to stay aloft. Nine disabled birds flew back to Tunisia, as did six undamaged aircraft.

Because of the dispersion caused by "friendly" fire, C-47's wandered about in the darkness as far north as Messina and as far south as Malta. As a result, more were hit by friendly and enemy fire. In all, out of 135 C-47's involved, 11 were shot down (most with all hands on board), 49 were severely damaged, and 47 others had bullet and/or shrapnel holes in them when they finally made it back to base. The paratroopers who did jump out were scattered all over eastern Sicily.

Miraculously, some of the Red Devils actually came to earth where they were supposed to. There was considerable confusion as the British landed in the zone of the 1st Parachute Machine Gun Battalion, temporarily under the command of Captain Otto Laun, as Schmidt was away, apparently conferring with Colonel Heilmann.[19] German and British paratroopers wore similar helmets, and many Fallschirmjaegern thought the Red Devils were Germans. Other machine gunners, watching the British descend in the three-quarter moon, recognized who they were and killed quite a few. One German participant recalled:

At 22.00 hours [ten P.M.] aircraft suddenly appear overhead and our own sentries are shouting "German paratroopers!" We know that reinforcements should be landing or making a drop some time. But shit! shit!—when the signal flares light up the eerie darkness—we can see yellow and red parachutes . . . British airborne troops overhead! . . .

Everything happening in a matter of seconds. . . . Great volleys of fire, a fantastic performance from our men behind the guns. More and more aircraft. . . . Our fellows behind the machine-guns are shooting like supermen . . . cones of machine gun fire cut through the darkness with their trajectory. . . .[20]

Some of the gunners had unwittingly registered their guns on the exact line of approach of the American aircraft. One platoon quickly shot down three gliders; another shot down four Dakotas. Other German paratroopers, finding the British helpless in their harnesses, rapidly began collecting prisoners. About a hundred elite British paratroopers were captured in this manner almost the instant they hit the ground.

It should be noted that there was a strange bond of comradeship between the German and British paratroopers fighting for Primosole Bridge. Red Devils, swinging helplessly from the orange trees, were not shot or bayoneted in their harnesses as one might expect in such a confused night battle; rather, the enemy paratroopers were allowed to unbuckle and fall to the ground, where they were taken prisoner. Captives were not shot, or even roughly handled, but were treated almost like guests. Seriously wounded prisoners on both sides received medical treatment first while lightly wounded friendlies quietly waited their turn. It was incredible behavior for World War II. "Straight leg" British infantry did not receive such preferential treatment; nor, of course, were the Italians so gently treated by the Red Devils.

Into this mass of chaos and confusion jumped Brigadier Lathbury. He evaded capture, quickly assembled about forty men, and rushed toward Primosole Bridge. When he arrived there, he found that it had already been captured by fifty men from the 1st Parachute Battalion, who had taken fifty Italians prisoner. Soon other Red Devils rallied on the position. They ripped the explosive charges set to destroy it off the structure and threw them into the water. Before long, there were 120 paratroopers in defensive positions around the critical span.

The British airborne landing caused fear and panic in Generale di Divisione Carlo Gotti's 213th Coastal Defense Division, and soon most of it had fled. Behind the 213th lay Port Defense Area "E" (Difesa Porto "E"), the port defenses of Catania, under Generale di Brigata Azzo Passalacqua. Like the defenders of Augusta and Syracuse, most of these troops deserted, forcing the German paratroopers to divert valuable manpower to Catania to guard against a possible amphibious landing north of Primosole Bridge. Some of the reduced units of Port Defense Area "E," however, would remain in the front lines with the German paratroopers until their city fell twenty-five days later.

When the glider force carrying the seventy-seven Red Devil artillerymen of the 1st Airlanding Anti-Tank Battery approached Sicily at eleven P.M., there was still considerable fighting in progress in the vicinity of the bridge and all chance of surprise was gone. Nearing the shore, they came under heavy antiaircraft fire. One glider released too early and crashed into the sea. Four others were shot down with all hands aboard. Another crashed into the Simeto, killing or wounding all but one man aboard. Four Horsas, however, crash-landed close enough to the bridge to join Lathbury with five antitank guns.

Once again paratrooper casualties had been too high and the

drop too widely scattered, and the operation had not succeeded in putting anything like the expected numbers of paratroopers on the bridge. Counting artillerymen and other late arrivals, Lathbury's force at the Primosole totaled only 12 officers and 283 men out of 1,856—less than 16 percent of the force. This was the last major airborne assault in the Sicilian campaign. On July 15 Alexander suspended all but small-scale operations until the causes for the failures of Fustian, Husky Two, and the other operations could be investigated and interservice cooperation could be improved.

East of the bridge another elite British unit went into action closer to the coast. This was Lieutenant Colonel John Durnford-Slater's 3rd Commando, which had taken part in the initial landings with the 5th Infantry Division. Landed by the Royal Navy at 10:30 P.M. on July 13 at Agnone, near the mouth of the Simeto, the Commandos quickly chased off an Italian coastal defense company and hurried inland toward the small Malati Bridge, which crossed the Leonardo River three thousand yards north of Lentini and five miles inland. If they were successful, the Commando might well succeed in cutting off the retreat of Brigade Schmalz. They were delayed by five miles of olive orchards, vineyards, and gullies but took the bridge against light opposition at four A.M. on July 14. After they chased the handful of Italian defenders away, they ripped off the explosive charges and dropped them into the water. The four hundred Commandos then awaited the Italian reaction, which was much more violent than expected.

The Italians counterattacked with a tactical battle group under Colonel Tropea, which included a motorcycle company and anti-tank units (possibly an AT battalion). They were supported by elements of Koerner's 115th Panzer Grenadier Regiment. The Commandos continued to hold the bridge, but as the day wore on, casualties mounted. They were peppered by antitank fire, harassed by snipers, and continuously shelled by mortars. By noon there was still no sign of the relief force from the south, the 3rd Commando was in very serious danger, and Colonel Durnford-Slater was worried. What if German forces came up from the south, instead of the relief force, which had obviously been delayed? Then his Commandos would be annihilated. That afternoon the colonel decided that he could wait no longer. He broke his unit into small groups and ordered them to make their way east and then south, to reach British lines, if they could. Most of them did, but the raiding party's casualties, as reported on July 18, were still high: twenty-eight killed, sixty-six wounded, and fifty-nine missing.

And where were the Northumbrians of the British 50th Infantry Division, who were supposed to relieve the Commandos at Malati and the paratroopers at Primosole Bridge?

On the morning of July 13, Major General Sidney Kirkman was summoned to Montgomery's headquarters, told that the airborne and Commando landings would take place that night, and ordered to relieve Lathbury and Durnford-Slater "with all possible speed."[21] For this purpose, Brigadier J. C. Currie's recently landed 4th Armoured Brigade (now in the Augusta area) was attached to his command, which already included the 69th, 151st, and 168th Infantry brigades. Specifically, Monty wanted the Northumbrians to be at Primosole Bridge early the following morning; which would require them to advance twenty-five miles in less than twenty-four hours. They would be supported on the right flank by the British 5th Infantry Division.

Kirkman's mission was, quite simply, an overly ambitious task. The Northumbrian Division had been marching and fighting for three days and was nearly exhausted. The temperature was 100 degrees Fahrenheit, and the dust clogged the men's noses and formed mud along the edges of their mouths. Major General de Guingand, chief of staff of the 8th Army, recalled, "I have never met in any part of the world such oppressive heat."[22] For an officer who had fought Rommel in the Western Desert, that was saying quite a lot.

Now the lack of motor transport really told on the 8th Army and in all sectors. Progress on the left flank was virtually halted at Vizzini, and the 1st Canadian could not be committed there as planned because of heat exhaustion. It should be noted that these soldiers from a country in the northern latitudes had spent the past three and a half years in England. They were the only division in 8th Army not acclimatized to the semitropical conditions of the Mediterranean. Also, much of their transport had been dispatched to the bottom of the sea by U-boats. They had been fighting well and advancing constantly, but had averaged only about three hours of sleep per night since they had landed. Reluctantly, on July 13,

Montgomery ordered them to rest in the Giarratana area for a day and a half.

On the British right flank the 5th Infantry Division was not in good shape, either. The men were tired and short of vehicles, many units were being forced to use "liberated" donkeys to keep themselves resupplied, columns stretched all the way back to the beaches, and their advance was being frustrated by Brigade Schmalz. Using two battalions of the 3rd Parachute Regiment and part of the 115th Panzer Grenadier, the skillful panzer veteran dug into his next delaying position. This one, described by the British Official History as "excellent," was in a wooded ravine near Villasmundo, along the coastal highway. Because of the terrain, it was hard to outflank. The British spearhead, the 15th Infantry Brigade, was blocked here at eight A.M. on July 13 but was unable to launch a concerted attack with artillery support until late afternoon. Even this made only slow progress. Two hours later Schmalz fell back to Villasmundo, where he conducted yet another delaying action, not retreating from his position until early on July 14. In the meantime, on Kirkman's left, the 6th Green Howards of the 69th Brigade had advanced down the unimproved Sortino-Carlentini Road, which was well beyond the right flank of Villasmundo. Kirkman pushed his men hard, obviously in the hope that he could reach Carlentini before Schmalz realized that he was being outflanked. Such a maneuver might well trap the ad hoc brigade. Unfortunately, the Green Howards found another panzer grenadier detachment on the formidable heights of Monte Pancali, three miles south of Carlentini. They were checked here at 4:30 P.M. on July 13.

When dawn broke on July 14, the 50th Division was still a good fifteen miles from the paratroopers and eight miles from the Commandos. The 6th Green Howards had been reinforced by the 7th Green Howards during the night, and the battle of Monte Pancali began. It was taken by the two British battalions at about ten A.M., with the Germans again making good their escape to the next blocking position. The Germans on the coastal road also fell back to the north. At about five P.M. on July 14, part of the 69th Brigade captured the Malati Bridge, which the Germans had not had time to destroy. At this point the 151st Brigade (6th, 8th, and 9th battalions, Durham Light Infantry) assumed the role of spearhead, replacing the 69th Brigade, which was now exhausted. The

151st pushed up the dusty gravel road (on Kirkman's left flank) very slowly. The Shermans of the 4th Armoured Brigade, which was following the 151st, were of no use whatsoever. They were held up by a blown bridge near Carlentini and could not proceed until almost seven P.M.

The British finally reached Lentini in the afternoon, only to find the streets obstructed by rubble and craters. Clearing the debris was not an easy task, for Schmalz had left behind small detachments of snipers and machine gunners. It took the Northumbrians some time to secure the town and resume their advance northward, into the night. For the defenders of Primosole Bridge, however, time had run out.

As the dawn of July 14 broke on the 295 British paratroopers at Primosole Bridge, they found themselves in a very isolated and dangerous position. No one knew where the 50th Infantry Division and its supporting Shermans were, but they were clearly not south of the Primosole, where they were supposed to be. These positions, just beyond the British perimeter, were being held by the 1st Parachute Machine Gun Battalion of the German Wehrmacht. As if they did not have enough problems, the unhappy British paratroopers were soon met by an unwelcome flood of Italians, who wanted to surrender. By the morning of July 14 more than five hundred of these men had surrendered to the 2nd Parachute Battalion alone. They were herded into a nearby farmhouse, where they were left unwatched, because Colonel Frost simply did not have enough men to guard them.

The British 1st Parachute Brigade was deployed with the 1st Parachute Battalion (Pearson) north of the bridge, and the 2nd Battalion (Frost) was deployed to the south, holding the vital hills of Johnny I, II, and III. Both "battalions," of course, were actually only company-sized units. The 3rd Parachute Battalion, which had been badly scattered, had only a few men on the bridge. They were attached to the 1st Battalion.

North of the bridge, the Italians deployed the 372nd Coastal Defense Battalion and an *Arditi* (Blackshirt anti-Commando) Battalion. The 372nd was of limited value, however, and many of its men had already deserted. Even the battalion commander had mysteriously disappeared. On the other hand, the Arditi Battalion mounted a few small-scale attacks, but it lacked heavy weapons and did not represent much of a threat by itself. The real danger lay to the south, where Major Schmidt's men began a deadly machine gun and mortar fire at dawn. The first German attack was turned back, but later that morning Johnny II fell in heavy fighting. Colonel Frost launched an immediate counterattack, but it was beaten back with losses.

At about nine A.M. Frost's naval forward observer managed to make contact with the British cruiser H.M.S. *Newfoundland*. Soon 6-inch shells began to fall on the German paratroopers, who suffered heavy casualties for the first time in the battle. After this, Schmidt mounted no more full-scale attacks; rather, he concentrated on blasting British positions with machine gun fire. British casualties mounted as the morning wore on. The dry grass caught fire, and the blaze did what the Germans could not do: it forced the British off Johnny I. Frost's perimeter was now dangerously restricted, and his ammunition was running low. One more all-out attack would have destroyed the British 1st Parachute Brigade because, as happened so many times in Sicily, British communications failed at a critical moment. The naval forward observer's (FO) radio went dead, and Frost had no way of directing the fire of the Royal Navy's heavy guns. Fortunately for the British, Schmidt did not know this and therefore he did not attack.

Meanwhile, at 10:30 A.M. a German dispatch rider reported to Captain Franz Stangenberg, a Luftwaffe staff officer in Catania. He had been carrying a message to Colonel Heilmann when he had been fired on by British paratroopers north of the Primosole Bridge.

Stangenberg decided to see for himself. He drove toward the Simeto but was soon turned back by automatic weapons fire. A little while later he returned with twenty men, but his counterattack was quickly beaten back.

At that point Stangenberg realized the gravity of the situation. The vital bridge had to be retaken, but no further reinforcements would arrive until that night. The British might well relieve the defenders by then, and the way to Catania would be open. Also, FJR 3 and Brigade Schmalz could conceivably be cut off as well. To avert these disasters, Stangenberg signaled General Heidrich and received permission to employ the only uncommitted German unit north of the Simeto: Captain Erich Fassl's 1st Company, 1st Parachute Signal Battalion, which had been dropped the previous afternoon. Originally scheduled to provide the other parachute units with communications, it had been pressed into the role of a coastal defense unit when the Italians deserted Catania. Stangenberg also impressed into combat duty every German serviceman he could lay his hands on, including clerks, cooks, mechanics, drivers, dispatch riders, truck drivers—anyone. In this manner he rapidly assembled an ad hoc battle group of about 350 men, including a German heavy flak battery and several antitank guns.

Stangenberg's first attack went forward at two P.M. and was promptly repulsed. The second attack, however, began to drive the British back. Three 88-mm antiaircraft guns, one of which was self-propelled, blasted Pearson's positions. Captain Fassl pushed almost to the bridge and captured several prisoners. Meanwhile, the Germans moved an 88-mm down the Catania Road and began methodically to blow away the two pillboxes on the northern end of the bridge at almost point-blank range. The British, without heavy weapons, could not effectively counter this deadly menace.

One by one the British Red Devils ran out of ammunition. At about five P.M. the survivors of the 1st Battalion rushed across the bridge, and the northern half of the perimeter collapsed. The 8th Army's foothold across the Simeto had been eliminated. Then, from the north bank, the 88's blasted the two pillboxes on the south side of the bridge into oblivion. A painfully wounded Brigadier Lathbury had little choice but to withdraw the remnants of his brigade to positions about 1,200 yards south of the river. Ringed by fire, Lathbury held on until midnight and then escaped into the darkness with the remaining Red Devils, leaving his wounded behind. Of the 295 defenders of the Primosole Bridge, 115 had been killed, wounded, or captured during the fighting of July 14. As the survivors worked their way slowly through the darkness to the south, most were convinced that they would be mopped up and captured the next day. Finally they halted for the night to sleep the sleep of exhaustion and despair, knowing in their hearts that they would be finished off on the morrow.

They would have felt much better had they continued their trek for another twenty minutes or so. The vanguard of the 4th Armoured Brigade and the 6th Durham Light Infantry was camped for the night only one mile away.

In the intervening hours, back at the bridge, the German paratrooper/medics carefully bandaged the wounds of their captured

British comrades and transported them back to the hospital at Catania as gently as they could.

But where was Group Schmalz at this time? Why was it not between the spearheads of the British XIIIth Corps and Catania, as it had been continuously since July 10?

The answer was simple. By the night of July 14 Group Schmalz had done its job. Primosole Bridge had been recaptured, and the British had been delayed sufficiently. The new German commander in Sicily, General Hans Hube (see Chapter 10), had set up a new *Hauptkampflinie* (main defensive line) to which Schmalz must now retreat. Running north from Lentini to the Simeto River lay a gradual, barren slope, which offered little cover and few defensive possibilities. To continue along the coastal highway would invite disaster—especially with the 4th Armoured Brigade not far behind and unknown numbers of British paratroopers still at large. Schmalz therefore was to sidestep to the west. A good road leading to Scordia intersected the coastal highway north of Lentini and offered an ideal avenue of escape in this direction. By using secondary roads, the brigade could then retire across the Gornalunga River at Gerbini. This maneuver would have the additional advantage of putting Schmalz nearer to a junction with Conrath and the rest of the Hermann Goering Division. Such a movement would no longer uncover Catania and the road to Messina. The Primosole was being held by the 1st Parachute Machine Gun Battalion, Battle Group Stangenberg, and the two Italian battalions and would be reinforced during the night by another airborne drop, which would deposit the 1st Parachute Engineer Battalion and a battalion from Lieutenant Colonel Erich Walter's 4th Parachute Regiment, as well as part of the 1st Parachute Artillery Regiment. Once he reached the Hauptkampflinie, Schmalz would take charge of the newly arrived units while retaining control of the 3rd Parachute and 115th Panzer Grenadier regiments.

It was a good, solid plan. Schmalz, however, had a great deal of trouble with it, not because of the British but because of the German paratroopers—especially the commander of the 3rd Parachute Regiment, Lieutenant Colonel Ludwig Heilmann, called "King Ludwig" by his men.

Heilmann had been born in Wuerzburg in 1903 and had spent his entire adult life in the service. He had enlisted in the Reichswehr in

1921, but his advancement had been stifled by the Treaty of Versailles, and he did not receive his commission until 1934. Heilmann was a company commander in the 21st Infantry Regiment when the war broke out, and after seeing action in Poland and France, he volunteered for the paratroopers in 1940. Transferred to the Luftwaffe, he was named commander of the IIIrd Battalion, 3rd Parachute Regiment (III/FRJ 3) after completing jump school. Heilmann saw action in the bitter battle for Crete and served on the Russian Front in 1941 and 1942, where he distinguished himself at the Vyborgskaya Bridgehead. In the spring of 1943 the 3rd Parachute Regiment, (now under Heilmann) was transferred to the 1st Parachute Division then forming in southern France.

Although his courage was almost legendary within the airborne arm, King Ludwig was arrogant, stubborn, and opinionated. His military experience was also limited primarily to rapid advances (Poland and France) and taking key positions and holding them at all costs (Crete and Russia). He had never taken part in the skillful type of mobile delaying action that Schmalz was conducting, nor did he appreciate its necessity or value. To him, as to Adolf Hitler, there was something dishonorable or cowardly about any retreat, no matter how necessary it was or how skillfully it was conducted.

About nightfall on July 14 Wilhelm Schmalz issued his orders for the withdrawal to the Hauptkampflinie. From Heilmann, whose regiment was on Schmalz's left flank, came the incredible reply, "Wherever German paratroopers are, there will be no retreat."[23] Schmalz continued to send urgent radio messages to Heilmann until the Shermans of the 4th Armoured were north of Lentini. By the time the proud paratrooper commander had second thoughts about his stubbornness, it was too late. The 3rd Parachute Regiment was completely cut off.

The fall of Lentini had repercussions elsewhere. For days General Guzzoni had been ordering, urging, and pleading with Lieutenant General Paul Conrath to move more quickly to close the gap between his Hermann Goering Division and the forces defending on the east coast, but without success. On the afternoon of July 14, however, when he received word that Lentini had fallen, Conrath decided to retreat in one movement to the Hauptkampflinie. Colonel Gian Felice Grosso, chief of staff of the Italian

XVIth Corps, begged him to make the move in two days, to give the Italians to the west of his division time to retreat, and Conrath reluctantly agreed. Later that day, however, at the urgent requests of von Senger and Kesselring (who were afraid the east wing was about to collapse), Conrath changed his mind again and decided to retire as rapidly as he could. He withdrew in three groups, which were of roughly the same composition as those which threatened the U.S. IInd Corps' bridgehead on July 11. Group West (Lieutenant Colonel Ohring) retreated from Caltagiorne through Ramacca, while Lieutenant Colonel Hahm's Group Center (including the IInd Panzer Battalion) fell back from Grammichele through Palagonia. Group East under Lieutenant Colonel Rabholz retreated from Vizzini through Militello and Scordia. All left behind strong rear guards.[24]

The Hermann Goering Division lost several tanks as a result of mechanical failures, but otherwise its withdrawal was entirely successful, and the gap between Conrath and Brigade Schmalz narrowed rapidly. On the other hand, this swift movement to the east *opened* a wide gap between the Goerings and the 15th Panzer Grenadier Division to the west. Major General Eberhard Rodt, commander of the 15th, was very unhappy about this—especially since it came as a complete surprise. When he awoke on July 15, he was informed that the Hermann Goering Division had vanished. Apparently neither Conrath nor Senger had seen fit to inform him that it was withdrawing to the Hauptkampflinie, even though the move left the east wing of Rodt's division sixteen miles forward of Conrath's west wing and also left a growing gap of at least nine miles between the two divisions. Rodt quickly pulled together a handful of troops (engineers and antiaircraft gunners) and sent them to screen his extreme eastern flank, but this did not alter the fact that both of Rodt's flanks were exposed and practically "in the air." Rodt's protests, however, were rejected, because Field Marshall Kesselring felt that as long as the 15th held its positions along the Piazza Armerina–Serradifalco line, the Allies probably would not attempt to break through the weak center and envelop the western flank of the Goering Division. The somewhat lesser danger of an attack against the eastern flank of the 15th Panzer Grenadier was accepted as a calculated risk.[25]

Meanwhile, as the gap between Conrath and Schmalz rapidly narrowed, more German paratroopers jumped into Sicily. Just before nightfall on July 14, 450 men from Captain Paul Adolff's 1st Parachute Engineer Battalion parachuted into drop zones south of Catania. Somewhat scattered because their He-111 pilots had flown too fast, the battalion was nevertheless re-formed in two hours and was marching south, where it relieved Fassl's signal company and Stangenberg's ad hoc battle group. Fassl and Stangenberg returned to Catania to resume their coastal defense duties, while Major Schmidt posted his machine gun units west of the bridge. Captain Adolff deployed two of his three companies, (the 1st and 3rd) astride Highway 114 south of the bridge. The third (2nd Company) he placed north of the bridge, in reserve. Here the parachute engineers awaited the British attack, which was not long in coming.

The second phase of the Battle of Primosole Bridge began on the morning of July 15. Seeing his chances for victory fading, Major General Kirkman ordered Brigadier R. H. Senior, commander of the 151st (Durham) Brigade, to launch an immediate daylight attack against the bridge. Senior protested that his men had marched twenty miles during the previous day and night and were unfit for such an attack, but his objections were overruled.

At 7:30 A.M. two British artillery regiments opened up against the German positions with their self-propelled 105-mm howitzers. Then the attack went in, spearheaded by the 9th Durham Light Infantry.

They never had a chance. The Durhams were cut down by machine gun fire as they approached the bridge, and most of them halted. One platoon managed to ford the river, but was met by paratroopers from Adolff's 2nd Company and the Italian Blackshirt Commando battalion. A hail of machine gun and mortar fire struck the Durhams from the sunken road north of the bridge. The 9th Durhams retreated out of range after suffering 100 casualties, including 34 killed. Three tanks from the 44th Royal Tank Regiment (RTR) were also knocked out. The fighting was over by 9:30 A.M.

Despite their failure, the Durhams' attack had weakened the defenses, mainly because the lieutenant in command of the 1st Engineer Company withdrew his unit across the bridge without orders, leaving only the 3rd Company of the parachute engineer battalion to hold the German bridgehead south of the Simeto. Meanwhile, undeterred by his losses, General Kirkman planned another, stronger attack for the night of July 16–17. It was to be coordinated with an amphibious landing that General Dempsey, the corps commander, planned to launch against Catania later that night. Besides, Kirkman would have more artillery by then. Two regiments were coming up, and two more were landing in Syracuse and might make it in time to participate in the battle. A short lull descended at Primosole, with both sides maintaining a cautious vigil.

In the meantime, Colonel Wilhelm Schmalz set up headquarters at Misterbianco and linked up with the Hermann Goering Panzer Division on his right on the morning of July 15. He had conducted a masterful retreat, and his air force staff had gained valuable experience in mobile ground combat. Far from congratulating himself on July 15, however, Schmalz was very worried. He had lost radio contact with Colonel Heilmann and the 3rd Parachute Regiment, whose last known location was more than ten miles behind enemy lines. It was feared that the entire unit might be lost.

While Schmalz improved his positions and Kirkman completed his preparations for the night's attack, Captain Fassl's company returned to the Primosole Bridge sector on the afternoon of July 15. Fassl did this on his own initiative. After inspecting Catania, which was virtually undefended, he decided that there was little his small command could do if the British launched a major amphibious assault. On the other hand, his signal troops might be of considerable use to Adolff's engineers. They dug in northwest of the bridge, on Adolff's deep right flank.

The night attack across the Simeto to secure Primosole Bridge began at one A.M. on July 16 with an eighty-minute artillery barrage. "To watchers and to the advancing troops," Pond wrote, "it seemed that no one could possibly survive such a saturation barrage."[26] Spearheaded by the 8th Durhams, the British waded into the muddy water well to the left of the bridge at 2:10 A.M. and crossed the river unopposed. Crossing the river, however, was no longer the same thing as continuing the advance, for the German paratroopers were well dug in and ready for the attack, fanatically determined to hold their positions. The first two companies of the 8th Durhams advanced north into the darkness about three hundred yards before they ran into a well-laid ambush. Almost all the men in the first two sections were killed before they knew what had hit them. The British commanders rallied their companies and mounted a frontal assault into the vineyards. Before dawn the fighting was hand to hand, with heavy casualties on both sides. In the end, however, the Fallschirmjaegern held their positions.

Meanwhile, two other Durham assault companies overran the 3rd Parachute Engineer Company and raced across Primosole Bridge with fixed bayonets. Ignoring the German fire on their right flank, they dug in north of the bridge. Here they were subjected to hours of small attacks by the parachutists, who constantly fired and changed positions, threw grenades and changed positions. Casualties were heavy, but the British clung to the new foothold across the Simeto.

The coming of dawn did not halt the battle. At daybreak the British bridgehead was only three hundred yards deep, but most of the 8th and 9th battalions of the Durham Light Infantry were north of the river. Only now did the British find that the main German position was a sunken road called Fosso Bottaceto, in which the Germans and a few Italians had taken refuge during the artillery barrage. They emerged unscathed as soon as it ended and then proceeded to tackle the Durhams.

The battle continued throughout the day. The temperature was "like a furnace."[27] Brigadier Senior tried to get some Shermans from the 44th Royal Tank Regiment across the bridge but was unsuccessful, and four of the steel monsters were quickly knocked out. The battle was clearly stalemated.

That afternoon some armored carriers took a chance and raced across the bridge, carrying two antitank guns with them. Then the Shermans tried again, but again were checked by the 88's. Two of them did manage to reach the northern bank, but were almost immediately blown apart. Then the Germans launched a fanatical counterattack and almost succeeded in pushing the British back into the river. Some men actually swam back to the southern bank before the German charge was turned back by mortars and machine guns. The counterattack might well have succeeded had Heilmann's FJR 3 been where it was supposed to be. It was not, however, so the German paratroopers retreated, but continued their intensive shelling and sniping. One British company was reduced to a strength of one officer and twenty men. Obviously the bridgehead would have to be reinforced or abandoned. General

Kirkman and Brigadier Senior decided to attack again that night.

Later, Dempsey and General Montgomery turned up at Kirkman's headquarters in an effort to get the advance going again. They agreed to postpone Dempsey's amphibious assault on Catania for twenty-four hours (it was, in fact, never launched) and ordered Kirkman to attack again on the night of July 16–17.

The Germans took advantage of this lull in the battle by parachuting in even more reinforcements from the 4th Parachute Regiment under the command of the fearless Lieutenant Colonel Erich Walter. One of the first German paratroopers, Walter had won his Knight's Cross in Holland in 1940, where he had commanded the Ist Battalion, FJR 1. He would win his Oak Leaves here, just north of Primosole Bridge.

There was no doubt in Major General Francis de Guingand's mind as to why the offensive had been halted: the German paratroopers had "fought with fanatical savagery."[28] Pond recorded that even those who were taken prisoner "remained arrogant and hostile in the face of all threats and interrogations. . . . Spitting in the faces of their captors, some officers would not answer any questions, refusing to give even name, rank and number."[29] De Guingand wrote later:

> During the fighting across the Simeto these incidents occurred. A wounded German was lying on a stretcher at a dressing station having his wounds dressed by one of our orderlies. Directly he recovered sufficient strength and turned over, seized the orderly's hand and plunged his teeth deep into it, shouting some Nazi invective. Another, when being interrogated by one of our officers, drew himself up to attention and spat deliberately into his face. A third, who was wounded, managed to stand up, pulled out his revolver, shouted "Heil Hitler" and shot himself.[30]

General de Guingand had a personal brush with one of the paratroopers, and it impressed him deeply. Albrecht Gunther, a twenty-eight-year-old lieutenant, had been brought to the 8th Army's chief of staff. Gunther had been cut off behind British lines. He had tried to get back to his unit by putting on a suit of civilian clothes but had been captured nevertheless. Lieutenant Gunther was a veteran of the Russian Front and had fought in Holland and

France before that—not that de Guingand was aware of it. "He refused to give anything except his rank and name," the chief of staff recalled. The general informed Gunther that as he had been caught in civilian clothes, he could be shot as a spy under international law; in fact, that was what was going to happen to him. "His face never showed the least reaction," de Guingand recalled.

"That is quite understood," the young officer replied. "I took the risk and failed—I deserve it. Heil Hitler!" Gunther then saluted and marched away.[31]

De Guingand did not have Gunther shot; he sent him to a prisoner-of-war camp and released the story to the British Broadcasting Company, in hopes that it might lead to better treatment of Allied POWs by the Germans.

Beginning at 1:30 A.M. on July 17, seven British artillery regiments saturated the ground in front of the Durhams, trying to obliterate the Fosso Bottaceto area. Shortly thereafter the Durhams advanced into enemy territory once more. In the darkness many paratroopers hid in trenches or vineyards and then, after being overrun, jumped up again and shot the attackers in the back. The battle degenerated into a series of firefights between small bands of infantry groping in the dark. During the confused fighting Fassl's signalers knocked out three Sherman tanks. By 6:30 A.M. the British attack had been pinned down. At seven A.M., however, a squadron of Shermans finally got across the bridge and forced its way through the orange groves and vines, crushing all resistance. Apparently the last of the German antitank guns had been knocked out in the artillery barrage. Aware that the time had come to destroy the bridge, if possible, Captain Paul Adolff tried to drive explosive-laden trucks over it in the manner used by present-day terrorists. All of his attempts failed, and Adolff himself was mortally wounded on the last try; he died the next day. He was posthumously promoted to major and awarded the Knight's Cross.[32]

Meanwhile, Captain Fassl's foxhole was overrun by a Sherman, and a few moments later he was taken prisoner by the Durham Light infantrymen. His company had been reduced to a strength of seventeen men. The surviving German paratroopers retreated to the Fosso Bottaceto, unmolested by the Durhams, which had lost 220 men. Smashed equipment, bodies, and dead mules lay everywhere.

By now, Lieutenant Colonel Walter's 4th Parachute Regiment was up and occupying the Fosso Bottaceto position, which would form the hard left flank of the German front for weeks to come. Walter assumed command of the retiring units, established contact with Group Schmalz to his west, and prepared for the next British onslaught. He was greatly aided in this effort by British weapons taken from British gliders and weapons canisters that had been lost in Lathbury's initial assault on the Primosole Bridge four days earlier.

After consulting with Dempsey, Kirkman prepared to attack again on the night of July 17–18. This time he had his entire division up and in the bridgehead, which was now almost two thousand yards deep. This time ten artillery regiments pounded the Fosso Bottaceto (which was called *"Der Panzergraben"* [the Tank Ditch] by the Germans), with the intention of blasting the paratroopers to bits. The 168th Brigade was then to push forward to the Fosso Bottaceto. Elements of the British 5th Infantry Division, now up on the right (coastal) flank, were to support the attack.

The Northumbrian Division struck at 7:15 P.M. Unfortunately, the British plan was based on a reconnaissance report that stated that Colonel Walter's main body had retired to the Fosso Bottaceto and was only holding the two thousand yards of ground south of it with weak detachments and outposts. In reality FJR 4, which consisted of the parachute engineer battalion and associated attachments, had re-formed in the Tank Ditch but then had once again moved forward to occupy hidden positions south of the Fosso Bottaceto. The artillery bombardment hit nothing, and resistance as usual was fierce. The attack was halted two hundred yards in front of the sunken road. The British then fell back to positions about a thousand yards south of the road and three thousand yards north of the bridge. The Battle of the Primosole Bridge was over, although the fighting in the area was not. The British Official History laconically reported, "Four days' hard fighting had failed to expand the Simeto River bridgehead sufficiently to warrant further attempts to force a way through to Catania on this axis."[33]

Meanwhile, much to Colonel Schmalz's relief and delight, more than nine hundred men of "King Ludwig" Heilmann's FJR 3 broke through British lines and regained contact with Brigade Schmalz on the Catania plain late in the afternoon of July 17.

The 3rd Parachute had had an adventure. Cut off east of the coastal highway, Heilmann had abandoned his vehicles and heavy equipment and marched northwest throughout the night of July 14–15 across difficult, swampy ground; by the dawn of July 15 he was southeast of Malati Bridge. Here he found his escape route blocked by the British, who, luckily for Heilmann, had not yet spotted his regiment and were unaware that they had cut him off. King Ludwig ordered his men to lie low in a nearby orange grove throughout the daylight hours of July 15. Then, leaving about seventy British prisoners in the hands of wounded paratroopers, he led his men quietly across the Lentini. That night some of the leading troops actually hid under the Malati Bridge, which was echoing with the sound of British boots and wheels—men and equipment on their way to the Primosole Bridge.

During the day the paratroopers hid out in olive groves, out of the sight of Allied reconnaissance planes, which were not looking for them, anyway. During the nights of July 15–16 and 16–17 they trekked cross-country, avoiding the roads, until they found the Hauptkampflinie.

Although Schmalz and Kesselring were delighted to see Heilmann, General von Senger und Etterlin was not. The German liaison officer with the Italian 6th Army recalled that the regiment had been cut off because Heilmann had been "too proud" to obey an order to retreat. "During all the fighting between 14 and 17 July," Senger wrote later, "this urgently needed regiment was absent; furthermore it could not be committed immediately after its return because it had lost all of its heavy weapons."[34] Because the paratroopers had to travel light, these had been abandoned in the olive groves.

Fridolin von Senger's subsequent report leaves little doubt that he would have relieved Heilmann of his command if he had had the power. However, von Senger was no longer the senior German officer in Sicily; in fact, his own days on the island were numbered. He had been superseded by General of Panzer Troops Hans Valentin Hube.

✧ 10 ✧

ENTER GENERAL HUBE

CALLED *"DER MENSCH"* (THE MAN) BY HIS TROOPS, HANS VALENTIN Hube, a West Prussian, was born on October 29, 1890, at Naumburg, a garrison town on the Saale River not far from Leipzig. He enlisted as a Fahnenjunker (officer-cadet) on February 27, 1909, shortly after his eighteenth birthday, and spent the rest of his life in the German army. He was commissioned *Leutnant* (second lieutenant) on August 22, 1908.

Young Hube's first outfit was the 26th Infantry Regiment, an old Prussian unit. Part of the 7th Infantry Division, it took part in the capture of Liège, the Battle of the Marne, and the subsequent trench warfare on the Western Front. During the Battle of Verdun, Lieutenant Hube was so badly wounded that his right arm had to be amputated. This injury would have ended the career of a less dedicated officer, but not Hube. He worked hard, overcame his handicap, and clamored for renewed employment. The personnel office finally yielded to his requests, and Hube performed so successfully that he was promoted to captain before the war ended on November 11, 1918.

Under the terms of the harsh Treaty of Versailles, the Reichsheer (as the new German Army was dubbed) was allowed to have only one hundred thousand men, only four thousand of whom could be officers. With more than thirty thousand officers available, they kept only the cream of the crop physically and mentally; nevertheless, Hans Hube was retained despite his disability. He was apparently the only one-armed captain in the Reichswehr (armed forces).

As a junior officer Hube was known for his determination, energy, and attention to detail. He strove to master every aspect of his profession. His promotions came slowly (typical in a small army), and he was not elevated to the rank of major until 1929, when he went through a special course in command. He was promoted to lieutenant colonel on June 1, 1934.

Hans Hube was an innovative and forward-thinking officer, which probably explains why he was placed in charge of a special motorized infantry battalion in 1934. When this experimental unit distinguished itself in the ensuing summer maneuvers, it added increased impetus to the demand for mechanization in the German Army and led to the creation of the first panzer divisions in 1936. Meanwhile, Hube was named commander of the prestigious infantry school in Doberitz, a suburb of Berlin. For years this was the largest infantry training facility in Germany, but Hube's rise was just beginning.

Effective October 1, 1935, Lieutenant Colonel Hube was commandant of the Olympic village, which was to be erected in the meadows adjoining Doberitz. He was the person chiefly responsible for the excellent living conditions and top-flight practice areas the worldwide concourse of contestants enjoyed during the games. He was also responsible for security.

Adolf Hitler was personally involved in all levels of preparation for "his" Olympics. It was to be the international showpiece in which a resurgent Germany would show the entire world its new wealth, strength through joy, and preeminence in sporting events. It was therefore only natural that Hitler conferred frequently with Hube, who proved to be the master of his assignment. Hitler was so impressed that he promoted Hube to full colonel on August 1, 1936.

After the games ended and the athletes returned to their far-flung homes, Hans Hube returned to the task of training infantry officers for combat. During the prewar period no separate academy for motorized infantry existed. Hube, however, introduced such courses at Doberitz, so his young subalterns would be able to cope with the new technology and the rapid movement of a motorized and mechanized battlefield.

The outbreak of the war in September 1939 caught Colonel Hube by surprise. He petitioned OKH (*Oberkommando des Heer,* the High Command of the Army) for a field command, and in early October he was appointed commander of the 3rd Infantry Regiment of the 21st Infantry Division. He took over on October 18.

Hube was not happy with his new assignment. Not only was the 21st a nonmotorized formation, it was an ultraconservative East Prussian unit with an almost hereditary officer corps. The forward-thinking Hube simply did not fit in with this mind-set. The division did not leave its cantonments around Mohrungen until the spring of 1940, and in the campaign against the Western Allies it was slated for employment opposite the forts of the Maginot Line—a truly secondary role. At that point Hube's contacts in Berlin came in handy. He may have even written to the Fuehrer personally, but this is not certain. In any event, on May 9, 1940—one day before the start of the invasion—Hube was replaced as regimental commander and transferred to the staff of Colonel General Fedor von Bock's Army Group B, located on the Rhine. Three days later it was reported that Major General Heinrich Krampf, commander of the 16th Infantry Division, was too ill to hold his post much longer. Early on May 15 Hube joined the division in Belgium and replaced Krampf, who was immediately returned to Germany for hospitalization.[1]

Although the 16th was still officially an infantry division, OKH had already slated it for conversion into a panzer unit, and one of its three infantry regiments (the 64th) had been largely motorized. Colonel Hube directed his new command with exceptional skill, particularly in the storming of Mont Damion on May 22–23. He was promoted to major general on June 1.

After France surrendered, the division was posted to Muenster for motorization, and the larger part of it was subsequently sent to Kassel for panzer training. In March 1941 Hube took his troops to Bulgaria, ostensibly for training but actually for the invasion of Yugoslavia, where they formed the principal reserve for Colonel General Ewald von Kleist's 1st Panzer Group (later Army). Yugoslavia collapsed so rapidly that the 16th Panzer was not committed to any heavy fighting, although it did take part in the triumphant entry into Belgrade. After this it was sent to Silesia, where it took part in the invasion of the Soviet Union.

Hitler invaded Russia on June 22, 1941, and Hans Hube came into his own. He earned a reputation as a brilliant tactician and an outstanding commander of mobile forces. He was one of the first to reach and breach the Stalin Line in July 1941 and took part in the encirclement at Uman, which netted more than a hundred thousand prisoners. On the night of September 14–15 his unit linked up with the 5th Panzer Division east of Kiev, completing the encirclement of several Soviet armies, and Hube held his positions despite repeated Soviet counterattacks. When the Kiev pocket was finally cleared, Germany had taken 667,000 more prisoners; it was the largest battle of encirclement of the war. Following this victory, Hube took part in the drive toward Rostov and the subsequent withdrawal to the Mius River, where, against heavy odds, his men repulsed several Soviet attacks in the winter battles of 1941–1942.

As a reward for his services in the East, Hube was decorated with the Knight's Cross (August 17, 1941) and the Oak Leaves to the Knight's Cross (January 21, 1942). He was promoted to lieutenant general on April 1, 1942, while his division was refitting for the next German offensive. However, the Soviets preceded them.

In mid-May 1942 General Friedrich Paulus's 6th Army was threatened with annihilation by the huge Russian forces east of Kharkov. The 16th Panzer Division was part of von Kleist's 1st Panzer Army, which rushed to the rescue. Hube fought one of his most famous battles (later called the Bacaklesa Encirclement) south of Kharkov and west of the Donets between May 17 and 22, 1942. During this action Hube's men took 31,500 prisoners and destroyed 224 vehicles and 69 tanks while helping take the pressure off the 6th Army. Within the next few weeks the 16th Panzer crossed the Donets and the Don and neared the Volga.

Meanwhile, General of Infantry Gustav von Wietersheim, commander of the XIVth Panzer Corps, made the mistake of criticizing Adolf Hitler's penchant for interfering in tactical matters, especially as they related to the current drive on Stalingrad. At the request of Fuehrer Headquarters, General Paulus summarily relieved him of his command on September 14, 1942, and Hube was offered the post.

It is very strange that Hans Valentin Hube was named von Wietersheim's successor, for he had concurred with Wietersheim's criticisms of the campaign, and the Fuehrer was well aware of it. Furthermore, once he assumed his new duties, the redoubtable Hube sent a list of complaints to Fuehrer Headquarters at Rastenburg, East Prussia—a list almost identical to that submitted earlier by Gustav von Wietersheim. Yet instead of being sacked, Hube, who had a reputation for utter honesty, was promoted to general of panzer troops on October 1, 1942—only six months after his promotion to lieutenant general. Very few German generals received such rapid promotions, and almost none who were as outspoken as Hube; but for some inexplicable reason, the Fuehrer swallowed criticism from this one-armed panzer officer when he might have thrown someone else into a concentration camp for saying the same thing. Even so, Hube's good advice was usually ignored at Rastenburg.

On November 19, 1942, the Soviets launched the most massive double envelopment of the war to date, and by November 23 Paulus's 6th Army, which included Hube's XIVth Panzer Corps, was surrounded. Hitler forbade a breakout attempt; Stalingrad would hold out until relieved, he announced. Hube was among the corps commanders who urged Paulus to break out on his own initiative, but Paulus refused. The tragedy of Stalingrad would be acted out to its ultimate conclusion.

It was the turning point of the war.

General Hube's corps in the northernmost sector of the pocket controlled two motorized divisions: the 3rd under Lieutenant General Helmuth Schloemer and the 29th, led by Major General Hans-Georg Leyser. The corps fought well, but by Christmas it was starving and almost out of fuel and ammunition. By then the situation was desperate throughout the shrinking fortress; as a result, the corps commanders and a few other general officers decided to override Paulus's veto of a breakout attempt. They voted to send Hube to Berlin to present their problems directly to the Fuehrer.

On December 26 Hube flew out of the cauldron, accompanied by his chief of staff, Colonel Eberhard Thunert, and his aide, Lieutenant Harro Eysen. He met with Hitler two days later in the Reichschancellory, his headquarters in Berlin.

Hitler was in a rational mood that day and listened carefully to Hube's detailed outline of the situation, which included status reports, lengths of front held by badly depleted units, and descriptions concerning the paucity of supplies in the fortress. Hitler interrupted occasionally with pertinent questions about particular situations within the pocket. Hube and Thunert were both amazed at Hitler's apparently inexhaustible knowledge of details about every unit trapped in Stalingrad. The meeting ended without any far-reaching conclusions, but Hitler asked Hube to return the next day.

On December 29 Adolf Hitler personally presented Hube with the Swords to his Knight's Cross with Oak Leaves and thanked him for his report. He appreciated Hube's help, the Fuehrer said, but there was really nothing to worry about. He explained to the West Prussian that orders were already being issued for three panzer divisions, all in France, to be hurried to the Russian Front to spearhead another relief attempt on Stalingrad. Hitler warmed to his subject. He showed them a map overlay, pointing out that by February he would have twelve panzer and more than thirty infantry units in place—surely enough to smash the intervening Russian forces! Until then 6th Army would be resupplied by a greatly augmented 4th Air Fleet. It was Hitler at his most persuasive. By the end of the meeting both Hube and Thunert were convinced of the inevitable success of the proposed counteroffensive. Thunert, a skilled and veteran staff officer who was certainly no fool, told Lieutenant Eysen that night, "All we have to do—not that it will be easy—is hold on!"[2]

After Hube and Thunert returned to their temporary quarters at Doberitz, the personnel office of OKH sent an officer to announce a ten-day leave for both officers. Thunert at once set off to visit his family at Kulmsee, while Hube, accompanied by Eysen, journeyed to the Austrian Tyrol to enjoy his favorite hobby: snow skiing. While the one-armed general enthusiastically negotiated the slopes, his aide enjoyed spending pleasant days in the grand lodge before a roaring fire, none too happy about returning to the bitter cold of hard-pressed Stalingrad.

On January 7, 1943, the three officers boarded their big transport plane to return to the Eastern Front. Two days later Hube's party landed back at Gumrak Airfield in Stalingrad. They were met by Paulus and his chief of staff, Major General Arthur Schmidt. When Hube spoke, their faces fell. They were clearly expecting a different kind of word than Hube gave them. The panzer general, however, did not lose his enthusiasm until he returned to his own headquarters and retook command from Lieutenant General Schloemer. Here he was brought face to face with the extent and reality of the deterioration of the German position since his absence. Here, in beleaguered Stalingrad the optimism generated in Berlin disappeared rapidly; even if the promised forces did arrive, Hube saw that there was no way the city could be held.

On January 16, via 6th Army's daily radio hookup with army

group headquarters, a Fuehrer Order arrived. Hans Hube was to report to Berlin for reassignment. Schloemer was to take charge of XIVth Panzer Corps.

Many men would have been elated to get off this sinking ship, but not Hube. He replied, also by radio, that he was determined to remain in Stalingrad with his men. He had led them into the trap, and he would either lead them out of it or die with them. In other words, he refused to obey Hitler's order.

Two days later a transport plane landed at Gumrak, and four mysterious men got out. The airplane taxied to a bombed-out runway and cut its motors; walking wounded and others waiting for transport out of the cauldron were warned off by bursts of machine gun fire.

The four officers presented their credentials to Colonel General Paulus, who summoned Hube, Colonel Thunert, Lieutenant Eysen, Colonel Walter Muller, and one other officer of the XIVth Corps staff. When they arrived at 6th Army Headquarters, the panzer officers were met with drawn pistols. The four mysterious officers were identified as members of the Waffen SS in the Fuehrer's personal service. The SS men tersely informed Hube and his staff officers that they were taking them back to Fuehrer Headquarters whether they liked it or not. They would be shot if they resisted. Hube and his companions were rushed to the airfield via commandeered vehicle, forced onto the waiting airplane by the SS guards, and flown out of the pocket. On the way back the transport was hit by Soviet antiaircraft fire and was disabled so badly that it barely made it back to the German lines.[3]

Hube was taken to Berlin, where the fall of Stalingrad was now viewed as inevitable. It had been decided that XIVth Panzer Corps would be rebuilt under the direction of Hube, Thunert, and the others. They were sent to Dnepropetrovsk in Russia to begin the task. During this period Adolf Hitler paid Hans Hube an interesting left-handed compliment at the military conference that was held at Rastenburg at 12:17 A.M. on Felbruary 1, 1943.

Hitler: I saw a letter—it was addressed to [Luftwaffe Colonel Nikolaus von] Below. I can show it to you. An officer in Stalingrad wrote: "I have come to the following conclusions about these people—Paulus, question mark; Seydlitz, should be shot; Schmidt, should be shot."

Zeitzler (the new chief of the General Staff of the Army): I have also heard bad reports about Seydlitz.

Hitler: And under that: "Hube—The Man!" Naturally one could say that it would have been better to leave Hube in there and bring out those others! But, since the value of men is not immaterial since we will need men in the entire war, I am definitely of the opinion that it was right to bring Hube out. . . .[4]

The new HQ, XIVth Panzer Corps remained in the Ukraine until early March, acting as a depot and distribution point for arriving panzer troops and new equipment. When the desperate battles to the east (the Donets, Rostov, the Mius, and Kharkov) were over and the front more or less stabilized, Hube and his new headquarters were transferred to France under the aegis of *Oberbefehlshaber West* (OB West, a term referring to the commander in chief, West, or his headquarters). Here it began to receive its organic (corps-level) units, including the 414th Artillery Command (Arko 414), the 60th Signal Battalion, and the 414th Supply Troop.[5]

In mid-June the rebuilt corps headquarters was sent to a suburb of Rome to take charge of any German units that Hitler might find it necessary to send to southern Italy. Hube conferred with the senior German officers in the Italian capital, including Kesselring, von Rintelen, and von Senger und Etterlin. He also made at least one visit to Sicily. Although he was reticent, Kesselring and von Senger both got the impression that the one-armed veteran of the Russian Front had little faith in a prolonged successful battle in Italy. By early July, however, he was headquartered in the Naples area supervising three reconstituted divisions, as well as several nondivisional artillery and flak battalions, all of which were moving into the Bari–Taranto–Salerno–Reggio di Calabria area of southern Italy.

On July 2 the redoubtable Colonel Thunert was summarily transferred to France, where he was named chief of staff of the LVIIIth Reserve Panzer Corps. To replace him, OKH sent an officer with considerable experience in the Mediterranean: Colonel Bogislaw von Bonin. It was only eight days before the Allies landed in Sicily.

Hube and von Bonin had never worked together before and apparently had never met; however, they had no problems and made a very effective, smooth-working team. After the war, and long after Hube's death, von Bonin wrote that his commander in Sicily "was a brave soldier, calm, well-balanced, equal to any situation, never in doubt and always ready to take over responsibility."[6]

It was through von Bonin that General Jodl, the operations officer at OKW, passed the High Command's orders to Hube. "The vital factor," Jodl said, "is under no circumstances to suffer the loss of three divisions. At the very minimum, our valuable human material must be saved."[7] Hube was privately instructed to assume command of all German formations and to ignore Italian orders.

After the Allies landed in Sicily, Hube moved his headquarters to Reggio, on the mainland side of the Straits of Messina, and tried to keep in close contact with the campaign in Sicily. He conferred frequently by phone and two-way radio with Kesselring in Rome and kept in touch with the Italian 6th Army Headquarters and the German Liaison Staff through Lieutenant Colonel Hans Meier-Welcker, Senger's operations officer.

Meanwhile, Reichsmarschall Hermann Goering was waging a battle of influence at Fuehrer Headquarters. He tried to get Hitler to name a Luftwaffe officer, General Rainer Stahel, as Commanding General, Sicily. However, his bitter enemy, Field Marshal Rommel, "managed to spike that gun," as Brett-Smith wrote, "and insisted on the excellent General Hube."[8]

Like his rival Rommel, Kesselring was delighted to have Hube as the German commander designate in Sicily, if for no other reason than that he did not want Hermann Goering meddling any further in his affairs in Italy. It did not seem to bother him that Hube was less optimistic than he was about the overall situation, because *everyone* was less optimistic than he was about the overall situation. After the war he said that as commander in Sicily, Hans Hube was "the right man in the right place, seconded by his excellent Chief of Staff." He added that cooperation between Hube and OB South was "absolutely ideal."[9]

The arrival of the steady, capable Hube had a calming effect on the Germans both in Sicily and in higher headquarters and on some of the Italians. Some pretty strange strategic thinking had been going on in certain circles. Mussolini, for example, wanted a massive and unrealistic commitment of German strength. On July 13 he called for another German motorized corps and a huge increase in combat aviation wings from the Luftwaffe. Then the Germans were to counterattack and drive the Allies into the sea, for, as the Duce said, "if the English cannot be dislodged then Sicily is lost."[10]

The Italian dictator was also shocked by a report from Colonel Wilhelm Schmalz. Bypassing normal command channels, the angry colonel sent a summary of Italian behavior at Augusta and Syracuse directly to OB South. The report reached Hitler's desk on July 14, and Hitler was outraged at his ally. The Fuehrer sharply demanded an explanation from the Italians. Mussolini, in turn, demanded a reply from Ambrosio.

The chief of Commando Supremo basically denied Schmalz's allegations. He did admit that "certain detachments" of the Augusta garrison had retreated under intense air and naval bombardment but went on to say, "Episodes of this kind happen in all armies." He claimed that generally speaking, the Italian Army was fighting well.

Schmalz, who was anti-Italian anyway, replied, "I cannot sanction any excuses about the behavior of the men at Augusta. . . . I believe that the whole thing goes much deeper than that: namely, there was no desire to prevent the enemy landing." He went on to accuse the Italians of lacking fighting spirit "because the will to fight comes from leadership." He concluded that he was sickened by Ambrosio's response.[11]

Mussolini, of course, accepted Ambrosio's explanation. Apparently the Italian dictator could not bring himself to accept the reality of the situation, i.e., that his military was unwilling to fight any longer and that Sicily *was* lost. The only questions that remained were how long the Allies could be tied up on the island and what units could be evacuated. Jodl saw the situation more realistically than did most. He told Hitler (also on July 13) that he did not think Sicily could be held for long and that they would do better to prepare for the defense of Italy.

In the meantime, the OKW staff, disenchanted with the feebleness of the Italian resistance and the ineptitude of its High Command, updated its plans to occupy northern Italy in case the Fascist regime collapsed.

Field Marshal Albert Kesselring also refused to believe that all was lost. Within forty-eight hours of his visit to Sicily he had decided that at least part of the island could be held indefinitely. On July 14 he met with Ambrosio in Rome and proposed that Sicily be reinforced with the 29th Panzer Grenadier Division and the rest of the 1st Parachute Division, as planned, and that naval forces (especially U-boats and small E-boats) and Luftwaffe forces should also be reinforced. With these units, he felt that northeastern Sicily could be held. He also informed Ambrosio that Headquarters, XIVth Panzer Corps, would be transferred from southern Italy to the island to command the German forces on Sicily. Unlike prior to the invasion, Ambrosio did not object.

Kesselring did not know it at the time, but he had promised more than he could deliver. It was true that Hitler already had authorized the transfer of the 29th Panzer Grenadier to Sicily, providing the supply and transportation facilities on the island could handle another division, but that was before Jodl and Rommel submitted memos and forcefully objected to sending new units to Sicily. On July 17, therefore, Hitler met with Jodl, Rommel, Keitel, Doenitz, and others. For the first time he accepted Jodl's view that Sicily could not be held indefinitely, and withdrew his permission to commit the 29th Panzer Grenadier. Hitler also agreed to allow the German army in Italy to withdraw northward if Mussolini's government fell.

Hitler's order of July 17 deferring the movement of the 29th Division was a source of great embarrassment to Kesselring, who could not explain the decision to Ambrosio and Roatta. Mussolini tried to override Hitler (!) and commanded the 29th to move immediately from southern Italy to Sicily and the 3rd Panzer Grenadier Division to move from Rome to Calabria. He was politely ignored. In fact, with the arrival of General Hube, the Germans had already begun to act as if the Italians did not exist.

General of Panzer Troops Hans Valentin Hube knew that he was in a tough situation, but he by no means considered it a hopeless one. As a corps commander who had been through the hell of Stalingrad, he had been in tougher situations than this. His orders, sent by the Fuehrer from his headquarters in East Prussia on July 13, read, "After the bulk of the Italian forces are eliminated [apparently a foregone conclusion] the Germans alone will be insufficient to push the enemy into the sea. It will therefore be the objective of the Germans to delay the enemy advance, and bring it to a halt west of Mount Etna."[12] Specifically, Hitler wanted the Allies halted along a defensive line running roughly from San Stefano through Adrano to Catania.

The instructions from the OKW Operations Staff (i.e., Jodl), dated that same day, enlarged upon Hitler's orders. They commanded that the OKW directive

> be kept secret from the Italians, and the [distribution] of which is to be limited to the smallest possible circle, even in German quarters. Hereafter it will be the task of the Corps Headquarters, in close co-operation with the head of the German Liaison Staff attached to the Italian 6th Army, to take over the overall leadership in the bridgehead of Sicily itself, while unobtrusively excluding the Italian headquarters. The remaining Italian formations are to be divided up and placed under the command of the various German headquarters.[13]

Verbally, via Colonel von Bonin, Jodl told Hube to "fight a delaying action and gain further time for stabilizing the situation on the mainland." In other words, as quietly and diplomatically as possible, Hube was to take complete control of the land battle and conduct operations with the twin aims of delaying the Allies as long as possible and saving as many German troops as possible. That is exactly what Hube set out to do.

There were problems initially. On July 13 General Guzzoni asked von Senger to agree that the withdrawal of the Hermann Goering and 15th Panzer Grenadier divisions would conform with the withdrawals made by the Italian units. In other words, the German shift to the east would be delayed so that the less mobile and less battleworthy Italian units could make good their escape, covered by the Germans. At this time speed was of the essence in blocking Montgomery, so Senger did not agree. He was backed up by Hube. Eventually, Guzzoni and the one-armed German agreed to form a new line running from the north coast at San Fratello through Cesaro–Adrano–Biancavilla–Monte San Nicolo to Stazzo, a few miles south of Catania. This was the Haupfkampflinie (main defensive line) referred to earlier. There was to be an orderly, timed withdrawal to this positon.

Meanwhile, the Americans continued their successful attacks against the Italian 6th Army. On July 13 Mobile Group H was enveloped by the Americans at the San Pietro airfield, and the Livorno was once again subjected to heavy air, naval, and ground attack at Mazzarino. Its infantry commander, Colonel Mona, was killed, and the division temporarily disappeared from the battle. The gap between the Hermann Goering and 15th Panzer Grenadier divisions thus grew even larger. Still Rodt was not authorized to withdraw from his exposed positions, which were becoming more and more dangerous.

The next day the XIVth Panzer Corps Headquarters began its move to Sicily. At the same time Kesselring visited Guzzoni at his new headquarters in the Passo Pisciero area, east of Randazzo. They had a frank talk during which the field marshal violated his instructions and told Guzzoni what General Hube's orders really were.

Guzzoni's reaction was exactly what Kesselring hoped it would be: he more or less accepted Hube as the dominant partner in the Sicilian enterprise. Colonel von Bonin, chief of staff of the panzer corps, recalled later that "after the arrival of General Hube, the Italian commander-in-chief never again made the slightest attempt of issuing any orders to the German forces. He himself was, or at least seemed to be, annoyed and ashamed about the complete collapse [of the Italian units]."[14] He was, however, not yet ready to hand over full responsibility for the defense to the Germans. Even though Alfredo Guzzoni was hurt and embarrassed by the performance of his army, he still had his pride and insisted on retaining control of the Italian elements of the 6th Army. This was acceptable to Hube, who knew better than to ask for everything at once.

On July 15, while his staff was busy reconnoitering the Haupf-kampflinie, Hube met with Guzzoni and Kesselring. They agreed that the XIVth Panzer Corps would take charge of the Hermann Goering, 15th Panzer Grenadier, and Livorno divisions and Brigade Schmalz, all on the left (eastern) flank of the army. Since Alexander's orders had temporarily eliminated the U.S. 7th Army as a threat, this would give Hube control of the only sector of real importance at the moment. Wisely, Hans Hube accepted this arrangement. After all, if General Patton eventually did succeed in reintroducing his American forces as a factor in the battle, Hube could deal with that at the appropriate time. At the moment, however, he had more pressing problems, such as securing his rear and fending off Montgomery's "left hook."

We agree with the distinguished military historian Colonel Albert Seaton, who wrote, "If the thrusting Patton had been allowed more freedom by Alexander, the British army group commander, 15th Panzer Grenadier Division might have been cut off in West Sicily."[15]

Certainly General Rodt was in an exposed position, especially after July 13, when Paul Conrath rapidly moved the H.G. Division to the east, toward the Caltagirone-Vizzini line, closing the gap between himself and Schmalz. This inevitably opened a gap between his right (western) flank and the 15th Panzer Grenadier, which was at that time trying to contain Truscott north of Licata. In justice to Conrath, it must be noted that he left behind rear guards to delay the Americans and Canadians; nevertheless, if Alexander had called on Patton, the U.S. 7th Army might easily have broken through the thin Axis center with Bradley's IInd Corps and quite conceivably could have advanced all the way to the coast, cutting off Rodt's 15th Panzer Grenadiers—the best Axis division in Sicily.

On the evening of July 13 Rodt's division held a line running from Serradifalco, south of Caltanisetta-Pietraperzia-Barrafranca, south of Piazza Armerina. There is no doubt that he was overextended and that Patton was in a position to deliver a devastating—if not fatal—blow.[16] Alexander, however, had no intention of calling on Patton for anything so ambitious. The Americans, whom he at this time (and later) considered second-rate soldiers, could not be trusted for anything but secondary missions, or so Sir Harold thought. On July 13 he signaled Alan Brooke, "Future operations will then envisage thrust towards Messina from Catania by XIIIth Corps. XXXth Corps drive to the north coast at San Stefano then turning east to join up with XIIIth Corps at Messina. When the island is split in two from north to south American 7th Army will be directed towards Palermo and Trapani."[17]

This movement took the pressure off the Germans. They quickly regained their equilibrium and—now that Hube and the XIVth Panzer Corps were running the show—never lost it again for the rest of the campaign.

We have already seen how Montgomery's eastern thrust (Dempsey's XIIIth Corps) was halted north of Primosole Bridge. We now turn our attention to the zone of Monty's left hook, which was to be delivered by Lieutenant General Sir Oliver Leese's XXXth Corps.

On July 13, during the Battle of Vizzini, the British XXXth Corps included the 51st Highland Division (with the Malta Brigade attached) and the 23rd Armoured Brigade, with the 1st Canadian Infantry Division in reserve. After Vizzini fell on the night of July 14–15, Leese returned the 1st Canadian to the battle. It was recommitted to the corps' far left flank and ordered to drive up Highway 124 toward Caltagirone, with the objective of taking Enna. Thus the outermost blow of Monty's left hook was to be delivered by his least motorized division and the only one in his army not yet fully acclimated to the semitropical conditions of the Mediterranean summer. It was also committed to an axis of advance along a single highway in a mountainous area, where all the advantages of terrain accrued to the defenders.

Meanwhile, on July 14 the 180th and 179th Regimental Combat teams of Middleton's U.S. 45th Infantry Division secured the Biscari airfield after a stiff fight and pushed to within two miles of Highway 124. If they had continued to advance, they would have cut off the retreat of the German rear guard, which was frustrating the Canadian advance. However, in accordance with Alexander's orders, the Thunderbirds turned around and retraced their steps back to the coastal highway, almost all the way back to the invasion beaches themselves. The Canadians would have to clear the hilltop towns along the highway on their own and then rapidly turn north, loop behind Mount Etna, and penetrate all the way to the northern coast. Their right (inner) flank was to be cleared by the Highlanders. Their left flank was initially to be covered by the American army.

The Canadians set out on the morning of July 15, advancing to the west along Highway 124. Their final objective was Enna, forty miles away "as the crow flies" but about seventy miles away as the Sicilian roads turned. Appendix 5 shows the division's order of battle.

The Canadians covered the first eight miles quickly enough. However, at nine A.M. they were halted at Grammichele by the rear guard of the Hermann Goering Division.

Grammichele was a town of thirteen thousand people, perched on a long ridge in the middle of a rare upland valley. Built in 1683 after an earthquake, it was a completely hexagonal town, constructed like a spiderweb. When the Canadians entered the town, they walked into an ambush. The Hermann Goerings quickly knocked out a tank, several armored personnel carriers, and a number of other vehicles. Most of the division was near at hand, however, and as the morning wore on, the Hermann Goering lost three medium panzers and an 88-mm gun. By noon the rear guard had had enough and retreated west along Highway 124, toward Caltagirone, harassed by Canadian artillery. The Canadian advance, however, was delayed by mines and by a shortage of personnel carriers, many of which had been lost at sea. The Canadians continued to advance through the darkness, although much more slowly than Montgomery would have wished, and were outside Caltagirone well before daylight on July 16. There they halted and prepared for a dawn attack.

When the Canadians struck on July 16, they found that the Germans had once again disappeared into the night. Caltagirone, a city of thirty thousand people, had formerly been the headquarters of the H.G. Division and, as such, had been heavily bombed by the Allied air forces. The Canadians found it "a veritable shambles, with the streets badly blocked by rubble and many fires burning."[18] They did what they could for the civilian wounded, who had already swamped the very inadequate local hospital. As the Canadian doctors, nurses, and medics worked, Sicilian nuns insisted on serving the wounded men coffee, which they had made from crushed acorns. Meanwhile, the advance continued toward Piazza Armerina.

On the morning of July 16 the Canadian vanguard met little resistance, except from the ubiquitous German mines. They took the village of San Michele di Ganzeria, at the junction of Highways 117 and 124, without opposition. Then they made the turn north, following Highway 117 toward Enna and Leonforte. In many ways Leonforte was now more important than Enna, for it was there that Highways 117 and 121 connected and Highway 121 provided lateral communications for the southern part of the Hauptkampflinie. This fact did not enter into Canadian operational planning for several days, however, because the Germans stopped them at Piazza Armerina.

As we have seen, the 15th Panzer Grenadier Division (minus one regiment) had been committed against the Americans in the west and was trying to delay the Americans and Canadians as long as possible while simultaneously avoiding a double envelopment. Eventually General Rodt hoped to link up with the right flank of the Hermann Goering Division near Dittaino Station and then gradually fall back to the Hauptkampflinie, but Field Marshal Kesselring still forbade him to retreat; even if his order was rescinded, the rapid advance of the Allies was going to make the maneuver difficult. Rodt's eastern (left) flank was especially exposed, since no one seemed to be able to find the remnants of the Livorno Division, which were supposed to be somewhere between the two German divisions. Therefore, the left flank was in a critical position. This zone was the responsibility of Lieutenant Colonel Ens's 104th Panzer Grenadier Regiment, which had only two battalions. Ens could spare only one of these to oppose the Canadians: Captain Rudolf Struckmann's IInd. His missions were to delay the Canadians for as long as possible without becoming decisively engaged and to keep the lateral roads to the east open as long as possible— at least until the other elements of the 15th Division could disengage from the U.S. 7th Army and withdraw from the west. Fortunately for Struckmann, he had the advantage of excellent defensive terrain and an understanding of how to use it.

The II/104th waited for the Canadians three miles south of Piazza Armerina, where the road made a sharp turn beneath commanding heights. Here the leading Canadian company was ambushed with fire from machine guns, mortars, and artillery. It "took a terrific battering," to quote the Canadian Official History, and fell back along Highway 117.[19]

The Canadians regrouped and returned that afternoon, struggling toward Struckmann's hill with the Edmonton Regiment, the Seaforth Highlanders (battalion), and the Princess Patricia's Canadian Light Infantry (also a battalion), all supported by two British artillery regiments. The Canadian tanks were not used in this battle because they were useless here: they could not elevate their guns sufficiently to bring fire on the II/104th Panzer Grenadiers.

The infantry battle lasted all afternoon, but in spite of the odds, the Germans—most of whom were veterans of the Afrika Korps—still held the heights at dusk and still commanded the highway to Piazza Armerina. The next day, however, Captain Struckmann knew that the battle would be lost; consequently, he pulled one of the favorite German tactics of the campaign. He withdrew under the cover of darkness and retreated to the next blocking position, liberally scattering mines and booby traps behind him so that the Canadians would not pursue too quickly. The terrain again worked in favor of the defenders. Because of the high iron content of the lava-deposited soil, mines in Sicily were much harder to detect than they were elsewhere and caused the Allies longer and more serious delays than would otherwise have been the case. Undetected mines would cause civilian deaths in Sicily for years to come.

The Canadians occupied Piazza Armerina by six A.M. the following morning. This town had previously been the headquarters of Rossi's XVIth Italian Corps, and the Canadians captured large stocks of supplies, petrol, and badly needed signals equipment. They watched in amusement as civilians rushed back and forth between their homes and the deserted military barracks, carrying abandoned furniture. The senior officers were not amused, however. A single German battalion had held up their entire division for twenty-four hours and had made good its escape. It was noon before the division could regroup and resume its advance up Highway 117 toward Enna. In the hills north of the town, however, they again met stiff resistance.

General Rodt's position, exposed since July 11, was becoming more and more desperate. As early as the night of July 14 Guzzoni, through von Senger, ordered Rodt to pull back to Leonforte. It is doubtful, however, that Rodt ever received this order. At 11:30 P.M. on July 14 Senger informed Kesselring of Guzzoni's instructions, and the Luftwaffe marshal immediately countermanded the order. Rodt was to hold his present positions in the Piazzi Armerina–Serradifalco area at all costs, he insisted, echoing the sentiments of his Fuehrer. Throughout July 15 and 16 he continually bombarded Rodt with "hold at all costs" orders. Throughout this period the gap between the two German divisions continued to grow, as did the gap between Rodt and the Italians in the sector north of Agrigento. Finally, at 3:25 P.M. on July 16, Rodt signaled that he had committed his last reserves and that a retreat would soon be imperative. Once again, however, Kesselring refused to give him freedom of action, but General Rodt had had enough. During the night of July 16–17 he began to withdraw on his own initiative, a decision that drew no response from Kesselring at Frascati. Hube, however, subsequently confirmed Rodt's decision as soon as he officially took charge of the battle on July 18.[20]

The Germans were also having their troubles in the area of reconnaissance. Because of the overwhelming superiority of the Allied air forces, flights by reconnaissance aircraft were possible only in exceptional instances. The German field commanders had to depend entirely on ground reconnaissance, and this had to be done on foot, placing, in the words of Colonel Max Ulich, "extraordinarily high demands on the physical strength of the 'lowland infantry,' who were neither accustomed to nor equipped for mountain climbing." Indeed, a good army or SS mountain division would have been a major boon to the XIVth Panzer Corps in Sicily. Colonel Ulich found that reconnaissance in mountainous terrain took five or six times as long as was the case in flat terrain, yet, he wrote after the war, "the reconnaissance patrols on foot, operating in high mountain regions, nevertheless accomplished tasks which had been considered as impossible to achieve."[21] As a result, German commanders were able to react with at least adequate speed in spite of enemy aerial supremacy, and no major Allied breakthroughs occurred during the entire campaign.

In the meantime, Monty's advance had in effect broken his army into *three* wings: the 1st Canadian Division on the left, the XIIIth Corps (5th and 50th divisions) on the right, and Major General Douglas N. Wimberley's 51st (Highland) Infantry Division in the center. "Lang Tom" Wimberley's objective on July 15 was to push rapidly ahead to secure bridgeheads across the Dittaino and Simeto rivers, simultaneously capturing the airfields in the Gerbini vicinity and threatening the rear of Brigade Schmalz. At division headquarters the crossing of the rivers appeared to be no great task. Even the forward troops were lighthearted. The Sicilian peasants they met were no longer reserved or apathetic; they were now quite friendly to the advancing Allies. The Highlanders, of course, did not realize that Paul Conrath had now succeeded in linking up with Schmalz and had brought up most of his battalions.

"Emboldened by the speed at which we had gone forward, we were too hasty," General Wimberley admitted later, "and took rather a bloody nose."[22]

The battered but unvanquished Luftwaffe panzer troops had regained their composure by July 16 and were rapidly gaining experience in holding actions, delaying tactics, and ambush techniques. As the main body of the division dug in along the Hauptkampflinie, strong rear guards fell back slowly, inflicting casualties and delay after delay on the Highlanders and their attached 23rd Armoured Brigade without ever being decisively engaged. Wimberley's advance slowed to less than ten miles a day. He cleared the town of Palagonia on the 16th, crossed the Gornalunga, and cleared Ramacca the next day. By nightfall on July 18 he held positions south of Mount Turcisi and was planning to break through the German line at Sferro with the objective of capturing Paterno. At the same time, on his right flank, the 152nd Infantry and the 23rd Armoured Brigade had pushed to within about two miles of Gerbini and the important airfields. Wimberley did not realize that he had reached the Hauptkampflinie, Hube's main line of defense. The Hermann Goerings dug in, determined to retreat no more.

The sector opposite the 51st Highlander Division was controlled by the newly committed 2nd Hermann Goering Panzer Grenadier Regiment and what was left of the Hermann Goering Panzer Regiment—forty-eight tanks in all. Mixed in were a few intact elements of the Napoli Division's 76th Infantry Regiment. On the 2nd H.G. Panzer Grenadier's right was the 1st Hermann Goering Panzer Grenadier Regiment, and on its left lay Brigade Schmalz.

The Highlanders advanced confidently on the night of July 18–19 but met unexpectedly heavy resistance. The battle lasted until the morning of July 21, but the climax came on the night of July 20–21. At that time the British 50th, 5th, and 51st divisions launched a coordinated night attack against Brigade Schmalz and the 2nd Panzer Grenadiers of the Hermann Goering Division. Supported by three artillery regiments and a squadron of the 46th Royal Tank Regiment, Lieutenant Colonel Mathieson's 7th Argyll and Sutherland Highlanders advanced two thousand yards and captured the main Gerbini airfield, where they were reinforced by the 1st Black Watch and part of the 7th Black Watch. The British position was still not a good one, however. On their right flank the 5th Infantry

Division had passed around the left flank of the nearly exhausted 50th Infantry Division and attacked the small town of Misterbianco, near the western suburbs of Catania. They had been stopped by Group Schmalz without making a dent in the German lines despite the supporting fire of nine Royal Artillery regiments. On the German left flank, Colonel Walter's paratroopers turned back yet another attempt by Kirkman's Northumbrians to expand their bridgehead, while the Goerings still held the hills that dominated the Gerbini airfield and were continually lobbing artillery shells on top of the Highlanders. Also, the lack of motorization within the British 8th Army was causing serious supply problems. In all divisions except the 1st Canadian, for example, artillery rounds were limited to thirty shells per day for twenty-five-pounders and only twenty per day for self-propelled guns. In addition, in the sector opposite the Highlanders, Conrath had reinforced the 2nd Grenadiers with his reconnaissance battalion and most of the IInd Battalion of his panzer regiment, and the young Luftwaffe riflemen, who were fast becoming veterans, were infiltrating British positions with considerable tactical skill. Wimberley's men had hardly any cover except for a few irrigation ditches, an orange grove, and a patch or two of cane.

At 10:30 A.M. the main counterattack came. This time the German infantry-panzer tactics were coordinated, and after a sharp fight the British retreated all the way back to the Dittaino River. The Argyll and Sutherland Highlanders alone had lost 160 men and 18 officers, among them Colonel Mathieson and the commander of the 46th Royal Tank Regiment (RTR), both killed in action. Eight British tanks had also been destroyed. German losses had not been light, either. On July 23, for example, the Hermann Goering Panzer Division reported that it had only twenty-three tanks ready for action, and only three of them were Tigers. Nevertheless, the latest threat had been defused, the Gerbini Airfield was back in German hands, and although the Luftwaffe had long since departed, at least the airfield had been denied to the RAF.

By July 21 even Montgomery was prepared to admit defeat at Gerbini. He ordered the Highlander Division to go over to the defensive. His efforts to score a decisive victory on the right flank and in the center of the 8th Army's front had come to nothing. But what about the all-important left flank? Had the Canadians succeeded in converting Montgomery's left hook into a knockout blow?

When we left Major General Simonds's 1st Canadian Infantry Division on the morning of July 17, it had just secured Piazza Armerina from the IInd Battalion, 104th Panzer Grenadier Regiment. Undiscouraged, the veterans of Poland, France, Africa, and the Eastern Front simply fell back to their next major delaying positions. These were the hills on either side of the Portello Grottacalda Pass, which lay eight miles north of Piazza Armerina and sixteen road miles southeast of Enna (about seven miles overland). Only a few hundred yards northeast of the hill, the side road from Valguarnera joined Highway 117. This was an important road junction for the Germans because here they could block the Canadian drive in two directions: northwest to Enna or northeast to Valguarnera, where commanding heights overlooked the Dittaino valley and the western Catania plain.

The terrain, as usual, favored the defenders. Immediately before the road forked, Highway 117 passed through a narrow gap in a long ridge that extended from the backbone of the Erei Mountains. The hills on either side of the pass were occupied by the bulk of the II/104th Panzer Grenadiers, which was now joined by its sister battalion, the I/104th, under Major Stellmacher. Meanwhile, Captain Struckmann's rear guards continued to delay and harass the Canadians south of Portello Grottacalda. At the same time, Ens's mortar sections set up positions on Monte della Forma, a square-topped hill on the western side of the pass. With an elevation of 2,700 feet, Monte della Forma was to be a key position in the upcoming battle.

The Canadians advanced slowly. The German rear guards blew up bridges as they retreated, and the entire Canadian advance was brought to a halt four miles north of Piazza Armerina while the Canadian engineers constructed another bridge across a gorge on Highway 117 to replace one destroyed by the panzer engineers. The advance could not resume until after four P.M., and it was five P.M. before the Canadian advance guard came under machine gun and mortar fire 1.5 miles south of Monte della Forma. The Canadian infantrymen quickly jumped off the tanks of the Three Rivers Regiment and followed them toward the German outpost line. The panzer grenadiers, in turn, fell back to their main line of resistance. Then the entire Carleton and York Regiment came up and pushed to within a mile of the pass, where they were checked. The Canadians halted, having gained only about five miles that day.

Despite the determination of the resistance and the lack of rapid progress anywhere, Montgomery ordered an all-out attack in all three sectors for the night of July 17–18. Dempsey was to break through Brigade Schmalz and take Catania; Wimberley's Highlanders were instructed to overrun Gerbini and push on to Paterno; and the Canadians, who formed the most important attack of all, were to advance north and then east, across the lower slopes of Mount Etna, capturing Leonforte, Regalbuto, and Adrano (Aderno) in turn. In his enthusiasm Montgomery even promised General Leese help from the U.S. 7th Army. He wanted the Americans to occupy the line northward from Caltanisetta to Petralia in order to secure the left rear of the XXXth Corps as the 1st Canadian Division swung right from Leonforte. Alexander duly forwarded Monty's instructions to Patton, who was naturally furious. "Monty is trying to steal the show again and with the assistance of Divine Destiny [Dwight D. Eisenhower] he may do so," Patton wrote to his wife on the 16th.[23]

Patton need not have been upset. The XIVth Panzer Corps halted all three of Montgomery's attacks.

Before daybreak on July 17 the Canadians resumed their attack with two infantry brigades supported by a tank regiment and five artillery regiments. Despite this tremendous firepower, the attack was halted. The Royal 22e Regiment was stopped within a few hundred yards of the pass and was almost cut off from the rest of the division by a well-timed German counterattack. After beating back the panzer grenadiers with difficulty, the Canadians dug in for the night.

The attack resumed at midmorning. This time the 3rd Brigade attacked with three regiments on line. The 1st Brigade on the right flank advanced in a similar formation. The battle raged all day in the hot sun, and the 1st Canadian Brigade had a particularly difficult time because of the rugged terrain it had to cross: deep ravines and dried-up, rocky streambeds overlooked by high hills and protected by steep slopes. The tanks carrying the forward observers and their radios could not negotiate this type of ground, so the assault companies were without artillery support for most of the day.

The German defenses held firm all morning, but as the sun sank, so did German fortunes. Monte della Forma finally fell at about five P.M., and the road junction was lost at nightfall. Meanwhile, the West Nova Scotia Regiment captured a hill that dominated the road to Enna, apparently with the intention of cutting off the German retreat. Colonel Ens, however, had no intention of retreating in that direction. Under the cover of darkness he fell back through Valguarnera, which the Canadians occupied later that night. The 104th Panzer Grenadier Regiment, meanwhile, fell back toward the north, keeping itself between the 1st Canadian Division and Leonforte (Map 8). Its two battalions had already done exceedingly well: they had once again held up an entire division for more than twenty-four hours.

The Canadians left Enna to be captured by the Americans and pursued the 104th northward, toward Leonforte. "Drive the Canadians hard," Montgomery ordered Leese,[24] and hard they were driven, up and down steep hills, across the barren Sicilian countryside, through an area where the communications, bridges, and culverts had been systematically destroyed by the retreating Germans. Mines seemed to be everywhere, and it was so hot that medical orderlies found it very difficult to get accurate temperature readings for several hours each day because the thermometers would not go below the 102-degree mark. The orderlies took to dipping them into cold water and hurriedly slipping them into the mouths of the wounded, hoping that the resultant readings indicated body temperature and not the temperature of the outside air.

As usual, there were indecisive rearguard actions. At a crossroads five miles north of Valguarnera the Canadian spearhead was halted by artillery, mortar, and machine gun fire. It had to take cover and go to ground because its own artillery had been delayed by another blown bridge. It was afternoon before the Allied engineers repaired the road and their own guns could be brought up. By nightfall the crossroads was in Canadian hands, but the German rear guard had escaped once more.

At last the Canadians were within sight of Mount Etna, the huge pinnacle that extends to an elevation of more than ten thousand feet above sea level. Leading south of the mountain, across the hills and smaller mountains, lay Highway 121, the main Palermo-Catania road, over which the Canadians would be fighting for the next three weeks. Between the hills and small mountains lay many of the Simeto River tributaries, which had eroded much of the region and left very rugged terrain. Dry now, these streambeds impeded the advance of vehicles and, with the hills and stone-built villages, provided the Germans with innumerable excellent defensive positions.

As he neared Leonforte on July 20, Simonds developed his division's advance on two axes: Brigadier Vokes's 2nd Canadian Brigade on the left would attack Leonforte, while on the right, Graham's 1st Brigade would attack Assoro, a village about two miles east-southeast of Leonforte. Both sites were again defended by Lieutenant Colonel Ens's 104th Panzer Grenadier Regiment, with the bulk of the unit concentrated at Leonforte. Assoro was held by a company-size detachment of about a hundred men and five panzers.[25]

The village of Assoro was located on the western slope of Assoro Mountain, on the least precipitous slope, across which ran the road connecting it to the valley; unfortunately for the Canadians, this road was well registered by Major of Reserve Karl Theodor Simon's 33rd Motorized Artillery Regiment as well as Captain Ahrens's 315th (Army) Flak Battalion. Lieutenant Colonel B. A. Sutcliffe, commander of the Hastings and Prince Edward Regiment, was given the task of spearheading the Canadian assault on Assoro, and on the afternoon of July 20 he went forward on a reconnaissance. He was quickly nailed by an 88; both Sutcliffe and his intelligence officer were killed. He was replaced by Major The Lord Tweedsmuir, the son of a former governor-general of Canada.

Lord Tweedsmuir was a young man who knew his business. He gathered that the Germans thought that an assault up the eastern slope was a physical impossibility, so he decided to try it. During the night his regiment worked its way up the mountain single file, toward the ruins at the summit. These ruins were the former castle of Roger II, a twelfth-century Norman king whose stronghold was located on the edge of the eastern cliff, a thousand feet above the valley. Tweedsmuir's instincts proved correct. Except for a small detachment in the ruins, the eastern slope was un-defended. The Hastings overran this German outpost at one A.M. on July 21 without losing a man.

Despite having captured the summit of Assoro Mountain, the Canadians were not in an enviable position. They were without direct artillery support and could not even bring up food and ammunition during daylight hours. The German artillery shelled the ruins and inflicted several casualties on the Hastings with their accurate fire. During the late afternoon the Assoro garrison launched a surprise attack and advanced almost to the top of the hill before the Canadians turned it back. The Hastings were then subjected to harassing fire from snipers and artillery and mortar fire throughout the evening and night.

In the meantime, Brigadier Graham had brought up most of the rest of his 1st Brigade. Early on the morning of July 22 he drove the Germans from the heights southwest of the town. The Cana-dian engineers then began filling in the demolished road, preparing to bring up their heavy weapons. Seeing that his position would soon be untenable, the German detachment commander at Assoro fell back two miles and rejoined his parent regiment in Leonforte, where a major battle was already in progress.

Early on the morning of July 21 the Seaforth Highlanders had advanced to within a mile of Leonforte, when they reached a severe road bend. Here they found a key bridge over a ravine blown up and the area swept by machine gun and mortar fire. They did not try to advance farther until the afternoon, when the rest of the brigade came up. The attack was abortive because the pre-liminary artillery bombardment fell short, and several rounds hit the Seaforths' battalion headquarters, causing thirty casualties and tremendous confusion. Brigadier Vokes wisely postponed the attack and replaced the Seaforths with the Edmonton Regiment.

The third attempt to take Leonforte began at nine P.M., sup-ported by the heaviest Canadian artillery concentration to date. This time the shells landed on the 104th Panzer Grenadier Regi-ment, which took cover in the town.

Leonforte, a large and modern place by Sicilian standards, had a peacetime population of twenty thousand. It extended up the mountain ridge almost to the summit. The foot soldiers of the Edmonton Regiment, supported by mortars and machine guns, advanced up the slope and into the town while the engineers below attempted to bridge the ravine.

The fighting inside Leonforte was heavy and fluctuating. Part of the town changed hands several times before a few of the Edmontons did a foolish thing: they shot some prisoners within view of some of their *Kameraden* who were still fighting. "This occurrence soon became known throughout the division and heightened its determination to resist," General Rodt noted later.[26] Furious, Colonel Ens's regiment counterattacked and, supported by panzers and machine gun fire, surrounded many of the Edmontons in the town. Leonforte became the scene of bitter house-to-house fighting as the grenadiers tried to wipe out Simonds's assault force, which took cover in the stone houses and turned every building into a small fortress. Meanwhile, the Canadian engineers worked feverishly to repair the road across the ravine so they could get antitank guns to their trapped comrades. Finally, despite German mortar fire, the road was made passable again at about two A.M., and at nine A.M. on July 22 Brigadier Vokes led a rescue force into Leonforte. This "flying column," which included Shermans, an infantry battalion, and an antitank battery, turned the tide of the battle. At ten A.M. the Edmontons were rescued, and by the afternoon the town was cleared, although German artillery continued to rain shells on it from the heights east and west of the town. These were cleared by 5:30 P.M., but only after both sides had suffered more casualties.

The early capture of the heights around Leonforte paid additional dividends for the Canadians, because the 104th Panzer Grenadier had to withdraw in broad daylight for a change. As the Germans retreated, they were pounded by Kittyhawk fighter-bombers and lost numerous vehicles and men north and east of the ruined city. By the next morning, however, the survivors had occupied their next delaying positions and awaited the next attack, which was some time in coming, because the British advance had at last run out of steam.

Despite the casualties Hube's battalions had suffered at Monte della Forma, Assoro, Leonforte, and the other battles, the men of the XIVth Panzer Corps had accomplished their main mission. Monty's left hook had been effectively blocked, and his advance up the east coast had been stalemated. The 8th Army had proved to be too weak to defeat the XIVth Panzer Corps decisively in three widely separated sectors at the same time. The opportunity the Allies had to win a quick and overwhelming victory in Sicily was forever lost. Even Montgomery was beginning to realize this. On July 19, for example, he went so far as to signal Alexander and suggest an offensive role for the Americans. It was too late now, however, for the Americans had already gone.

PATTON BREAKS LOOSE

GEORGE S. PATTON WAS A HAPPY MAN ON JULY 12, THE THIRD DAY of the invasion. True, he felt that he had been given a raw deal by the British (i.e., by Alexander and Montgomery), but he had made the best of a bad situation. His 7th Army had justified his faith in it, and all his initial objectives had been taken or were about to fall. The main airfields in his zone had been captured, and the Luftwaffe had been eliminated as a factor in the battle. Lacking further specific instructions from Alexander, Patton ordered the IInd Corps to continue pushing inland while Truscott launched an offensive along the coast toward Agrigento and Porto Empedocle. Agrigento was the gateway to western Sicily, and the 7th Army needed Porto Empedocle, a good artificial port, to augment the minor harbor capacities of Gela and Licata.

Despite the legitimate supply needs of the U.S. 7th Army, Patton was forced to camouflage his advance from the prying eyes of Headquarters, 15th Army Group. Alexander was unwilling to let him take Agrigento, because the attempt might bring about a major engagement. Ignoring his C-in-C's obvious lack of confidence in his American soldiers, Patton assured Sir Harold's HQ that Truscott's drive was nothing more than a "reconnaissance-in-force." The army group commander could hardly object to this and did not; Patton did not forget the incident, however.

Agrigento, located on a hilltop three miles from the coast and twenty-five miles west of Licata, was a town with a history. Pindar's "loveliest city of the mortals," it had been founded by the Greeks in 582 B.C. It had been known as Akragas in ancient times, when it was said to have had a population of a quarter of a million people, including the philosopher Empedocles, for whom its port was named. It had been notorious throughout the ancient world for its pleasure-loving gentry, who grew wealthy selling olives to the Carthaginians. It began to decline after it was seized by Hannibal in 406 B.C., and all that remained of the old city were three ruined Doric temples facing the sea.[1] Reduced to a population of 34,000 in 1943, Agrigento was now significant only because it commanded the approach to Porto Empedocle and the two main roads to Palermo, the capital of Sicily. This was significant enough, however, to make it the most important road center in southwestern Sicily, and Italian Colonel Augusto de Laurentiis blocked it with about all that was left of his rapidly disintegrating 207th Coastal Defense Division, which now included the 10th Bersaglieri Regiment (minus one battalion), the 19th Blackshirt Battalion, the 35th and 160th Coastal Artillery battalions, the 22nd Artillery Battalion, and the 77th Anti-Aircraft Battalion.[2] De Laurentiis, therefore, had enough artillery left in the hills around and beyond the town to make Truscott proceed somewhat cautiously. He assigned the task of taking Agrigento and its port to Colonel Harry B. Sherman's 7th Infantry Regiment, which he reinforced with the 3rd Ranger Battalion and two artillery battalions.

On the afternoon of July 12 Agrigento, Porto Empedocle, and the surrounding areas were shelled by the U.S. Navy and subjected to repeated low-level attacks by fighter-bombers. The gunners of the 77th Anti-Aircraft Battalion—a Fascist militia unit—fled in terror, leaving the 207th Coastal Defense Division almost devoid of antiaircraft protection at a critical time. The bad example of the militia caused panic and confusion among other units, and the divisional artillery commander stemmed the tide only through strenuous efforts. Even so, the American air and naval bombardments caused heavy casualties, especially to the artillery. By nightfall only one gun of the 2nd Battery, 22nd Artillery Battalion, was still firing. Other units were in a similar condition.

Sherman began his advance on July 13. Initially the Italians put up heavy resistance, and the reinforced 35th Bersaglieri Battalion even managed to launch a determined counterattack on the Castrofilippo-Napo Road, pinning down an American battalion. The Italian battalion commander was wounded six times in the fighting and lost an arm as a result. By the time it retreated late that night, the 35th Bersaglieri had fewer than two hundred men left. Nevertheless, it conducted an orderly withdrawal toward Castrofilippo and halted an American pursuit force near that town the next day.[3] Elsewhere, however, resistance began to crumble.

Advancing along the coastal highway, Colonel Sherman's task force was blocked on the Naro River, four miles east of Agrigento, by the 73rd Bersaglieri Battalion and the remnants of the 35th and 160th Coastal Artillery battalions. Soon, however, the defenders were being battered by the U.S. cruisers *Birmingham* and *Brooklyn*, the American light cruiser *Philadelphia*, the British monitor *Abercrombie*, and a few destroyers. All this was too much for the 207th, which crumbled. The 73rd Bersaglieri Battalion held its positions and was surrounded north of the coastal highway by the rapid American advance on July 14. It continued to resist for two days but was effectively written off because Colonel de Laurentiis retreated to Agrigento with the remnants of his command, where he decided to make a last stand built around the remnants of Colonel Storti's 10th Bersaglieri Regiment. De Laurentiis was quickly pursued by the Americans, who overran the 35th Coastal Artillery Battalion, invested the city, and methodically began to knock out the rest of the Italian artillery. By early afternoon on July 16 Colonel Sherman's guns had silenced the last of the Italian batteries, and his infantrymen had loosely surrounded the ancient city. Uncontrolled fires were burning everywhere when the Americans broke through the Italian perimeter, and they were soon fighting the last reserves in the streets. Seeing that his position was hopeless, Colonel de Laurentiis raised the white flag. He and most of his staff surrendered to an American battalion commander. He had been a divisional commander for less than four days. Meanwhile, at 4:30 P.M., the 3rd Ranger Battalion stormed Porto Empedocle. They took seven hundred prisoners and lost one man killed and twelve wounded. The Italian 207th Coastal Division had ceased to exist.

In the battles of Agrigento and Porto Empedocle, Truscott's units had captured more than six thousand men, fifty field pieces, and more than one hundred vehicles. They had provided Patton with a lightly damaged port with a capacity of eight hundred tons per day, about the same as Licata but twenty-five miles closer to the front. The U.S. Navy's minesweepers went to work immediately to clear a German-laid minefield, and the harbor became operational on July 18.

It was a good thing the sailors worked so rapidly, for General Patton needed Porto Empedocle immediately. He was already driving on Palermo.

Lieutenant General George S. Patton was not known for his restraint, but he had been remarkably patient thus far in the Sicilian campaign. He had accepted his secondary role in the invasion without protesting, had swallowed insults (real or implied) from Montgomery, and had not even lodged a protest when Alex handed Highway 124 over to the 8th Army, even though this transfer did the Germans much more good than it did the Anglo-Americans. Now, however, Patton had had just about enough.

Patton had first balked at a Montgomery slight when the two had exchanged liaison teams at the start of the campaign. To the 8th Army Headquarters Patton sent an experienced detachment, which included a full colonel, a major, two half-tracks, and a communications section. Monty reciprocated by sending one "white-kneed lieutenant, who arrived with a suitcase tied with a string."[4] Patton, rightly feeling provoked, sent the young officer back, along with a message to Montgomery informing the 8th Army commander that he could not have boys in his war room. He also requested that Monty send him Colonel Robert Henriques, whom Patton liked and had worked with before. Montgomery had little choice but to accede to this request, although he did not like it.

On July 15 Colonel Henriques visited 8th Army HQ, where Montgomery gave him the impression that he considered his American counterpart distinctly inferior to himself not only militarily but intellectually. "Tell Patton," Monty said peremptorily, "that when he gets to the north coast, he's not to go towards Palermo, but is to face east—better say right, then he'll understand. He's not to get in my way, but is to make faces and draw off the Germans from my front."[5]

Henriques relayed the message to Patton, but in more diplomatic terms. Patton, however, was astute enough to realize that Montgomery and Alexander were combining to deny him and his army the glory of capturing Palermo, the capital and the largest city on the island. After some tossing and turning that night, Patton was unable to sleep. At three A.M. on July 16 he awakened Henriques and asked him if it was probable that he would receive an order not to go to Palermo. Now the British colonel told Patton the whole undiluted story. In a rage, the insulted California aristocrat ordered his reserve division, the 9th Infantry, up from North Africa. Shortly afterward he received a message from Alexander, confirming his original instructions from Montgomery. Patton quickly sent a message to Alex, requesting a face-to-face meeting in North Africa the following day.

The fateful conference took place at La Marsa, Tunisia, on July 17. Accompanying Patton was General Wedemeyer, the U.S. chief of war plans—an obvious indication of the importance the Americans attached to this meeting and a hint that was not lost on Alexander. He was receptive when Patton protested his latest orders and presented an alternative to Montgomery's plan.

General Patton proposed that a new American corps be created in Sicily, that it be given 7th Army's armor, and that it attack toward Palermo, the largest city in Sicily, with a population of four hundred thousand. Alexander explained to the forceful American that he was planning to do just what Patton suggested, but his chief of staff had failed to issue the order.[6] Patton, of course, did not believe this remarkable explanation for one moment, but he acted as if he did; he had, after all, gotten what he wanted.

As a result of his inept handling of Americans in general and of Patton in particular—not to mention his catering to and favoritism toward Montgomery—Alexander had brought about a most undesirable situation. Patton was now heading northwest with most of his army, while Rodt was heading east with his 15th Panzer Grenadier Division to join Hube in his Hauptkampflinie. Montgomery was heading nowhere—precisely because he was deprived of the American help he had heretofore insisted he did not need, except to protect his left flank. This fact finally dawned on Montgomery on July 19, when he sent Alexander a message suggesting a limited offensive role for the Americans. This indicates how much the resistance on his front had stiffened. That night Alexander duly passed those instructions along to Patton, signaling him that 7th Army was to drive north from Petralia to cut the island in half (i.e., to conform with Monty's plans). Only then was he to drive on Palermo. It was too late by then, however, because the Palermo offensive was already well under way and the U.S. 7th Army Headquarters had gone into business for itself. Patton's chief of staff pretended that the message had been garbled in transmission and, after some delay, asked the 15th Army Group to repeat its instructions. By the time this process was completed, the Americans were on the outskirts of the Sicilian capital.

There is little doubt that Patton headed in the wrong direction when he drove on Palermo. Both Bradley and Truscott agreed with this assessment, as did Montgomery and the American Official History. Nigel Hamilton wrote that

> as resistance before Eighth Army stiffened, and as Monty belatedly began to cast his eye around for more troops to break open the enemy's stretched defences, he found that Seventh Army had departed in the opposite direction. Like a horse that has bolted—Alexander having meekly opened the stable door—Patton was racing westwards.[7]

Montgomery, of course, was quite critical—not of Patton, but of his own chief. Alexander, he complained, was doing nothing, while the 7th and 8th armies each fought their own individual battles. He was quite right, too, although his own conduct was hardly above reproach. In fact, the Sicilian campaign was one of the poorest ever handled by Sir Bernard Law Montgomery and *the* worst in the generally distinguished career of George S. Patton.

And what was General Guzzoni doing while Patton was organizing his forces for the conquest of western Sicily? He was conforming to Hube's plan to defend the northeastern corner of the island, while meant he was evacuating his mobile forces from western Sicily as rapidly as he could.

Alfredo Guzzoni realized when Agrigento fell that he would either have to move the Italian XIIth Corps from western to eastern Sicily or lose it. For reasons that have never been made clear, he had a new corps commander to work with. Commando Supremo had replaced Mario Arisio on July 12 with Generale di

Corpo Francesco Zingales. This personnel move is especially puzzling when one considers that Arisio was one of the best Italian commanders, that he worked well with the Germans, that it was customary for an Italian commander to carry much of his staff with him, and that both Arisio and his officers were familiar with local conditions in Sicily, whereas Zingales and his officers were neophytes. Still, given the conditions under which he had to work, it is difficult to criticize Zingales's subsequent conduct of the retreat. He received the order to withdraw his headquarters and the Aosta and Assietta divisions eastward to the Nicosia-Cerda line early on the morning of July 17. Here he was to set up defensive positions along Highway 120. The withdrawal was to be covered by the Italian elements of Tactical Group Schreiber, which was still fighting the U.S. 3rd Infantry Division north of Agrigento. In addition to his regular mobile divisions, Zingales was also ordered to pull out Mobile Groups A and C, leaving behind Mobile Group B. This group, plus all the static coastal defense units and anything else left behind in western Sicily, was placed under the command of Generale di Divisione Giovanni Marciani, commander of the 208th Coastal Defense Division.

The movement was beginning rather late in the campaign, for as early as July 12 Guzzoni had ordered the Aosta Division to withdraw all the way to Cesaro (on the western slope of Mount Etna), while Assietta was instructed to be prepared to halt a possible American advance from Licata and Agrigento toward Palermo. Later that day, however, Commando Supremo warned the 6th Army to expect additional landings in western Sicily. This warning was based on the opinions of staff officers in Rome, but Guzzoni did not know that. Thinking that the message was based on sound military intelligence, he countermanded his original order and posted Aosta to the San Cipriello–Ficuzza sector, twelve to fifteen miles southeast of Palermo. This misunderstanding was to cost the XIIth Corps severe casualties in the next two weeks.[8]

Zingales began his withdrawal on July 17. General Romano's Aosta Division was soughwest of Palermo, and it had to be moved a hundred miles to the Petralia-Nicosia Road, while General Erberto Papini's Assietta Division had to shift simultaneously to the north coast, where it was to take up positions between Termini Imerese and Cefalù.

It was too late now to carry Mobile Groups A and C with the two semimobile divisions, since they would be needed as rear guards, so Zingales created the ad hoc Mobile Group West under Colonel Rossi to cover the retreat and prevent Patton's spearheads from plowing into the rear of the withdrawing Aosta and Assietta divisions. Rossi's new command controlled Mobile Groups A, B, and C, which were about to clash with three divisions of Patton's victorious 3rd Army.

On July 18 Patton issued his orders for the drive on Palermo. He created a new corps on his left flank, placed it under his deputy army commander, Major General Geoffrey Keyes, and charged it with capturing the city. The new command, dubbed Provisional Corps, was given the 82nd Airborne, 3rd Infantry, and 2nd Armored divisions. Meanwhile, on the 7th Army's right flank, Bradley's IInd Corps was also ordered to advance. Allen's 1st Infantry Division was to take the western half of the Enna road net (including the city) while Middleton's 45th Division advanced northward along Highway 121 to cut the northern coastal road west of Palermo. Map 10 shows Patton's change of direction and the attempt of the Italians to deal with it.

Keyes jumped off at five A.M. on July 19, with the 82nd Airborne on his left and the 3rd Infantry on his right. The 2nd Armored was in corps reserve at Campobello, preparing to exploit a breakthrough toward Palermo.

Opposition to Keyes's advance was generally weak. Most of the Italian mobile units and all the Germans had been pulled out, leaving only the ineffective and demoralized Italian static divisions, which had, in effect, been abandoned by the Italian 6th Army because of a lack of transportation. Many of these men were Sicilian, and their morale was rock bottom.

"It was a pleasure march, shaking hands with Italians. . . ." Brigadier General Maxwell Taylor, deputy commander of the 82nd Airborne Division, recalled later, adding, "Nicest war I've ever been in!"[9]

It was also a rapid advance. The 504th Parachute Infantry Regiment advanced twenty-five miles by nightfall on July 19, capturing hundreds of prisoners along the way. The 3rd Infantry Division had similar experiences, advancing up to fifty-four miles in

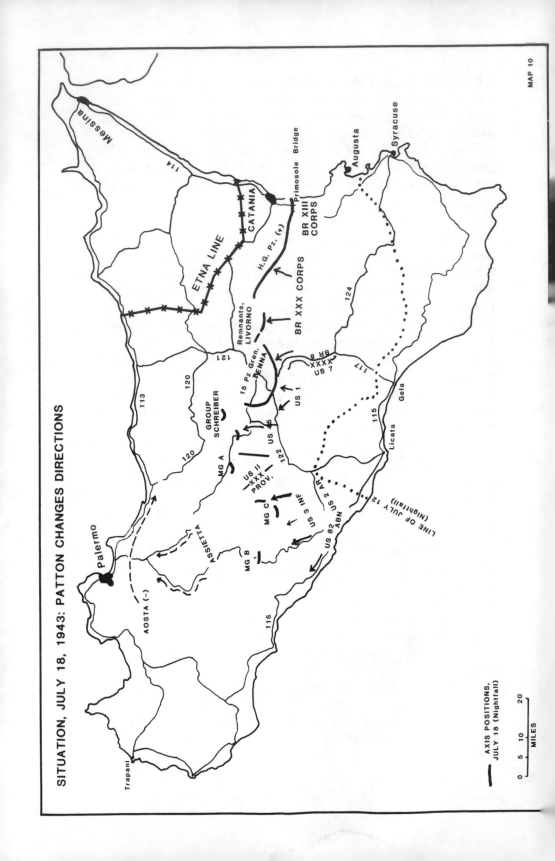

STITUATION, JULY 18, 1943: PATTON CHANGES DIRECTIONS

MAP 10

Messina

Palermo

Trapani

AOSTA (–)

ASSIETTA

MG B

MG C

MG A

GROUP SCHREIBER

113

120

120

121

115

US 45

US 1

US II PROV.
XXX

US 3 INF

US 82 ABN

US 2 AR

122

15 Pz Gren.

ENNA

Remnants, LIVORNO

ETNA LINE

CATANIA

114

H.G. Pz. (+)

BR XIII CORPS

Primosole Bridge

Augusta

Syracuse

BR XXX CORPS

124

BR 8
XXXX
US 7

117

Gela

Licata

115

LINE OF JULY 18 (Nightfall)

AXIS POSITIONS,
JULY 18 (Nightfall)

0   5   10   20
        MILES

thirty-three hours—on foot. At the same time, elements of the 1st Infantry Division took Enna, Guzzoni's former headquarters. This town had held out for thirty-one years against the Saracens in the Middle Ages. Now it fell without a fight.

"We're kicking the Krauts' and Spaghetti Benders' asses all over Sicily," a buoyant Patton told reporters,[10] jubilantly but not quite accurately. On his far-right flank the 1st Infantry Division was making only very slow progress against Lieutenant Colonel Fritz Fullriede's 129th Panzer Grenadier Regiment; elsewhere, however, the U.S. 7th Army advanced with incredible speed against the demoralized Italians, fanning out from Agrigento and Porto Empedocle in every direction, "like floodwater spreads after the dam is broken,"[11] as Map 11 indicates. Only Mobile Groups A, B, and C and Tactical Group Schreiber put up resistance worthy of the name. The static units of General Marciani's 208th Coastal Defense Division were facing the impossible task of halting Patton's young, aggressive, and superbly equipped Americans with an odd collection of sixty thousand demoralized, overaged, and ill-equipped policemen and Fascist militiamen who had no interest in dying for the glory of Mussolini's fading empire. Most of them wanted to go home—and many of them did just that.

To block the American spearheads, Colonel Rossi deployed his mobile groups at bottlenecks on the road nets. Mobile Group B delayed along Highway 118 on the right, while Mobile Group A delayed on the left, along Highway 121, north of Caltanissetta. Mobile Group C defended on the unimproved roads in Rossi's center. To the left (eastern) flank of Mobile Group West, Schreiber's tactical group was to fall back to the north, on the right flank of the 15th Panzer Grenadier Division.

On the night of July 17–18 Mobile Group C, reinforced by three 149-mm batteries from the 122nd Artillery Battalion, checked the American advance at Passo Fonduto, a narrow spot on the road fifteen miles north of Agrigento. After some heavy fighting the Italians fell back to Casteltermini. The following afternoon (July 19), this village was also taken by the Americans. That night Mobile Group C held blocking positions at Acquaviva against heavy attacks until four A.M. When it retreated, the group was in remnants and the 122nd Artillery Battalion had lost its last gun to a direct hit. It rallied at Cammarata Station on the ruined railroad and

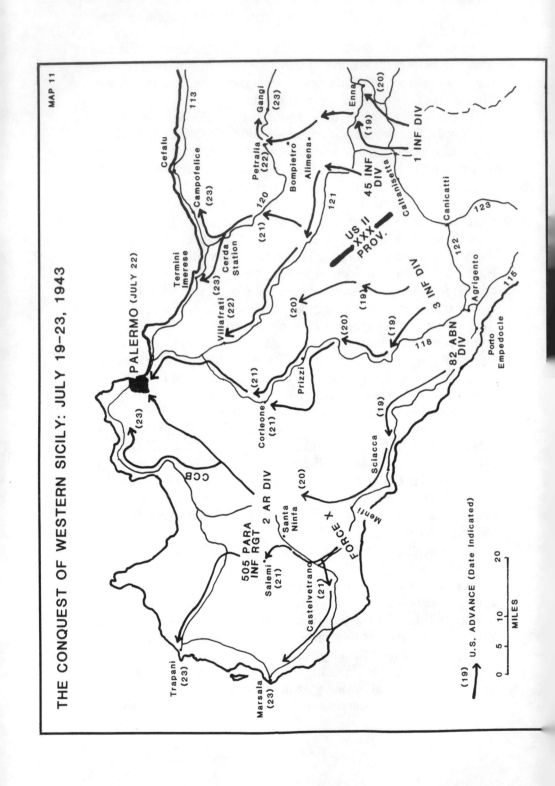

THE CONQUEST OF WESTERN SICILY: JULY 19–23, 1943

MAP 11

PALERMO (JULY 22)

Trapani (23)
Marsala (23)
Castelvetrano (21)
Salemi (21)
Santa Ninfa
505 PARA INF RGT
2 AR DIV
CCB
Corleone (21)
Prizzi
Menfi
Sciacca (19)
FORCE X
(20)
(21)
(20)
(19)
(19)
(20)
(19)
(19)
82 ABN DIV
Porto Empedocle
Agrigento
115
122
123
Canicatti
Caltanisetta
3 INF DIV
118
121
US II XXX PROV.
45 INF DIV
1 INF DIV
Enna
(20)
(19)
Gangi (23)
Petralia (22)
Bompietro
Alimena
120
(21)
Cerda Station
Villafrati (22)
Termini Imerese
Campofelice (23)
Cefalu
113
(23)
(23)

(19) U.S. ADVANCE (Date Indicated)

MILES
0   5   10   20

actually turned back an American attack at six A.M. This was followed, however, by an intensive artillery preparation and then by another attack at nine A.M. This time Mobile Group C could not withstand the pressure. It surrendered at 11:45 A.M. on July 20, opening Truscott's path into the rear of the retreating divisions of the XIIth Corps.

Mobile Group B was also overwhelmed. On the night of July 19 the vanguard of the U.S. 3rd Infantry Division, after a twenty-seven-mile foot march in the terrible Sicilian heat, pushed on to the heights overlooking the humble little town of San Stefano Quisquina. Here Mobile Group B, reinforced with the XIIth Corps's 1st Anti-Tank Battalion, made a last-ditch effort to halt the American advance. The fighting was fierce all morning on July 20, but by 1:30 P.M. the Americans were in a position to launch a coordinated attack on the town from three sides. Even so, San Stefano Quisquina did not fall until five P.M. The Italians lost more than 100 vehicles and 750 prisoners. Meanwhile, the U.S. 82nd Airborne Division took Menfi and Sciacca on the southwestern coast against token resistance on July 20, and elements of Middleton's 45th Infantry Division wiped out Mobile Group A and most of the 48th Artillery Battalion on Highway 121 on July 21.

Tactical Group Schreiber was also destroyed on July 21. The Americans, supported by tanks, had split it in half near Villalba railroad station on July 19, but Schreiber had managed to reconcentrate at Alimena that evening, blocking Middleton's way to Highway 120 and the coast. Everything seemed to be going well in this sector until two A.M. on July 21, when strong American units outflanked the group to the east and launched a surprise attack on the 17th Blackshirt Battalion, which was crushed. (This flank was supposed to have been screened by Cavalry Squadron Palermo but obviously was not. What happened to it is not known; apparently it just melted away.) In any event, at seven A.M., while Schreiber tried to organize a counterattack, the Thunderbirds attacked the III/30th Infantry Regiment and quickly surrounded it. The battalion surrendered at 8:30 A.M., and at 10 A.M., Sherman tanks rolled into Alimena. Tactical Group Schreiber ceased to exist, and it became every man for himself. Most of the group was captured, but a few men, including General Schreiber, made their way to German lines to the east. One final tragedy took place north of Alimena at 10:30 A.M., when German forward observers (FOs) spotted the remnants of the 19th "Centauro" Artillery Battalion, which was trying to escape the Americans. Mistaking it for a U.S. unit, the FOs called artillery fire in on it and wiped it out.

At noon, with Tactical Group Schreiber gone, about twenty American tanks pushed forward in the direction of Bompietro, but were halted by Group Fullriede of the 15th Panzer Grenadier Division. The Battle of Alimena was over.

After overwhelming the Italian rear guards, General Patton's rapidly moving spearheads plowed into the rear of the withdrawing columns of the Aosta and Assietta divisions. Most of them had already escaped, but several units had been delayed by transportation problems and/or Allied air attacks. The IInd Battalion of the 22nd Artillery Regiment was destroyed, as was Aosta's mortar battalion, the IInd Battalion of Aosta's 5th Infantry Regiment, the IInd and most of the IVth battalions of Assietta's 25th Artillery Regiment, and the III/29th (Assietta) Infantry Regiment. When the Assietta Division reached its new assembly areas between Cerda and Cerda Station, it included the I/ and II/29th Infantry Regiment, the II/30th Infantry Regiment, the remnants of the I/30th, two batteries of the IIIrd Battalion, 25th Artillery Regiment, two batteries of the 121st Artillery Regiment, and two batteries of the 157th Artillery Battalion. Its 48th Artillery Regiment was down to one gun. The Aosta Division was in a similar state of disrepair.[12]

During the night of July 20–21 Geoffrey Keyes committed the U.S. 2nd Armored Division on the left flank of Truscott's 3rd Infantry, sparking a race for the Sicilian capital that partisans for both divisions later claimed they won. On the other side of the hill, meanwhile, the Italian and German commanders woke up to the fact that Palermo was doomed, and the mobile units that were still intact were rapidly ordered eastward. Most of the German anti-aircraft units and supply troops were evacuated in time by railroad, trucks, or naval lighters, three of which were sunk by Allied airplanes. Very little equipment could be brought off, however. Colonel Mayer, the German antiaircraft commander at Palermo, was not able to withdraw his guns in time, but at least he destroyed them, which in most cases the Italians did not. Meanwhile, the small Axis naval contingents hastily departed for Naples, while the airport commander blew up his petrol tanks just before the few remaining aircraft took off. At that point even Reichsmarschall Hermann Goering took an interest in the evacuation of Palermo. He sent orders commanding Admiral Ruge to evacuate the porphyry sarcophagi of the Emperors Henry VI and Frederick II from the cathedral, but these orders were quietly ignored. Ruge did not have time to evacuate all of the German supplies; he had neither the time nor the inclination to engage in plundering.

On July 21 elements of the 82nd Airborne Division occupied the important road junction of Castelvetrano and took four hundred prisoners, who surrendered without a fight, but with "great pomp and ceremony," according to the 2nd Armoured Division's historian.[13] All totaled, almost four thousand Italians surrendered to the American vanguards that day, and there was no significant opposition anywhere. Many of the infantry units of the 202nd Coastal Defense Division "self-demobilized" (i.e., simply vanished). There were, however, still isolated incidents of heroism. With a few of his men, the commander of the 20th Coastal Defense Battalion fought to the last round. Then he stood up, threw down his weapon, bared his chest, and shouted, "Here's a good target!" He was immediately shot dead.[14]

Patton's men closed in on Palermo on July 22. They were now in the zone of tough Generale di Brigata Giuseppe Molinero's Port Defense "N," and his preparations for the defense of the city were quite solid. Each road into Palermo was blocked by infantry companies supported by antitank guns, occupying numerous improved positions built by conscripted civilian laborers; nevertheless, each defensive task force just melted away. The only organized resistance took place at Portella della Paglia, where a single Italian company under Major Mistretta put up a short fight. The Americans were hampered more by blown bridges and scattered mines than by anything else.

The 2nd Armored Division had outrun its supply lines and was being propelled by captured Italian gas without any ill effects on the Shermans. The American infantrymen, who had also outrun their supply lines and had to resort to drinking the local water, could not make the same statement. Still, they were more than a match for their opponents, whose resistance was rapidly crumbling. General Marciani went forward, apparently to try to rally his troops, but instead ran into a forward patrol of the 2nd Armored Division, which took him prisoner. The responsibility for the defense of Palermo devolved onto Generale di Brigata Giuseppe Molinero,[15] who was captured a few hours later.

The scar-faced General Molinero recognized the hopelessness of the situation and offered to surrender the city to General Keyes, who promptly accepted. Keyes and Molinero entered the city that evening, and the formal capitulation took place in a ceremony at the Royal Palace at seven P.M. By eight P.M. elements of the 2nd Armored and 3rd Infantry divisions were entering the city from opposite ends. An hour later General Patton entered the Sicilian capital, where streets full of people greeted him with shouts of "Long live America" and "Down with Mussolini." Patton observed later that the provincial governor had fled, "but we captured two Generals, both of whom said that they were glad to be captured because Sicilians were not human beings, but animals."[16] As if to underscore his words, the city was swept with an orgy of rioting and looting that night.

Patton's soldiers entered Palermo in strength on July 23 and found a city battered by bombs. Earlier that spring Allied bombers, attempting to raid the Roccadaforte airport and the waterfront, had missed. They had gutted much of the city, including several palaces and churches. They had also started the destruction of the harbor, a process completed by the Germans. The Americans found forty-four ships sunk in the harbor; its value as a port was nil. Seventh Army immediately rushed two engineer regiments to the port, because it was absolutely vital to have the harbor functioning as rapidly as possible. Patton's army simply could not be sustained from the small and now distant harbors of Gela, Licata, and Porto Empedocle.

The engineers did an excellent job under the circumstances. The harbor was first opened to shipping on July 27, and by the next day it was operating at 30 percent of capacity. That same day Naval Operating Base Palermo was established, and by July 30—only eight days after its capture—the port of Palermo was operating at 60 percent of its normal capacity. By August 1 the U.S. Navy was able to simultaneously unload twelve transports, which were carrying troops of the U.S. 9th Infantry Division to Sicily. At the same time the men of the U.S. 727th Railway Operating

Battalion also performed a minor miracle. They had the Sicilian railroad system operating at partial capacity in the south and central parts of the island and by July 29 had the northern shore rail line operating from Palermo to Cefalù, which was now in the hands of Middleton's 45th Infantry Division. As a result of these efforts, the American army would be at least adequately supplied when it turned east toward Messina.

Meanwhile, George S. Patton set himself up in a style befitting a conquerer, although he steadfastly insisted that his old friend Geoffrey Keyes be given credit for the capture of Palermo. Patton took up residence in the royal palace and, disliking the local water, decided to drink only champagne. Unfortunately, the thirsty general and his staff soon exhausted the local supply. When he learned that a local bootlegger was in jail, Patton had him released and gave him an order for a large amount of champagne. When the man delivered the booze, Patton had him sent back to jail—apparently without paying him for the champagne.

As Patton and the engineers set about solving their logistical problems, Middleton's 45th Infantry Division cut the northern coastal road (Highway 113) at Station Cerda at nine A.M. on July 23. The former National Guardsmen had advanced eighty miles on foot in five days over very difficult terrain, against sporadic resistance from the remnants of the Italian units that once formed the left flank of Tactical Group Schreiber. After reaching the sea, the American vanguard advanced eastward along the coastal road toward Messina until it was stopped near Campofelice by Colonel Max Ulich's 15th Panzer Grenadier Regiment, the advance unit of Major General Walter Fries's 29th Panzer Grenadier Division. Here Middleton halted to await resupply and reinforcements from the rest of 7th Army.

That same day Major General Ridgway's 82nd Airborne Division, with Colonel Darby's Task Force X attached, began the task of clearing western Sicily. This was not to be a difficult operation. Colonel Darby's men occupied Mazara del Vallo and Marsala on July 23, and the small port of Castellammare del Golfo surrendered to Colonel Tucker's 504th Parachute Infantry Regiment on the afternoon of July 24 without a fight. The big prize, however, was Trapani, which Ridgway attacked at four P.M. Vice Admiral

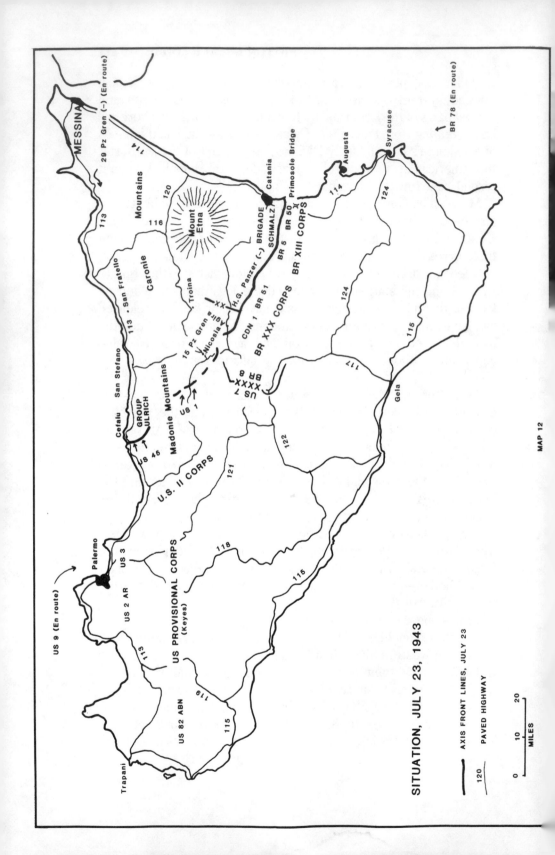

SITUATION, JULY 23, 1943

━━━ AXIS FRONT LINES, JULY 23

━━━ PAVED HIGHWAY

120

MILES

0   10   20

MAP 12

Giuseppe Manfredi surrendered Naval Fortress Area Trapani to him at about seven P.M. The Americans suffered one casualty when a paratrooper severely burned himself while firing his own weapon. The next day the small Italian garrison of the Egadi Islands in Trapani harbor also surrendered to General Ridgway.

This was the last act of the campaign in western Sicily. The Provisional Corps, which now consisted of only the 82nd Airborne and 2nd Armored divisions, settled down to occupation duties until it was dissolved on August 20. During the Battle of Western Sicily, it had captured 189 guns of 75 mm or larger, 359 vehicles, 45 tanks, and thousands of Italian soldiers. It had also demonstrated the power and mobility of the American Army. Its newly earned status was amply demonstrated on July 23, when Montgomery sent Patton a message of congratulations and invited him to spend a night at 8th Army Headquarters, where they could discuss the capture of Messina. Map 12 shows the situation at the end of that day—in essence at the end of the first phase of the campaign.

Patton arrived at Syracuse on July 25, and Monty greeted him cordially. Much to his surprise, the British commander offered 7th Army both major northern roads (Highways 113 and 120) for the drive on Messina. Although Patton was still privately suspicious, Montgomery's motives were straightforward enough: he now wanted the help of Patton and the four proven divisions, which he planned to bring against the right wing of Hube's XIVth Panzer Corps.

Alexander also arrived in Syracuse on July 25, but only after Monty and Patton had settled on their strategy. Alex was quite brusque with his two principal subordinates (presumably because they had seen no need to consult him when they had decided how to end the campaign), but, in the end, he approved their plans. On August 1, after a few preliminary operations, the U.S. 7th and British 8th armies would launch a coordinated offensive, the goal of which was to force all Axis forces to surrender or evacuate the island. In physical terms, this meant that both armies had the same goal: Messina, the primary military objective of the campaign since the planning stage had begun. Both generals wanted it, and Patton in particular was obsessed with capturing it. The first phase of operations was now over. The second phase—the "Race for Messina"—was about to begin.

THE BATTLES OF THE HAUPTKAMPFLINIE

ON JULY 24 FIELD MARSHALL KESSELRING AND HIS CHIEF OF STAFF, Major General Siegfried Westphal, visited Mussolini in the famous Palazzo Venezia, the fifteenth-century palace that had housed the Austro-Hungarian Embassy until World War I. Contrary to his custom, the dictator kept the Germans waiting half an hour. Mussolini then emerged and "with jovial excitement" asked Kesselring, "Do you know Count Grandi? He just visited me. We have spoken out our minds, we are moving along the same line. He is completely loyal to me."[1]

That night the Fascist Grand Council met and voted nineteen to eight (with one abstention) to turn command of the armed forces over to the king, in effect presenting Mussolini with a vote of no confidence from his own party. The motion was introduced by none other than Count Dino Grandi, and it was supported by Galeazzo Ciano, Mussolini's own son-in-law.

General Westphal wrote later, "judgment of character was not one of Mussolini's strong points."[2] The next morning the Duce visited the royal residence at Villa Savoia, where King Victor Emmanuel forced him to resign. Outside the palace a few moments later the stunned former dictator was arrested by a squad of carabinieri, was hustled into a waiting ambulance, and disappeared. He was replaced by Marshal Pietro Badoglio, a longtime political backstabber and a known anti-Nazi.

After a day of excited rumors, news of Mussolini's overthrow and arrest was broadcast from Rome that evening, along with official proclamations from Badoglio and the king. There was dancing in the streets as the Italian people sang, paraded in jubilation, and wept with joy. They thought that the overthrow meant the end of the war. Mobs attacked Fascist party officers, desecrated Fascist statues and monuments, and tore down every Fascist symbol they could find, including those on the lapels of private citizens. There were incidents of Fascist militiamen being caught before they could get home to change. These unfortunates were stripped, ridiculed, and sent home in their underwear. "The King struck one resolute blow at their leader, and without any resistance or violence the whole Fascist structure collapsed," Badoglio wrote. "Fascism fell, as was fitting, like a rotten pear."[3] "The fact is, the whole Fascist movement went pop, like a soap bubble!" General Jodl exclaimed to Adolf Hitler.[4] By dawn the next day, not a Fascist emblem was to be seen and all the Fascist leaders had gone underground or into hiding. It was as if Mussolini, his party, and their alliance with Adolf Hitler had never existed.

When Adolf Hitler learned that his partner had been deposed, his reaction was one of alarm bordering on panic. He ordered Jodl to begin preparing for the evacuation of Sicily immediately. "The fellows down here [in Sicily] have to be saved under all circumstances," the excited Fuehrer snapped. "They are of no use down here. They have to get back. Especially the paratroopers and men from the 'Goering.' Their equipment doesn't matter a damn. Let them blow it up or destroy it; but the men have to get back."[5]

Hitler paused long enough in his tirade to make some jokes about General Hube, who saw no sense in destroying the heavy equipment of an entire panzer corps and who reported that the military situation in Sicily and Italy was quite stable. "You see how dangerous it is when 'apolitical generals' get into such a political atmosphere," he smirked.[6]

Hube was quite accurate in his assessment of the situation. General Guzzoni, who apparently had no idea of the political machinations going on in Rome, sincerely expressed complete surprise at Mussolini's overthrow. He issued a communiqué to his army, stressing loyalty to the Axis and stating that the war would continue, and Hube believed him—quite correctly, as events later proved. The evacuation of Sicily had already been accepted as long-term policy, but the overthrow of Mussolini, while serious, was no cause for panic at Hube's headquarters. The panzer troops still held the Hauptkampflinie and would for the foreseeable future. What mattered now was that XIVth Panzer Corps continue to tie down the U.S. 7th and British 8th armies while Hitler, Kesselring, and others secured his rear by infiltrating German troops into Italy and simultaneously prepared to occupy the entire peninsula if need be. This was the strategy the Germans eventually adopted.

On July 26 the German public was coolly informed that Mussolini had resigned because of ill health but that this involved no change in Italian policy. Hitler pretended that he fully accepted the declarations of loyalty from Badoglio and Victor Emmanuel. "We still have to plan ahead," a calmer Fuehrer told his staff. "Undoubtedly in their treachery they will proclaim that they will remain loyal to us. Of course they won't. . . . We'll play the same game while preparing everything to take over the whole area with one stroke, and capture all that riffraff."[7] Meanwhile, he picked another apolitical soldier to deal with what he called "Italian treachery": Field Marshal Erwin Rommel, whom he had recently sent to the Balkans.

The first German military reaction to the Italian coup took place within hours of the Desert Fox's return to Rastenburg. That night the 305th Infantry Division began to move from the interior of France toward Nice, where the Italian 4th Army was concentrated. At the same time the 44th Infantry Division "Hoch und Deutschmeister" began to move toward the vital Brenner Pass. Both divisions were placed under Rommel's command, as were the troops of the Mittenwald Mountain Warfare School and three battle groups of Tiger tanks. Rommel was to direct operations from Bavaria, where his Headquarters, Army Group B, was camouflaged as "High Command Rehabilitation Unit, Munich." For the time being Rommel and his staff were ordered not to show their faces in Austria, much less in Italy.

On the other side of the hill the overthrow of Mussolini also took the Allies by surprise. It was impossible for them, as yet, to state even the most basic terms of peace with Italy other than unconditional surrender. "The Allies even lacked a set of armistice terms for an Italy offering to surrender," the U.S. Official History states.[8] President Roosevelt's reaction was ambiguous. He cabled Churchill and backed off slightly from his previous policy of demanding unconditional surrender, although he added that if the Italians did make peace overtures, the terms should be as close to unconditional surrender as possible.

Churchill's attitude was also ambiguous. He wanted to gain the active aid of the Italian armed forces in defeating the Germans even if it meant that the Italian government would retain sovereignty on the mainland. Nevertheless, on July 27 he told the House of Commons, "We should let the Italians . . . stew in their own juices a bit." Neither he nor Roosevelt seemed to appreciate that time was of the essence if a German occupation was to be forestalled. At that moment Italy was, in fact, a political power vacuum, but this situation was transitory. Nature hates a vacuum, whether it is physical or geopolitical, and Adolf Hitler could not be counted upon to remain inactive forever. The only person on the Allied side who seemed to grasp this fact, however, was Dwight D. Eisenhower.

General Eisenhower realized immediately that the Allies had an opportunity that would not present itself again. On July 26, the day after Mussolini's arrest, he ordered Lieutenant General Mark Clark, commander of the U.S. 5th Army in North Africa, to speed up the detailed planning of Operation Avalanche, the main Allied amphibious assault on the Italian mainland. One division was to be put on immediate alert and was to be prepared to sail to Naples on command. Via radio broadcasts, he urged the king to make immediate contact with the Allied supreme commander (himself) for the purpose of arranging an armistice. He also drew up a set of armistice terms and asked for authority to negotiate the Italian surrender on behalf of the Allies.

On July 27 Eisenhower privately regretted the existence of rapid communications, because without the interference of his political bosses he believed that he could now directly offer the Italians sufficiently favorable terms to pull them away from the Germans. Had he been able to do so, he would have been able to land unopposed on the peninsula with his U.S. 5th Army, thus cutting off the XIVth Panzer Corps, which would eventually have to surrender. With the help of the Italian armed forces, much of Italy could have been occupied at little cost to the Allies, because the Germans were at that time too weak on the ground to stop them. Eisenhower was, however, prevented from acting by his superiors. The next day, July 28, General Marshall telegraphed Ike and informed him that the British government (i.e., Churchill) believed that a surrender of Italy involved political and economic as well as military conditions. The British viewed Eisenhower's authority as being limited to purely local surrenders. Franklin

Roosevelt agreed and stated that Eisenhower should not fix general terms without the approval of both governments.

Eisenhower responded the next day by requesting authority from both governments empowering him to state general surrender terms; otherwise, he warned, "the prospect of obtaining Italian cooperation in seizing vital ports and airfields might be lost."[9] No such authority was forthcoming, however, and the opportunity was lost. As a result of the rejection of Eisenhower's plea, no individual or team of diplomats was empowered to negotiate for the Allies. The Allies could not speak with one voice, they would not even attempt to contact the Italians, and their surrender terms remained inflexible.

To make matters even worse, the Allied political leaders tipped their hand to Hitler. On July 28 Churchill made a speech to the House of Commons in which he stated that nothing short of "wholesale unconditional surrender" could prevent Italy from being "seared and scarred and blackened from one end to the other."[10] The next day he spoke to President Roosevelt on the transatlantic telephone. The two leaders gossiped gaily about the "imminent armistice with Italy" with total disregard for security, completely unaware that the conversation was being monitored by SS intelligence experts. Hitler received a transcript of the conversation the next day. From it, the Fuehrer correctly deduced that Roosevelt was in secret contact with the king but that several weeks would pass before Italy could defect because the terms of the armistice had not yet been worked out.[11]

Hitler now knew that he need not take chances; he would be able to infiltrate his units gradually into Italy without provoking a joint Italian-Allied reaction. He also knew that Hube could continue his delaying action in Sicily, confident that his rear was not in danger—at least for the moment. At Fuehrer Headquarters there would be no further talk of blowing up the panzers, abandoning the heavy equipment, and fleeing across the Straits of Messina with just the "valuable human material." Now Hube was free to fight a prolonged action, inflicting as many casualties on the Allies as possible while simultaneously planning a controlled, phased evacuation of the island.

During the week of July 23–30, when Rome, London, Washington, and Rastenburg were beehives of activity, a lull descended along most of the German front. Patton had to mop up western Sicily, regroup, and turn east against Hube, while Montgomery awaited the arrival of the British 78th Infantry Division before launching his next major offensive. Hube used the period of relative quiet to pull back his outposts while he consolidated his main battle positions along the Hauptkampflinie (the Main Defensive Line), which extended from San Stefano on the north coast, due south to Nicosia, southeast to Agira, east to positions south of Regalbuto, and southeast again to Catenanuova, Sferro, and Gerbini. It reached the east coast four miles south of Catania. These planned operations were temporarily disrupted on the night of July 22–23, when the 171st Blackshirt Battalion went over to the enemy and uncovered Mistretta, creating a vacuum northeast of Group Fullriede.[12] Hube was forced to give ground for a few days, but he managed to prevent a breakthrough, and by July 26 he had his regiments fairly well sorted out and organized into three sectors. The right (northern) flank he assigned to Major General Walter Fries's 29th Panzer Grenadier Division, part of which was still in transit. Remnants of the Assietta Division, under the command of Generale di Brigata Francesco Scotti until July 26, were also assigned positions in this sector, which extended from San Stefano to a point south of Mistretta. The center was the responsibility of Major General Rodt's 15th Panzer Grenadier Division, which included the remnants of General Giacomo Romano's Aosta Division and elements of Livorno. The German 382nd Panzer Grenadier Regiment (two battalions) was also attached to Rodt's division.

Paul Conrath's Hermann Goering Division held the German left (southern) flank from positions north of Leonforte to the sea near Catania. Group Schmalz, which still held the far left flank just north of the Primosole Bridge, was again under Conrath's command. The 3rd and 4th Parachute regiments were still attached to the H.G. Division, as were the 115th Panzer Grenadier Regiment, the 923rd Fortress Battalion, and Fortress Battalion Reggio. Part of this sector was occupied by elements of Generale di Brigata Azzo Passalacqua's Port Defense "E" (Catania) and the few extant elements of the 213th Coastal Defensive Division and the very few intact remnants of the Napoli Division.

Behind the Hauptkampflinie, which was also known as the San Stefano Line, German engineers were already preparing a second defensive zone, the Etna Line, extending from San Fratello to Troina to Adrano and Acireale, on the east coast north of Catania. In many sectors this line was stronger than the Main Defensive Line, and the territory between them was filled with many excellent intermediate delaying positions. A breach in the San Stefano Line would in no sense be fatal to the German defense so long as the defenders retreated in time and avoided a decisive engagement.

While Hube and his subordinates adjusted their units for the next onslaught, Patton and Montgomery decided that, beginning on August 1, the U.S. 7th Army would advance eastward along two axes: the northern coastal road (Highway 113) and the parallel inland route (Highway 120). Their initial objective would be the north-south San Stefano–Nicosia Road, which gave Hube lateral communications in his northern sector. Initially, Middleton's 45th Infantry Division would advance along the coastal route while Allen's 1st Infantry Division took the inland route. Bradley's IInd Corps would direct both advances. The British were also to resume the offensive on August 1, with Leese's XXXth Corps launching the main attack. Its objective was to break the Hauptkampflinie and the Etna Line and capture Adrano. It was to be spearheaded by Major General Vivian Evelegh's fresh 78th Division, which was to advance along the Axis Catenanuova-Centuripe-Adrano. Simond's 1st Canadian Infantry Division on Evelegh's left was to advance through Regalbuto and the Salso valley while the 51st Highland Division supported Evelegh on his right. Simultaneous with the XXXth Corps' attack, Dempsey's XIIIth Corps was to create the impression that the main attack was going to be launched in the Catania sector in order to tie down the German reserves.

Facing Patton's main attack was the bulk of Major General Water Fries's 29th Panzer Grenadier Division in defensive positions along the northern coastal road. This unit was commanded by a veteran panzer officer who had a reputation as a skillful commander of motorized forces.

Walter Fries, a big, good-looking Prussian, was born at Guesternheim/Dillkreis on April 22, 1894. Raised in the Prussian military tradition, he joined the 80th Fusilier Regiment as a Fahnenjunker on October 1, 1912, when he was eighteen years of age. He was commissioned second lieutenant of reserves on January 19, 1915. In the meantime World War I broke out, and Fries's regiment was sent to the Western Front, where it formed part of the 21st Infantry Division, a unit Allied intelligence rated as first-class throughout the war.[13] Fries became a company commander in the 80th Fusiliers in August 1915 and led this unit until the Armistice. During the process he was awarded both grades of the Iron Cross (i.e., 1st and 2nd classes).

At the end of the conflict Fries returned to Germany, where he was released from the defeated army on December 30, 1918. In 1919 he became a second lieutenant in the state police of his native Prussia. He applied himself diligently to his work during the years of the Weimar Republic, rising to first lieutenant in 1920, captain in 1925, and major in 1934. That same year he became police adjutant to General Goering, the police president of Prussia. Apparently Walter Fries did not care for this duty (or for Herr Goering), for he put in several requests for a transfer to the active military. Finally, in March 1936 he got his wish and was appointed major on the staff of the newly activated 34th Infantry Division at Heidelberg (Wehrkreis XII), with a date of rank of July 1, 1935.

Walter Fries first became associated with the 29th Division in October 1935, when he received his first troop command: the IInd Battalion of the division's 15th Motorized Infantry Regiment. The 29th (then an infantry division) was stationed at Kassel at the time and was in the process of motorizing. Fries, who had already gained valuable experience in the use of motor vehicles while an officer in the Prussian police, was entering on the ground floor as far as the panzer arm was concerned.

Fries was very happy with his new unit and did well in his new command. He was promoted to lieutenant colonel on March 1, 1938, and led his battalion in the invasions of Poland, Belgium, and France, again winning both classes of the Iron Cross. In November 1940 he was advanced to regimental command when he took over the newly motorized 87th Regiment of the 36th Motorized Infantry Division at Kaiserslautern. The new commander made the 87th one of the crack regiments in the Wehrmacht and was rewarded with a promotion to full colonel on March 1, 1941. Fries and his regiment fought in the northern sector of the Eastern Front during Operation Barbarossa and played a major role in the overrunning of the Baltic states and in the defensive fighting south of Leningrad in early 1942. For his exploits Walter Fries was decorated with the Knight's Cross in December 1941.

The veteran 36th Division was sent to the Rzhev salient in 1942, where Walter Model's 9th Army was boxed in on three sides by the numerically superior Soviets. Again and again Fries's well-drilled and indomitable regiment acted as a fire brigade for the whole perimeter, checking several Russian attempts to break the lines and surround the 9th Army. Finally, on September 3, Fries was defending around Leuschino, the corner post of the entire defensive perimeter. He had successfully repulsed several heavy Soviet attacks there in August despite terrible losses. His lines held on this day as well, but his luck did not. An entire stick of enemy artillery shells slammed into his command post, killing or severely wounding everyone inside. Fries was rushed back to Germany, where his left leg and left arm had to be amputated. No one believed he would ever recover.

Fries fooled them all. With iron determination he not only lived but recovered rapidly. He was fitted with a prosthetic leg and, by almost superhuman effort, was back on limited active duty on January 3, 1943, as an instructor to third-year students at the Doberitz Infantry School. Meanwhile, the war in the East had gone badly for the Third Reich, and Germany needed all its experienced panzer officers. Within two months the wounded colonel was sent to France to take command of the 29th Panzer Grenadier Division, the reincarnation of his old 29th Motorized, which had been destroyed at Stalingrad.

The new division was created primarily from the 345th Motorized Infantry Division, which was officially absorbed by the 29th Panzer Grenadier on March 1, 1943, the day Fries assumed command.[14] He moved it to Toulouse in May, to Nice in June, and to the Foggia-Lucera area of Italy by early July. The division was fully motorized by July 1. Table 5 shows its order of battle in July 1943. Fries was promoted to major general effective June 1, 1943. When the Allies landed in Sicily on July 10, he immediately rushed his division to the Tyrrhenian coast near Palmi, less than twenty miles from the Straits of Messina, and awaited developments.

In addition to Fries, the 29th Panzer Grenadier Division had a roster of talented and experienced officers, led by their three regimental commanders: Colonel Max Ulich of the 15th Panzer

TABLE 5

ORDER OF BATTLE, 29th PANZER GRENADIER DIVISION

Commanding General: Major General Walter Fries
  Ia: Lieutenant Colonel (General Staff) von Stuenzer
  Ib: Captain (General Staff) Oster
  Adjutant: Captain von Bassewitz
  Division Medical Officer: Colonel Dr. Neis

15th Panzer Grenadier Regiment: Colonel Ulich
  Ist Battalion: Captain Hufschmidt
  IInd Battalion: Captain Baron von Humboldt
  IIIrd (Jaeger) Battalion: Captain Dyck

71st Panzer Grenadier Regiment: Lieutenant Colonel Krueger
  Ist Battalion: Major von Tschischwitz
  IInd Battalion: Captain Schneider
  IIIrd Battalion: Captain Spohr

29th Motorized Artillery Regiment: Colonel Dr. Polack
  Ist Battalion: Captain Kammerer
  IInd Battalion: Captain Keil
  IIIrd Battalion: Captain Woebbeking

129th Panzer Battalion: Captain Nill
129th Panzer Reconnaissance Battalion: Major Ziegler
29th Engineer Battalion: Captain Holzapfel
313rd Army Flak Battalion: Major Schlunk
29th Signal Battalion: Captain Grotz
Division Supply Trains: Major Hagen
Division Motor Park: Lieutenant Colonel Dyke

SOURCES: Kurowski, *Tor,* pp. 164–65; Fries, *MS # T-la.*

Grenadier; Lieutenant Colonel Walter Krueger of the 71st Panzer Grenadier; and Colonel Dr. Fritz Polack of the 29th Motorized Artillery.

Max Ulich was born in a suburb of Berlin on March 25, 1896. He volunteered for duty with the Imperial Army at the outbreak of the Great War (August 2, 1914) and was commissioned second lieutenant in the 24th Infantry Regiment on June 2, 1915. This Brandenburg unit, one of the best in the German army, spent the entire war on the Western Front, and Lieutenant Ulich served with considerable merit. As a result, after the Armistice he was selected for the elite four-thousand-man officer corps of the Reichsheer.

Ulich's service in the Reichswehr was undistinguished. By 1937 he had only reached the rank of major and was on the instruction staff of the inspectorate of infantry. In 1939, however, he was promoted to lieutenant colonel and assumed command of the Ist Battalion of the 15th Motorized Infantry Regiment, a unit he was associated with until late 1943, except for the period from May to mid-September 1941, when he commanded the instruction staff of the infantry school at Doberitz. Ulich assumed command of the 15th Regiment on September 20, 1941, and was promoted to full colonel on December 1 of the year. He fought in Poland, Luxembourg, Belgium, France, and Russia, where the 15th Motorized was largely destroyed in the Stalingrad pocket. Ulich took the remnants back to France for regrouping and then on to Sicily as the vanguard of the 29th Panzer Grenadier Division.

Fritz Polack was born at Gera, Thuringia, on October 22, 1892. He joined the Imperial Army as an officer-cadet in 1911, was commissioned in 1912, and served in the foot artillery in World War I. Mustered out in April 1920, Polack returned to school and received his doctorate in political theory from Friedrich Schiller University. He rejoined the army as a captain in December 1934 and by 1938 was a major, commanding the IIIrd Battalion, 29th Artillery Regiment. After the campaign in Poland he was transferred to the *Lehr* (Demonstration) Artillery Regiment in February 1940 and was promoted to lieutenant colonel on August 1, 1940. He became commander of the Lehr Regiment in May 1941 and on February 1, 1942, was promoted to full colonel. All this time he continued to turn out capable young officers, NCOs, and men for the Wehrmacht.

Dr. Polack, however, was unhappy with a training assignment in wartime. In October 1942, in response to his repeated requests, Polack was sent to the Russian Front, where he assumed command of the 140th Panzer Artillery Regiment of the newly formed 22nd Panzer Division. He remained with this ill-fated unit until December, when his regiment was dissolved and he was transferred to the artillery staff of Baron von Weichs's Army Group B. When the army group headquarters was pulled out of Russia in

March 1943, Polack was sent to France to take over command of the 29th Motorized Artillery Regiment.

The junior regimental commander of the 29th Division, Lieutenant Colonel Walter Krueger, was a Sudeten German. Born in 1902, he migrated to Bavaria with his family in 1920, after the Treaty of Versailles turned the Sudetenland over to the newly created nation of Czechoslovakia. Young Krueger entered the police service and remained there until the end of the Weimer Republic and the advent of National Socialism. Commissioned into the Reichswehr (soon to be the Wehrmacht) as a captain, he went to war with the elite Grossdeutschland Motorized Infantry Regiment, where, as a major, he commanded the IIIrd Battalion during the bitter battles before Moscow during the winter of 1941–1942. In March 1943, after further service on the Russian Front, he was sent to France and named commander of the 71st Panzer Grenadier Regiment.

As we have seen, the commitment of the 29th Panzer Grenadier Division to the Battle of Sicily was an on-again, off-again affair. The I/15th Panzer Grenadier Regiment (Captain Georg Hufschmidt) was the first battalion across, being ferried over on July 14, but then Hitler's first halt order arrived. The I/15th was attached to Rodt's 15th Division and was not returned to its parent formation until the Sicilian campaign was over.

From July 14 to 18, the 29th Division was held in reserve at Reggio, while the 15th Panzer Grenadier Division was responsible for the entire sector from the right flank of the Hermann Goering Division to the north coast east of Palermo. Hube, of course, knew that this sector would be too large for one division once Patton took the Sicilian capital. With this in mind, he secured permission to ferry across Group Ulich on July 18.

Group Ulich consisted of the IInd and IIIrd (Jaeger) battalions of Colonel Ulich's own 15th Panzer Grenadier Regiment, led by Captain Baron von Humboldt and Captain Dyck, respectively. The group was augmented by the IIIrd (heavy) Battalion of the 29th Motorized Artillery Regiment and the 1st Company of the 29th Engineer Battalion. It was held in corps reserve in the Taormina–Francavilla sector until July 22, when Hube ordered it to take up positions along the northern coastal highway between Cefalù and Palermo. It was temporarily attached to Rodt's 15th Panzer Grenadier Division, whose forward command post was now located near Nicosia.

Ulich's road march to Cefalù was not easy, because every Axis airplane on the island had been evacuated or destroyed. Allied fighters and fighter-bombers were everywhere, and Ulich's men lost fifty vehicles and a battery of artillery before they even saw an American infantryman.

Meanwhile, on July 21 Hitler reluctantly ordered the rest of the division to cross into Sicily. Kesselring passed the order on to Fries on July 22, and the bulk of the division made the trip across the straits via Siebel ferry on July 23. The only divisional units that did not make the crossing, other than a few supply elements, were the 129th Panzer Reconnaissance Battalion and the 129th Panzer Battalion (minus one company), which remained on the mainland to provide coastal protection.[15]

The order committing the 29th Panzer Grenadiers did not come one day too soon for Hans Valentin Hube, who now had at least a chance of holding his northern flank against George S. Patton. As the mass of Fries's troops rushed across the straits, the IIIrd Jaeger Battalion of Group Ulich dug into positions commanding the coastal road east of Termini Imerese; simultaneously, the forward patrols of Middleton's 45th U.S. Infantry Division advanced down the road from the west. After making contact with the Americans, Ulich conducted a delaying action while awaiting reinforcements.

During the next two days—July 24 and 25—Group Ulich was joined by the 71st Panzer Grenadier Regiment, the bulk of the 29th Motorized Artillery Regiment, and Fries and his headquarters. Hube now had established a thin but continuous line from coast to coast, occupied from north to south by the 29th Panzer Grenadier Division, the 15th Panzer Grenadier Division, the Hermann Goering Panzer Division, and Brigade Schmalz. Within the zone of each German unit were a number of Italian units, which were variously causing trouble for or lending assistance to their Teutonic allies.

Considerable friction had existed between the Germans and the Italians in Sicily prior to the fall of Mussolini. The Germans were afraid that the Italians would run away without fighting, and the Italians were afraid that the Germans would retreat without warning them, as they had sometimes done in Africa and Russia. The Germans—especially the Goerings—used some pretty desperate measures to solidify the backbones of their Italian comrades. "The Germans have, on several occasions, put mines in behind the Italians," General Patton wrote in his diary, "so that when the Italians attempt to run, they get blown up. This naturally does not make the Italians love the Germans."[16] Indeed, Lieutenant General Conrath's contempt for the Italians was well known. On August 24, for example, he officially reported to OB South that "90% of the Italian Army are cowards and do not want to fight."[17] This type of attitude naturally transmitted itself throughout the division and exacerbated the problem of cooperation.

The fall of Mussolini on July 25 increased the friction but did not bring about a wholesale defection of Italian units—thanks in part to the efforts of General Guzzoni[18]—although the number of individual desertions did increase. Most of the Italian army had already ceased fighting. Of the original four mobile divisions, only Aosta and Assietta still had some combat power, and they were being used only to cover gaps, screen outposts, and occupy relatively quiet sections of the front when no German units were available. They were not used to fighting in major battles unless it was absolutely unavoidable.

Command relationships had also changed since Hube and his staff set up their tactical headquarters east of Randazzo, on the northern slope of Mount Etna, on July 16 and 17. In theory, XIVth Panzer Corps was under the command of the Italian 6th Army; in reality, this relationship was reversed. Hube, however, genuinely respected the elderly Guzzoni, who was obviously embarrassed by the painfully obvious fact that Commando Supremo was not sending any reinforcements to Sicily. Hube was very careful not to offend or further humiliate him. Prior to Patton's arrival on the northern coast, for example, Hube made no effort to assume command of that sector. As Patton neared Palermo, however, this situation changed because Hube did not want his right flank guarded solely by his unreliable allies. On July 22 he asked Guzzoni to give him command of all ground forces in Sicily. The 6th Army commander refused on the grounds that such a move would be too much of a blow to Italian prestige; nevertheless, with the commitment of the 29th Panzer Grenadier Division, Hans Hube nominally took charge of all ground forces in Sicily, and Guzzoni knew it, even though the Italian XIIth Corps still exercised command of some Italian units in the west, including a few that were still engaged in combat.

On July 25 Hube met with General Francesco Zingales, the XIIth Corps commander, and the two reached a compromise whereby Zingales would remain in command of the San Stefano–Nicosia sector (including the advanced elements of the 29th Panzer Grenadier Division) until it became necessary to retire to the Etna Line (i.e., the sector from San Fratello to Troina). At that time all XIIth Corps units would revert to the command of the XIVth Panzer Corps. Later that day Guzzoni confirmed this arrangement, which was in no way changed by the fall of the Fascist government the same day. As a result, Hube achieved his goal of acquiring de facto command of all units in combat in Sicily. He still continued to discuss his plans with Guzzoni via General von Senger, however, largely out of a sense of courtesy, because Alfredo Guzzoni made few attempts to influence the course of operations after this date. Even Commando Supremo recognized this arrangement, and on July 30 ordered Guzzoni to turn over command of all units still in the combat zone to XIVth Panzer Corps as of noon, August 2. Headquarters, 6th Army, still remained in Sicily, however, directing coastal defense units and other elements in the rear area.

The cooperation and sense of comradeship that existed between the top commanders in Sicily did not extend to the rank and file on the island. After the fall of Mussolini the already low morale of the Italians deteriorated even further as more and more men deserted. There were incidents in which entire units headed to the rear without orders, with their equipment. German elements, whose transport had been ravaged by Allied fighter-bombers, took to halting the convoys and relieving them of their vehicles, often at gunpoint. Sometimes the Italians resisted, and this usually resulted in shots being fired and often entailed fatal casualties. Friction between the nominal allies increased at an exponential rate as the Germans assumed a more and more disproportionate share of the fighting.

Guzzoni did what he could to keep his army in the field, but with little success. Remarkably, enough, he was even now planning offensive operations. Guzzoni correctly believed that the Allies would be too cautious to invade the mainland until after they had ejected 6th Army from Sicily; consequently, he called for sub-stantial reinforcements, with which he intended to launch a major counterattack. He hoped to inflict severe casualties on the Allies, enabling him and Hube to tie them down until the winter rains came. If this could be accomplished, he thought, Eisenhower would not be able to invade Italy until 1944.

Guzzoni's proposal did not receive an enthusiastic response. Although the German panzer general did not overtly oppose it, Guzzoni sensed that he had no intention of holding Sicily in-definitely, much less building up for a major offensive. For this reason Guzzoni opposed the idea of withdrawing 6th Army Headquarters to the mainland.

Matters came to a head on August 5 when Hube, who was worried about possible Allied landings on the toe of Italy, sug-gested to Guzzoni that his HQ be withdrawn to Calabria so that he could assume command of the defenses there. Also, the perimeter in Sicily was shrinking to the point that the Italian Army headquar-ters was superfluous. Guzzoni turned down this request because he felt that it would be improper for him to make such a suggestion to Commando Supremo. Hube would have to submit his idea through OB South, the Italian general said.

This is precisely what General Hube did. On August 8 OB South recalled General von Senger and replaced him with Lieutenant Colonel Hans Meier-Welcher.[19] The next day Guzzoni received orders from Rome extending his zone of command into Calabria. At noon the following day (August 10) he bowed to the inevitable and crossed the Straits of Messina, never to return. Headquar-ters, XVIth Italian Corps (General Carlo Rossi) departed with him, followed by the remnants of the Livorno and Assietta divisions. Hans Valentin Hube was now the sole Axis commander on the island.

Hube's relationship with the Luftwaffe commanders was much worse than the relationship he had with the Italian generals. Hans Hube held the Luftwaffe leadership responsible for the Stalingrad debacle, in which his beloved 16th Panzer Division had perished, and stated his views on the subject quite clearly. During his discussion with Hitler in late January 1943 he pointed out with contempt that not one Luftwaffe general had remained in the pocket and even said to the Fuehrer, "Why not kill an air force general or two?" This remark did not endear him to Wolfram von Richthofen, whose 4th Air Fleet was responsible for supplying the 6th Army in Stalingrad. The Baron confided in his diary that he looked around for "a wall to run up" when he heard about it from Goering.[20] This did not improve army-Luftwaffe cooperation when Richthofen assumed command of the 2nd Air Fleet in Italy and Sicily. Hermann Georing did not forget about it, either, and unsuccessfully opposed Hube's selection as commander of the ground forces in Sicily.

Whatever one thinks of Hube's views on the Luftwaffe generals in the Stalingrad campaign, his contemptuous attitude toward them in the Sicilian campaign was certainly justified. Even though their last aviation unit had long since gone, Buelowius's IInd Air Corps, the senior Luftwaffe headquarters in Sicily, steadfastly refused to hand over its excellent communications network (left over from the days of the North African campaign) to the ground forces. It was too busy using it to send reports critical of Hube and the army to Hermann Goering. The Luftwaffe ground service support units also behaved badly. Von Senger complained,

> Elements of the Luftwaffe ground forces began to set fires to [supply] dumps that might still be saved and thereby spread panic. They carried furniture with them—and left secret files behind! Hube implored me to report these facts to Kesselring and to Field Marshal von Richthofen in Rome after my return there.[21]

Lieutenant Martin Poeppel, a platoon leader in the parachute machine gun battalion (and thus a member of the Luftwaffe) would have agreed with Hube. On July 18 his unit occupied a position hastily abandoned by an antiaircraft unit. He wrote in his diary,

> It's a miserable sight, everything lying around. Stores with clothing and equipment, a complete orderly room with secret division orders lying open and in full view, also tailor's equipment and a superb shoemaker's workshop. They were carrying on a real peacetime lifestyle here, but its irresponsible to leave everything lying around when they retreated.[22]

Perhaps Hube's bitterness toward the Luftwaffe was exhibited in his attitude toward Richard Heidrich, the commander of the 1st Parachute Division. Heidrich was openly enraged at what he considered to be Colonel Schmalz's abandonment of Heilmann's 3rd Parachute Regiment at Lentini and wanted the brigade commander punished. Hube, however, took a different view of the incident and backed a recommendation to award Schmalz the Oak Leaves to his Knight's Cross. Heidrich also requested that he (Heidrich) be allowed to cross the Straits of Messina with his headquarters and take charge of Hube's left flank, where most of his division was actively engaged in combat. This request was rejected by the one-armed panzer general on the thin excuse that since Heidrich's men were so few, they did not warrant the employment of a divisional headquarters and would remain under the operational control of the Hermann Goering Panzer Division (i.e., under the despised Colonel Schmalz, who commanded the division's left wing). Whether Hube took this attitude because of the Schmalz-Heidrich feud or because he trusted the former army colonel more than he did General Heidrich is not known. Perhaps it was both. Heidrich was still furious over Hube's decision years later, but there was little he could do about it. He spent most of the Sicilian campaign on the Italian mainland, doing nothing. In fact, the 1st Parachute Division was not reunited under Heidrich's command until after the Battle of Salerno ended (i.e., after September 17), and by then battle losses had reduced it to 50 percent of its former strength.[23]

Although the major Allied offensive was supposed to begin on August 1, it actually started considerably earlier in both the Canadian and American zones. As Patton's 7th Army closed in on Palermo, his 45th Infantry Division reached the sea at Station Cerda, near the coastal town of Termini Imerese, at nine A.M. on July 23. Termini, thirty-one miles east of Palermo, fell without a fight, but the Thunderbirds' vanguard ran into the newly arrived Group Ulich just west of Campofelice. The Americans cleared the town but were soon halted again by heavy fire from a ridgeline across the Roccella River.

The Thunderbirds resumed their offensive that night and advanced fairly rapidly in spite of blasted bridges, demolished roadbeds, and liberally scattered mines. Colonel Ulich gradually fell back to excellent positions behind the Tusa River, along the Tusa and Pettineo ridges, which the Americans reached on July 26.

It took Middleton's troops four days to dislodge Max Ulich from his strong positions. Fighting was heavy, and Tusa Ridge was nicknamed Bloody Ridge by the Americans, who finally pushed beyond it on July 29. Meanwhile, other elements of the 45th Infantry Division worked their way to Mistretta (ten miles from San Stefano) and threatened to envelop the town from the south. By now General Fries was up with much of his division and had taken charge of the battle. Even though he accepted the idea that San Stefano must fall soon, the one-armed, one-legged general wanted to slow the American advance as much as possible. He reinforced Ulich with an infantry battalion from the 71st Panzer Grenadier Regiment and two more battalions of Dr. Polack's motorized artillery and instructed him to counterattack at dawn.

Colonel Ulich did not use his new guns immediately, because he felt he could obtain the advantage of surprise if he attacked without the customary artillery preparation. He was right. When the grenadiers struck at 4:30 A.M., they achieved surprise all along the line and pushed the Americans back toward Tusa Ridge. The former national guardsmen absorbed the blow, however, and at one P.M. halted the attack with the help of the heavy guns of their divisional artillery. Neither side launched another major attack that day, and that night Fries, recognizing that his counterattack had failed, ordered a retreat. The Thunderbirds occupied the town of San Stefano the following morning and were relieved here by Truscott's 3rd Infantry Division, which had been resting near Palermo for a week.

In Palermo, over highballs at the Royal Palace, Truscott had told Patton that if he wanted to beat Montgomery to Messina, his 3rd Infantry was the division to do it. Now, however, the tough divisional commander was opposing a first-class German unit on terrain well suited for the defense; in addition, he was largely confined between the sea and the cliffs to the narrow coastal road, which was heavily mined. Unlike the drive on Palermo, the going was slow and the casualties much heavier. There would be no more mass surrenders and advances of 40 miles a day; it would take Truscott eighteen days to cover the 105 miles from San Stefano to Messina. Resupplying his regiments became a major problem for Truscott. Linklater, the British official historian, wrote,

The north-coast road, which the Americans were using, was a nightmare route for the quartermasters. Often a mere ledge on the steep hill-side, it had offered German Engineers the most tempting prospects of demolition; and they had invariably yielded to opportunity and their natural inclination. From Palermo to Messina every bridge had been blown, and here and there, as though before a landslide, the road had completely vanished.[24]

General Walter Fries's task was not a simple one either, however. Of the three modes of warfare—air, sea, and ground—his side could compete only on the ground. Allied fighter-bombers freely roamed his rear, shooting up armored and motorized vehicles almost at will in the barren countryside. He also had to deal with Task Force 88 from the U.S. Navy.

Task Force 88, which was unofficially known as "General Patton's Navy," was created at Palermo on July 27. Its function, which was similar to that of the U.S. 7th Fleet ("MacArthur's Navy") in the Pacific, was to support Patton's 7th Army. The task force included the flagship *Philadelphia,* the cruiser *Savannah,* six destroyers, and dozens of amphibious, supply, and auxiliary vessels. Its missions were to defend Palermo (in case the Italian Navy became uncharacteristically aggressive); to provide gunfire support for the 3rd Infantry Division as it advanced along the coast; to provide amphibious craft for "leapfrog" landings in the German rear; and to ferry heavy artillery, supplies, vehicles, and ammunition to the advancing troops in order to relieve the congestion on the railroad and the single northern coastal road. TF 88 was led by Rear Admiral Lyal A. Davidson, who Professor Morison described as a "tall, lanky flag officer, firm in decision and quiet of speech, [who] never lost his temper under the most trying circumstances, and inspired confidence in everyone around."[25] This imperturbable officer was an excellent choice to command TF 88 and, as a result of his talents, German casualties were much heavier than they otherwise would have been.

Davidson was continually harassed by Luftwaffe bombers and dive-bombers (now operating from primitive bases in southern Italy) because, as the U.S. Navy's Official History records, "Adequate air cover was never provided to the ships operating along this coast." Incredibly enough, the U.S. air force refused to permit naval vessels to communicate directly with the pilots lest some naval commander attempt to control its fighter squadrons. The Luftwaffe, Morison states, apparently got wind of "this strange state of affairs." It adopted the tactic of sending a decoy aircraft ahead of a bomber strike force, and this single pilot would often draw away TF 88's entire close air support in pursuit while the real attack came in. The ships' radar operators detected the main formation, of course, but they could not communicate with friendly aircraft, which were off on a wild-goose chase. "Fortunately," Morison writes, "the anti-aircraft gunners in Task Force 88 became very expert, through abundant experience; beating off enemy air attacks without benefit of C.A.P [close air patrols] became almost daily routine."[26]

Despite its reduced numbers and the extended range from its bases in southern Italy, the Luftwaffe's attacks were more successful than Morison's statement might imply. The raids off the northern coast were conducted with more skill and a higher rate of success than had been the case in the battles against the initial landing forces off the southern coast. The most important raid came at dawn on August 1, when forty-eight German bombers successfully evaded American radar and swooped down on Palermo harbor. The first airplane dropped flares; the rest dropped very heavy bombs. A destroyer was damaged, as was a minesweeper and one of the vital LSTs. A British freighter took a direct hit and sank, but the greatest damage occurred when the flyers attacked an ammunition train and blew up nine hundred tons of ammunition that had been painstakenly stockpiled and that Bradley's IInd Corps badly needed. The Luftwaffe visited Palermo again at 4:45 A.M. on August 4, causing further damage. Friendly fighters did not respond until half an hour after the raid was over. Needless to say, George S. Patton was less than pleased with these proceedings.

While Middleton was driving on San Stefano, Major General Allen's 1st Infantry Division on the American right flank was struggling forward along Highway 120, in the barren Sicilian interior, toward Nicosia, Troina, Cesaro, and Randazzo. Bradley's two wings were separated from each other by the rugged Caronie (Nebrodi) Mountains, which contained the highest peaks in Sicily other than Mount Etna. The very difficult terrain denied Bradley any chance of coordinating the two prongs of his advance, but things were worse in the zone of the Big Red One. The narrow, winding highway in its sector was dominated by mountains on both sides and, unlike Highway 113 to the north, had no beaches on which amphibious attacks might be launched to turn German strongpoints. Naval gun support of the type that aided Middleton and later Truscott—and inflicted heavy casualties on Group Ul-ich—was out of the question this far inland. The Americans were, in fact, fighting two distinct battles out of mutual supporting distance of each other.

The 1st Infantry Division had actually begun its advance toward Highway 120 on the morning of July 21, the day it destroyed Group Schreiber. Later that day, however, the Americans were halted south of the highway by a small German combat group that Colonel Fullriede had stationed behind Schreiber's men in case of just such an emergency. The German detachment then retreated north-ward, up the dirt road from Alimena to Petralia, toward Highway 121, scattering mines and blowing up bridges as it went. The destruction of the bridge south of Bompietro was especially criti-cal, because it halted the Big Red One for almost twenty-four hours. It was noon on July 22 before the bridge was repaired and the advance resumed, although much more slowly than before.

The vanguard of the 1st Infantry Division reached Highway 120 east of Petralia on the morning of July 23. By nine A.M. the village was cleared, and the hard-drinking General Allen pivoted east, beginning his advance along Highway 120. His initial objective was Nicosia, a major crossroads town about twenty miles away. Late that afternoon he reached Gangi, about half the distance to Nico-sia, and found the town abandoned; however, it would take Allen five days to cover the remaining ten miles.

This sector was defended by the remnants of General Romano's Aosta Division and by Group Fullriede, the reinforced 129th Pan-zer Grenadier Regiment under the command of Lieutenant Colonel Fritz Fullriede. Fullriede had already pulled back his main forces to a defensive line covering Nicosia in a rough arc, leaving only a combat outpost line, supported by some light artillery, to oppose the Americans. On July 24, when the enemy resumed its advance, he gave up Hill 937, eight miles from Nicosia, without a fight. That night, however, General Rodt paid Fullriede a visit. Rodt's situation had improved significantly in the past few days. On July 20 the left flank of Lieutenant Colonel Ens's 104th Panzer Grenadier Regiment had at last made contact with the right flank of the 2nd H.G. Panzer Grenadier Regiment, thus closing the gap that had existed between the two main German divisions since July 10. Also, the arrival of Group Ulich had relieved Rodt's men on the far right flank of their responsibilities and had thus given him a new reserve, which he now assigned to Fullriede. He also ordered his regimental commander to counterattack the Big Red One the following morning.

At dawn on July 25 the guns of Major Simon's 33rd Motorized Artillery Regiment opened up and administered a surprise pounding all along the 26th RCT's front. Colonel Bowen's 26th RCT had only occupied Hill 937 with a single platoon, and when the lieutenant in command was hit, it fell back to the west. Fullriede quickly occupied the abandoned heights with a German infantry battalion. Colonel Bowen, pressed hard by General Allen, quickly counterattacked with two battalions. Supported by six artillery battalions, Bowen retook the hill at about two P.M. By nightfall he had pushed on to Hill 962, six miles from Nicosia.

Colonel Bowen resumed his advance at dawn on July 26, but his assault force was quickly thrown back to its starting line. Colonel Fullriede then launched a violent counterattack against Hill 962 and overran the crest, only to be thrown back again by the stubborn Americans. The top of Hill 962 became a no man's land in which no German or American could live for long because of the other's artillery. The 26th RCT did not secure the hill until that evening, when the panzer grenadiers withdrew to their next defensive line.

The battle began to go Allen's way on July 27. The 16th RCT south of the highway was stopped cold, and the 26th RCT was pinned down by German counterattacks, but the 18th Infantry on the northern flank made considerable progress against Fullriede's weak right flank, which was covered mainly by elements of the Aosta Division. By nightfall the U.S. 18th Infantry, aided by the Goumiers, had captured Monte Sambughetti, a 4,500-foot hill mass about two miles west of Highway 117, the San Stefano–Nicosia Road

That night at about 8:30 P.M. Allen probed the German center with the light tanks of the 70th Tank Battalion plus elements of the 753rd Medium Tank Battalion. Three American tanks were knocked out in this reconnaissance in force (along with one German antitank gun), but it convinced Hube that Nicosia could not be held another day. In fact, even General Hube had finally become a little nervous. On July 25 he had seen fourteen unidentified warships off the coast of northern Sicily, and feared that they might be an Allied amphibious landing force heading for the toe of the Italian peninsula. He alerted Axis units all the way back to Calabria to be prepared to repel invaders. In fact, the ships were American destroyers and minesweepers out on a more or less routine patrol. Nevertheless, this incident, coupled with the arrest of Mussolini, lent additional urgency to Hube's desire to consolidate his defensive positions in preparations for the inevitable evacuation of the island. Consequently, about nine P.M. on July 27, he ordered Rodt to abandon Nicosia despite the initial objections of General Guzzoni. Colonel Fullriede withdrew that same night without bothering to inform the Italians on his right. When it learned that the Germans had gone, the Aosta Division hastily withdrew, but not all the Italians got the word. At least seven hundred of them were captured by ten-thirty the following morning, when the 1st Infantry Division finished clearing Nicosia. The Americans who occupied the city said that they were "eager to surrender."[27] Meanwhile, Colonel Fullriede's men retreated to the next delaying position, which extended south to north from Gagliano (just north of Agira) to Cerami (on Highway 120) to Capizzi (three miles north of Cerami). At its nearest point, the main German line was still only about eight miles east of Nicosia.

As the Americans slugged it out with Hube's right wing for San Stefano and Nicosia, General Sir Bernard Law Montgomery prepared to launch an all-out offensive against his left. It was preceded by an advance on Monty's left flank by the 1st Canadian Division, which was ordered to take Agira and Regalbuto before the main advance began against Adrano, which Montgomery considered to be the key to outflanking Catania (Map 13).

Agira, a medieval town perched high on a mountain ridge, was defended by Colonel Ens's 104th Panzer Grenadier Regiment. The battle began on the night of July 22–23, when the Germans caught the Canadian spearhead in its assembly areas with a surprise bombardment and smashed it. Nevertheless, the Canadians, supported by seven artillery regiments and more than a hundred

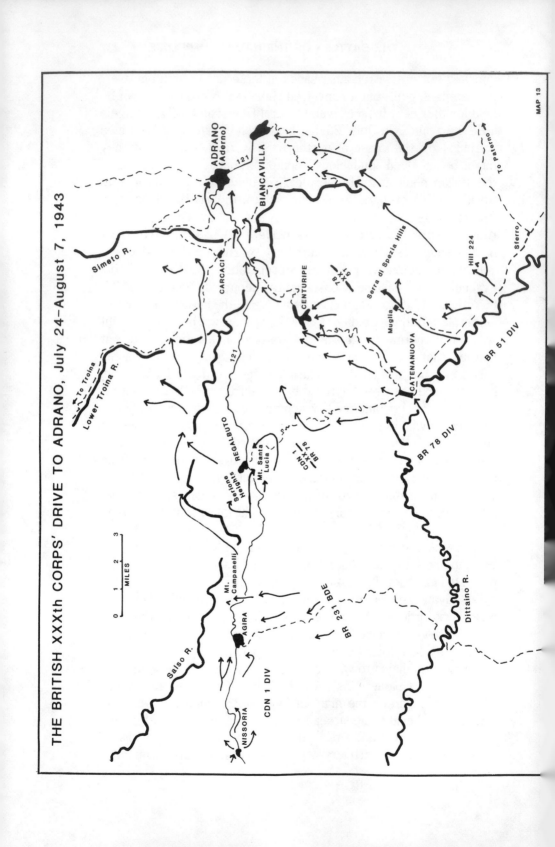

THE BRITISH XXXth CORPS' DRIVE TO ADRANO, July 24–August 7, 1943

ADRANO (Aderno)

BIANCAVILLA

121

CARCACI

Simeto R.

To Troina

Lower Troina R.

CENTURIPE

78 XX 1

Serra di Spezia Hills

Muglia

CATENANUOVA

121

REGALBUTO

Serione Heights

Mt. Santa Lucia

CDN 1 XX 78 BR

BR 78 DIV

BR 51 DIV

Hill 224

Sterro

To Paterno

MILES

0 1 2 3

Mt. Campanelli

AGIRA

BR 231 BDE

Dittaino R.

Salso R.

CDN 1 DIV

NISSORIA

MAP 13

Kittyhawk fighter-bombers, gradually pushed the Germans back in heavy fighting. Agira fell on July 28, when Ens's battered regiment withdrew north of the Salso River, where it joined forces with Group Fullriede near Gagliano to join the battle against the Americans. The 1st Canadian Division, meanwhile, continued its advance eastward along Highway 121 into the zone of the Hermann Goering Panzer Division, which extended its flank to the right to block any further Canadian advances.

Lieutenant General Paul Conrath was proving to be a much more competent defensive commander than he was a panzer commander in the attack. Like Montgomery, he recognized that Adrano was the key to the entire Etna Line. Conrath, however, wanted to halt the Canadians well short of that, at Regalbuto and Centuripe on the Hauptkampflinie. These two towns formed the main strongpoints in front of Adrano, but Regalbuto was especially critical, so Conrath ordered the Hermann Goering Panzer Engineer Battalion to take over its defense and augmented it with a company of eight panzers, a battery of artillery, an infantry company from the 3rd Parachute Regiment, and a few rocket launchers *(Nebelwerfern)*. The garrison commander was also placed directly under Conrath's personal command. He ordered his men to hold their positions at all costs.

On July 28 the Canadian Division advanced through almond and olive groves to within a mile of the town. In the early morning darkness the Malta Brigade was forming up to spearhead the division's attack, when it was caught in its assembly areas by a surprise Nebelwerfer attack. Despite severe casualties, it pushed on, only to run into an ambush. Caught in a cross fire by the paratroopers and Luftwaffe panzer engineers, it had no choice but to fall back to its starting points. It did not storm the ridge overlooking Regalbuto until 2:35 A.M. on July 31, after a severe series of firefights.

Daylight breaks early in Sicily in the summer, and when it came on July 31, the Germans were ready with a spirited counterattack spearheaded by the paratrooper company. The fighting was desperate, and the 2nd Devons, which had already lost two hundred men out of the seven hundred they had when they landed in Sicily on July 10, now lost over one hundred more. Nevertheless, they held their positions and even managed to counterattack and dislodge the

Germans from a foothold they had established on the eastern slope of the ridge.

With the ridgelines west of the town lost, the Luftwaffe ground soldiers retreated into Regalbuto itself and prepared to defend it house to house. Now the 1st Canadian Infantry Brigade joined the battle and unleashed a major assault on the hilltop fortress at two A.M. on August 1, but it was not successful. After the Royal Canadian Regiment was repulsed southwest of the town, the 48th Highlander Battalion advanced on Regalbuto from the northwest. They were also checked and were pinned down to the point where they were unable to get food or medical supplies until the next day.

On August 1 Canadian and British artillery pounded Regalbuto all day and into the night, and all available air support was concentrated against eastbound traffic, which was expected to fill the road between Regalbuto and Adrano when another all-out infantry assault began on the afternoon of August 2.

There was no attack. On the morning of August 2 the 48th Highlander sent a patrol toward Regalbuto and found the place deserted. The Germans had once again pulled a vanishing act just before a major Allied attack. Even so, an estimated forty German vehicles were destroyed on the road between Regalbuto and Adrano, and the Hermann Goering Panzer Engineer Battalion had been eliminated as a viable combat force.

While the bulk of the 1st Canadian Division was struggling toward Regalbuto, Brigadier Penhale's 3rd Canadian Infantry Brigade was ordered to secure a bridgehead north of the Dittaino River and take the town of Catenanuova as quickly as possible. General Leese planned to funnel the British 78th Infantry Division into this bridgehead just before Monty launched his major drive for Adrano (the key to Catania) on August 1.

After attacks on July 27 and 28 failed, Penhale launched an all-out assault on the night of July 29–30, supported by seven artillery battalions. The infantry surged forward, following the artillery curtain that advanced one hundred yards every minute to a line one thousand yards north of the village. Catenanuova fell with surprising ease because of what the Canadian Official History called "an unusual case of German cowardice." The 923rd Fortress Battalion, which had been charged with defending the town, bolted and ran away when the West Nova Scotia Regiment attacked.

"The battalion fled in the direction of Centuripe in a shameful manner without enemy pressure," Field Marshal Kesselring reported, adding, "The immediate dissolution of the battalion has been ordered." In addition, Field Marshal Keitel initiated court-martial proceedings against the battalion commander and the officers who had fled with their men.[28]

The rout of the 923rd forced Conrath to commit elements of the 3rd Parachute Regiment north of Catenanuova, but it was too late to prevent General Leese from establishing his bridgehead, into which he committed Major General Evelegh's 78th Infantry Division, which was scheduled to spearhead Montgomery's all-out offensive. This drive was scheduled to begin on the night of August 1–2, but Evelegh moved it up twenty-four hours, in order to take advantage of any German disorganization the collapse of the 923rd Fortress Battalion might have caused.

Evelegh's hopes that the Germans would still be disorganized were soon dashed. The British Official History recorded that the brigade advanced "under a deadly fire from well-placed light machine guns and mortars. In such conditions ground can often be gained only in small bites, laboriously."[29] The opposition was no longer furnished by an ill-trained, hastily formed march battalion but by the Ist Battalion of the 3rd Parachute Regiment, elements of the IInd Battalion of the same unit, and a battery and an antitank troop from the Hermann Goering Division. The British gained ground only very slowly. (This sector had originally been commanded by Lieutenant Colonel von Carnap of the Hermann Goering Division, but he had been killed on July 30. The sector was then handed over to "King Ludwig" Heilmann, the commander of the 3rd Parachute Regiment.)

By now the Allies were attacking in strength all along the line. Many of the Germans had been in the front lines since July 10, and Hube's three under-strength divisions and Brigade Schmalz had been opposing twelve Allied divisions, the Malta Brigade, and assorted Ranger battalions and Royal Commandos. Seven of these divisions were attacking on August 1, supported by vastly superior artillery, undisputed air supremacy, and in the coastal sectors the big guns of the Royal and U.S. navies. Exhaustion was beginning to set in. Hube's men were still able to delay Monty's drive, but they were no longer able to stop it. And there were no more reserves.

On Evelegh's right flank the 51st Highlander Division advanced two brigades abreast, with the 50th Royal Tank Regiment in support. They were opposed by part of Group Schmalz: Ist Battalion/2nd Hermann Goering Panzer Grenadier Regiment, reinforced by a dozen PzKw IV tanks. The attack began at 11:30 P.M. on July 31 when Brigade Schmalz was suddenly hit by a barrage from the 51st Division's artillery. "All 8th Army's assaults started in the same way," Pond wrote later, and "the Germans were by now used to it and their reaction was to get as many men as possible under cover, leaving just a few sentries and look-outs. As the shelling ended, or went over, they reoccupied their defensive positions and came up fighting."[30] Colonel Schmalz estimated that the enemy fired approximately thirty thousand shells on one kilometer of front in a one-and-a-half-hour period. He lost two men killed and eight wounded.

The Highlanders reported that their advance was "stubbornly opposed" by the Goerings and slowed by extensive minefields, but they continued to advance into the Serra di Spezia Hills until they reached Hill 224, which they took in hand-to-hand fighting. They could advance no further, however, until their artillery support was brought up. At this point Schmalz's troops counterattacked with their panzers. They retook Hill 224 and reached Angelico Farm, about a mile to the south, where they came under the fire of the Scottish Horse Artillery and six field regiments. The counterattack was quickly smashed, and all twelve panzers were knocked out. The Highlanders then resumed their advance toward their two objectives: the Simeto River and the town of Biancavilla, two miles southeast of Adrano and about eight miles northwest of the long-abandoned airfields at Gerbini.

Meanwhile, the 78th Infantry Division reached the outskirts of Centuripe during the predawn darkness of August 2, but here Heilmann made a stand, and the British division was unable to clear the town completely during the rest of the day. Fighting was very heavy, and the 78th was subjected to two sharp counterattacks. At nine P.M. that night, however, General Conrath told Heilmann to begin to withdraw from the place, and this time

Heilmann obeyed orders. Early the next morning the Irish Brigade entered the ruins of Centuripe; meanwhile, Heilmann's veteran rear guards retired across the Salso, a tributary of the Simeto.

They were only 3.5 miles from the critical position of Adrano.

The capture of Centuripe opened up the Hauptkampflinie, or the outer ring of the main German defenses south of Etna. Hube's bent and battered line now ran from Adrano through Biancavilla to Paterno. One breach of the line would outflank Catania, where Colonel Schmalz's men had been pinning down the British XIIIth Corps for so long. "The Germans, however, had quickly realized the danger they were in about Catania," Linklater wrote. "They began to thin out. Laying innumerable mines, demolishing everything that gun-cotton would usefully wreck, and leaving behind them strong rear-guards to hold and hinder the pursuit. . . ."[31]

Unfortunately for the Wehrmacht, General Dempsey, the commander of the beleaguered XIIIth Corps, noticed that Conrath and Schmalz were thinning out their lines, so he planned an attack of his own.

Since they had secured the Primosole Bridge on July 17, the men of the XIIIth British Corps had been more or less pinned down by Schmalz's brigade. They were dependent on the single bridge for much of their supplies, and it was the continuous target of Axis mortars and field guns. On July 23 it was hit and broken, and it could not be reopened until July 25. The next day Primosole Bridge was put out of action again and was not repaired until July 29. Two days later German artillery again made it unusable for supply vehicles. In addition to supply problems, the battle was stalled in an area infested by malarial mosquitoes. Lax discipline in this regard caused numerous casualties on both sides. During August, for example, the Hermann Goering Panzer Division lost 1,669 men in battle (killed, wounded, and missing), compared with 2,605 lost to illness—mainly malaria.

More or less constant German sniping, mortaring, and harassment fire caused further serious losses to the British XIIIth Corps. The 50th Infantry Division alone had suffered 1,500 casualties by the end of July, including 100 officers. Nevertheless, when General Dempsey noticed that Conrath was thinning out his line on August 3, he threw both divisions into the attack that very night.

Dempsey's men did not advance far before they were stopped by strong rear guards from the Hermann Goering Division; nevertheless, they were advancing for the first time in more than two weeks. By the following afternoon the British 5th Infantry Division had gained four miles and was fighting in the southern outskirts of Catania. The battle continued throughout the night, but the British could go no farther. That night, in compliance with Hube's orders, General Conrath and Colonel Schmalz evacuated Catania, and Brigade Schmalz fell back to prepared positions around Acireale, covered by the Koerner Regiment. Catania formally surrendered to Lieutenant J. B. Gardner of the 9th Durham Light Infantry, who led the first patrol into the city. After a twenty-three-day battle, the British entered it without firing a shot.

✧ 13 ✧

THE ALLIES CLOSE IN

THE FALL OF THE HAUPTKAMPFLINIE DID NOT UNDULY DISTURB General Hube, who simply fell back to his next main line of defense, the Etna Line, which extended from San Fratello on the north coast to Troina and Adrano—the main inland strongpoints— and ended at Acireale on the eastern coast. The Americans and British pursued him quickly, so that the battles of the Hauptkampf-linie and the Etna Line merged and were indistinguishable to many of the men involved.

On the right (interior) flank of Bradley's IInd Corps, the 1st Infantry Division assembled around Nicosia to attack Cerami and Troina, a town five miles farther east.

They expected little trouble. The divisional intelligence staff reported on July 29, "Germans very tired, little ammo, many casualties, morale low." Two days later IInd Corps echoed this report, concluding, "Indications are Troina lightly held."[1]

Events on the ground seemed to confirm those reports. The Big Red One jumped off at dawn on July 31 and took Cerami by nine A.M. against very light opposition. Local civilians reported that the Troina garrison had very few troops, a few antitank guns, and one antiaircraft battery. Allen was convinced that it could be seized rapidly, without elaborate preparations, if his lead regiment pushed on quickly. He sent the 39th Infantry Regiment, a fresh unit recently attached to him from the 9th Infantry Division, to do the job alone. The three thousand men of the 39th, however, were stopped cold west of Troina (Map 14).

General Allen had badly underestimated the Germans' strength and determination to hold this hilltop town in the heart of the Etna

THE BATTLE of TROINA, August 1-6, 1943

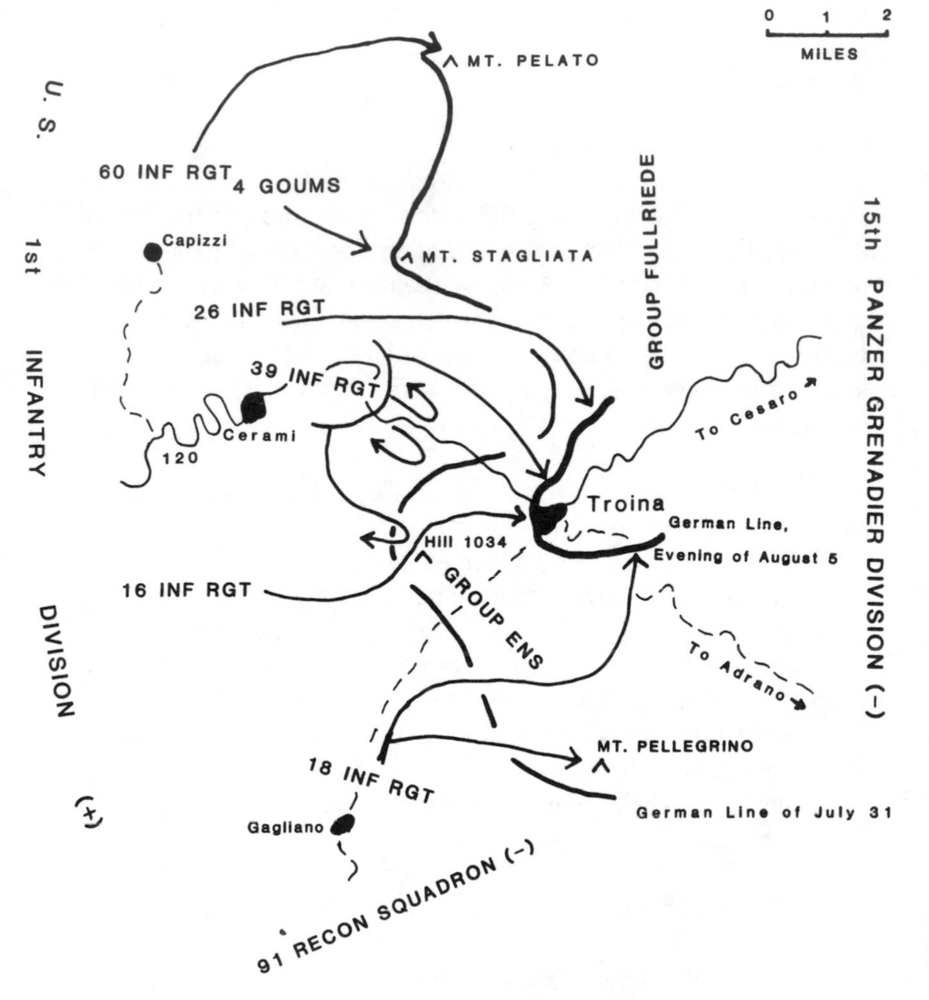

0   1   2
MILES

^ MT. PELATO

U. S.

GROUP FULLRIEDE

15th PANZER GRENADIER DIVISION (−)

60 INF RGT 4 GOUMS

1st

Capizzi

^ MT. STAGLIATA

26 INF RGT

To Cesaro →

39 INF RGT

INFANTRY

Cerami

120

Troina

German Line,

Evening of August 5

Hill 1034

16 INF RGT

GROUP ENS

To Adrano →

DIVISION

MT. PELLEGRINO
^

18 INF RGT

German Line of July 31

(+)

Gagliano

91 RECON SQUADRON (−)

MAP 14

Line. Before the battle was over, five American infantry regiments—all of the 1st and most of the newly arrived 9th U.S. Infantry divisions—would be committed to the fighting, which would be the bloodiest the Americans would experience in the entire Sicilian campaign.

The defense of Troina was masterminded by Hans Hube and conducted by Major General Rodt and Lieutenant Colonels Ens and Fullriede of the 15th Panzer Grenadier Division.

Troina was a town of 12,000 people, situated 3,674 feet above sea level on a high, dominating bluff that gave the defenders excellent fields of observation in all directions. It was the highest town in Sicily. Barring the passage of Highway 120, Troina was surrounded by a series of parallel north-south ridges and dozens of hills, which could be used to protect the German flanks. Forward observers could also use the hills to call in artillery fire on American assembly areas. The intervening valleys were almost completely barren, offering the attackers no cover or concealment from the defenders on the high ground.

General Hube had prepared for Troina's defense well in advance. While the Allies were still struggling toward the Hauptkampflinie, Colonel Albrecht Grell, who later commanded the 129th Panzer Grenadier Regiment in Italy, was assigned the task of delineating the projected new positions with representatives of Rodt's engineer battalion, the panzer grenadier and artillery regiments, and other units.[2] The remnants of the Aosta Division were pulled back to Troina, where they were used as laborers, along with anybody else Grell could find. Redoubts were dug, minefields laid, fields of fires cleared, and supplies organized. Finally, on the night of July 27–28, Rodt ordered his major units to fall back on the Troina heights, leaving strong rear guards to delay the Americans another two or three days.

On July 28, as Rodt retreated, nature intervened on his side. Under the cover of a heavy storm—the first rainfall since the campaign began—he fell back to the Troina heights, posting the 129th Panzer Grenadier Regiment (Fullriede) northeast of the town and the 104th Panzer Grenadier (Ens) to the southeast. After setting up his headquarters at Castello Maniace, Rodt had second thoughts about making a stand with his depleted division. He spoke to General Hube and asked permission to continue his retreat to the east, because his division had already lost 1,600 men—almost 40 percent of its preinvasion combat strength. Hube rejected this request because he had already guessed that the Allies planned to advance from Troina to Adrano and Randazzo, in order to force the collapse of the entire Etna Line. Troina was to be held, he said, until he gave permission to abandon it. After this discussion, Rodt grouped the majority of his remaining panzers east of the town in positions from which they could launch counterattacks if the Americans broke through.

The battle began in earnest on August 1. After his defeat the previous day, Allen decided to conduct a coordinated assault, using four infantry regiments supported by no fewer than twenty-four artillery battalions. Unfortunately for Allen, the terrain was so poor and so well covered by German fire that much of the artillery could not be deployed effectively on August 1; nevertheless, his attack went forward at five A.M. His plan was simple: The 39th Infantry Regiment was to spearhead the attack from the west, while the 18th Infantry Regiment attacked from the south and the 26th Infantry Regiment seized the high ground north and northeast of the town. The 16th Infantry Regiment was held in reserve, to be committed when the opportunity presented itself.

The 39th Infantry Regiment was only four miles west of Troina when it entered the zone of Group Fullriede, but as Craven and Cate wrote, "blown bridges, damaged roads, numerous mine fields, and enemy resistance of the most determined and vicious type" brought the advance to a quick halt north of Highway 120.[3] To the south, however, in the zone of Group Ens, the Americans slowly pushed to within two miles of the town and captured the important Hill 1034. This success was achieved because the 104th Panzer Grenadier Regiment had been more badly battered in the earlier battles and was less well organized than was Group Fullriede. However, at nightfall, Colonel Ens rallied his forces and counterattacked with two hundred men. This stroke was a complete success. It recaptured Hill 1034, threw the Americans back more than a mile, and reduced one U.S. battalion to a strength of three hundred men.

August 2 was a day of minor American attacks that resulted in almost no gains. Fullriede and Ens continued to strengthen their positions while General Allen prepared for another all-out attack on August 3. This attack began at three A.M. and continued for

THE ALLIES CLOSE IN • 249

nine hours. Even though it was supported by four regiments of artillery, it made little progress because of careful German preparations. Shell after shell from Captain Huettig's Nebelwerfer (rocket-launcher) unit and fire from several batteries of field guns landed on American positions, driving the troops to ground. However, the Americans used close air support properly for the first time in the campaign, with ground liaison officers having direct contact with the pilots. These tactics had not yet been perfected, however, and American bombs frequently landed within American lines. U.S. dive-bombers actually circled Allen's command post at Cerami, obviously mistaking it for Troina, which is five miles away. Fortunately they hesitated before attacking, and the divisional artillery commander was able to hurriedly contact an air liaison officer, who diverted the dive-bombers to the correct target. Elsewhere, a column of American tanks was strafed by American airplanes, which ignored their recognition panels. On another occasion a flight of A-36's actually attacked General Bradley, but he was luckier: they missed.

The American attack had definitely shot its bolt by noon, and Colonel Ens launched a concentrated counterattack against the U.S. 16th Infantry Regiment, which Allen had unsuccessfully committed to an attack on the southern face of Hill 1034. Only the fire of six American artillery battalions saved the exposed regiment from being overrun.

Despite his undeniable defensive victory, General Rodt's position was far from enviable as darkness fell on August 3. He had lost several hundred men since the battle had begun, and the strength of some of the grenadier companies was dangerously low. Also, the Canadians and the British 78th Infantry Division were threatening to cut Highway 120 east of Troina, an act that would seal the doom of the bulk of his division. That night Hube gave Rodt the last of his corps reserves, to enable him to hold open an escape route east of town; however, because neither Hitler nor Kesselring had yet authorized the evacuation of the island, Hube felt compelled to hold the Etna Line as long as possible. He again ordered Rodt to stand fast.

The fifth day of the battle began on August 4 and was as fierce as the previous four. Eighteen American artillery battalions and waves of fighter-bombers (thirty-six per wave, each armed with five-hundred-pound bombs) hammered Troina and its approaches into rubble. The ground attack, however, was a failure. Group Fullriede especially conducted a skillful and aggressive defense, infiltrating American positions and launching innumerable local counterattacks. Late in the afternoon Fullriede was forced to commit his last reserves to keep the Americans at bay, but he held his positions. The Germans were assisted by Lieutenant Colonel Gianquinto's Ist Battalion of the 5th (Aosta) Infantry Regiment, one of the few Italian units still fighting with spirit. The Ist even managed to take forty American prisoners in one successful counterattack. Indeed, counterattack was the order of the day. During the Battle of Troina, the Germans and Italians launched twenty-four medium-scale counterattacks and a host of smaller ones. American casualties were so high that General Bradley was appalled.

The sixth day of the Battle of Troina began at dawn on August 5 with no end in sight. The U.S. XIIth Air Support Command was again assigned the task of providing direct dive-bomber support. General Bradley went forward to Cerami with Major General Edwin J. House, Patton's tactical air commander, to watch a dive-bomber attack on Troina—an attack that never took place. Then, far to the south, they saw a flight of A-36's heading for home.

"Holy smokes!" Bradley exclaimed. "Now just where in the hell do you suppose they've dropped their bombs?"

"I'll be damned if I know!" House replied. "Maybe we'd better get back to your headquarters and see what went wrong."

When they got back, the telephone was already ringing. "What have we done that your chaps would want to bomb us?" General Oliver Leese, commander of the XXXth British Corps, asked.

"Where did they hit?" Bradley groaned.

"Squarely on top of my headquarters," Leese said. "They've really plastered the town."[4]

The American ground attack was again halted north and west of Troina with only minor gains, but it finally made some significant progress south of the town. Here the U.S. 18th Infantry Regiment managed to seize and hold Mount Pellegrino, about four miles south of the ruins of Troina. From here, American forward observers directed the artillery fire, which broke up several small German attacks and knocked out ten of Rodt's artillery pieces. American casualties were also heavy, however, and some companies were down to sixty-five men.

Meanwhile, General Rodt again requested permission to withdraw three miles because of the depleted and exhausted state of his units. Hube at first denied his request, but that evening the Goering Division reported that the British XXXth Corps was pushing back its right flank and presenting an even greater threat to the left flank of the 15th Panzer Grenadier Division. That night Hube gave Rodt, Fries, Conrath, and Schmalz orders to retreat by phases to what Guzzoni called the Tortorici Line, a series of defensive positions running from Cape Orlando on the north coast, through Poggio del Moro, Randazzo, and Mount Etna, to Giarre on the eastern shore.

The following morning at about eight A.M., as the British entered Catania, elements of the Big Red One entered Troina. They could advance little farther, however, because the stubborn rear guards of the 15th Panzer Grenadier Division still held them up short of the key road junction of Randazzo, using thick minefields, skillfully placed artillery concentrations, and demolitions. Except for low-level air attacks, the 15th withdrew without interference.

The Americans did not pursue aggressively because of the severe casualties they had suffered at Troina. U.S. Major General John P. Lucas, Ike's observer at 7th Army Headquarters, considered this to be the toughest battle the Americans had fought since World War I. Also, Bradley and Patton had serious misgivings about Allen's conduct of operations. His division had lost 1,600 men at Troina, 40 percent of its combat strength. Morale in the 1st Infantry Division was low, and discipline was poor.[5] General Bradley decided that the situation had become intolerable and, with Patton's blessings, relieved Allen of his command, replacing him with Major General Clarence R. Huebner, a former private in the Big Red One who had risen through the ranks. Bradley also sacked Brigadier General Theodore Roosevelt, Jr., the assistant divisional commander and son of the former U.S. president. Patton was less keen on relieving Roosevelt, but in the end acquiesced to Bradley's wishes. Meanwhile, Major General Eddy's 9th Infantry replaced the 1st in the line and prepared for its own battle against the survivors of the 15th Panzer Grenadier Division.

And what about the northern coastal sector? What was happening on Hube's right flank while he held the British 8th Army in front of Nissoria, Agira, Adrano, and Catania, and Terry Allen was bogged down in the bloodbath of Troina?

The reader will recall that Middleton's Thunderbirds had pushed elements of Fries's 29th Panzer Grenadier Division out of San Stefano on July 31. During this retreat, a shell from an American ship struck a bridge over the Santo Stefano River, forcing the Assietta Division to give up most of its remaining artillery.[6] Hube then decided to withdraw his right flank to the San Fratello–Cesaro–Troina line, which he resolved to hold until Hitler or Kesselring decided to evacuate Sicily (Map 15). This line was anchored by the very strong position of Monte Fratello, a 2,400-foot height that dominated the coastal highway and the road to Cesaro.

Meanwhile, at the end of July, Truscott's 3rd Infantry Division struggled slowly forward down the coastal road. At places the road ceased to exist as a result of German demolitions. Also, every spring issuing from the barren hills was found to be heavily mined. General Truscott had trouble even getting water to his forward troops; nevertheless, the advance continued, propelled largely by supplies delivered by "liberated" Sicilian mules and horses, which Truscott organized into supply columns. (The superior performance of ad hoc horse and mule supply units led General Patton to comment later that if he had had an old-fashioned cavalry division, complete with mule trains, he would have gotten to Messina much more quickly.) Thanks to these innovative supply techniques, the American vanguards were able to continue their drive toward Messina, until they reached the Furiano River (the forward outpost of the San Fratello position) on the afternoon of August 3. They tried to bounce the Germans out of this position via a rapid attack, but were quickly met with enfilade fire from both flanks and were thrown back.

The 3rd Infantry Division renewed its attacks against the San Fratello position at six A.M. on August 4 and was again stopped cold. The divisional artillery did little to support this hasty attack. Because of the terrain and the improvised nature of the road, most of the batteries barely had time to come up in the darkness and deploy; they had no time to register their guns. On the other side, however, Truscott found that the guns of Colonel Dr. Polack's

29th Motorized Artillery Regiment were fully registered and had been for days. After four hours of fighting, Lucian Truscott finally admitted defeat and called off the attack. He would try again the following day.

For the Battle of San Fratello, Major General Fries had deployed Lieutenant Colonel Krueger's newly arrived 71st Panzer Grenadier Regiment on his right (coastal) flank and the remnants of the Italian Assietta Division (now under General Ottorino Schreiber) in the center—the least vulnerable part of his line. The left (interior) flank was held by Colonel Ulich's 15th Panzer Grenadier Regiment. These dispositions had proved perfectly sound in the first three days of the battle, but General Fries was still a worried man despite his initial successes. He was concerned that the fall of Troina had uncovered his left flank and was deeply worried about a possible Allied amphibious landing in his rear. During the night of August 5–6 he sent most of his support units, along with a few combat elements, farther back to the east. The main combat forces, however, remained in the San Fratello positions.

Fries would have been even more concerned if he had been able to read the mind of General George S. Patton. The 7th Army commander, who realized that the terrain would deprive him of his customary swift armored thrusts, had decided to employ amphibious landings to speed up his advance. Unfortunately, Admiral Davidson's Task Force 88 could only provide him with two LSTs, seven LCTs, and one LCI—barely enough shipping to transport a reinforced infantry battalion. Patton nevertheless decided to use these vessels to outflank San Fratello and possibly cut off the retreat of the 29th Panzer Grenadier Division. He and Truscott picked Lieutenant Colonel Lyle Bernard's 2nd Battalion, 30th Infantry Regiment, to do the job. Attached to this battalion were a platoon of tanks and two batteries of field artillery. Simultaneously, Admiral Davidson assigned the cruisers *Philadelphia* and *Savannah* and six destroyers the task of covering the landings. Map 16 shows Patton's first (and subsequent) amphibious attacks, along with the final Anglo-American conquest of northeastern Sicily.

The Battle of San Fratello resumed on August 6, a day on which Truscott launched a series of uncharacteristically uncoordinated

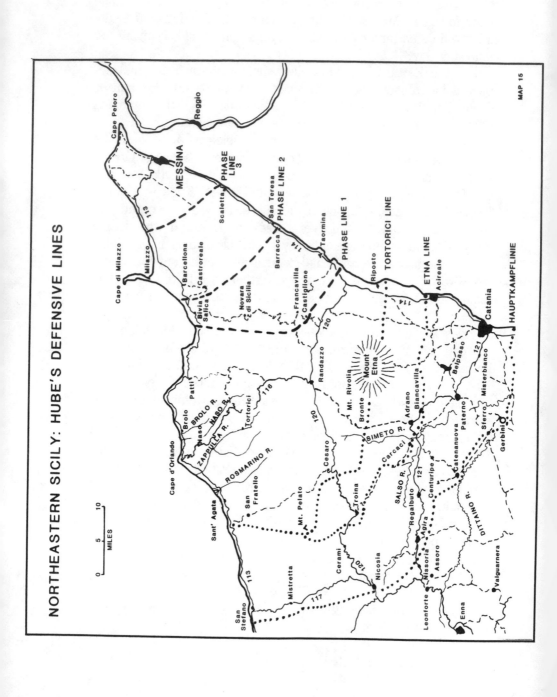

NORTHEASTERN SICILY: HUBE'S DEFENSIVE LINES

MAP 15

piecemeal attacks against the German line. All were repulsed without much difficulty. That afternoon, after consulting wth Patton and Bradley, Truscott ordered an amphibious assault for the next day.

Late that afternoon Lieutenant Colonel Bernard's battalion was marched toward its embarkation point near San Stefano, when four objects appeared out of the sky. To everyone's surprise, they turned out to be airplanes from the Luftwaffe, which had somehow learned that a small amphibious task force was assembling at San Stefano. The little harbor was protected by antiaircraft guns, of course, and two of the intruders were shot down, but the embarkation point was strafed and bombed, and—worst of all— one of the vital LSTs was damaged beyond repair. Truscott had no choice but to postpone the landing twenty-four hours until another LST could be rushed in from Palermo. The brave pilots had bought Hube another day.

August 7 saw the climax of the San Fratello battle. After a morning of unsuccessful attacks, the U.S. 3rd Infantry Division finally broke into the San Fratello position just before nightfall and stormed Hill 673, seriously threatening Fries's left flank. The general's ensuing orders to Max Ulich were clear: the Americans would have to be dislodged. That night, following a barrage of forty-five minutes, the colonel threw his 15th Panzer Grenadier Regiment into one of the most savage counterattacks of the campaign. For almost two hours a bitter struggle raged across the face of the hill, which was defended by two depleted American infantry battalions. Sometimes the fighting was hand to hand. In the end the panzer grenadiers could not prevail, and they broke off the attack about two A.M. on August 8.

General Fries had had enough. His positions had been shelled almost continuously by the big guns of the U.S. warships and by Truscott's divisional artillery all day long. He was also increasingly concerned about the prospect of an American landing in his rear. (By then he knew about the task force assembling near San Stefano.) During the night he pulled out the rest of his division, leaving the remnants of the Assietta Division on San Fratello Ridge to cover his withdrawal.

Fries's move was very well timed, for the American landing force was already at sea. The Luftwaffe had tried to disrupt it again

THE CONQUEST OF NORTHEASTERN SICILY

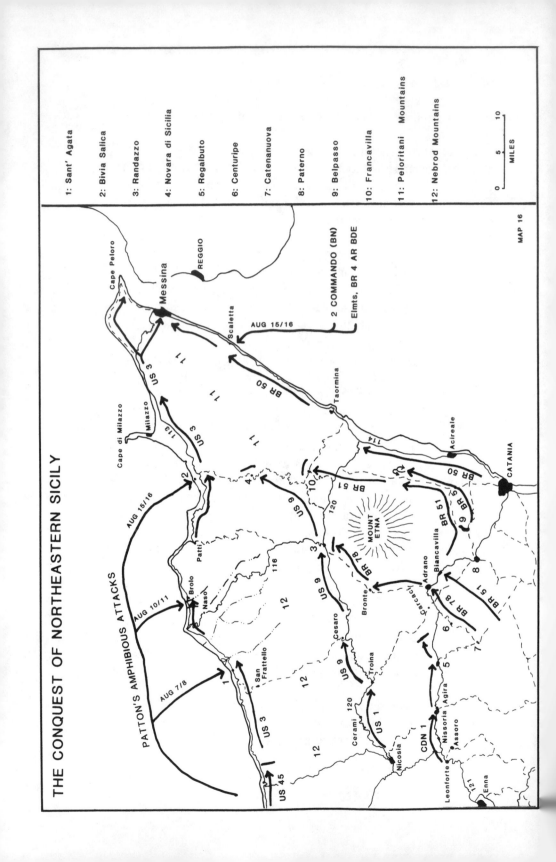

PATTON'S AMPHIBIOUS ATTACKS

AUG 15/16

AUG 10/11

AUG 7/8

US 45

US 3

1: Sant' Agata

2: Bivia Salica

3: Randazzo

4: Novara di Sicilia

5: Regalbuto

6: Centuripe

7: Catenanuova

8: Paterno

9: Belpasso

10: Francavilla

11: Peloritani Mountains

12: Nebrod Mountains

0   5   10
MILES

MAP 16

Cape Peloro

Messina

REGGIO

Scaletta

AUG 15/16

2 COMMANDO (BN)

Elmts, BR 4 AR BDE

US 3

US 3

11

11

11

BR 50

Taormina

Cape di Milazzo

Milazzo

113

AUG 15/16

2

US 9

4

10

120

MOUNT ETNA

BR 51

114

Acireale

BR 50

BR 9

CATANIA

Patti

Brolo

Naso

AUG 10/11

116

12

12

San Frattello

12

1

3

US 9

Cesaro

US 9

Troina

Bronte

BR 78

Adrano

Carcaci

Biancavilla

BR 78

BR 51

9

6

8

BR 51

7

Cerami

120

US 1

Nicosia

CDN 1

Nissoria

Agira

Assoro

Leonforte

5

121

Enna

and had even succeeded in damaging the newly arrived LST, but hasty repairs had made it seaworthy once more. The task force sailed through the night and "hit the beaches" near Sant' Agata, nine miles east of Mount Fratello, at 3:15 A.M. on August 8. By 4:08 A.M. every soldier from the 2nd Battalion was ashore. When they advanced toward the coastal road, however, they found that most of the 29th Panzer Grenadier Division had gone.

Most, but not all. As the Germans withdrew along the coastal road, a shell from an American destroyer struck the highway bridge over the Rosmarino River, about a mile from the American beaches. This bridge had already been wired for demolition, and the American shell set off the charges, blowing the bridge prematurely. The dry riverbed had also been mined, so there was no possibility of crossing the river at that point. As a result, a long traffic jam was created just about the time the Americans landed. After knocking out two Italian Renault tanks and a Panzer Mark IV, Colonel Bernard's men quickly overran the mass of confusion, killing or capturing 350 Germans in the process. Four panzers were captured, and at least sixty (perhaps as many as a hundred) other vehicles were captured or destroyed. The premature detonation also cut off Captain Schneider's IInd Battalion of the 71st Panzer Grenadier Regiment, but Schneider was wise enough to swing inland, well south of the traffic jam and the American landing forces. Later that day he crossed the Rosmarino River about four miles south of the coast, thus avoiding encirclement, even though he did lose vehicles and equipment in the rough and generally trackless terrain. For the bulk of the Assietta Division, however, there was no such escape.

Morale was already bad among the Italians, but when Fries withdrew on the night of August 7–8, he deliberately abandoned the remnants of Assietta to their fate, and they knew it. Except for a few small units that had been withdrawn earlier, the survivors of the division were still holding Mount Fratello, and they felt understandably betrayed. They had no desire to die for the Germans or the Badoglio government. When the men of the 3rd Infantry Division resumed their attack at dawn on August 8, they met very little opposition; in fact, Assietta surrendered in droves. One American battalion alone took almost a thousand prisoners, and Truscott had little trouble linking up with Bernard east of the Rosmarino River late that afternoon.

Patton's first amphibious assault thus came to an end. It was not successful in cutting off the 29th Panzer Grenadier Division, but it had helped overcome the San Fratello position, a victory that unhinged the northern anchor of the Etna Line, virtually destroyed the Assietta Division, and forced Fries to fall back to the Zappula River and the Cape Orlando–Randazzo Road. Patton had already covered more than two thirds of the distance between Palermo and Messina, but the XIVth Panzer Corps still barred his way to the prize.

As Patton's men pursued Fries's panzer grenadiers east of the Rosmarino, Montgomery's Tommies were pursuing Conrath and Schmalz north of the Salso and the Simeto. They were, however, running out of space as the genius of Hube's strategy now became apparent. As the XIVth Panzer Corps withdrew into the apex of the Messina triangle in northeastern Sicily, Hube's front became shorter and shorter; therefore, he was able to take troops out of his front line and send them back to the mainland without reducing the density of his frontline strength. Monty, by contrast, found the shortening front a major disadvantage because he was forced by geography to pull units out of the line, since he no longer had the space to employ them all.

The first to go into reserve was the 1st Canadian Infantry Division. It fought its last battle of the Sicilian campaign in the vicinity of Carcaci on August 5 and 6, when it covered the left flank of Evelegh's drive on Adrano. Here the Canadians brought up their 4th Reconnaissance Regiment and smashed a sizable portion of the German 3rd Parachute Regiment, which did not expect an armored attack at this point and was without antitank guns. After hiding out in lemon and orange groves on August 5, the paratroopers broke into groups of twos and threes and made their way as best they could back to the main body of the Hermann Goering Division, which was now defending on the Adrano-Bronte Road. Early the following morning, August 7, the British 78th Infantry Division pushed the remnants of two battalions of the 3rd Parachute out of Bronte. That same day Montgomery pulled the Canadians out of the line, followed the next day by the British 5th Infantry Division, which was pinched out of the line after it captured Paterno and Acireale on August 6 and 8, respectively. Headquarters, XIIIth Corps, was also withdrawn.

Meanwhile, the Hermann Goering Panzer Division was occupying new defensive positions north of Catania, while Rodt's 15th Panzer Grenadiers were digging in on a new fortified line around Cesaro—the so-called Trotorici Line (Map 15). Both divisions had already sent much of their heavy equipment back to the Messina by night, where it awaited the order to evacuate the island.

The British 78th Infantry Division—Monty's left hook—still constituted the 8th Army's main effort, but the German resistance against it stiffened. The terrain north of Bronte was appalling, with the Etna wilderness on the British right, the river Troina on the left, and four German battalions—liberally supported by mortars—to the front. Vehicles could hardly leave the road as the Tommies struggled forward toward Randazzo. The battle now consisted largely of a British advance guard clearing a path through extensive and systematic minefields and pushing back the German rear guard. This meant that the progress was extremely slow, even for the Sicilian campaign. It was August 12 before the British reached Maletto, only four miles north of Bronte. On the right flank British progress was equally meager. On August 11, for example, the 50th Infantry Division finally took Riposto, a village on the main coastal highway, only sixteen miles north of Catania. It had taken the division a week to cover this ground along the narrow coastal plain between Etna and the sea. Hube's rear guards still blocked the road to Messina.

After his victory on the Rosmarino on August 8, Patton's spearhead was only seventy-five miles from Messina; Montgomery, however, was twenty-three miles closer at his nearest point, so Patton pushed on relentlessly. General Fries ordered Lieutenant Colonel Krueger's 71st Panzer Grenadier Regiment to hold west of the Zappulla River, while Ulich's 15th checked the American advance along Highway 116, south of Naso. Most of Dr. Polack's 29th Motorized Artillery Regiment was posted in the northern sector to help Krueger delay Truscott's division, but it did little good initially. On August 9 the Americans pushed back the 71st Panzer Grenadier, and the following day they reached the Zappulla, repelled a German counterattack, and crossed the river. The stiffening resistance had taken its toll on the infantrymen of the 3rd, however, and they were halted short of Naso Ridge. In the meantime, Patton decided to speed up the advance by ordering a second amphibious assault for the night of August 10–11.

George S. Patton was well pleased with the success of his Sant' Agata landings and on August 9 directed Bradley and Truscott to launch a second one on the night of August 9–10 (Map 16). The assault force would be the same: Lieutenant Colonel Lyle Bernard's 2nd Battalion/30th Infantry Regiment reinforced with five tanks, two batteries of artillery, and a fifteen-mule ammunition train. This time the target would be Monte Cipolla, a steep hill midway between the Brolo and Naso rivers that completely dominated the northern coastal highway, the narrow coastal plain, and the beaches. Its capture would effectively cut off Krueger and probably cause the destruction of his regiment. Bradley and Truscott objected to the plan, but Patton heatedly overruled their objections. The landings would take place as scheduled, he roared, implying that he would find someone else to direct the battle if they would not. Thus cowed, Truscott agreed to direct operations as Patton dictated. He could not, however, because of the Luftwaffe. On August 9 a German airplane on a harassing mission spotted LST-318 near its staging area of Caronia (twelve miles west of Sant' Agata), and damaged it beyond repair. The landings now had to be delayed twenty-four hours until a replacement could be sent from Palermo.

In the meantime, Truscott lined up his division for the assault on Fries's weakened 29th Panzer Grenadier. He realized that this battle might devolve into one to save a trapped landing force, so he planned an all-out attack for the morning of August 11. Meanwhile, on the afternoon of August 10 the American landing force marched to its staging area, boarded its landing craft, weighed anchor at six P.M., and sailed east into the night. They landed in waves on a beach west of the tiny town of Brolo between 2:30 and 4:00 A.M. Initially they were undetected.

To meet Truscott's land-based assault, Fries had positioned his 71st Regiment astride the coastal road and along Naso Ridge. To the south, Ulich's 15th Panzer Grenadier Regiment held positions south of Malo, covering the eastern side of the Zappulla River. To his rear, in and east of the town of Brolo, he stationed his divisional reserve: the headquarters detachment of the 29th Motorized Artillery Regiment; the Headquarters Battery, 29th Anti-Aircraft Battalion (with two four-barrel 20-mm antiaircraft guns); elements of the Ist Battalion, 71st Panzer Grenadier Regiment; and a few Italians, now thoroughly intermixed with the Germans. It was a weak reserve, consisting mainly of headquarters troops, but it was all Fries could muster under the circumstances. He had stationed them at just the right place to meet the emergency he was about to face, however. All of these units were placed under the command of Fritz Polack, who set up headquarters on Monte Cipolla, the very objective of Patton's landing.

In the predawn darkness of August 11 all the Germans appeared to be asleep. Still undetected, Colonel Bernard's men began to advance inland at four A.M. to cover the 450 yards between the beach and Monte Cipolla, when a German staff car and a half-track blundered into the American infantrymen. Bernard's men quickly knocked out the half-track and blew up the staff car with a bazooka. The explosions woke up Colonel Polack, who gathered fifteen of his men and launched an immediate counterattack against the Americans, who were now avancing up Monte Cipolla. Several GIs were killed, but Dr. Polack soon recognized that he could not hold the position against an American battalion. He hastily returned to headquarters, burned his secret papers (including a copy of Hube's evacuation plans), and fell back to Brolo, from which he telephoned Walter Fries with the news that the Americans were behind him. The Battle of Monte Cipolla had begun.

When he occupied the high ground at 5:30 A.M., Colonel Bernard had effectively cut off the retreat of the 29th Panzer Grenadier Division. He had also placed Colonel Polack in a position where he had no choice but to retake the steep, conical hill, especially with General Fries's orders ringing in his ears: counterattack immediately with everything you have.

This was to be the only serious threat the Allies were ever to present to the German evacuation of Sicily.

Meanwhile, Colonel Lyle Bernard was having his own problems, for he had already lost all five of his supporting tanks. Three had gotten stuck in ditches as they blundered toward Monte Cipolla in the predawn darkness, and he had no way of extracting them. The other two had been damaged trying to knock down stone fences enroute. Thus he had no armor for the battle ahead. To make matters worse, Polack quickly took the precaution of sending patrols into the no man's land between Monte Cipolla and the sea just at the moment when Bernard's mule train attempted to join him on the heights. It was caught in the open by a German ambush; thirteen of the fifteen mules were killed, and the column scattered. Bernard and his men would be low on ammunition all day long.

The first attack on the hill, other than minor probes, began at about eight A.M. It was delivered from the south by the 6th Company, IInd Battalion/15th Panzer Grenadier Regiment. Bernard met it with his infantry and his mortars. Seventy of the hundred attackers were killed or wounded, and the 6th Company practically ceased to exist; however, Bernard almost completely exhausted his mortar ammunition in the process. On the other hand, he still had the eight guns of Batteries A and B, 58th Armored Field Artillery Battalion, and they had an adequate supply of ammunition on hand. He still had enough firepower to win the battle, although the situation was growing desperate both for Colonel Bernard and General Fries.

Truscott had launched his attack at dawn and was making slow progress in heavy fighting. At nine A.M. Fries tried to break out of the trap with his own resources by weakening his front at Naso Ridge and attacking Monte Cipolla from the west, using elements of Krueger's 71st Panzer Grenadier Regiment. This attack was broken up by gunfire from the cruiser *Philadelphia*, by friendly aircraft sent over the Brolo sector at the request of General Truscott, and by Bernard's own artillery. Shortly thereafter Fries sent his grenadiers forward again, this time supported by panzers. Again they were beaten back by the Americans.

The battle raged back and forth all day. Colonel Polack launched another major attack at two P.M., but it was blasted by the big guns of Task Force 88, which included a battleship, two cruisers, and two destroyers. Almost simultaneously the attackers were hit by an air raid and the 155-mm guns of the 3rd Division's artillery, which had pushed to within 26,000 yards (and maximum range) of Monte Cipolla. This was too much for Colonel Polack's troops, who quickly dispersed. Three panzers, however, remained undamaged.

Meanwhile, at 2:20 P.M., under the cover of a smoke screen, Truscott's men broke across the Zappulla River and slowly pushed Krueger and Ulich back toward Brolo, although they were frequently delayed by the ubiquitous German land mines. It seemed Patton was about to achieve his objective of destroying the bulk of the 29th Panzer Grenadier Division and opening the road to Messina. The survival of the XIVth Panzer Corps hung in the balance that afternoon, when fate intervened: Colonel Bernard's shore-to-ship radio fell silent about 2:30 P.M. Communications from shore had been erratic all day, but now Admiral Davidson was worried. He had already blasted all his prearranged targets and was unwilling to continue firing without directions from the ground forces for fear of killing American soldiers. Also, he was concerned that his ships would become sitting ducks if the Luftwaffe attacked in force. After waiting forty minutes, during which he was unable to raise Bernard, he withdrew toward Palermo.

There is no question that Admiral Davidson made the right decision, but the loss of his big guns crippled the American defense of Monte Cipolla. Shortly after Davidson sailed away, Colonel Polack attacked Bernard's beaches in an effort to complete the isolation of the 2nd Battalion. He was entirely successful. The men on the beaches were mainly support troops who had no heavy weapons. Helpless against tanks, they jumped into their DUKWs and escaped into the sea. Then, at 3:10 P.M., Polack resumed his attack on Monte Cipolla, this time supported by Krueger's artillery, the two 20-mm antiaircraft guns, and the three panzers. As the attackers pushed through the lemon groves near the base of the hill, Battery B of the 58th Armored Field Artillery Battalion was forced to displace. Two guns and their ammunition half-tracks were caught on the road by the panzers and were destroyed. The third engaged a German tank over open sights. Both guns fired at the same time, and both scored direct hits. Both exploded into hundreds of pieces and burned furiously. Seeing this, the crew of the fourth American gun abandoned its isolated piece and fled for the protection of the infantry. Bernard had lost half his remaining firepower, but he quickly committed Battery A—his last reserve—to the battle. Another panzer was knocked out by the U.S. gunners, and Polack's last tank fell back, destroying the abandoned American gun as it retreated. Colonel Bernard had held his positions, but just barely. He and his men were beginning to feel very isolated on top of Monte Cipolla.

In the meantime, at four P.M., the 7th Army signaled Admiral Davidson and asked him to return to Brolo, which he promptly did. This time he was met by eight FW-190 fighter-bombers. The ships had to maneuver rapidly to escape destruction, and there were several near misses. Naval antiaircraft gunners shot down most of the attackers but could do nothing to influence the land battle because radio contact with the landing force could not be reestablished. The ships did rescue the beach parties that had escaped in DUWKs when confronted by the panzers, but this was their only positive accomplishment.

Meanwhile, back at Monte Cipolla, overeager American pilots finished Colonel Polack's job for him. Seven A-36's from Ponte Olivo Airfield, unable to communicate with the ground, dropped two bombs on Colonel Bernard's command post, killing or wounding nineteen men. Then they spotted Battery A at the foot of the hill. Mistaking it for German artillery, the American aviators reduced all four guns to burning piles of wreckage. Colonel Bernard's men fired the last of their mortar ammunition and fell back to a defensive perimeter on the top of the hill, certain that they would have to make a last-ditch stand as soon as dawn broke on August 12. Since they had only rifles with which to defend themselves, their position seemed hopeless. Colonel Bernard ordered them to be prepared to escape and evade in groups of twos and threes at daylight—a real every-man-for-himself order!

They need not have worried. Isolated on the hilltop, without heavy weapons, they no longer constituted a threat to the coastal highway, so General Fries promptly lost interest in them. He was more concerned with extracting his division from Patton's trap. At ten P.M. the vehicles of Colonel Krueger's regiment sped down the coastal road past Monte Cipolla to safety. Colonel Ulich's command also withdrew east of the hill to the next delaying line. Neither side attempted to disturb the other; both had had enough.

The 1st Battalion of the 30th Infantry Regiment linked up with its sister battalion on Monte Cipolla at 7:30 A.M. on August 12. The 2nd Battalion had lost ninety-nine men killed or missing and seventy-eight wounded. In addition, the amphibious battle group had lost five tanks and eight guns. German losses were about the same, except that they lost fewer heavy weapons. "Patton had come close to trapping a good part of Fries's division and perhaps even to rolling up the whole northern sector of Hube's front," Blumenson wrote later, "but the battalion sent to make the landing had been too small for the job."[7] Admiral Ruge, the German Naval Commander, Italy, was unimpressed by the American amphibious efforts. He commented that he did not see why this sort of operation had not been attempted earlier, more frequently, and on a larger scale.

He was right on all three counts.

Meanwhile, on the interior flank of Bradley's IInd Corps, the U.S. 9th Infantry Division replaced the Big Red One and was driving on Randazzo, the last strongpoint on the Tortorici Line with which the Americans had to deal.

Randazzo was a very important position because it controlled Hube's last lateral road (Map 16). Once it fell, the last link connecting the Germans on the east coast to those in the north would be cut. The Axis forces would thus be split in half, and Hube would have little choice but to abandon the interior of the island and retreat to Messina along either coastal road. Because of the importance of Randazzo, the British 78th Infantry Division was committed to support the Americans, as were large elements of the U.S. air corps and the RAF. The town soon became one of the most heavily bombed positions in the Sicilian campaign. It suffered through 1,180 bombing sorties and many fighter runs, but the Allies attacked with little success. General Rodt conducted his usual competent defense. After a series of delaying actions, Eddy's 9th Division took Cesaro on August 8 but was checked on the Simeto River on August 9. That evening he launched a night attack but failed again. On August 10 the 9th Infantry finally secured a foothold across the Simeto but could not advance any farther because of stiff German resistance. The American advance resumed on August 11, but Eddy could gain only three and a half miles, primarily as a result of thick German minefields.

Finally, on August 12, the Allies began to gain ground all along the front. The British 78th Infantry took the village of Maletto and drove into the high ground south of Randazzo while the Americans closed in from the north. At 9:30 A.M. the following morning American patrols entered Randazzo, only to find that the Germans had gone. They found only shattered, burning ruins.

Indeed, the Germans were breaking contact all along the line. They were, in fact, considerably thinned out already; the evacuation of Sicily had already begun, and the race for Messina was about to reach its conclusion.

And what was happening on the mainland while Hube was tying down an entire Allied army group in Sicily with his single panzer corps?

Simply put, Hitler was capturing Italy. True, the process was not completed before Hube started to evacuate the island, but it was so far advanced by then that its successful completion was inevitable.

As soon as he was installed as premier of Italy, Marshal Badoglio began to try to halt the flow of German troops into Italy, while Hitler tried to accelerate it. The Fuehrer assigned this task to Field Marshal Erwin Rommel, who was no friend of the Italians.

Rommel soon made it clear that he would not hesitate at provoking a war with Italy, if necessary, to secure the peninsula for Nazi Germany. When Mussolini was overthrown on July 25, Hube's rear was almost totally exposed to a combined Italian defection and an Allied invasion of the mainland. The Desert Fox, however, acted quickly to rectify the situation. The crisis came on the morning of July 31, when Generale di Corpo Alessandro Gloria, commander of the Italian XXXVth Corps, refused to let Rommel's 44th Infantry Division "Hoch und Deutschmeister" cross into Italy via the vital Brenner Pass. Rommel responded by ordering his men to prepare to cross the border, using force if necessary and coordinating their advance with elements of the 26th Panzer Division, which had already crossed the border but was still in the vicinity. At least one German general expected codeword Achse, the signal for the German invasion of Italy, to be issued at any moment.

It was Badoglio who backed down. At 6:10 P.M. Roatta's chief of operations, Generale di Brigata Umberto Utili, telephoned Gloria and told him to let the Hoch und Deutschmeister Division pass. It was quickly followed by the 305th Infantry Division, the Headquarters, LXXXVIIth Mountain Corps, the 76th Infantry Division, the 94th Infantry Division, the 1st SS Panzer Division "Leibstandarte Adolf Hitler," the 2nd Panzer Division, and the 65th Infantry Division. They were followed by other units, including the 2nd Parachute Division, which landed outside Rome one afternoon—much to the surprise of the Italians *and* Field Marshal Kesselring, who had not been informed. Table 6 shows the order of battle of the German forces in Italy during the third week of August—a marked contrast to their weakness a month earlier.

T A B L E 6

GERMAN ORDER OF BATTLE IN ITALY, SECOND HALF OF AUGUST 1943

Army Group B: Field Marshal Erwin Rommel
  LIst Mountain Corps: General Feuerstein
    65th Infantry Division
    305th Infantry Division

  LXXXVIIth Corps: General von Zangen
    76th Infantry Division
    94th Infantry Division

  IInd SS Panzer Corps: SS General Hausser
    24th Panzer Division
    1st SS Panzer Division "Leibstandarte Adolf Hitler"

  Army Group Reserve:
    44th Infantry Division
    71st Infantry Division
    Brigade Doehla

XIth Air Corps: General Kurt Student
  3rd Panzer Grenadier Division
  2nd Parachute Division

OB South: Field Marshal Albert Kesselring

  10th Army: Colonel General von Vietinghoff

    XIVth Panzer Corps: General Hans Hube
      15th Panzer Grenadier Division
      Hermann Goering Panzer Division
      16th Panzer Division

    LXXVIth Panzer Corps: General Herr
      29th Panzer Grenadier Division
      26th Panzer Division (+)
      1st Parachute Division (−)

Forming in Sardinia: 90th Panzer Grenadier Division
Forming in Corsica: SS Brigade "Reichsfuehrer-SS"

NOTE: The 3rd and 4th Parachute regiments of the 1st Parachute Division were attached to the 26th Panzer Division.
SOURCE: Molony, vol. V, p. 213.

While all this was going on, Badoglio made bungling peace overtures to the Allies with an ineptitude that typified his government. Nothing came of them, of course.

Meanwhile, the 2nd Parachute Division consolidated its positions north and south of Rome, while elements of the 26th Panzer Division were used to reinforce the 3rd Panzer Grenadier, which was still at Lake Bolsena and still in a position to threaten the Italian capital from the north. No major German units had moved south of the Rome area in some time. The Germans seemed to be preparing to seize Rome and La Spezia and set up a defensive line in the northern Appenines.

This is exactly what Erwin Rommel was planning. On August 16 he finally moved to northern Italy, setting up headquarters at Lake Garda near the Brenner-Verona Railroad. He ordered all his forces to be prepared to take action against the Italians, if necessary. The following day divisions of his army group were marching south, establishing defensive positions between Pisa and Rimini, in the area later known as the Gothic Line. Without Italian help, Rommel believed, the peninsula south of this point could not be held, and the Desert Fox was convinced that Badoglio and the king were planning to abandon the Axis at the first opportunity. According to Rommel's concept of operations, the XIVth Panzer Corps should evacuate Sicily, but only when it was absolutely necessary; then the forces under the command of Kesselring's OB South should conduct a planned retreat to the northern Appenines, where they would be absorbed by Army Group B. Kesselring's headquarters could then be dissolved or transferred elsewhere while Rommel directed the defense of Hitler's southern flank.

Not surprisingly, Kesselring disagreed with his rival on every point, including the loyalty of the Badoglio regime. Even now he was convinced that all was well in Italy. On August 5 he wrote to Hitler, "At the moment it is certain that the Italian leadership and armed forces want to cooperate with us."[8]

Small wonder that, at this point, Hitler favored Rommel and his plan over Kesselring. Nevertheless, that same day OKW temporarily canceled its plan for seizing Rome, a decision largely based on Kesselring's assertion that he could tie up a dozen Allied divisions in Sicily indefinitely. The weakness in his argument was that southern Italy—and thus the XIVth Panzer Corps—was still vulnerable to an Allied amphibious attack. At the moment only the

16th Panzer Division and a few miscellaneous battalions were guarding Calabria and southern Italy. Kesselring, therefore, asked for reinforcements so that he might have at least one division in Calabria, at Puglia, and in the Naples-Salerno area.

General of Artillery Jodl, chief of operations at OKW, emphatically objected. He pointed out to Hitler that the XIVth Panzer Corps was in danger of being cut off and called on the Fuehrer to evacuate Sicily and southern Italy and retreat to the northern Appennines.

As was frequently the case when he was confronted with opposing strategies, Hitler vacillated. On August 5 he rejected Kesselring's request to reinforce southern Italy but could not make up his mind to evacuate Sicily.

He never did. The order to begin evacuating the island came from Field Marshal Albert Kesselring on August 8. Early that morning the town of Bronte fell to the British 78th Infantry Division, San Fratello fell to Truscott, the British XIIIth Corps pushed eight miles beyond Catania and was exerting heavy pressure on the Hermann Goering Division, and the U.S. 9th Infantry Division took Cesaro from the rear guards of the 15th Panzer Grenadier Division. Later that day General von Senger flew to Kesselring's headquarters at Frascati and reported that the situation in Sicily was serious if not exactly critical. All units were holding fast, but the pressure on them was great, and they could not hold on much longer. German combat units had been depleted by almost a month of heavy fighting. Half the panzers had already been lost, and the grenadiers were outnumbered between six to one and ten to one. Supplies, for the first time in the campaign, were beginning to run low, and the bridgehead was becoming dangerously restricted.

Realizing that Hitler was not going to reinforce southern Italy, and that the four divisions in Sicily were in serious danger, Kesselring concluded that it would soon be time to get the XIVth Panzer Corps out of there, and that *someone* was going to have to make a decision. He authorized Hube to evacuate the island. The date when this operation was to begin, as well as its timing and the full conduct of operations, he left to the judgment of his corps commander.

✧ 14 ✧

OPERATION LEHRGANG: A PANZER CORPS ESCAPES

OF THE GERMAN EVACUATION OF SICILY, SAMUEL ELIOT MORISON, the distinguished American naval historian, wrote, "The final episode in the campaign has never received proper attention; partly for want of information, partly because nobody on the Allied side has cared to dwell on it. This is the Axis troops' evacuation of Sicily across the Straits of Messina, an outstanding maritime retreat of the war, in a class with Dunkirk, Guadalcanal and Kiska."[1]

The aerial defenses for the Straits of Messina began to take shape prior to the invasion, when Luftwaffe Major General Rainer Stahel, commander of all antiaircraft units in Sicily, began organizing the flak defenses for the straits. The genesis of the German evacuation of Sicily dates from July 14, four days after the Allied landings began. On that day Kesselring appointed Colonel Ernst-Guenther Baade "Commandant of the Straits of Messina." Baade had, in effect, superseded General Stahel in the most important sector—a move that indicates how much Kesselring trusted the flamboyant eccentric—or how little he trusted Stahel, who had been Goering's nominee for Commanding General, Sicily, instead of Hube. Perhaps to minimize Goering's influence on the defense of this critical sector, Kesselring relegated Stahel to coastal defense duties in the Palermo area.[2]

Baade's mission was to organize and coordinate all available means to protect the two-mile water passage between Messina and the mainland and to maintain the flow of supplies to the XIVth Panzer Corps. To accomplish this, he was given unusually far-reaching authority, including unconditional control over all artillery, antiaircraft artillery, and naval units in the Messina area and in the Villa San Giovanni and Reggio sectors of the mainland.

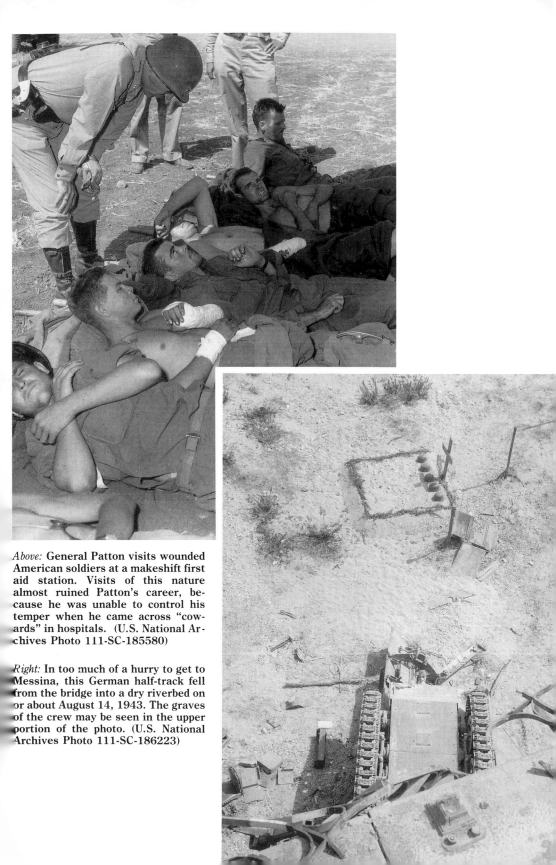

Above: **General Patton visits wounded American soldiers at a makeshift first aid station. Visits of this nature almost ruined Patton's career, because he was unable to control his temper when he came across "cowards" in hospitals. (U.S. National Archives Photo 111-SC-185580)**

Right: **In too much of a hurry to get to Messina, this German half-track fell from the bridge into a dry riverbed on or about August 14, 1943. The graves of the crew may be seen in the upper portion of the photo. (U.S. National Archives Photo 111-SC-186223)**

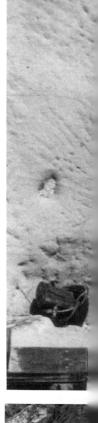

Top left: **An American private from the 7th Infantry Regiment, 3rd Infantry Division, is being given blood plasma by a medic after he was wounded by shrapnel near San Agata, Sicily, on August 9, 1943. A barefooted Sicilian family watches from their home in the background. (U.S. Army War College Photo)**

Bottom left: **German prisoners of war being interrogated near Cefalù, July 24, 1943. These men were members of Group Ulrich of the 29th Panzer Grenadier Division. The U.S. intelligence officer (at right) is wearing the patch of the U.S. 45th Infantry Division on his left sleeve. The men are eating U.S. Army C rations (or K rations). (U.S. National Archive Photo 111-SC-185458)**

Top right: **American forward observers from the 1st Infantry Division direct artillery fire on German positions in the town of Troina, Sicily, August 2, 1943. The Battle of Troina was the fiercest the Americans faced during the Sicilian campaign. (U.S. Army War College Photo)**

Bottom right: **U.S. troops pursue the Germans along a blown-out roadbed a few miles past Gioiosa Marea, August 14, 1943. Demolitions such as this one significantly slowed the Allied advance and materially contributed to the success of the German evacuation of Sicily. (U.S. National Archives Photo 111-SC-180347)**

Above: **Italian soldiers surrender in a small town near Messina, August 15, 1943. These men seem happy to be out of the war and some of them are actually carrying suitcases for their journey to the prisoner-of-war camps. German POW's were usually a much more sullen lot—and never surrendered en masse. (U.S. National Archives Photo 111-SC-179872)**

Right: **Generale d'Armata Alfredo Guzzoni, one of the better Italian generals, was recalled from retirement to command the 6th Army in Sicily. Although he handled the initial operations with some skill, Generale Guzzoni was gradually displaced as Axis commander in Sicily by Hans Hube. (Bundesarchiv, Kolbenz)**

Right: An 88-mm gun, destroyed near a pillbox complex, near Gesso, Sicily. This photograph was taken in January 1944. (U.S. Army War College Photo)

Below: Graves of German soldiers killed near Troina, August 1943. An American convoy is seen in the background. Note the rough nature of the barren terrain, which the German defenders used to maximum advantage. (U.S. National Archives Photo 206-AA-89z-10)

Top: **Major General Troy H. Middleton** *(left),* **commander of the U.S. 45th Infantry Division, discusses tactics with Lieutenant General Omar N. Bradley** *(center),* **IInd Corps commander, and Lieutenant General George C. Patton in a Sicilian olive grove, July 25, 1943. At this time, Middleton's division was pushing down the northern coastal road against stiff opposition from Group Ulrich of the 29th Panzer Grenadier Division. (U.S. Army War College Photo)**

Bottom: **A meeting in Sicily, August 1943. Left to right are Colonel George A. Smith, Jr. (C.O., U.S. 18th Infantry Regiment), Colonel Pappy Flint (C.O., U.S. 39th Infantry Regiment), Major General Vivian Evelegh (C.G., British 78th Infantry Division) and Brigadier E. E. Cass (C.G., British 11th Infantry Brigade). (U.S. National Archives Photo 111-SC-187002).**

Top left: Victor Emmanuel III, king of the Italians. Born in Naples in 1869, he was king from July 29, 1900, until May 9, 1946, when he abdicated in favor of his son, Umberto II. When the Italian people voted to dissolve the monarchy later that year, Victor went into exile in Alexandria, Egypt, where he died on December 28, 1947. (U.S. National Archives Photo 306-NT-95.271)

Above right: Italian Marshal Pietro Badoglio on a state visit to Berlin, 1937. Badoglio, who the Duce sacked as Chief of Commando Supremo in December 1940, replaced Mussolini as ruler of Italy on July 25, 1943. He escaped the German capture of Rome in September 1943, and remained head of an Italian rump government until the capture of Rome in June 1944. He then retired from public life and died on November 1, 1956. (U.S. National Archives Photo 242-HLB-2326-3)

Below: The Italian delegation signs the instruments of surrender at Cassibile, Sicily, at 5:15 p.m. on September 3, 1943. Left to right are Major General Walter "Beetle" Smith, Eisenhower's Chief of Staff; Commodore Roger M. Dick, Royal Navy, Cunningham's Chief of Staff; Major General Lowell W. Rooks, Eisenhower's Operations Officer; Captain de Haan, Strong's aide; Generale di Bragata Giuseppe Castellano, the Italian representative; and Consul Franco Montanari of the Italian Foreign Ministry. Brigadier Kenneth W. D. Strong, Eisenhower's Chief of Military Intelligence, is directly behind Generale Castellano. (U.S. National Archives Photo 111-SC-183172)

Above: An American soldier looks out at Messina, the strategic objective of the Sicilian campaign. The mainland of Italy can be seen in the background. In a five-day period, General Hube successfully evacuated his XIVth Panzer Corps over these straits without significant loss of life—an achievement that has been largely ignored by military historians. (U.S. National Archives Photo 208-AA-89z-13)

Below: The U.S. Army cemetery near Caronia, Sicily. Note that the soldiers' dog tags appear on the crosses to identify the graves. (U.S. Army War College Photo)

A truly interservice organization, Baade's command initially included several Luftwaffe flak batteries, Captain Kurt Paul's 771st Engineer Landing Battalion (an army ferrying unit that had served in North Africa), and part of the 616th Naval Artillery Regiment. All totaled, Admiral Doenitz would supply Colonel Baade with 1,723 naval gunners and several naval antiaircraft batteries during the campaign. Also subordinate to Baade were the German Naval Commander, Messina Straits Defenses, Captain *(Kapitaen zur See)* von Kamptz, and the German Naval Officer in Charge of Sea Transport, Messina Straits, Commander *(Fregattenkapitaen)* Baron Gustav von Liebenstein. Liebenstein's 2nd Naval Landing Division, in turn, directed Lieutenant Commander *(Korvettenkapitaen)* Wehrmann's 2nd Landing Flotilla, Lieutenant Commander Zimmermann's 4th Landing Flotilla, and (later) Lieutenant *(Kapitaenleutnant)* Einecke's 10th Landing Flotilla.[3]

As early as July 16 reports indicated that the German ferry service was operating efficiently. Blumenson wrote that Baade "ran a cold and efficient, machine-like service entirely apart from the operation conducted by the Italian military authorities."[4] By August 1 he and Commander von Liebenstein controlled thirty-three naval barges and L-boats, twelve Siebel ferries, seven MFBs,[5] thirteen small landing craft, and seventy-six motorboats, all protected by ten batteries of coastal defense artillery and numerous antiaircraft guns. The mainstay of the ferrying operation was the Siebel ferry, a double-ended, pontoon-supported motorized raft that had been invented by an aircraft designer named Fritz Siebel.

In the early 1920s Siebel had befriended an unemployed ex-fighter pilot named Hermann Goering. In 1940 the same Hermann Goering—now Reichsmarschall—hired Siebel to study seized French aircraft factories, and this led the inventor into an interest in designing barges for the invasion of Great Britain. The Siebel ferry was eighty feet long and fifty feet in beam. It could carry about 450 men or ten loaded trucks (sixty tons), make a speed of eight to ten knots, and mount up to three 88-mm antiaircraft guns. Small of draft and highly maneuverable, it could be loaded quickly and was designed so that it could be disassembled and transported overland for employment anywhere. In May and June 1943 the Luftwaffe sent a dozen Siebels to Sicily, where they were given to the highly competent naval reserve officer Baron von Liebenstein.

Gustav von Liebenstein was born in Rastatt, the son of a major general. He joined the Imperial Navy in 1909 as an officer-cadet and received a commission in 1912. He fought in World War I, served on a torpedo boat during the Battle of Jutland, and eventually commanded his own MTB. Discharged as a lieutenant commander (probably in 1920), he was not recalled to active duty until 1940. He commanded a minesweeping flotilla in the North Sea from May 1942 to February 1943, after which he was transferred to Italy as commander of the 2nd Landing Flotilla. He was posted to Sicily as commander of the 2nd Naval Landing Division shortly thereafter.

Before Liebenstein and Baade arrived, the ferrying situation was chaotic. Sea transport was conducted independently by navy, Luftwaffe, and army engineer commands, often operating with little concern for each other. The establishment of a unified command improved matters considerably. Also, Baron von Liebenstein instituted what was perhaps the first roll-on/roll-off cargo system in military history. Prior to his innovation, trucks arriving at Reggio were unloaded and their cargos were placed on ferries, often by hand. Once they reached Sicily, they had to be reloaded onto trucks for transport to the depots or to the troops. Liebenstein's system of ferrying fully loaded trucks was much more efficient. The average time required to load a Siebel ferry was reduced to twenty minutes, a remarkable increase in efficiency over previous methods. When the Hermann Goering Panzer Division arrived in late June, for example, Liebenstein was able to ship over 3,600 men, 610 vehicles, and 750 tons of supplies in a single day.[6]

Throughout May, June, and July Liebenstein ran an efficient supply service. He changed his embarkation and landing places frequently to avoid Allied air attacks, and by late July he and his boatmen were thoroughly familiar with potential staging areas and crossing points on the Messina Straits and knew the strengths and weaknesses of each one. This advanced knowledge would be priceless in the operation ahead.

On July 26, the day after Mussolini's overthrow and arrest, Hitler ordered OB South to "make preparations for the evacuation of German troops from Sicily, Sardinia and Corsica."[7] The next day Kesselring met with his senior German commanders in Rome.

Colonel Bogislaw von Bonin, chief of staff of the XIVth Panzer Corps, represented General Hube. During the meeting Kesselring said, "If the Italians should leave the alliance with Germany, XIVth Panzer Corps will immediately disengage from the enemy and evacuate all troops from Sicily." Evacuation preparations were to begin at once, and cooperation between the XIVth and LXXVIth Panzer Corps on the mainland was to be ensured.[8] The following day, after a briefing by von Bonin, Hube ordered Baade and von Liebenstein to start preparing an evacuation plan.

Although the evacuation of troops would not begin for two more weeks, the evacuation of excess supplies began in late July under the direction of special staffs that would later ensure the orderly embarkation of troops and equipment at the ferrying sites. Although some supplies had been lost when Syracuse and Augusta fell and some supplies left over from the Tunisian campaign had been abandoned at Trapani, most of the German depots were in northeastern Sicily and were successfully evacuated. The only major loss suffered by the German logistical staffs consisted of about two thousand railroad cars that they were unable to salvage. Most of them were captured by the Allies at the end of the campaign.[9]

In addition to the supply depots, Hube ordered that all nonessential noncombatant installations be withdrawn to Calabria, including workshops, camps of all sorts, and most medical establishments. On the mainland a specific area was allotted to each division to serve as a supply base. During the evacuation these bases would eventually be used as an assembly area and rally point for each division. Command of these rear area bases fell to Lieutenant General Richard Heidrich, commander of the 1st Parachute Division, who was without any important duties at this time.

As the time for the evacuation attempt neared, Colonel Baade was reinforced and was able to concentrate a tremendous density of antiaircraft guns on either side of the straits. These guns and their crews came mostly from the 3rd and 22nd Flak brigades (under Colonels Nieper and Mueller, respectively) of the 5th Flak Division and were lent to the XIVth Panzer Corps by General of Fliers Ritter Maximilian von Pohl, the officer responsible for the flak defenses of southern Italy. His generosity was probably due to an appeal from his fellow Luftwaffe officer, Kesselring. In any event, General Galland later wrote:

The fact that anything at all reached the Italian mainland was solely due to the flak batteries. Their unique concentration protected the continuous ferry traffic so effectively that the hordes of Allied planes of all types could only half complete their mission from a great height.[10]

The British Official Naval History[11] noted that the straits were covered by four batteries of 280-mm (11.2-inch) guns, two 152-mm (6-inch) Italian batteries, and many mobile 3- to 4-inch guns, for a total of perhaps 150 medium and heavy guns. These excluded the heavy artillery battalion of the 15th Panzer Grenadier Division (II/15th Motorized Artillery Regiment under Captain Meyrhofer), which had also been placed at Baade's disposal. It included two batteries of 170-mm guns, which had a range of more than ten miles.[12] Morison, the U.S. naval historian, estimated that there were about 150 German 88-mm and Italian 90-mm dual-purpose guns divided between the Sicilian and Calabrian shores as well as a great many smaller pieces.[13] The U.S. army estimated that there were perhaps 500 guns guarding the two- to five-mile crossings, of which at least 333 were antiaircraft guns.[14] Allied bomber pilots subsequently stated that the flak over the Messina corridor was thicker than any they had ever seen, including that over the Ruhr—and that is saying something. A typical remark came from an Allied air staff officer who said that the antiaircraft fire over Messina was "the heaviest ever encountered in the Mediterranean—heavier than 'Flak Alley' between Bizerta and Tunis, and greater than the inner artillery of London."[15] Map 17 shows the Messina flak corridor and the detailed dispositions of the Axis batteries.

In addition to the flak corridor, all evacuation routes were protected by patrols of minesweepers, E-boats, and Italian mini-submarines. Admiral Ruge reported that the Royal Navy ships always turned away from the straits when they saw Axis patrols. He also noticed that there were never any aircraft over the straits an hour after dawn or before nightfall, times in which the Germans learned to make maximum use of their supply vessels. "The Anglo-Saxon habit of lunch hour also helped considerably," he added sarcastically.[16]

On July 29 Kesselring took the evacuation planning one step further when he met with the Ia's (operations officers) of each

German division in Sicily: Colonel Heckel of the 15th Panzer Grenadier, Lieutenant Colonel Stuenzer of the 29th Panzer Grenadier, and Lieutenant Colonel Bergengruen of the Hermann Goering. Presumably Lieutenant Colonel Ernst-Ludwig Birck, the Ia of the XIVth Panzer Corps, was also present, but this is not clear from the records. After this conference, Kesselring reported to Hitler that it would be possible to evacuate the island in three nights. Hans Hube, however, politely ignored Kesselring's preliminary planning. He obviously felt that such a hasty withdrawal would be too expensive in terms of equipment losses, and he was no doubt right. Four days later, on August 2, he submitted his own plan to OB South. Code-named Operation "Lehrgang," it called for all troops and equipment to be evacuated in five successive nights. The fact that he later decided to add an additional night in the middle of the operation is testimony to his coolness, his nerve, and his desire to save as much equipment as possible. Kesselring approved the plan and told Hube that he would let him know when to start the evacuation. He then signaled OKW that all was ready.

General Hube's plan called for the XIVth Panzer Corps to retreat to Messina in stages by night. He designated five general lines of resistance, which were to be held for one day each and then abandoned that night. Later these would evolve into four major lines, designated the Tortorici Line (previously discussed) and Phase Lines 1, 2, and 3, with several intermediate positions and phase lines. Every step backward into the apex of the triangle formed by northeastern Sicily would release troops, who would proceed to assembly areas and then to the ferry sites on order. On the last evening the rear guards would march directly from the fifth line of resistance to the boats, completing the operation. General Hube himself planned to accompany this group back to the mainland.

Meanwhile, Hans Hube was receiving annoying orders from Hitler through OKW. One of them forbade him to inform the soldiers that an evacuation was being organized. Hube decided to ignore these instructions and, as early as August 2, let it be known that preparations to evacuate the island were in progress. This had a tremendously positive effect on morale, for the troops were worried that they might fall victim to one of Hitler's "hold at all cost" orders, as had happened to the 6th Army at Stalingrad and to Army Group Afrika at "Tunisgrad." On August 4, because of

MAP 17

THE MESSINA FLAK CORRIDOR, early August, 1943

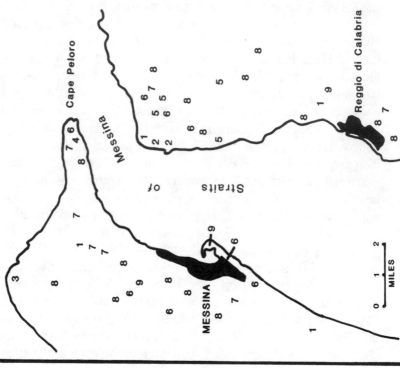

Cape Peloro

Messina

Straits of

MESSINA

Reggio di Calabria

0 1 2
MILES

AXIS BATTERIES:

1: 280mm

2: 170mm

3: 152mm

4: 120mm

5: 105mm

6: 90mm Dual Purpose

7: 90mm Anti–Aircraft

8: 88mm

9: 76mm

NOT SHOWN: Guns less than 76mm,

including numerous 20mm mobile batteries

heavy Allied pressure, Hube acted on his own initiative and ordered the evacuation of all noncombat units that could be spared. This move took considerable courage, because OKW had specifically instructed him not to evacuate any units without direct orders from the High Command (i.e., Hitler himself).

By the first week in August, Baade's command included three naval flotillas, the army engineer landing battalion, two or three engineer fortification battalions, and two port maintenance companies, for a total of 134 small naval vessels, ferries, and barges (excluding minesweepers and patrol boats, which screened the evacuation but did not normally carry troops). In consultation with Commander von Liebenstein, Colonel Baade developed six ferry routes, each of which included several landing places on each shore. From these, Hube selected the four he considered the most practical, all of which were north of Messina. A fifth route south of the city was surveyed and designated for emergency use only; in fact, it was never used except for some supply units that left the island prior to August 8.

From north to south, Hube assigned the first route, at the northern tip of Sicily, to the 15th Panzer Grenadier Division. The second route, also near the tip, was given to the 29th Panzer Grenadier Division. Route 3, located two miles north of Messina, was to be used by the corps headquarters, general headquarters, and miscellaneous troops, the 131st Flak Regiment, and Major General Stahel's troops. It was also supposed to accommodate any overflow from the other routes. The fourth route, a mile north of Messina, was assigned to the Hermann Goering Division and the attached elements of the 1st Parachute Division. Routes 1 and 2 were the responsibility of Captain Kurt Paul's 771st Engineer Landing Battalion. Routes 3, 4, and 5 were the responsibility of the 2nd, 4th, and 10th Flotillas, respectively. Map 18 shows the evacuation routes.

The 771st Engineer Landing Battalion controlled several Siebel ferries, at least eleven L-boats (large, open boats put together using pontoons, each capable of carrying two trucks),[17] some W-boats, and a great many I-boats. (W- and I-boats were motorboats.) The 2nd Flotilla consisted of twenty MFPs (naval barges) and two MALs (naval artillery lighters). The 10th Flotilla had eight Siebel ferries, two heavily armed combat Siebel ferries, about ten

THE EVACUATION: AUGUST 11–17, 1943

Torre di Faro

Ganzirri

ROUTE 1

ROUTE 2

Scilla

Cannitello

Pezzo

Villa S. Giovanni

Paradiso

Salvatore

ROUTE 3

ROUTE 4

113

MESSINA

Catano

Gallico

ROUTE 5
(EMERGENCY)

Pistunina

114

0   1   2

MILES

REGGIO

MAP 18

I-boats, and two W-boats. The 4th Flotilla was similarly equipped. All totaled, in the second half of July, Liebenstein had thirty-three MFBs, twelve Siebel ferries, two MALs, eleven L-boats, seventy-one I-boats, and five W-boats. To protect these vessels, Captain Kamptz had very little: four 100-ton minesweepers (armed with five 20-mm guns and some 35-mm's) and one senior officer's boat *(SG 14)*, an old French colonial-service gunboat of a thousand tons armed with one 88-mm and four 37-mm antiaircraft guns plus three sets of quad-mounted 20-mm AA guns.[18]

General Hube specified that the troops were to cross only during the hours of darkness. Weapons and equipment could be ferried over day and night, at Baade's discretion, on the basis of a strict order of priority: antitank weapons, artillery, self-propelled weapons (including panzers and assault guns), trucks, and motorized vehicles, in that order. All material not transported was to be destroyed. Italian troops and equipment could also be ferried by German boats, but only if all available German soldiers and matériel were evacuated first.

Traffic controllers were assigned to direct each stage of the withdrawal and loading. The area formed by the Milazzo-Scaletta-Messina triangle was designated a prohibited zone. Troops were allowed to enter only on the direct orders of a road traffic controller. All assembly points were linked to the ferry sites by telephones, so that there would be no traffic jams on the roads or on the beaches for the Allied fighter-bombers to blow away. Typically, troop units would be withdrawn from the front line and moved to the rear, where they would lie hidden and well dispersed in numerous gullies until it was almost time for them to board the ferries; then they would be signaled to proceed. The barges, rafts, and ferries would be waiting for them when they reached the shore, ready to cast off as soon as the army and Luftwaffe ground units were on board. A meticulously planned series of camouflaged assembly areas, phase lines, and checkpoints was set up by the staff officers of the XIVth Panzer Corps to ensure a steady movement of men and equipment across the straits, without creating bottlenecks.

General Hube also had his stern side. Realizing that panic could break out in an evacuation, he ordered that discipline was to be rigidly maintained. Incidents of indiscipline were to be instantly suppressed, and the violator(s) were to be shot or clubbed to death.[19] General Conrath carried this order one step further and decreed that, in his sector, the rifle was a soldier's ticket off the island, and that individuals without their weapons were to be left behind. "The *most rigid discipline* is the main condition for the success of all future movements," the divisional warning order read. "Anyone not co-operating will be shot. Examples of individuals always work wonders."[20]

The plan called for the evacuation of eight to ten thousand men per night, beginning with the Hermann Goering Division, which was to withdraw around both sides of Mount Etna and head for the evacuation points. Elements of the 15th Panzer Grenadier were to evacuate from the northern route at the same time, but most of Rodt's division was to cross before the Hermann Goering made its escape. Fries's 29th Panzer Grenadier Division was to go last and, along with a detachment of tanks from the Hermann Goering Panzer Regiment, was to form the rear guard for the final evacuation.

It is interesting to note that Hube's plan denied the Italian units the use of Messina without his prior approval. Roadblocks manned by armed guards were erected at all entrances to the city, forcing unauthorized individuals and units to use other routes.

The Italian ferrying operations were conducted entirely independently of the German effort. Whereas the German ferry service operated efficiently from the start, the Italian service was on the verge of breaking down completely at the beginning of the campaign. From the moment the invasion began many Italian soldiers were trying to escape to the mainland on any pretext, while Sicilian soldiers on the mainland were attempting to return to the island, loudly affirming that they wanted to defend their homeland, when in fact they intended to desert and join their families as soon as possible. The Italian sailors manning the ferries accommodated both groups, and everyone else who wanted to cross in either direction. "The Italians were far more humane in their conduct of ferries" than were the Germans, Martin Blumenson wrote. They were usually willing to grant passage to or from Sicily to soldiers on leave and even to civilians (or even men in civilian clothes) "for the most obscure reasons and on the most transparently flimsy excuses." The Italian sailors would overload boats and ignore schedules, safety regulations, timetables, and common sense; also, because they failed to maintain them, their engines were constantly breaking down.[21] Commander von Liebenstein's men were much more efficient and much less understanding toward individuals.

Acting independently, General Guzzoni decided on July 31 to begin evacuating Italian forces on August 3, a task he assigned to Rear Admiral Pietro Barone, commandant of Messina. According to Colonel von Bonin, Guzzoni made this decision at the urgent request of General Hube, who wanted as many Italian units out of the way as possible *before* he started his own evacuation.[22]

Although the Italians started their planning much later than did the Germans, and much later than should have been the case, Admiral Barone did a very competent job under the circumstances. He assigned one senior Italian army officer and one senior naval officer to each of his four embarkation points, and, after a poor start, the Italian ferry service operated with reasonable efficiency, although it was hampered by mechanical problems during most of the evacuation.

To evacuate the remnants of the 6th Italian Army, Admiral Barone had only two small steamboats, four motorized rafts, one 932-ton train ferry (the *Villa*), and one 2,800-ton train ferry, the *Cariddi*. Unfortunately, the *Villa*, which was capable of lifting three thousand men per trip, caught fire on August 12, during the peak of the evacuation, and was out of commision for forty-eight hours. During this period the motorized rafts saved the situation by transporting twenty thousand men.

The *Cariddi* was even less fortunate than the *Villa*. It was unable to move on its own power, but the Italians nevertheless docked it at the roadstead north of Messina (two of their evacuation points were north of the city) and loaded it with heavy artillery and other equipment. They intended to tow it across the straits but could not find a tugboat, and it had to be scuttled as the Allies entered Messina. This, plus one motorized raft sunk by Allied aircraft, constituted the only serious losses the Italians suffered during the evacuation.

As a result of breakdowns, fires, and engine malfunctions, the Italians were unable to transport their heavy equipment, so Hube and his subordinates generously offered to help by taking over whatever they could on a space-available basis. When they got to the other shore, however, the junior partners learned the limits of German generosity. The soldiers of the Wehrmacht, reasoning that the Italians were not going to use their equipment against the Anglo-Americans anyway, usually confiscated it and incorporated it into their own units—especially trucks and other motorized vehicles. The Italians were furious about this, of course, but there was very little they could do about it.

On August 2 Montgomery signaled Alexander that he expected to storm Adrano on the night of August 5–6. Once that happened, he said, he expected Hube to begin evacuating the island. What, he asked, did the Allies plan to do in the event of such a contingency?

This was a very good question, one that never really received an answer. On August 3, the day the Italian evacuation began, Alexander learned of it, probably from the British intelligence network, which had thoroughly infiltrated Commando Supremo much earlier. From Sicily, Alex signaled Admiral Cunningham in Malta and Air Chief Marshal Tedder in Tunis that the Germans were preparing to evacuate Sicily and might begin pulling out at any time. He asked them to be prepared to "take immediate advantage of such a situation by using full weight of Navy and Air Power. You have no doubt coordinated plans to meet this contingency. . . ."[23]

They had no plans, coordinated or otherwise. The astonishing fact is that no Allied plan for halting the Axis evacuation ever existed. Admiral Cunningham gave the matter careful thought, but decided that he could not employ his heavy warships in the area of the straits until the strong German coastal defense batteries had been knocked out. Indeed, Cunningham did not believe there was any effective way to halt the evacuation by sea or air. The only way to stop it, he felt, was for the ground forces to overrun the evacuation points.

Postwar historians have generally concluded that Sir Andrew was wrong in not launching an all-out attempt to block the evacuation.[24] It is doubtful that the German defenses could have withstood a maximum effort from the combined Allied navies and air forces for long, especially when one considers that the Germans were running low on antiaircraft ammunition. By August 12, only one of Liebenstein's flotillas had 45 percent of its basic load of antiaircraft ammunition; the other two had less than 20 percent. Only the 771st Engineer Landing Battalion had more than half of its normal allocation. The shore batteries were equally low on shells.

But Admiral Cunningham had been a young destroyer captain in 1915 and had been there during the Royal Navy's disastrous attempt to silence the Turkish batteries in the Dardanelles during the Gallipoli campaign. He had never forgotten the slaughter—could never forget it. He would not commit his precious capital ships to a duel with the batteries on the straits, which bore a strong resemblance to the Dardanelles, even on a map.

Even if he had been willing, it is doubtful that he could have obtained a simultaneous maximum effort from the air force. With no strong-willed person in overall command, the degree of coordination necessary to smash the XIVth Panzer Corps or disrupt its evacuation simply could not be obtained by the far-flung Allied headquarters in 1943.

Without a positive physical barrier between Sicily and the mainland—which the Royal Navy could not or would not provide—the Anglo-American air forces could not halt Operation Lehrgang. Even if they had been able to control the straits in the daytime, the highly mobile landing craft could have continued the evacuation at night. The air forces, however, could have accomplished a great deal more than they did.

Air Chief Marshal Tedder did put his air forces to work against the ferries and evacuation points immediately after receiving Alexander's request, but it was less than an all-out effort. Crews were exhausted, flak fire was horrible, and the air combat units were already attacking railroads, bridges, and airfields on the mainland in preparation for the invasion of Italy. In fact, the only serious attempt at stopping the German escape was Patton's amphibious landing at Brolo.

"The trouble is that there is no high-up grip on this campaign," Montgomery lamented on August 7. He was certainly right about that. Alexander, Cunningham, and Tedder were about six hundred miles apart, so coordination and even discussion were impossible. Indeed, the entire Allied campaign in Sicily suffered from a distinct lack of coordination from beginning to end.

The U.S. Army's Official History of the campaign states that the weakness in Baade's defenses was his shortage of high-altitude guns. It speculates that if U.S. Major General James Doolittle's Northwest African Strategic Air Force (NASAF) had been used against Messina, the evacuation might have been disrupted,[25] but even this is doubtful. We will never know for sure, however, because Allied strategic bombing missions in late July and August were concentrated against lines of communications targets and airfields in Italy. Even during the actual evacuation of Sicily, the Anglo-Americans continued to use their strategic bombers in raids against the mainland. On August 13, for example, the 12th U.S. Air Force attacked Rome with 106 B-17's, 102 B-26's, and 66 B-25's, escorted by 135 P-38's—409 airplanes in all. In other major raids during the first seventeen days of August, the Americans bombed Bologna and the RAF Bomber Command attacked Milan four times (August 7, 12, 14, and 15), Turin three times (August 7, 12, and 16), and Genoa (August 7). A host of smaller raids were flown against targets in southern Italy. Hube's men were also attacked, primarily by fighters and fighter-bombers, but they hardly received the undivided attention of the Allied air forces.

Things were difficult enough for Hans Valentin Hube, who was growing alarmed at the rate at which his divisions were losing ground. Late on the afternoon of August 10 he issued the order for Operation Lehrgang to commence on the night of August 11–12.

When Hitler was told of the evacuation order, he accepted it as a fait accompli, in marked contrast to his attitude on many other occasions, when he stubbornly insisted that German army units hold every inch of ground no matter what the cost. General Warlimont credits Jodl with calming the Fuehrer on this occasion and keeping his infamous temper from exploding.[26]

The evacuation began on schedule. From the start one coastal road along each side of the straits served all embarkation and debarkation points, and despite the German precautions, there were serious problems and occasional traffic jams. The evacuation was temporarily halted at 8:45 P.M. on August 11 because of a raid by British Wellington bombers. Afterward the troops were generally slow in reaching their embarkation points, and, as a result, the ferries operated at less than full capacity much of the evening. It was not a bad start, but it was not an overwhelming success, either.

The following day, August 12, the ferries operated at irregular intervals, carrying equipment. That night the evacuation of troops resumed, but the soldiers, moving back at night over unfamiliar terrain, were frequently late. At one point a large group of ferries waited three hours and then returned to the mainland, almost empty. The men they were supposed to transport arrived a few minutes later.

Things got worse as the night wore on. Around eleven P.M. the evacuation had to be stopped altogether because of the failure of the telephone connection between Messina and the mainland. It did not resume until two A.M. on August 13, and even then it was harassed by Allied night bombers until five A.M. According to the war diary of the LXXVIth Panzer Corps, 615 officers, 19,924 men, 2,185 vehicles, 34 tanks, 34 self-propelled guns, 15 heavy antitank weapons, 21 artillery pieces, and 11 antiaircraft guns were evacuated during the first two nights.[27] About half the men were German—probably somewhat less. The evacuation was behind schedule. To get it back on track, Colonel Baade and Commander von Liebenstein decided to ferry troops back during the daylight hours on August 13, in spite of Hube's original instructions.

At the exact moment when hundreds of German troops were huddled together in ferries and small landing craft in the middle of the Straits of Messina, more than four hundred American aircraft appeared—over Rome. While the 12th U.S. Air Force bombed the Italian capital, Ernst-Guenther Baade ferried thousands of veteran grenadiers and panzertruppen across the water, virtually unmolested. By the evening of August 13 a total of 15,000 German troops, 1,300 vehicles, 21 panzers, and 22 assault guns had been evacuated to the mainland, including the entire 15th Panzer Grenadier Division. The evacuation was back on schedule.

In the meantime, the Germans at and near the front had not yet reached Baade's protective flak umbrella and were forced to deal with hundreds of Allied fighters and fighter-bombers in an ever-diminishing area. The northern coastal road in particular became known as Death Alley by the Germans. They minimized their casualties by maintaining large intervals between units, convoys, and individual vehicles within convoys, and by distributing their engineers throughout the various columns, to clear the road and push aside demolished wrecks. Such antiaircraft weapons as were still available were distributed throughout the convoys.[28]

Besides the ubiquitous Allied airplanes, the Germans had to deal with occasional salvos from Anglo-American warships. At one point, the Allies attempted to cut off the German retreat by destroying the coastal highways with naval gunfire. Their targets were certain points where the road had been built into cliff faces. By pounding the overhead rock, they caused rockslides to obliterate the highway. The Germans, however, soon noticed that the salvos came at regular intervals, and this enabled the engineers to clear a single lane of traffic. The military police would then push traffic through until it was time for the next salvo, and the process would then repeat itself. There were few casualties, and, like all the others, these attempts at disrupting the retreat failed.

George Patton and Sir Bernard Montgomery, meanwhile, were pushing toward Messina, with Patton especially determined to reach the prize before his rival did. On August 13 Patton brought the Big Red One back into the line and pushed forward with three infantry divisions (the 1st, 3rd, and 9th), but with little success. On the coastal flank, Truscott was brought to a temporary halt by a "spectacular demolition." At Cape Calava, near the village of Patti, the coastal road (hewn here from solid rock) entered a tunnel. When the Americans arrived, however, both the tunnel and the road had vanished, leaving only a huge scar on the face of the cliff. The American engineers had to build a wooden footbridge to circumvent the handiwork of their German counterparts, but it was suitable only for infantry. Artillery, trucks, and supplies had to be ferried around by landing craft.[29]

That same day, on the other coast, Monty launched a two-pronged attack with his 5th and 50th Infantry divisions. The battle raged along the southern slopes of Mount Etna, but the British gained little ground against the remaining elements of the Hermann Goering and 1st Parachute divisions. General Conrath conducted a leisurely delaying action and, that evening, gave up Taormina, a former resort town twenty-nine miles from Messina. (The German engineers had blocked the road so thoroughly, however, and had left behind so many mines and booby traps that the British would not reach this point until August 15.) Then, leaving a strong rear guard in Hube's second phase line, Conrath continued to move the bulk of his forces northward, toward the evacuation points.

As the ground battle neared its conclusion, the air battles did not go well for either side. The declining Luftwaffe aviation units did virtually nothing; the Allies pounded Messina and the beaches north of the city. During the first week of August (1–7) they attacked the Messina–Cape Peloro area with 815 sorties. This average of just over one hundred sorties per day was not significantly improved on during the evacuation, however. From August 8 to 17, for example, medium bombers and fighter-bombers flew 1,170 sorties, mostly against vessels in the straits but sometimes against naval craft and landing points on the southern Italian shore. Between August 8 and 14 the obsolete British Wellingtons flew an average of eighty-five sorties per night, almost exclusively against the evacuation beaches. They did little damage, however.

The greatest Allied air effort took place from August 15 to 17, after most of the panzer corps had gone. During this period, attacking through heavy flak, Wellingtons, Mitchells, Bostons, Baltimores, Warhawks, and Kittyhawks flew around the clock, bombing and strafing troop-laden craft on the evacuation beaches, in the straits, and along the mainland. During Operation Lehrgang Allied air forces claimed the destruction of 23 vessels, direct hits on 43 others, and near misses (i.e., damaging but not fatal injuries) on 204 others.

Had these claims been even close to accurate, the XIVth Panzer Corps would have been destroyed, for the Allied pilots reported the damage or destruction of more vessels than Commander von Liebenstein had. In reality, however, German naval losses were minor. Total Axis naval losses in Lehrgang consisted of six German vessels and one Italian vessel sunk or damaged beyond repair and eight other vessels damaged.

The evacuation was never delayed more than three hours by Allied air attacks and Baade's timetable was never seriously disrupted, because the light ferries were simply too agile and too well defended to be destroyed by bombers, and the fighters and fighter-bombers were too often shot down or turned back by the Axis flak wall. Exhaustion of the Allied air crews was also a factor in this battle, for they had been operating almost continuously since D-Day, and the strain was beginning to tell on them. In any case, Colonel von Bonin later noted that the Allied air forces caused much more trouble by destroying the roads and railroads in southern and central Italy than by anything they did over the Straits of Messina.

On August 14 General Alexander first became aware that the German evacuation was under way when the XIVth Panzer Corps broke contact with the 8th Army all along the line. He signaled Tedder and suggested that he commit strong forces to the straits to disrupt the evacuation. Tedder, however, had already committed most of his wings to raids on the mainland that day. He was able to release only a few medium and light bombers, plus a few fighters and fighter-bombers. Baade's antiaircraft guns prevented these planes from doing any serious damage.

Patton, meanwhile, was anxious to cut off the retreat of the 29th Panzer Grenadier Division and was desperate to beat Montgomery to Messina. On the morning of August 15 he ordered Keyes, Bradley, and Truscott to prepare another amphibious landing behind German lines. This time the target would be the beaches of Spadafora, east of Milazzo. Truscott objected and was backed up by General Bradley. The 3rd Infantry, they said, was now advancing so rapidly down the coastal highway after capturing Patti on August 14 that the landing would be useless and might well come ashore behind American lines. Patton's emotions had run away with him again, however, and he would not listen to reason. The argument between the generals grew heated until Patton became very angry—angry enough to threaten both Bradley and Truscott with demotion to the rank of colonel if they did not do as he commanded. This, naturally, settled the matter.

On August 15, as the 157th Regimental Combat Team of the 45th Infantry Division prepared to launch Patton's third amphibious landing, Truscott's division continued its rapid advance. Falcone fell, and a few hours later the U.S. 3rd and 9th Infantry divisions met at Montalbano, which Fries had evacuated some time before. Early the next morning the 157th RCT landed at Bivio Salica, about twenty-five miles west of Messina. Two officers from the 3rd Infantry Division strolled down to the beach to greet them. Truscott and Bradley had been right: the spearhead of the 3rd Infantry were now on the Milazzo plain, fifteen miles west of Messina. The landing had taken place behind American lines.

Meanwhile, to the southeast, Montgomery was also moving toward Messina, but only very slowly because of a multitude of German mines. The 50th Infantry Division finally reached Taormina on August 15, and the 51st Highlander and 78th Infantry divisions joined hands near Linguaglossa later that day, completing the circuit around Mount Etna. The 8th Army did not regain contact with the rear guards of the Hermann Goering Division until late on August 15. Most of the division had already escaped by then.

On August 13 Admiral Cunningham asked Montgomery point-blank why he did not use "the priceless asset of sea power" to cut off the German retreat up the coastal highway, but Monty had seen no need to engage in such a risky venture. On August 15, however, he changed his mind, an indication that he also wanted to capture Messina (although probably not as badly as Patton did). The following morning the four hundred men of the British 2nd Commando, reinforced with engineers, artillery, and a squadron of tanks from the 4th Armoured Brigade, came ashore three miles north of Cape d'Ali—sixteen miles north of Taormina and only about ten miles south of Messina. By this time, however, Conrath's rear guard had fallen back to Hube's third phase line, which was located a few hundred yards *north* of the British beaches. The Commandos were quickly brought under fire by the Goerings, who remained between them and Messina.

Now the real race for Messina began, because the leader of the 2nd Commando was Lieutenant Colonel J. M. T. F. Churchill. A distant cousin of the prime minister, "Mad Jack" also had the Churchillian spirit and was determined to beat the Americans to the port. He was just the man to do it, too. The unorthodox Colonel Churchill had quite a reputation within the elite British Commandos. His favorite weapon, for example, was the bow and arrow. As second in command of the 3rd Commandos, he had led his men to shore in a raid in Norway, playing the bagpipes. The bagpipes were now safely stored in the back of his jeep, along with a huge Scottish sword, as he turned north, toward Messina. He was followed by Brigadier J. C. Currie, commander of the 4th Armoured Brigade and the overall commander of the landing force, who (according to Churchill) was similarly equipped. Both, however, like the Americans, were soon slowed by rear guards and blocked by demolitions. The race for Messina proceeded at a snail's pace, both in the interior and along both coastal highways.

As the frustrated Allies struggled toward Messina, Hube put the finishing touches on his tactical masterpiece. On the evening of August 12 he ordered German units in all sectors to pull back to Phase Line 1. This move shortened his line considerably and allowed him to pull out the division in his center—Rodt's 15th Panzer Grenadier—which went directly to the rear assembly areas for evacuation. Much of the Hermann Goering Division had already been pulled back, and the 29th Panzer Grenadier Division was thinned out considerably as well.

The remaining men of the XIVth Panzer Corps held Phase Line 1 until the early morning hours of August 13–14, when Hube signaled them to withdraw to Phase Line 2. Most of the 29th Panzer Grenadier Division did not stop here, but continued on to the evacuation points. By nightfall only a single reinforced battalion of the 29th remained on the coastal road to hold the division's front. It was now that Hube decided to extend the evacuation one more day in order to get as much equipment off the island as he could. The rear guard of the 29th Panzer Granadier was ordered to hold Phase Line 2 until the night of August 15–16, which it did. It then fell back to Phase Line 3.

During the halt on Phase Line 2, operations were progressing so smoothly that Hube decided to send Kesselring some "suggestions for the final communique after the conclusion of the evacuation." His main idea was to describe the operation as a big success, in order to rekindle flagging morale at home. This was a good point, considering that morale in the Third Reich had reached its lowest point to date after the firebombing of Hamburg from July 24 through August 2, during which fifty thousand people were killed and more than a million were left homeless. This came on top of the defeat of the huge German offensive at Kursk on the Eastern Front and the fall of Mussolini—Nazi Germany's most prominent ally. German casualties now exceeded two million. War weariness had set in, and morale would not sink this low again until 1945.

Hube pointed out to Kesselring that the British propaganda

machine had sold the Dunkirk "catastrophe" (Hube's word) as a great success but that "the end of the Sicilian campaign is actually a full success. After the initial fiasco, the fighting as well as the preparation and execution of the evacuation, with all serviceable material and men (including the wounded) went according to plan."

The one-armed panzer leader was certainly right about the issue of public opinion. His successful operation in Sicily gave German morale a much needed shot in the arm at a critical time.

Finally, Hube lauded the work of the flak units, but sharply objected to any praise for any other Luftwaffe units for assisting the troops on the ground. Likewise, praise for the Italians should be omitted, except for their artillery. The Prussian panzer general concluded his memo with a pointed observation: "I consider it as especially harmful when, as happens time and again, one encounters communiques that do not correspond in any manner with the actual situation . . . and that appear ridiculous to those who were there."[30]

Hube's wishes were only partially ignored. In the final communiqué Hitler praised the Italian artillery, as Hube suggested. He also heaped praise on the Luftwaffe, however.

Late in the day on August 15 Fries and Conrath reported that the Allies had regained contact with their rear guards. Consequently, on the night of August 15–16 Hube fell back to Phase Line 3, which he was satisfied he could hold until all the German troops (except the last rear guards) were off the island.

There were not many left. Patton and Montgomery continued to struggle forward, but they were delayed by mines, demolitions, and blown bridges. Each Allied army had by then been restricted by geography to a front of one division: the British 50th and the U.S. 3rd. Once more the Germans had broken contact, and in fact, the last shooting in Sicily—other than strafing and long-range artillery fire—had already taken place when a company of the IInd Battalion, Hermann Goering Panzer Regiment, had skirmished with a British vanguard at Barracca, a village south of San Teresa, on the 15th.

On August 16 the British advance along the coastal road was slowed by German mines, demolitions, and long-range artillery fire and by a landslide that reportedly was caused by gunfire from the

Royal Navy. That evening the last of the Hermann Goering Division and their attached paratroopers left Sicily (except for a single tank detachment, temporarily assigned to the rear guard of the 29th Panzer Grenadier Division). Once on the mainland, the Goerings followed the 15th Panzer Grenadier Division north, where they again joined the Headquarters, XIVth Panzer Corps, in the Salerno-Naples area. The 29th Panzer Grenadier, the 1st Parachute, and Group Baade remained behind the Calabria, as part of Lieutenant General Traugott Herr's LXXVIth Panzer Corps.

Meanwhile, as night fell on August 16, the leading elements of the U.S. 3rd Infantry Division approached the Casazza crossroads and ridgeline on the outskirts of Messina, about four miles west of the city. That afternoon, on the orders of General Truscott, a battery of American guns fired on German positions around Villa San Giovanni—the first land-based artillery shells from the Western Allies to strike the European mainland since the fall of Greece.

That night the evacuation began to wind down. The last of the rear guards, two hundred men from the 29th Panzer Grenadier Division, abandoned the Casazza crossroads and headed for the evacuation points. Shortly thereafter Generale di Brigata Ettore Monacci, commander of the Italian army troops at the Messina naval base, set off the mines and demolished the port facilities. He left before midnight—the last high-ranking Axis officer to depart Messina. A reinforced platoon of the U.S. 3rd Infantry Division entered the city shortly afterward, followed that morning by other patrols.

Two miles to the north, however, the evacuation continued. At 5:30 A.M. on the morning of August 17 the two one-armed generals, Hube and Fries, boarded a ferry and left. They were followed forty-five minutes later by the last vessel, carrying the last of the rear guard—a battle group from the 29th Panzer Engineer Battalion, augmented by elements of the IInd Battalion, Hermann Goering Panzer Regiment.

As the last of the panzer engineers sailed toward Italy, they towed a bottle of wine in the sea to cool it and then cracked it open when they reached the other shore. One of them wrote that "with the mainland under our feet, and with the knowledge that we had not been left behind to fall into the hands of the enemy, we could breathe again." The diarist of the IInd Panzer Battalion also recorded his feelings:

The campaign in Sicily is over. We were far from fond of the country in which we have been fighting, but for all of that we felt strange when the ferry pulled away from Messina, and we had to leave the island to an enemy who was superior to us only in the material sense.[31]

There was still plenty of fight left in the German units. One paratrooper wrote in his diary:

Hardly anyone thinks of home. Oh, it would be wonderful to be there, but we're soldiers, the Fuehrer's best troops. . . . We'll be ready for action again. In my old Company command post I left a message behind for Tommy, expressing the hope that we'd soon meet again, on another battlefield.[32]

At 6:35 A.M. Baron von Liebenstein reported that Operation Lehrgang was completed. Hube passed this report on to Kesselring and praised the reserve naval officer for not having given up a single German soldier, weapon, or vehicle to the enemy. An hour later a German patrol boat picked up the last Axis soldiers to escape Sicily: eight Italians paddling across the straits in a raft.

At about daybreak British vanguards from the 2nd Commando and the 4th Armoured Brigade passed through Tremestieri, two miles south of Messina, but there they were halted by a demolished bridge across a deep ravine. It was well after daylight before they could effect repairs—too late for them to win the race for Messina for General Montgomery.

At seven A.M. an American patrol brought the mayor and a group of officials and local dignitaries to the ridgeline overlooking the city, where they formally surrendered Messina to General Truscott. An hour later Colonel Michele Tomasello of the Italian army staff arrived to offer the formal capitulation of the few Italian forces still left in Messina. However, because General Keyes had ordered him to wait for Patton before entering the city, Lucian Truscott sent Brigadier General William W. Eagles, his assistant divisional commander, into Messina, to prepare the formal surrender ceremony. Eagles recalled later that he was also instructed "to see that the British did not capture the city from us after we had taken it."[33]

George Patton arrived at the ridge at ten A.M. "What in hell are you all standing around for?" he yelled at Truscott and his staff. Then he entered Messina, which was still under long-range German artillery fire. As his cavalcade roared through the streets, shell fragments actually hit the car behind him. Unperturbed, George Patton accepted the formal surrender of the final strongpoint from Colonel Tremestieri shortly after ten A.M. The British vanguard arrived a few minutes later, and its commander, Lieutenant Colonel "Mad Jack" Churchill of the 2nd Commando, congratulated Patton for getting there first. Brigadier Currie arrived a few minutes later. "It was a jolly good race," he told Patton as they shook hands. "I congratulate you."[34] The Sicilian campaign was over. General Patton and the Americans had won the race for Messina.

Or had they?

Almost as soon as the battle ended, propagandists on both sides claimed successes that bore little resemblance to reality. The Italians, for example, claimed that the Allies had lost 83,850 men killed, wounded, or missing. According to German estimates, casualties reduced the combat effectiveness of the Allied forces by one third. They reported having destroyed 361 tanks and armored cars, 63 guns (including antitank guns and rocket launchers), 281 aircraft and 11 gliders shot down by ground forces alone, and 29 landing craft destroyed.

The Luftwaffe's claims were even more unrealistic. It claimed hits on 367 transports (totaling 1.5 million tons of shipping), 55 of which were sunk. It also claimed to have hit a battleship, nineteen cruisers, nineteen destroyers, and many landing craft, among which four destroyers and several landing craft were sunk.[35]

Actual Allied losses were considerably less. During the thirty-eight days of the Battle of Sicily, the U.S. 7th Army lost 8,781 men (2,237 killed or missing, 5,946 wounded, and 598 captured), and the British 8th Army suffered 11,843 casualties (2,062 killed or missing, 7,137 wounded, and 2,644 captured). In addition, the U.S. Navy lost 546 killed or missing and 484 wounded and the Royal Navy lost 314 killed or missing, 411 wounded and 4 captured. The U.S. Air Force reported its losses at 28 killed, 88 missing, and 41 wounded.

On the other side, the Italian 6th Army lost 147,000 men, and Hube's German units lost about 12,000 men killed or captured,[36] although Allied propagandists soon elevated this figure to 32,000 or more. Actual German losses, including wounded, probably totaled about 20,000[37]—or roughly the same as Allied losses.

As complete as their aerial victory was, the Allies also grossly exaggerated the magnitude of their success. Alexander claimed that more than 1,000 Axis aircraft had been destroyed, while Churchill[38] and Craven and Cate[39] put Axis losses at 1,100 aircraft—more than all the airfields in Sicily could hold altogether.[40]

According to Colonel Lioy of the historical division of the Italian Air Force, several Sicilian airports had air cemeteries, made up of hulks of destroyed or discarded airplanes that had accumulated over the years. Lioy estimated that there might have been five hundred such relics in Sicily before Husky started. He said that the total number of operational aircraft destroyed in the Allied bomber offensive against Sicily was not much in excess of a hundred and that the total number destroyed from July 3 to August 17 did not exceed two hundred.[41]

B. H. Liddell Hart and Samuel Eliot Morison seem to agree with Colonel Lioy's statistics. Hart, for example, wrote that the total number of Axis airplanes lost was "not more than 200, compared with the 1,100 claimed by the Allies."[42] In fact, Axis statistics show that only 225 German and 95 Italian aircraft were lost on all war missions from all causes, including accidents, from July 1 to September 5. The Allies claimed to have shot down 740 German and Italian airplanes in the same period and to have destroyed hundreds more on the ground.[43]

The Luftwaffe and Italian Air Force were also guilty of overstating enemy air losses. They claim to have shot down 640 Anglo-American airplanes from July 1 to September 5,[44] whereas the actual total was less than 400.[45]

Losses were naturally higher in some units than in others, and, unfortunately, the detailed German strength and casualty reports did not survive the war. One of the most battered units was Colonel Koerner's 115th Panzer Grenadier Regiment, which had fought as part of Brigade Schmalz throughout the campaign and had lost 641 men—a third of its authorized strength of 2,337. However, it had received almost three hundred replacements during the battle and was only 16 percent below its authorized strength level when it returned to the mainland. It was, however, classified as "practically immobile" when it returned to the mainland.[46] Losses in Ulich's 71st Panzer Grenadier Regiment also amounted to 33 percent, but it apparently received fewer replacements and was thus less battleworthy when it reached Italy.

Eberhard Rodt's 15th Panzer Grenadier Division was not badly damaged when it returned to the mainland. It reported losses of only 10 to 15 percent of its men, although losses were naturally higher in the panzer grenadier and engineer units than they were in support units.

The Hermann Goering Division was greatly reduced in Sicily, but more from malaria than from casualties. It reported its losses for August as 393 killed, 1,193 wounded, and 83 missing, along with 2,605 sick, almost all from malaria. On August 28 it was 6,139 men below its authorized strength of 18,446, even though it had received 1,725 replacements during the month.[47]

The German panzer battalions suffered the highest losses of all XIVth Panzer Corps units, because they were so vulnerable to Allied air attacks. The four tank battalions engaged in Sicily lost about two thirds of their armor and had to be rebuilt completely. The Tiger company (2/504th) was apparently disbanded. It had been almost totally destroyed.

Of the Italian coastal defense units, only the 213th Division survived the Battle of Sicily. Originally posted in northeastern Sicily, it was hardly engaged in the fighting and joined the Hermann Goering Division during the evacuation. Most of its losses came through desertion.

All four of the Italian mobile divisions were reduced to remnants after the battle. Casualty reports for Aosta, Assietta, and Napoli are unavailable (if they were ever recorded), but Livorno—the best of the Italian units—lost 214 of its 515 officers and 7,000 of its 11,400 men. It had lost one regimental commander killed, along with three battalion commanders (two infantry and one artillery). Three infantry and two artillery battalion commanders were wounded.[48]

If the defenders' losses were great, however, so were their accomplishments. From a peak strength of sixty thousand men, Hube's XIVth Panzer Corps, marginally assisted by a few extant Italian units, tied down the U.S. 7th and British 8th armies for more than a month. These Allied armies had a peak strength of 217,000 and 250,000 men, respectively. Although facing twelve

Allied divisions with three under-strength German divisions and most of a fourth, Hube managed to tie up an entire Allied army group while Hitler funneled division after division into mainland Italy and effectively neutralized the immediate threat to his southern flank. Then Hube managed to escape with his corps intact, in spite of a clear Allied superiority on the ground and supremacy in the air and on the sea. Incredibly, the Allies did not even attempt to destroy his evacuation vessels. They lay under the protection of Baade's flak guns on August 17, and that night, unchallenged by Allied aircraft or motor torpedo boats, they made their way north, hugging the shore. After reaching Naples they were used to evacuate German troops from Sardinia and Corsica, where they rescued the 90th Panzer Grenadier Division and the "Reichs-fuehrer-SS" Brigade, along with several smaller units.

Operation Lehrgang itself was a masterpiece. Even the British Official History labeled it "brilliantly successful."[49] In six days, according to OB South figures, Baade and his subordinates ferried out 39,569 German troops (4,444 of whom were wounded), along with 9,605 vehicles, 94 guns (excluding those of Group Baade), 47 tanks, 1,100 tons of ammunition, 970 tons of fuel, and 15,700 tons of other equipment and supplies. In excess of 12,000 Germans, 4,500 vehicles, and nearly 5,000 tons of supplies had been sent back to the mainland before Operation Lehrgang began—mostly nonessential supply and service support units. OKW put the total number of Germans who left the island at sixty thousand. The Italians had also done fairly well during Lehrgang, evacuating 62,182 men, 41 guns, 227 vehicles, 1,000 tons of ammunition and fuel, and 14 mules. Another seven thousand men and sixty guns had been evacuated between August 3 and 10, bringing the Italian total to around seventy thousand men evacuated.

The bulk of the German forces got away in good order and in reasonably good condition. Kesselring reported that the four German divisions were "completely fit for battle and ready for service" shortly after the campaign ended. This was more or less true, in spite of the fact that they had suffered heavy vehicle losses to the Allied fighter-bombers. The miraculous German recovery was no miracle; it is explained by the fact that they took, confiscated, or stole (depending on one's point of view) hundreds of vehicles from the Italians during the evacuation. Indeed, the 15th Panzer Grenadier Division not only made good its vehicular losses during the

Battle of Sicily, but actually acquired so many new vehicles that it formed a transport reserve when it reached the mainland. Indeed, most large German units seem to have been more mobile *after* the campaign than before it, except for the depleted panzer battalions. The generals were naturally thrilled about this, but the mechanics were not. For example, Fries's 29th Panzer Grenadier Division had 463 motorcycles, 517 armored cars, 1,094 trucks, and 274 other "special vehicles" after the campaign.[50] It also reported having some four hundred different types of vehicles in its inventory after returning to Italy. Acquiring spare parts for these and fixing vehicles with which they were not familiar must have caused the repair shop personnel nightmares for months after the battle ended.

Praise for Hube's evacuation was universal in 1943, and the verdict of history is the same. General von Senger called it a "glorious retreat," while Kesslring compared it favorably to Dunkirk. More to the point, however, are the remarks of Colonel General Heinrich von Vietinghoff, commander of the newly activated 10th Army in southern Italy, who later declared Hube's achievement to be "of decisive significance for the entire later course of the campaign in Italy," adding that his most valuable forces in the Italian campaign had come from Sicily. And this from the man who directed operations at Salerno, the Volturno River, Monte Cassino, the Gustav Line, and other areas.[51]

Finally, it must be noted that the capture of Sicily itself was a burden, not a blessing, to the Allies. Impoverished before, it was now devastated as well, and its port and communications infrastructure had to be completely rebuilt. In addition, further Allied troops were more or less permanently tied up occupying the place.

The Battle of Sicily almost cost the Americans the services of one of their best army commanders, Lieutenant General George S. Patton, Jr., who had slapped two soldiers for exhibiting what he considered cowardly behavior. A muckraking American journalist whose name is unimportant published the story, which led to Patton's being bypassed for command of the army group that invaded Normandy. He eventually did obtain command of the U.S. 3rd Army in France and led it in a number of brilliant victories until the final German capitulation. His immediate superior in these campaigns was his former subordinate, General Omar Bradley.

Although Badoglio did not seem to realize it for some time, Hube's skillful delaying action and subsequent evacuation of Sicily—coupled with his own ineptitude—robbed the Italian government of the last, slim chance it had to defect from the Axis and escape German occupation. The new pro-Royalist government continued to approach the diplomatic situation as if it had all the time in the world—until Generale di Brigata Giuseppe Castellano interjected himself into the picture.[52]

Long an anti-German, anti-Fascist conspirator, Castellano met with Roatta, Utili, the king, and Ambrosio and finally obtained permission to journey to Allied headquarters with a peace initiative. He did so against the wishes of Badoglio's foreign minister, who at first even refused to issue him an individual passport. Castellano nevertheless flew to Madrid and met with the British ambassador on August 15. After Churchill and Roosevelt finally decided to allow this approach (i.e., negotiations through military channels), a series of complicated negotiations ensued. Finally, on September 3, 1943, Castellano arrived at Alexander's headquarters in Sicily, where he secretly signed the armistice terms, which were based on the principle of unconditional surrender. The agreement came too late to help Italy, however. By the end of August there were seventeen German ground divisions in Italy: enough, events would prove, to dismantle the Italian army, capture the peninsula, and almost defeat the Allied invasion of the mainland at the same time.

It is undoubtedly true that the Allies made a mistake by going into Sicily. In May 1943, after the fall of Tunisia, there was probably still time to launch an invasion of northwestern Europe in the summer or early fall of 1943, as George C. Marshall advocated. Baldwin was correct when he commented that "Sicily was a strategic compromise conceived in dissension, born of uneasy alliance—a child of conflicting concepts and unclear in purpose. The campaign was fought because 'something had to be done.' "[53]

U.S. Admiral Ernest J. King felt the same way. He said that the invasion of Sicily was "merely doing something for the sake of doing something."[54] The distinguished American military historian, Martin Blumenson, was also quite critical of the invasion, and especially of Allied timidity. "The whole Allied plan," he wrote, "had been governed by the anticipation of strenuous resistance, and thus was one of caution and conservatism. The Allies had avoided gamble and risk, playing it safe; and in the final analysis they made a power drive—a frontal assault that was inexcusable in the rugged ground of Sicily."[55]

Colonel Seaton agreed when he wrote, "If the Italian resistance is largely disregarded, then less than four scratch German divisions held between eight and twelve allied divisions for a period of more than four weeks. In the German war diaries the enemy was described, almost daily, as 'timid' and 'cautious.' "[56]

Although these authors agree with Blumenson and Seaton, we feel that the greatest Allied mistake of the campaign was their choice of targets. If the Allies *had* to launch an invasion in the Mediterranean in the summer of 1943, the logical targets would have been Sardinia or the Italian mainland, especially Calabria. Southern Italy was virtually undefended in early July 1943. An invasion here would have trapped the Italian 6th Army, along with the 15th Panzer Grenadier and Hermann Goering Panzer divisions, in Sicily and might well have enabled the Allies to capture the peninsula as far as the Alpine passes—or at least as far as the northern Apennines. By invading Sicily, and especially by landing on the southern and eastern shores, the Allies adopted a self-defeating strategy. John Grigg had a brilliant strategic insight when he wrote, "In a sense, Italy was not knocked out of the war, but *brought into it*—at a place where the Germans were able to engage very large Allied forces, with immensely large communications, on ground naturally favouring the defense, for the best part of two years."[57]

If the Allies simply *had* to invade a Mediterranean island in the summer of 1943, their target should have been Sardinia. True, they would have met stiffer opposition in the air, but they would have faced only one partially formed German division (Division Sardinia, later renamed the 90th Panzer Grenadier Division) under a rather mediocre commander. Also, since Sardinia is separated from the mainland by one hundred miles of sea instead of two hundred, it is highly doubtful that the Germans would have been able to reinforce it significantly or to have made such a successful getaway. Finally, once Sardinia fell, Corsica would have been untenable. When the major Allied landings on the Italian mainland came, they could have taken place one hundred miles *north* of Rome instead of one hundred miles south of it. Geopolitical factors such as the Badoglio government aside, this would have saved the U.S. 5th and British 8th armies a year of heavy fighting up the Italian peninsula and would have put the industrial targets of Austria and southern Germany within easy range of the Anglo-American bombers a year earlier. Perhaps this is what British Member of Parliament Aneurin Bevan had in mind when he said, "Indeed, I am bound to say, if the House will forgive the metaphor, that the Allied High Command have approached the Italian mainland like an old man approaching a young bride, fascinated, sluggish and apprehensive."[58]

Admiral Franco Maugeri, the director of Italian naval intelligence during World War II, would have agreed with Bevan. In his memoirs he wrote that the Allies'

> entire strategic conception and tactical execution of the war in Europe lacked imagination, daring, boldness and vision after the North African landings. It almost seemed as though the Allied command had exhausted all of its inventive genius and courage in that one operation.[59]

Toward the end of the campaign, General Eisenhower was also thinking that the Allies had adopted too conservative an approach. On August 14, as Hube's evacuation neared its end, Eisenhower's friend and naval aide, Captain Harry C. Butcher, confided to his diary:

> Ike now thinks we should have made simultaneous landings on both sides of the Messina Strait, thus cutting off all Sicily and obtaining wholesale surrender and saving time and equipment, particularly landing craft, which would have permitted a rapid rush to the mainland itself.[60]

By that time it was too late, however. Indeed, despite their knowledge of German troop dispositions gleaned from both Ultra intercepts and more traditional intelligence sources, the Allies apparently never even considered what the Axis feared most: an invasion of Calabria *before* the close of the Sicilian campaign. General Guzzoni was very anxious about this possibility, even before the Allies landed on Sicily, and he continued to look nervously over his shoulder throughout the campaign. Nor was this a matter of timidity on his part; as we have seen, his anxiety was shared even by the normally inperturbable Hans Hube. Colonel General von Vietinghoff, whose 10th Army was given responsibility for defending this sector, considered the failure of the Allies to invade southern Italy prior to the conclusion of the Sicilian campaign to be one of their most serious mistakes of the war. Overwhelming the one and a half German divisions there, he believed, was well within the capabilities of the Allies, and such a landing would have sealed the fate of the XIVth Panzer Corps in Sicily. Without these forces, Vietinghoff argued, central and southern Italy could not have been defended.[61] After the war he wrote:

> from the German standpoint it is incomprehensible that the Allies did not seize the course of the initial actions, just as soon as the German troops were contained. On both sides of the Straits—not only in the northeast corner of the island but in southern Calabria as well—this would have been possible without special difficulty.[62]

Both Kesselring and his chief of staff, General Westphal, agreed with this assessment. Kesselring commented after the war that "a secondary landing on Calabria would have turned the landing in Sicily into an annihilating victory" for the Allies.[63]

B. H. Liddell Hart, one of the foremost military historians of this century, wrote:

> Much to Kesselring's relief, the Allied High Command had not attempted a landing in Calabria, the "toe" of Italy, behind the back of his forces from Sicily—to block their withdrawal across the Straits of Messina. He had been anxiously expecting such a stroke throughout the Sicilian campaign, while having no forces available to meet it.[64]

After the war Hitler's principal military adviser, Colonel General Jodl, explained to his captors why he had not devined their strategy in the Mediterranean. He could not credit, he said, that the Allies' strategy was to fight their way step by step, mile by mile, over the difficult mountainous terrain, all the way up the Italian peninsula.[65] This, in fact, was not what the Allies intended, but events certainly worked out that way. Colonel Seaton wrote:

It may be said of course that the allies had no clear strategic aim in the Mediterranean after the occupation of Sicily and the Americans were the unwilling partners, in that they did not want to be in the Mediterranean in the first place. But they were subsequently drawn more deeply into the adventure by the inviting prospect of a possible Italian collapse, since this held out the expectation of a rapid occupation of the whole Italian peninsula.[66]

The main assault on the Italian mainland began at Salerno on September 8, 1943, and it occurred simultaneously with the announcement of the Italian surrender. The Germans, however, did not retreat to the northern Apennines as the Allies expected and as Field Marshal Rommel advocated. Instead they counterattacked, and fiercely. The Allied army group was soon bogged down in heavy fighting; simultaneously, Student's XIth Air Corps captured Rome. Badoglio, Ambrosio, the king, and their principal advisers fled the city and eventually reached Allied lines. Meanwhile, the Italian Army either dissolved itself or was captured and disarmed by the Germans. Many of the Italian soldiers—especially those in Rommel's zone in the north—were sent to Germany as laborers. The war in Italy would not end until April 1945. The Battle of Sicily had been a turning point: the Allies' best opportunity to win a decisive victory in the Mediterranean had gone by the wayside.

EPILOGUE

WITH THE BATTLE OF SICILY OVER, THE MEN WHO FOUGHT THERE were scattered to the four winds. Soon, for many of them, the thirty-eight days they had fought on the island in the Mediterranean became only a vague memory, mixed in with many others.

Hans Valentin Hube received no German laurels for his brilliant campaign, because his ungrateful Fuehrer did not usually understand or appreciate the achievements of retreating troops. Ironically, on the recommendation of General Guzzoni, the Italians presented him with one of their highest decorations: the Grand Cross of the Military Order of Savoy. General Hube fought at Salerno and briefly served as acting commander of the 10th Army before being sent to Romania to take over the rebuilding of the 1st Panzer Army in September 1943. He was replaced as commander of the XIVth Panzer Corps by General of Panzer Troops Herman Balck. Shortly thereafter, the observation airplane in which Balck was riding piled up. The general suffered multiple fractures and had to stay in the hospital for months. Hube was recalled to Italy for the last time, and for about three weeks once again commanded his old corps. Then he returned to the Eastern Front, where he distinguished himself as a panzer army commander. Among other things, he prevented the XIth and XXXXIInd Corps from being wiped out in the Cherkassy pocket, and, after being encircled by the massive Soviet spring offensive of 1944, Hans Hube cut his way out and carried the entire 1st Panzer Army with him—one of the most brilliant breakouts of the war.

In contrast to the Sicilian aftermath, Adolf Hitler was ecstatic over the general's latest triumph. He summoned Hube to Berchtesgaden and, on April 20, 1944—Hitler's own birthday—

promoted Hube to colonel general and decorated him with the Swords and Diamonds to his Knight's Cross with Oak Leaves. Hube's adjutant, Major von Schwanenfeld, overheard his boss discussing his next assignment with Lieutenant General Rudolf Schmundt, the army personnel chief. Hube was soon to take over command of Army Group South Ukraine, now temporarily under the command of Ferdinand Schoerner.

Fortunately for Major von Schwanenfeld, he was scheduled to go on leave, so he did not accompany the general on his flight back to the Russian Front. Hube never returned. The engine malfunctioned, and the airplane plunged into the Bavarian Alps only a few miles from Berchtesgaden, killing everyone on board. The body of the defender of Sicily was recovered and sent to Berlin for an impressive state funeral. Adolf Hitler personally delivered the eulogy—a rare gesture indeed, especially this late in the war. The guard of honor was formed by veterans of Hube's old division, the 16th Panzer. Three field marshals, five colonel generals, and seventeen full generals followed his casket to its interment at the Invalides in Berlin.

Meanwhile, in Italy, Marshal Badoglio announced the Italian capitulation via a broadcast on public radio at 7:15 P.M. on September 8, 1943. The next day, with the U.S. 5th Army (the British Xth and U.S. VIth corps) ashore at Salerno, the remnants of the Italian 6th Army dissolved themselves. Most of the men simply went home. A month later Alfredo Guzzoni was arrested by the Gestapo, but was released after only four weeks of relatively mild incarceration because the senior German officers who had fought in Sicily lodged vigorous protests, stating that Guzzoni had done the best he could in Sicily with the forces at his disposal. Guzzoni then went into retirement but was arrested again in 1944 by the Italian Socialist Republic, as Mussolini's rump government was called. This time the former 6th Army commander actually went to trial, but again his former comrades in Sicily came to his aid as witnesses for the defense—most notably General von Senger. After his release, Guzzoni resumed his retirement, apparently in Rome. At least that is where he resided after the war.

Generale d'Armata Alfredo Guzzoni died of pulmonary complications in a Roman hospital on April 15, 1965, and was buried in

Rome two days later with full military honors. He was eighty-eight years old.

Almost as soon as the German XIth Air Corps (2nd Parachute and 3rd Panzer Grenadier divisions) began to attack Rome on September 8, 1943, Badoglio, the king, and the crown prince fled, heading for Allied lines, followed shortly afterward by Ambrosio and Roatta. After their departure the leaderless Italian divisions were quickly defeated by the Germans. Badoglio continued to head the rump Italian government until the Allies recaptured Rome in June 1944. Then he retired to private life, where he wrote his memoirs, which should be classified as historical fiction. He died on November 1, 1956, at Grazzano Monferrato, where he had been born eighty-five years before.

Generale di Brigata Emilio Faldella, Guzzoni's former chief of staff, joined the anti-Fascist resistance in 1943. In 1945 he tried to capture Mussolini alive, so that he could be put on trial, but was unsuccessful. After the war he wrote several military histories in which he tried to separate the Italian Army and the Fascist party. He died on September 9, 1975.

Most of the prominent Fascists were less fortunate than Guzzoni and Faldella. Following his arrest, Mussolini was taken to Ponza, then to the island of Maddalena, and finally to the mountain stronghold of Gran Sasso, where he was freed and taken to Germany after a daring rescue directed by SS Captain Otto Shorzeny. The Duce returned to Italy in October 1943 and established the Italian Socialist Republic, a puppet state for the Third Reich. It is clear that Benito Mussolini was now a broken man, constantly oscillating between lucidity and self-delusion. On April 27, 1945, he was arrested by Italian partisans, and the next day, near the village of Giulino di Mezzegra, he was summarily shot, along with his mistress, Clara Petacci. Their bodies, and those of some of their supporters, were mutilated, dragged through the streets of Milan, and hung upside down in a public square, where they were displayed as objects of ridicule.

Before he died Mussolini extracted vengeance on his son-in-law, Count Galeazzo Ciano, who had played such a prominent role in his overthrow. Shortly after assuming power, the Badoglio government placed the former foreign minister under house arrest for "illicit enrichment." Ciano escaped and—incredibly—sought refuge in Germany. The Nazis held him until the establishment of the Italian Socialist Republic; then they turned him over to Mussolini.

Count Ciano was tried in Verona on January 8–10, 1944, along with five other former members of the Fascist Grand Council who had voted against Mussolini. All except Tullio Cianetti, the former minister of corporations, were sentenced to death. (Cianetti was sentenced to thirty years imprisonment.) Edda Mussolini Ciano tried to intervene on her husband's behalf by means of pleas to her father and threats to have Galeazzo's secret diaries published, but Mussolini refused to halt the executions. Count Ciano faced the firing squad on January 11.

Although Hitler planned to name Rommel commander in chief in Italy at the time of the evacuation of Sicily, he eventually changed his mind and settled on Kesselring. He did this because the Luftwaffe marshal's strategy of holding as far south as possible more closely paralleled the Fuehrer's ideas than did Rommel's. The Desert Fox was sent to the Western Front, and Kesselring took command of OB South (later Southwest) and Army Group C until the fall of 1944. During this period he successfully held the Allied armies south of the Italian capital for months. Rome did not fall until June 4, 1944—partially because of his own brilliance and that of his subordinates and partially because of the ineptitude of some of his opponents. Kesselring then continued his delaying actions in the Gothic and Genghis Khan lines until October 23, 1944. On that day his car collided with a long-barreled gun, and the unconscious field marshal had to undergo emergency brain surgery the next morning.

Alfred Kesselring could not return to duty until January 15, 1945. On March 8 he was recalled to Berlin, where he was named OB West, replacing Gerd von Rundstedt, who was sacked for losing the Rhine River bridge at Remagen. There was little Kesselring could do, however, to stabilize the deteriorating situation on the Western Front. After Hitler's death on April 30 the marshal considered committing suicide, but decided against it. He was taken into custody by the Allies at the Berchtesgadener Hotel on May 15.

Kesselring was tried as a war criminal for the shooting of 335

Italian civilians in the Ardeatine catacombs near Rome on March 24, 1944, and for inciting 1,087 other murders through orders that he issued. He was sentenced to death, but the sentence was opposed by former Prime Minister Churchill (who had been defeated for reelection by Clement Attlee) and by his old opponent, Alexander, now governor-general of Canada. In the end Kesselring's sentence was commuted to life imprisonment by General Sir John Hastings, Alex's former chief of staff. After an operation for throat cancer, Kesselring was released from prison as an act of clemency on October 24, 1952.

Following his release, the old field marshal retired to Bad Wiessee in Bavaria to write his memoirs. He maintained his right-wing political views and became president of the Stahlheim (Steel Helmut), a nationalistic veterans' organization despised by many anti-Nazis. He was largely a figurehead, however, because he had developed a serious heart condition and his last years were plagued by ill health. Field Marshal Kesselring died in a sanatorium at Bad Nauheim on July 20, 1960, at the age of seventy-four. He was buried in a small cemetery in Bad Wiessee. All that appears on his tombstone is his name and rank.

With the Red army less than a mile away, Adolf Hitler committed suicide in the Fuehrer Bunker in Berlin on the afternoon of April 30, 1945. Shortly before he died he rendered a partial verdict on his own foreign policy when he said, "It is, in fact, quite obvious that our Italian alliance has been of more service to our enemies than to ourselves."[1]

As in Sicily, the XIVth Panzer Corps distinguished itself in Italy during the heavy fighting of 1943, 1944, and 1945. When Hube departed for the last time on October 23, 1943, he was succeeded by Lieutenant General Fridolin von Senger und Etterlin, the former liaison officer to Guzzoni's 6th Italian Army. Since he had left Sicily, Senger had served as Wehrmacht Commander, Corsica, and had performed brilliantly in the evacuation of German forces from that island. Now he directed XIVth Panzer Corps in its retreat up the Italian peninsula, during which he established his reputation as an excellent defensive commander. He is especially famous for his defense of Monte Cassino.

Fridolin von Senger was promoted to general of panzer troops on January 1, 1944, and eventually received the Oak Leaves to his Knight's Cross. Because of his diplomatic skills and command of the English language, Senger was named head of the German commission that negotiated the surrender of German forces in Italy to the 15th Army Group in April and May 1945. Senger maintained his diplomatic aplomb even when he was attacked by U.S. General Mark Clark's dog, which bit through his boot and into his leg, inflicting a wound that required medical attention.

Released from a prisoner-of-war camp in England in May 1948, Senger returned to Germany, where he became headmaster of a small school at Salem on Lake Constance. Later he became a military correspondent for the Suedwestfunk Broadcasting Service and for the *Deutsche Zeitung* and was a consultant on rearmament for the Adenauer government. He died at Freiburg on January 4, 1963.[2]

Colonel Ernst-Guenther Baade, replete with kilt and claymore, kept his headquarters after Sicily, but not his troops. The various naval, flak, and artillery units were either returned to their parent units or speedily redeployed to other assignments throughout Europe. Baade's *Sonderstab* (special staff) remained attached to the XIVth Panzer Corps and at various times controlled construction engineer units, flak battalions, and *Ostbataillone:* units composed of Ukrainians and White Russian volunteers who joined the Germans to fight communism.

On December 20, 1943, Baade succeeded the undistinguished Major General Carl-Hans Lungershausen as commander of the 90th Panzer Grenadier Division, which he led in the Monte Cassino fighting, in the Gothic Line battles, and in the retreat to the Arno. Baade proved himself to be an excellent defensive commander and a superb handler of troops, despite his unorthodox behavior.

The year 1944 was very eventful for Baade. Decorated with the Oak Leaves to his Knight's Cross in February and with the swords in November, he was promoted to major general on February 1 and lieutenant general on August 1. On December 9, however, he was wounded by a sniper and, upon recovery, was sent to a brief training course for senior officers.

In early 1945 General Baade became acting commander of the LXXXIst Corps on the Western Front, but was soon relieved of his command because of his outspoken criticism of Nazi interference in military affairs, and was placed in the Fuehrer Reserve. Recalled to duty in the last weeks of the war, Baade was named inspector of *Volkssturm:* last-ditch inductees (mostly boys of fourteen and old men of sixty or more). Baade was instructed to arm these men and put them in position for a last-ditch defense of the Reich. The veteran of the Afrika Korps, however, was not eager to sacrifice innocents for a lost cause in which he personally had never believed, so he paid lip service to the post and did more evading than assigning.

It is not exactly certain what happened to Baade in the last, chaotic days of World War II, but it is clear that he was threatened by a high-ranking SS man (his own National Socialist Political Officer) in Schleswig-Holstein. Baade proceeded to shoot the Nazi and went into hiding. He escaped Nazi vengeance, but, on May 8—the last day of the war—he finally ran out of luck. An Allied warplane strafed the car in which he was riding (near his estate in Schleswig-Holstein), killing him instantly. The body was burned and then lost in the ensuing confusion: a most unjust end to a flamboyant personality and excellent soldier.

Eberhard Rodt's subsequent career was not as exciting as Baade's. He continued to lead the 15th Panzer Grenadier Division in Italy, France, and western Germany until the time of the surrender, except for the period October 1944 to mid-January 1945, when he was recovering from wounds inflicted by an Allied fighter-bomber. He was promoted to lieutenant general on March 1, 1944, and was awarded the Oak Leaves in the last week of the war, but never received the decoration. After his release from a POW camp in 1947 he slipped into oblivion. At last report (1957) he was living in Hinterstein.

Alfred Jodl received his Oak Leaves the same day as Rodt, but did not slip into oblivion. Promoted to colonel general on January 30, 1944, he was hanged as a war criminal at Nuremberg in October 1946.

Walter Fries was promoted to lieutenant general on New Year's Day, 1944, and was awarded the Swords to his Knight's Cross on August 11, 1944. He continued to lead the 29th Panzer Grenadier Division in Italy until the end of August 1944, when he went into reserve, probably to take leave at Kassel. He was then sent to the central sector of the Eastern Front, where he assumed command of the XXXXVIth Panzer Corps on the Vistula on September 21.

Promoted to general of panzer troops on January 1, 1945, he was one of the scapegoats held responsible for the Soviet breakthrough to the Oder later that month. In spite of the fact that this charge was completely unjustified, and despite the overall brilliance of his record, the veteran general was never reemployed. Captured at Kassel by the Americans on April 4, 1945, he retired to the town of Weilberg after being released from the POW camps. He was still living there in the late 1950s.

Paul Conrath's career after Sicily was undistinguished, although, ironically, he was the only senior commander (division or above) to receive a reward for the campaign (the Oak Leaves to the Knight's Cross, awarded to him on August 23, 1943). Conrath continued to lead the Hermann Goering Panzer Division in Italy and later in Russia. He was finally recalled to Berlin in April 1944, and held no further field commands. He seems to have been employed exclusively in relatively minor staff positions and was commander of replacement and training units for the 1st Parachute Army at the end of the war. Nevertheless, he was promoted to general of paratroopers on January 1, 1945. Captured by the Western Allies at the end of the war, he was a prisoner of war until 1947. He died in Hamburg in 1979, at the age of eighty-two.

Conrath was succeeded as divisional commander by Wilhelm Schmalz on April 16, 1944. Two weeks later Schmalz was promoted to major general, the same day the division was redesignated *Fallschirmpanzerdivision* Hermann Goering (the Hermann Goering Parachute Panzer Division), the parachute designation being strictly honorary. Like Conrath, Schmalz received the Oak Leaves to the Knight's Cross for his performance in Sicily, becoming the 358th recipient on December 21, 1943.

Schmalz led his division on the Eastern Front until October 1, 1944, when it was expanded into a corps (the Hermann Goering Parachute Panzer Corps), which he led in the final battles in Poland and East Prussia. Schmalz was promoted to lieutenant general on January 30, 1945, and after a period as a POW retired in southern Germany. He died in 1983.

Lieutenant Colonel Fritz Fullriede was recognized as a defensive hero of Sicily and, on September 1, 1943, was given the task of commanding the Grenadier Training School of the Waffen SS. Exactly one year later he joined the Hermann Goering Division as commander of its replacement brigade. He also served for a time as commander of the 2nd Lehr Regiment, a spit-and-polish ceremonial force that appeared in the newsreels of the day and frequently escorted the Reichsmarschall.

In February 1945, as the Russians overran eastern Germany, Fullriede was named commandant of Fortress Kolberg and commander of Special Purpose Division 612. He held the city for weeks, but, when it finally fell on March 20, Fullriede capably extricated many of his defenders through enemy lines after destroying most of the city's vital equipment. For this feat Hitler decorated him with the Oak Leaves on March 23.

On April 15 Fullriede was given command of the newly activated Special Purpose Division 610, which took part in the defense of Berlin. He surrendered the remnants of his command to the Soviets on May 2, 1945, the day Berlin capitulated.

Fritz Fullriede was more fortunate than were most who fell into Russian hands in 1945. He was accused of having committed war crimes in the Netherlands in 1940, so the Soviets handed him over to the Dutch authorities for trial. He was found innocent of all charges and set free in June 1946, much to the annoyance of the Soviets, who would have sentenced him to ten years' imprisonment for so-called obstructionism (i.e., for serving in the Wehrmacht). As of 1957 Fullriede was living in retirement at Bad Tolz.

Karl Ens continued to lead the 104th Panzer Grenadier Regiment in southern Italy until the end of March 1944, when he was reassigned to command the 101st Grenadier Regiment, then rebuilding in Poland. Ens's new regiment was assigned to Lieutenant General Karl Thoholte's 18th Artillery Division, an experimental unit made up primarily of elements of the defunct 18th Panzer Division. This hybrid division fought well, but suffered so many casualties on the Eastern Front in the summer of 1944 that it had to be disbanded.

Colonel Ens was wounded twice in these battles. After his recovery he was named commander of reserve panzer and panzer grenadier units in *Wehrkries* XXI (the XXIst Military District, located in central Poland). When the giant Soviet offensive of January 1945 overwhelmed this region, Ens's units were assigned to combat. He and his staff were captured east of the Oder in early February, and the colonel disappeared. Presumably he died in Soviet captivity, like so many others.

Colonel Max Ulich, who had so skillfully commanded the 15th

Panzer Grenadier Regiment of the 29th Panzer Grenadier Division on the northern coast of Sicily, fought in the defensive battles in Italy until November 1943, when he fell ill and was invalided back to Germany. He was not declared fit for duty until the end of March 1944, when he was named chief of staff of Wehrkries VII, headquarters in Munich. He was promoted to major general in December.

Ulich remained in this backwater of the war until April 1, 1945. . Then, with disaster in the wind and an enraged and suspicious Fuehrer disposing of more generals than the Allies were, Ulich was given command of the 212th Infantry Division for the last-ditch defense of the Bavarian Alps. Twenty-seven days later, however, Ulich surrendered to the Americans, along with his entire command.

General Ulich contributed to the U.S. Army's Historical Commission Survey[3] before being released from the POW camps in 1947. As of 1959 he was residing peacefully in Munich.

Colonel Dr. Fritz Polack re-formed his crack 29th Motorized Artillery Regiment in Calabria in August 1943 and led it in Italy until the beginning of 1944, when he was named Special Adviser to the Artillery Branch of the High Command of the Army. He was promoted to major general on July 1 and, on August 24, 1944, returned to Italy and to the 29th Panzer Grenadier Division, to succeed Walter Fries as divisional commander.

General Polack was highly respected by both his own men and the enemy. He led the 29th in its last battles and surrendered the remnants of the division at Castelfranco, north of the Po, at the end of the war. Released from prison in 1946, Polack resumed his career as a professor of political science. He took a fellowship to England and, returning for a brief visit in 1956, died suddenly of a stroke. He was brought home to Turingen and buried, with many of his veterans in attendance.

Commander Baron von Liebenstein was awarded the German Cross in Gold for his efforts in Sicily and, after a similar performance in pulling the German forces out of Corsica, was awarded the Knight's Cross. His unit was disbanded shortly thereafter, and the baron fell ill. After several weeks' hospitalization he was named chief of staff to the German naval commander, the Netherlands, with the rank of captain. He held this post from January 1944 until the end of the war. After his release from a prisoner-of-war camp, ex-Captain von Liebenstein held an important corporate post in Mannheim. He died in 1967 at the age of seventy-five.

Vice Admiral Friedrich Ruge was recalled to Berlin in August 1943. On the recommendation of Lieutenant General Alfred Gause, Rommel's chief of staff, Ruge was named naval adviser to the commander in chief of Army Group B at about the time Rommel took over responsibility for the defense of the most important sectors of the Atlantic Wall. The two became close friends, and, after the war, Ruge wrote a book about the field marshal.[4] In mid-August 1944 Ruge was relieved of his duties and placed in Fuehrer Reserve for his criticism of the High Command of the Navy (OKL) and for his anti-Nazi attitude. After the war he wrote a number of books about naval warfare and became an internationally respected historian, as well as the first inspector general of the West German Navy. He died in 1985.

Field Marshal Rommel's life was near its end when he met Ruge. He opposed the Allied invasion of Normandy with great skill, but on July 17, 1944, was critically wounded by an enemy fighter-bomber. While he was recovering, the Gestapo discovered that he had been involved in the July 20 plot to overthrow Hitler. The Desert Fox was given the choice of suicide or court-martial. To save his family, Rommel chose death and took poison on October 14, 1944.

Johannes "Macki" Steinhoff led the 77th Fighter Wing in Italy and on the Eastern and Western Fronts until December 1944, when he took part in the "Revolt of the Fighter Pilots,"—an attempt by prominent members of the fighter branch to persuade Hitler to remove Goering as commander in chief of the Luftwaffe. Steinhoff was temporarily named commander of JG 7, a jet wing, but in January 1945 he joined Galland's JV 44—an experimental squadron equipped with jet-powered fighters. On April 8, 1945, Steinhoff (now a colonel) attempted to take off from a hastily repaired runway and, at approximately 125 mph, hit a partially filled bomb crater and lost his landing gear. In the ensuing crash the Me-262 jet burst into flames, and Steinhoff was horribly burned. Nevertheless, after enduring terrible pain and months in a burn unit, Steinhoff returned to aviation and rose to the post of commander of the West German Air Force in the 1970s. Many Americans saw him accompanying President Reagan at Bitburg in the 1980s. During World War II, Johannes Steinhoff scored 176 confirmed victories and was awarded the Swords to his Knight's Cross in July 1944.

Most of the members of the 77th Fighter Wing were not as lucky as their former commander. JG 77 fought against ever-increasing odds in the retreat up the Italian peninsula, then went to France to oppose the Normandy invasion, then to Romania, and finally to the Reich itself. It fell into Russian captivity at the end of the war.

Adolf Galland served as *General der Jagdwaffe* (general of the fighter arm) from November 1941 until January 1945, when Hermann Goering dismissed him from his post after the Revolt of the Fighter Pilots. Adolf Hitler, however, ordered Goering to reemploy him in some capacity, so the Reichsmarschall gave him command of an experimental jet fighter squadron. Although the post was hardly commensurate with his rank (lieutenant general), Galland did his best and recruited an elite group of fighter pilots. On April 24, 1945, he shot down a U.S. Marauder bomber, his 104th and final victory. Following his release from British captivity in 1947, Galland assisted Juan Perón in organizing the Argentinian Air Force. He returned to Germany in 1955, established an aerospace consulting firm, married his secretary, and fathered a son in 1966. He was living in Bonn in the 1980s.

Colonel "King Ludwig" Heilmann continued to lead the 3rd Parachute Regiment in the Italian campaign, where it won enduring fame during the defense of Monte Cassino. After the fall of Rome Heilmann was promoted to major general and was given command of the 5th Parachute Division, which had been decimated in Normandy and now consisted mainly of former Luftwaffe ground personnel fighting as infantry. Although the 5th fought with little tactical skill, Heilmann was awarded the Swords to his Knight's Cross during the Battle of the Bulge, shortly before he was captured by the Americans. He was released from a British POW camp in 1947 and died in October 1959.

Colonel Erich Walter, commander of the 4th Parachute Regiment, was awarded the Oak Leaves for his distinguished performance in Sicily on March 2, 1944. (He had won the Knight's Cross as a major in 1940, when he commanded the Ist Battalion of the 1st Parachute Regiment in Holland.) Colonel Walter fought in the

Italian campaign and, on October 1, 1944, was named commander of the 2nd Hermann Goering Parachute Panzer Grenadier Division on the Eastern Front. He held this post until March 8, 1945, when he left his command, apparently as a result of illness or wounds. He received the Swords to his Knight's Cross on February 1, 1945, and on April 20 was promoted to major general. Unfortunately for Walter, his home lay in eastern Germany. Arrested by the victors, he died of starvation in a Soviet camp near Weimar on December 26, 1948.

Field Marshal Wolfram von Richthofen, commander in chief of the 2nd Air Fleet, made one more bid for glory during the Battle of Salerno (September 9–17, 1943). Here Vietinghoff's 10th Army attempted to push Mark Clark's U.S. 5th Army into the sea. Despite being outnumbered ten to one, Richthofen's units struck with reckless abandon, attacking numerous ground targets and sinking several enemy ships. He was, however, unable to prevent Montgomery's 8th Army from pushing up the Italian peninsula, and on September 17 Richthofen was forced to evacuate Foggia, giving up the best airfields on the Italian peninsula in the process.

Salerno was the last hurrah for the Luftwaffe in the Mediterranean. The personal prestige of Baron von Richthofen also began to deteriorate rapidly. The depleted air elements of the Luftwaffe played no role in the battles of Monte Cassino and Anzio or in the subsequent retreats up the peninsula. Meanwhile, Richthofen developed an inoperable brain tumor and was in great pain much of the time.

Richthofen's final humiliation occurred on October 28, 1944, when the 2nd Air Fleet was downgraded and redesignated Luftwaffe Command South. Stripped of his status as an air fleet commander, Richthofen retired on November 28. He was replaced by General of Fliers Ritter Maximilian von Pohl.

Field Marshal von Richthofen maintained his admiration for the Fuehrer until the end. He lived to see the fall of the Third Reich, but just barely. The nephew of the Red Baron died in Austria on July 12, 1945.

NOTES

CHAPTER 1: THE GREAT BLUNDER

1. Dwight D. Eisenhower, *Crusade in Europe* (Garden City, N.Y.: Doubleday, 1949), p. 90 (hereafter cited as Eisenhower, *Crusade in Europe*); William B. Breuer, *Operation Torch* (New York: St. Martin's, 1985), p. 76.

2. As a major in the SS, he was killed in action in Hungary in 1945.

3. Erwin Rommel, *The Rommel Papers,* ed. B. H. Liddell Hart, (New York: Harcourt, Brace, 1953), pp. 363–4 (hereafter cited as Rommel, *Papers*).

4. Ibid., p. 365.

5. Ibid.

6. David Irving, *The Trail of the Fox* (New York: Dutton, 1977; reprint ed., New York: Avon, 1978), p. 293.

7. Ibid., p. 294.

8. At Hitler's order, only one copy of the transcript of this vital conference (Number S 29/42) was ever made, and it was apparently destroyed in the last days of the Third Reich. The last surviving participants (Keitel and Goering) were hanged at Nuremberg in 1946. We consulted several sources concerning this conference, and none of them agree exactly. Our version is a composite of these sources and may not be perfect in every detail, although we are satisfied that we have captured the spirit of this important meeting. Other useful accounts of this historic conference are found in Rommel, *Papers,* pp. 364–5; Paul Carell, *Foxes of the Desert* (New York: Dutton, 1960; reprint ed., New York: Bantam, 1972), pp. 313–4; and Desmond Young, *Rommel: The Desert Fox* (New York: Harper & Row, 1950), pp. 178–9.

9. Adolf Galland, *The First and the Last* (New York: Henry Holt, 1954; reprint ed., New York: Ballantine, 1969), p. 157 (hereafter cited as Galland).

10. Paul Joseph Goebbels, *The Goebbels Diaries*, ed. and trans. Louis P. Lochner (Garden City, N.Y.: Doubleday, 1948; reprint ed., New York: Universal-Award House, 1971), entry of December 18, 1942 (hereafter cited as Goebbels, *Diaries*).

CHAPTER 2. UNEASY ALLIES

1. Leonard Mosley, *Marshall: Hero for Our Time* (New York: Hearst, 1982), p. 227 (hereafter cited as Mosley, *Marshall*).

2. Albert C. Wedemeyer, *Wedemeyer Reports!* (New York: Henry Holt, 1951), p. 192 (hereafter cited as Wedemeyer).

3. Omar N. Bradley, *A Soldier's Story* (Chicago: Rand McNally, 1951), p. 105 (hereafter cited as Bradley, *Soldier's Story*).

4. Carlo D'Este, *Bitter Victory: The Battle of Sicily 1943* (New York: Dutton, 1988), p. 338 (hereafter cited as D'Este, *Bitter Victory*).

5. Ibid., pp. 340–1.

6. Ladislas Fargo, *Patton: Ordeal and Triumph* (New York: Faracorn, 1963; reprint ed., New York: Dell, 1970), p. 273.

7. B. H. Liddell Hart, *History of the Second World War* (New York: Putnam, 1972), vol. II, p. 439 (hereafter cited as Hart, *Second World War*).

CHAPTER 3: THE DETERIORATING AXIS

1. Elizabeth Wiskemann, *The Rome-Berlin Axis* (London: Oxford University Press, 1949), p. 1 (hereafter cited as Wiskemann).

2. Telford Taylor, *Munich* (Garden City, N.Y.: Doubleday, 1979; reprint ed., New York: Vintage, 1980), p. 166.

3. Henri Nogueres, *Munich* (New York: McGraw-Hill, 1965), p. 152n.

4. Trumbull Higgins, *Soft Underbelly* (New York: Macmillan, 1968), p. 1 (hereafter cited as Higgins, *Soft Underbelly*), citing Winston S. Churchill, *Step by Step: Speeches, 1936–1939* (London: 1949), p. 333.

5. D. J. Goodspeed, *The German Wars, 1914–1945* (Boston: Houghton Mifflin, 1977; reprint ed., New York: Bonanza, 1985), p. 17.

6. Heinrich von Vietinghoff, "Overall Situation in the Mediterranean," Foreign Military Studies *MS # D-116* (Headquarters, U.S. Army Europe: Historical Division).

7. Richard Collier et al., *The War in the Desert* (Alexandria, Va.: 1979), p. 32.

8. Wiskemann, p. 296; Albert N. Garland and Howard McG. Smyth, *Sicily and the Surrender of Italy,* United States Army in World War II, Mediterranean Theater of Operations (Washington, D.C.: U.S. Govern-

ment Printing Office, 1965), p. 38 (hereafter cited as Garland and Smyth).

9. Siegfried Westphal, *The German Army in the West* (London: Cassell, 1951), p. 139 (hereafter cited as Westphal, *West*).

10. Burkhart Mueller-Hillebrand, *Germany and Its Allies: A Record of Axis Collaboration Problems* (Frederick, Md.: University Publications of America, 1980), p. 118 (hereafter cited as Mueller-Hillebrand, *Allies*). Mueller-Hillebrand served on the staff of OKH and eventually became chief of the organizational branch. He was chief of staff of the 3rd Panzer Army in 1945.

11. Higgins, *Soft Underbelly*, p. 69.

12. Garland and Smyth, p. 37.

13. Pietro Badoglio, *Italy in the Second World War* (London: Oxford University Press, 1948; reprint ed., Westport, Conn.: Greenwood, 1976), p. 48 (hereafter cited as Badoglio).

14. Wiskemann, p. 277.

15. Badoglio, p. 32.

16. "Fuehrer Conferences on Naval Affairs, 1943," in *Brassey's Naval Annual 1948*, ed. Rear Admiral H. G. Thursfield (New York: Macmillan, 1948), p. 324 (hereafter cited as Fuehrer Conferences on Naval Affairs, 1943).

17. Paul Deichman, in Siegfried Westphal et al., "Der Feldzug in Italien, Apr. 1943–11 Mai 1944" (Headquarters, U.S. Army, Europe: Historical Division) (hereafter cited as Westphal et al., *MS # T-1a*).

CHAPTER 4: THE DEFENDERS

1. Albert Kesselring, *Kesselring: A Soldier's Record* (New York: Morrow, 1954), p. 191 (hereafter cited as Kesselring, *Soldier's Record*).

2. Fridolin von Senger und Etterlin, "War Diary of the Italian Campaign: Sardinia and Corsica," Foreign Military Studies *MS # C-095* (Headquarters, U.S. Army, Europe: Historical Division) (hereafter cited as Senger, *MS # C-095a*).

3. "Fuehrer Conferences on Naval Affairs, 1943," p. 324.

4. Ibid., p. 327.

5. G. W. L. Nicholson, *The Official History of the Canadian Army in the Second World War: The Canadians in Italy* (Ottawa: Clouter, 1956), vol. II, p. 51 (hereafter cited as Nicholson, *Canadians*).

6. David Irving, *The War Between the Generals* (New York: Congdon & Lattes, 1981), p. 57.

7. Hugh Pond, *Sicily* (London: William Kimber, 1962), pp. 10, 17–8 (hereafter cited as Pond, *Sicily*).

8. William B. Breuer, *Drop Zone Sicily: Allied Airborne Strike, July 1943* (Novato, Calif.: Presidio, 1983), p. 23 (hereafter cited as Breuer, *DZ Sicily*).

9. Pond, *Sicily*, p. 11.

10. Felix Gilbert, ed. and trans., *Hitler Directs His War* (New York: Award, 1960), p. 71 (hereafter cited as Gilbert). Hitler was probably referring to the fact that Roatta headed the Italian military intelligence service before the war.

11. From this time on, Headquarters, Italian 6th Army, was simultaneously known as Armed Forces Command, Sicily, although this term will not be used in this book for the sake of simplicity.

12. Franz Kurowski, *Das Tor zur Festung Europa* (Neckargemuend: Vowinckel Verlag, 1966), p. 17 (hereafter cited as Kurowski, *Tor*).

13. Magna E. Bauer, "Axis Tactical Operations in Sicily, July–August, 1943" *MS # R-114* through *MS # 146* (hereafter cited as Bauer, followed by the appropriate manuscript number, in this case *MS # R-117*). These are on file at the Army War College, Carlisle Barracks, Penn.

14. Colonel Faldella replaced Generale di Brigata Guilio Vanden-Heuvel as chief of staff of the 6th Army. Faldella was born in 1897 and had distinguished himself in World War I, in which he was wounded and decorated with the Military Order of Savoy and several other medals.

15. Samuel Eliot Morison, *History of the United States Naval Operations in World War II*, Volume IX: *Sicily-Salerno-Anzio* (Boston: Little, Brown, 1962), pp. 49–50 (hereafter cited as Morison, *USN*, Volume IX).

16. On July 10 both the Assietta and Aosta divisions had about eleven thousand men. See Hanson W. Baldwin, *Battles Won and Lost* (New York: Harper & Row, 1966), p. 198.

17. Nicholson, *Canadians*, vol. II, p. 57.

18. Westphal, *West*, p. 139.

19. Martin Blumenson, *Sicily: Whose Victory?* (New York: Ballantine, 1968), p. 39 (hereafter cited as Blumenson, *Sicily*).

20. Breuer, *DZ Sicily*, p. 9.

21. Nicholson, *Canadians*, vol. II, p. 58. The Einsatzstab created the 15th Panzer Grenadier Division in Sicily and the 90th Panzer Grenadier Division in Sardinia.

22. Georg Tessin, *Verbaende und Truppen der deutschen Wehrmacht und Waffen-SS im Zweiten Weltkrieg, 1939–1945* (Osnabrueck: Biblio Verlag, 1973), vol. IX, p. 4 (hereafter cited as Tessin).

23. Kesselring, *Soldier's Record*, p. 193.

24. Tessin, vol. IV, p. 10, and vol. IX, p. 10; Eberhard Rodt, "Studie

ueber den Feldzug in Sizilien bei der 15. Panzer Grenadier Division, Mai-August 1943," Foreign Military Studies *MS # C-077* (Headquarters, U.S. Army Europe: Historical Division) (hereafter cited as Rodt, *MS # C-077*).

25. Richard Brett-Smith *Hitler's Generals* (Novato, Calif.: Presidio, 1977), p. 179 (hereafter cited as Brett-Smith); Wolf Keilig, *Die Generale des Heeres* (Friedberg: Podzun-Pallas-Verlag, 1983), pp. 15–6 (hereafter cited as Keilig, *Generale*).

26. Keilig, *Generale*, p. 280.

27. Rolf Stoves, *Die Gepanzerten und Motorisierten deutschen Grossverbaende: Divisionen und selbstaendige Brigaden: 1935–1945* (Friedburg: Podzun-Pallas-Verlag, 1986), p. 153.

28. R. James Bender and George Petersen, *"Hermann Goering": From Regiment to Fallschirmpanzerkorps* (San Jose, Calif.: R. James Bender, 1975), p. 7 (hereafter cited as Bender and Petersen, *H.G.*).

29. Bruce Quarrie, *Fallschirmpanzerdivision "Hermann Goering"* (London: Osprey, 1978; reprint ed., Warren, Mich.: Squadron/Signal, 1978), pp. 4–5 (hereafter cited as Quarrie, *H.G.*).

30. *Kriegstagebuch des Oberkommando des Wehrmacht* (Frankfurt-am-Main: Bernard und Graefe Verlag fuer Wehrwesen, 1961), July 1, 1943 (hereafter cited as KTB OKW).

31. Fridolin von Senger und Etterlin, "Liaison Activities with Italian 6th Army," Foreign Military Studies *MS # C-095* (Headquarters, U.S. Army Europe: Historical Division) (hereafter cited as Senger *MS # C-095*).

32. Bender and Petersen, *H.G.*, p. 77.

CHAPTER 5: PANTELLERIA: THE PLAN AND THE AIR BATTLES

1. This brigade, part of the Italian 6th Army, was made up largely of local reservists. It was commanded by Generale di Brigata Achille Maffei, a cavalry officer.

2. Eisenhower, *Crusade in Europe*, p. 165.

3. Blumenson, *Sicily*, p. 28.

4. Garland and Smyth, p. 71.

5. United States Air Force Historical Group, *The Army Air Forces in World War II*, vol. II: *Europe: Torch to Pointblank, August 1942 to December 1943*, eds. Wesley Frank Craven and James L. Cate, (Chicago: University of Chicago Press, 1949), p. 425 (hereafter cited as USAAF).

6. Eric Linklater, *The Campaign in Italy* (London: His Majesty's Stationery Office, 1951), p. 20 (hereafter cited as Linklater, *Italy*).

7. Blumenson, *Sicily*, p. 28; Garland and Smyth, p. 72.

8. Blumenson, *Sicily*, p. 28.

9. USAAF, vol. II, p. 429.

10. Blumenson, *Sicily*, pp. 32–3.

11. Kesselring, *Soldier's Record*, p. 195.

12. Garland and Smyth, p. 203. Higgins (*Soft Underbelly*, p. 64) suggests that because it led to the transfer of the Hermann Goering Division to Sicily, the disadvantages of taking Pantelleria might have outweighed the advantages.

13. Werner Haupt, *Kriegschauplatz Italien 1943–1945* (Munich: Motorbuch Verlag, 1978), p. 22 (hereafter cited as Haupt, *Italien*). OKW KTB, 7 July 1943 (vol. VI, p. 736).

14. The previous divisional commander, Major General Rudolf Licht, had been a disappointment. His talents lay mainly in training new formations rather than in active field command.

15. The sources on Fridolin von Senger und Etterlin's career include Keilig, *Generale;* the correspondence of Friedrich von Stauffenberg; Senger, *MS # C-095;* and Senger's autobiography, *Neither Fear Nor Hope* (New York: Dutton, 1964) (hereafter cited as Senger, *Neither Fear Nor Hope*); Ferdinand and Stefan von Senger und Etterlin, "Senger," in Correlli Barrett, ed., *Hitler's Generals* (London: Weidenfeld and Nicolson, 1989), pp. 382, 392.

16. Senger, *MS # C-095.*

17. Senger, *MS # C-095a.*

18. Senger, *MS # C-095.*

19. Ibid.

20. Linklater, *Italy*, p. 27.

21. Senger, *MS # C-095.*

22. Ibid.

23. Order of battle sources include Bauer, *MS #R-125;* D'Este, *Bitter Victory;* Haupt, *Italien;* Rodt, *MS # C-077;* and Tessin.

24. Kesselring, *Soldier's Record*, p. 194.

25. Wolfgang Dierich, *Die Verbaende der Luftwaffe 1935–1945: Gliederungen und Kurzchronikeneine Dokumentation* (Stuttgart: Motorbuch Verlag, 1976), pp. 58–9.

26. Johannes Steinhoff was born in Bottendorf, Saxony, on September 15, 1913. By late 1939 he was a second lieutenant and commander of the 10th Squadron of the 26th Fighter Wing on the Western Front. Later transferred to JG 52, he became a squadron leader on the Eastern Front and had thirty-five victories in August 1941, when he was promoted to first lieutenant and awarded the Knight's Cross. Promoted to captain in

February 1942, he was named commander of II/JG 52 and shot down his hundredth enemy airplane on February 2, 1943. He was awarded the Oak Leaves to his Knight's Cross on September 2, 1942.

27. Johannes Steinhoff, *The Straits of Messina: Diary of a Fighter Commander* (London: Andre Deutsch, 1971), pp. 59–60 (hereafter cited as Steinhoff, *Messina*).

28. Ibid., p. 62.

29. Ibid., p. 24.

30. Pond, *Sicily,* p. 13.

31. "Fuehrer Conferences on Naval Affairs, 1943," p. 321.

32. Royal Air Force Historical Branch, *The Rise and Fall of the German Air Force, 1933–1945,* ed. Cyril March (London: Her Majesty's Stationery Office, 1948; reprint ed., New York: St. Martin's, 1983), p. 254 (hereafter cited as March).

33. Walter A. Musciano, *Messerschmitt Aces* (New York: Arco, 1982), pp. 85–6 (hereafter cited as Musciano, *Aces*).

34. Kesselring, *Soldier's Record,* p. 194.

35. Galland, p. 157.

36. Steinhoff, *Messina,* pp. 132–33.

37. OKW KTB, 25 June 1943.

38. March, p. 259.

39. USAAF, vol. II, p. 441; Morison, *USN,* vol. IX, p. 57.

40. USAAF, vol. II, p. 438.

41. Steinhoff, *Messina,* pp. 58, 196–7.

42. Pond, *Sicily,* pp. 27–8; Christopher Shores, *Luftwaffe Fighter Units: Mediterranean, 1941–44* (London: Osprey, 1978), p. 36 (hereafter cited as Shores).

43. USAAF, vol. II, p. 445; Morison, *USN,* vol. IX, p. 60.

44. Conrad Seibt, "Stockpiling Supplies for Sardinia and Sicily (May and June, 1943)," Foreign Military Studies *MS # D-090* (Headquarters, U.S. Army Europe: Historical Division) (hereafter cited as Seibt, *MS # D-090*). Major General Seibt was a Luftwaffe logistical expert who had been largely responsible for the success of the German airborne assault on Crete in 1941.

CHAPTER 6: THE ALLIES APPROACH

1. "Fuehrer Conferences on Naval Affairs, 1943," p. 324.

2. Morison, *USN,* vol. IX, p. 40.

3. Kenneth Macksey, *Kesselring: The Making of the Luftwaffe* (New York: David McKay, 1978), p. 143 (hereafter cited as Macksey, *Kesselring*); "Fuehrer Conferences on Naval Affairs, 1943," pp. 323–5.

4. "Fuehrer Conferences on Naval Affairs, 1943," pp. 321–5.

5. Morison, *USN*, vol. IX, p. 37.

6. Ibid., pp. 37–40.

7. Ibid., p. 79.

8. Breuer, *DZ Sicily*, p. 23.

9. Pond, *Sicily*, p. 62; Blumenson, *Sicily*, p. 47; Garland and Smyth, p. 110; Albert Seaton, *The Fall of Fortress Europe* (New York: Holmes and Meier, 1981), p. 72 (hereafter cited as Seaton, *Fortress Europe*); OKW KTB, July 9, 1943; Breuer, *DZ Sicily*, p. 27.

10. Nicholson, *Canadians*, vol. II, p. 78, citing OB South SITREP, 10 July 43. SITREP is military shorthand for a situation report.

11. Senger, *MS # C-095;* Garland and Smyth, pp. 110–1.

12. Fred Majdalany, *The Fall of Fortress Europe* (Garden City, N.Y.: Doubleday, 1968; reprint ed., New York: Modern Literary Editions, 1968), p. 231 (hereafter cited as Majdalany, *Europe*).

13. Bauer, *MS # R-127;* Blumenson, *Sicily*, pp. 47–50; Garland and Smyth, p. 111.

14. Breuer, *DZ Sicily*, pp. 26–7, 63.

15. Garland and Smyth, p. 111.

16. Blumenson, *Sicily*, p. 50.

17. Morison, *USN*, vol. IX, p. 70, citing Admiral Ruge, "The Evacuation of Sicily."

CHAPTER 7: D-DAY

1. Morison, *USN*, vol. IX, p. 161, citing Thucydides, *Peloponnesian War*, trans. Crawley, vol. IV, xx.

2. Breuer, *DZ Sicily*, pp. 32, 36–7; USAAF, vol. II, pp. 446–7.

3. Robert Wallace and the editors of Time-Life Books, *The Italian Campaign* (Alexandria, Va.: Time-Life Books, 1981), p. 22 (hereafter cited as Wallace, *Italian Campaign*); Molony, vol. V, pp. 79–81; Pond, *Sicily*, p. 70; Breuer, *DZ Sicily*, pp. 32–46; USAAF, vol. II, pp. 446–7.

4. Molony, vol. V, pp. 57–9; Blumenson, *Sicily*, p. 60.

5. Bauer, *MS # R-127;* Pond, *Sicily*, p. 110; Molony, vol. V, pp. 80–1; Breuer, *DZ Sicily*, pp. 47–9.

6. Morison, *USN*, vol. IX, p. 155.

7. Sources for the Canadian attack include Nicholson, *Canadians*, vol. II, pp. 40–75; Pond, *Sicily*, pp. 79–82; Morison, *USN*, vol. IX, pp. 155–6.

8. Hamilton, *Master*, pp. 295–6.

9. Morison, *USN*, vol. IX, p. 158, citing L. S. B. Shapiro, *They Left the Back Door Open* (1944), p. 48.

10. Nigel Hamilton, *Master of the Battlefield: Monty's War Years, 1942–44* (New York: McGraw-Hill, 1983), p. 298 (hereafter cited as Hamilton, *Master*).

11. Breuer, *DZ Sicily*, p. 90.

12. Bradley, *Soldier's Story*, pp. 129–30.

13. The 429th Coastal Defense Battalion was part of the 134th Coastal Defense Regiment, 18th Coastal Defense Brigade.

14. Morison, *USN*, vol. IX, p. 90.

15. Sources for the 3rd Infantry Division's actions on D-Day include Morison, *USN*, vol. IX, pp. 75–90; Blumenson, *Sicily*, p. 55; Wallace, *Italian Campaign*, p. 22; Bauer, *MS # R-137;* and Alexander P. Shine, *Stepchildren: The Rangers of World War II* (Cambridge, Mass.: Harvard University Press, 1970), p. 14 (hereafter cited as Shine, *Stepchildren*).

16. S. W. C. Pack, *Operation "Husky"* (New York: Hippocrene, 1977), p. 66 (hereafter cited as Pack, *Husky*).

17. Pack, *Husky*, p. 62.

18. Wallace, *Italian Campaign*, p. 24.

19. Steinhoff, *Messina*, pp. 149, 162.

20. Morison, *USN*, vol. IX, p. 101.

21. D'Este, *Bitter Victory*, p. 289.

22. Kurowski, *Tor*, p. 69; Hellmut Bergengruen, "Kampf der Panzer Div. 'Hermann Goering' auf Sizilien vom 10.–14.7. 1943," Foreign Military Studies *MS # C-087b* (Headquarters, U.S. Army Europe: Historical Division). Bergengruen revised his original manuscript several times.

23. Bauer, *MS # R-137*. Lieutenant Colonel Bergengruen served only as acting commander of the 1st Hermann Goering Panzer Grenadier Regiment and Kampfgruppe Links. He apparently held this temporary post until July 13 and then resumed his duties as Ia of the division. The original task force commander was court-martialed by General Conrath.

24. Sources for the Axis counterattack include Bauer, *MS # R-137;* Bergengruen, *MS # C-087a;* Garland and Smyth, pp. 126–54 and Map VII; Pond, *Sicily*, pp. 89–92; Wallace, *Italian Campaign*, pp. 22–3; Blumenson, *Sicily*, pp. 58–60; Breuer, *DZ Sicily*, pp. 68, 99–106; Morison, *USN*, vol. IX, p. 104; Senger, *MS # C-095;* and Kurowski, *Tor*, pp. 68–70.

25. Breuer, *DZ Sicily*, p. 202.

26. James M. Gavin, *Airborne Warfare* (Washington, D.C.: Infantry Journal Press, 1947), p. 16.

27. Garland and Smyth, pp. 157–8; Nicholson, *Canadians*, vol. II, p. xx; Breuer, *DZ Sicily*, p. 202; James M. Gavin, *Airborne Warfare* (Washington D.C.: *Infantry Journal Press*, 1947), p. 6.

28. Garland and Smyth, p. 157; Walter Fries, "The Battle for Sicily," Foreign Military Studies *MS # T-2* (Headquarters, U.S. Army, Europe: Historical Division) (hereafter cited as Fries, *MS # T-2*).

29. Bergengruen, *MS # C-087a* and *MS #C-087c*.

30. Senger, *MS # C-095*.

31. George S. Patton, *War As I Knew It* (Boston: Houghton Mifflin, 1947; reprint ed., New York Pyramid, 1966), p. 63 (hereafter cited as Patton, *War As I Knew It*).

32. Breuer, *DZ Sicily*, p. 202.

33. Kesselring, *Soldier's Record*, p. 196. Also see Fries, *MS # T-2*.

34. On the nights of July 12 and 13, Force Z of the Royal Navy shelled the city of Trapani and two of the Egadi Islands off the western cape of Sicily in order to create the impression that Allied troops were about to land in that sector. This diversion might have been successful on July 10, but it came too late: none of the major Axis commanders were fooled on July 12.

35. Rodt, *MS # R-138*; Bauer, *MS # C-077*.

36. Bauer, *MS # R-141*. The remnants of the Italian 12th Artillery Regiment may have been absorbed by Tactical Group Schreiber, but this is uncertain.

37. Sources for the Axis plans and dispositions on the night of July 10–11 include: Bauer, *MS # R-137*; Kurowski, *Tor*, pp. 70–4; Blumenson, *Sicily*, p. 62; Garland and Smyth, pp. 163–4, 191–2; Pond, *Sicily*, p. 92; Senger, *MS # C-095*; Rodt, *MS # C-077*; Nicholson, *Canadians*, vol. II, p. 78, citing OB South, SITREP of 10 July 43; and Morison, *USN*, vol. IX, p. 174.

CHAPTER 8: COUNTERATTACK AND RETREAT

1. Bauer, *MS # R-138*. The right-hand column of the Livorno attack was apparently under the command of Lieutenant Colonel Bruni.

2. Morison, *USN*, vol. IX, p. 113.

3. D'Este, *Bitter Victory*, p. 293.

4. Sources for the counterattack of July 11 include Pond, *Sicily*, pp. 92–9; Breuer, *DZ Sicily*, pp. 123–6, 132–5, 137; Senger, *MS # C-095*;

Blumenson, *Sicily*, pp. 62–4, 66–7; Wallace, *Italian Campaign*, pp. 23–4; Shine, *Stepchildren*, p. 13; Fargo, *Patton*, p. 289; Bauer, *MS # R-138*; Morison, *USN*, vol. IX, pp. 110–9, 145; Quarrie, *H.G.*, p. 14; Bender and Petersen, *H.G.*, pp. 29–30; Garland and Smyth, pp. 164–72, 189; Rodt, *MS # C-077*; Bergengruen, *MS # C-087a* and *MS # C-087b*.

5. Hamilton, *Master*, pp. 300–1.

6. Donald E. Houston, *Hell on Wheels: The 2nd Armored Division* (Novato, Calif.: Presidio, 1977), p. 159 (hereafter cited as Houston, *Hell on Wheels*).

7. Bauer, *MS # R-138*.

8. Bauer, *MS # R-139*.

9. Garland and Smyth, p. 177.

10. Sources for the airborne operation of July 11 include USAAF, vol. II, p. 454; Morison, *USN*, vol. IX, p. 141; Breuer, *DZ Sicily*, pp. 138–45; Garland and Smyth, pp. 175–84; Pond, *Sicily*, p. 100–4.

11. Pond, *Sicily*, p. 108.

12. Bauer, *MS # R-138*.

13. Bauer, *MS # R-139*.

CHAPTER 9: PRIMOSOLE BRIDGE

1. Kesselring, *Soldier's Record*, p. 196.

2. C. J. C. Molony et al., *The Mediterranean and Middle East*, vol. V: *The Campaign in Sicily, 1943, and the Campaign in Italy, 3rd September 1943 to 31st March 1944* (London: Her Majesty's Stationery Office, 1973) (hereafter cited as Molony, vol. V).

3. Senger, *MS # C-095*.

4. Ibid.

5. Blumenson, *Sicily*, p. 82.

6. Senger, *MS # C-095*.

7. Ibid.

8. Nicholson, *Canadians*, vol. II, pp. 82–3.

9. Kurowski, *Tor*, pp. 84–5. The final drop, which would have involved the reinforced 1st Parachute Regiment, was never made.

10. Carlo D'Este, "Where Devils Collide," *World War II*, vol. III, no. 2 (July 1988), p. 28 (hereafter cited as D'Este, "Devils").

11. Kesselring, *Soldier's Record*, p. 196.

12. Senger, *MS # C-095*.

13. Molony, vol. V, p. 88.

14. Bradley, *Soldier's Story,* p. 138.

15. Bauer, *MS # R-139.*

16. Pond, *Sicily,* p. 115.

17. Martin Poeppel, *Heaven and Hell: The War Diary of a German Paratrooper* (Tunbridge Wells, U.K.: Spellmount, 1988), pp. 117, 153 (hereafter cited as Poeppel).

18. D'Este, "Devils," p. 29.

19. Poeppel, p. 122.

20. Ibid.

21. D'Este, "Devils," p. 28.

22. Sir Francis de Guingand, *Operation Victory* (New York: Charles Scribner's Sons, 1947), p. 299 (hereafter cited as de Guingand, *Operation Victory*).

23. Pond, *Sicily,* p. 141.

24. Bauer, *MS # R-139.*

25. Rodt, *MS # C-077;* Bauer, *MS # R-139.*

26. Pond, *Sicily,* p. 147.

27. Ibid., p. 141.

28. De Guingand, *Operation Victory,* p. 298.

29. Pond, *Sicily,* p. 142.

30. De Guingand, *Operation Victory,* pp. 298–9.

31. Ibid., p. 299.

32. D'Este, *Bitter Victory,* p. 392.

33. Molony, vol. V, p. 105.

34. Senger, *MS # C-095.*

CHAPTER 10: ENTER GENERAL HUBE

1. Krampf eventually recovered and as a lieutenant general was the 4th Army Artillery commander on the Eastern Front at the end of the war.

2. Personal communication from Harro Eysen to Friedrich von Stauffenberg, Buenos Aires, 1952.

3. Ibid.

4. Gilbert, pp. 59–60.

5. Tessin, vol. III, p. 290.

6. Morison, *USN,* vol. IX, p. 218, citing Bonin MS.

7. Senger, *MS # C-095.*

8. Brett-Smith, p. 114.

9. Kesselring, *Soldier's Record,* p. 198.

10. Seaton, *Fortress Europe,* p. 73.

11. Pond, *Sicily,* p. 132.

12. Morison, *USN,* vol. IX, p. 172.

13. July 43.

14. Hanson W. Baldwin, *Battles Won and Lost* (New York: Harper & Row, 1966), p. 453 (hereafter cited as Baldwin, *Battles*).

15. Seaton, *Fortress Europe,* p. 77.

16. Senger, *MS # C-095.*

17. Molony, vol. V, p. 107.

18. Nicholson, *Canadians,* vol. II, p. 90.

19. Ibid., p. 93.

20. Rodt, *MS # C-077;* Bauer, *MS # R-139.*

21. Max Ulich, "Reconnaissance During the Battle of Sicily," Foreign Military Studies *MS # D-089,* Headquarters, U.S. Army, Europe: Historical Division.

22. Pond, *Sicily,* p. 156.

23. Martin Blumenson, *The Patton Papers* (Boston: Houghton Mifflin, 1972–1974), Volume II, p. 289 (entry of 16 July 1943) (hereafter cited as Blumenson, *Patton Papers*).

24. Pond, p. 170.

25. The Canadian Official History reported that the defenders of Assoro were the men of the IIIrd Battalion of the 104th Panzer Grenadier Regiment; however, the 104th had no third battalion. The defenders probably were a combat group from the regimental reserve, augmented by elements of the 215th Panzer Battalion.

26. Pond, *Sicily,* p. 172.

CHAPTER 11: PATTON BREAKS LOOSE

1. Morison, *USN,* vol. IX, p. 176.

2. Bauer, *MS # R-141.*

3. Ibid.

4. Pond, *Sicily,* p. 205.

5. Ibid., p. 206.

6. Blumenson, *Patton Papers,* p. 290. Patton called Alexander's excuse "pretty weak."

7. Ibid.

8. Bauer, *MS # R-141.*

9. Hamilton, *Master,* p. 319.

10. Breuer, *DZ Sicily,* p. 186.

11. Bauer, *MS # R-142.*

12. Ibid.

13. Houston, *Hell on Wheels,* p. 171.

14. Bauer, *MS # R-142.*

15. Molinero, a fifty-nine-year-old infantry officer, had been a generale di brigata since January 22, 1939. He had served as commander of Military Zone Milan in 1941.

16. Patton, *War as I Knew It,* entry of July 23, 1943.

CHAPTER 12: THE BATTLES OF THE HAUPTKAMPFLINIE

1. Albert Kesselring, "Special Report on the Events in Italy Between 25 July and 8 September 1943," Foreign Military Studies *MS # C-013.*

2. Westphal, *West,* p. 137.

3. Badoglio, p. 46.

4. David Irving, *Hitler's War* (New York: Viking, 1977), vol. II, p. 597 (hereafter cited as Irving, *Hitler's War*).

5. Gilbert, p. 95.

6. Ibid., p. 100.

7. John Strawson, *Hitler's Battles for Europe* (New York: Charles Scribner's Sons, 1971), p. 178.

8. Garland and Smyth, p. 273.

9. Ibid., p. 273.

10. Irving, *Hitler's War,* vol. II, p. 600.

11. Ibid., pp. 600–601.

12. Bauer, *MS # R-143.*

13. U.S. Army General Staff, Intelligence Section, *Two Hundred and Fifty-one Divisions of the German Army Which Participated in the War (1914–1918)* (Washington, D.C.: U.S. Government Printing Office, 1920).

14. Tessin, vol. 9, p. 237.

15. Joachim Lemelsen, *29. Division* (Bad Nauheim: Podzun, 1955), p. 267.

16. Patton, *War As I Knew It,* July 18, 1943.

17. D'Este, *Bitter Victory,* p. 439, citing Lieutenant General Paul Conrath, "Brief Experience Report on the Fighting in Sicily," 24 Aug. 43, *Report 14,* Historical Section (GS), Canadian Army Headquarters.

18. General Guzzoni was privately pleased that Mussolini had fallen, because he blamed the Duce for the failure of Fascism.

19. Hans Meier-Welcker had previously served on the General Staff of the 251st Infantry Division in the Rzhev salient on the Russian Front.

20. David Irving, *Goering* (New York: Morrow, 1989), p. 375–6.

21. D'Este, *Bitter Victory,* p. 455, citing Senger, *An Cosantoir,* July 1950.

22. Poeppel, p. 126.

23. Rudolf Boehmler and Werner Haupt, *Fallschirmjaeger* (Dorheim: Verlag Hans-Henning Podzun, 1971), p. 151.

24. Linklater, *Italy,* p. 38.

25. Morison, *USN,* vol. IX, p. 191.

26. Ibid., p. 192.

27. Blumenson, *Sicily,* p. 114.

28. Nicholson, *Canadians,* vol. II, p. 141, citing a German 10th Army communication. The 923rd Fortress Battalion had been formed in Italy on June 16, 1943, as a march unit and had been attached to the Hermann Goering Division. Because of the shortage of German troops, it was not possible to dissolve it immediately after its rout, as Kesselring had ordered. Remnants of the battalion were rallied and sent back to the line; it was not dissolved until September 25 (Tessin, vol. XIII, p. 130).

29. Molony, vol. V, p. 159.

30. Pond, *Sicily,* p. 164.

31. Linklater, *Italy,* p. 42.

CHAPTER 13: THE ALLIES CLOSE IN

1. Garland and Smyth, pp. 324–5.

2. Colonel Grell was on the staff of the XIVth Panzer Corps, but it is not clear if he was the corps engineer officer or merely an officer on special assignment.

3. USAAF, vol. II, p. 469.

4. Bradley, *Soldier's Story,* p. 152.

5. Baldwin, *Battles,* p. 457.

6. Bauer, *MS # R-144.* Assietta lost the 2nd Battery of I/22nd Artillery

Regiment; the 12th Battery, IV/22nd Artillery; and the 301st Battery, 75th Artillery Battalion.

7. Blumenson, *Sicily*, p. 143.

8. Ralph S. Mavrogordato, "Hitler's Decision on the Defense of Italy," in *Command Decisions*, Office of the Chief of Military History, United States Department of the Army (New York: Harcourt, Brace, 1959), p. 310 (hereafter cited as Mavrogordato, *Command Decisions*); Richard D. Law and Craig W. H. Luther, *Rommel: A Narrative and Pictorial History* (San Jose, Calif.: R. James Bender, 1980), p. 231.

CHAPTER 14: OPERATION LEHRGANG: A PANZER CORPS ESCAPES

1. Morison, *USN*, vol. IX, p. 209.

2. Coastal defenses in the Catania (west coast) area were assigned to Colonel Sonnenberg. Rainer Stahel was later Luftwaffe commandant of Rome (1943) and as a lieutenant general commanded Luftwaffe rear area units in Hungary in 1944.

3. The 10th Landing Flotilla was not available in May and apparently was not assembled in the Messina area until July.

4. Blumenson, *Sicily*, p. 96.

5. MFPs—*Marine-faehrpraehme*—were literally designated "naval perambulators." Called "formidable" by the U.S. Navy's official historian, they were beaching craft that were 163 feet long and capable of making ten knots while carrying a hundred tons of cargo. They were partially armored and heavily armed to repeal air or surface attacks. Their armament included at least one 75-mm gun, and some of them carried 88's. As barges they drew only 4.5 feet of water and thus were immune from attack by PT boats, whose torpedos would not run true in depths of less than eight feet (Morison, *USN*, vol. IX, pp. 189–90).

6. D'Este, *Bitter Victory*, pp. 497–500.

7. Nicholson, *Canadians*, vol. II, p. 168, citing Enno von Rintelen, *Mussolini als Bundesgenosse* (Tuebingen, 1951), p. 224.

8. Garland and Smyth, p. 374.

9. Conrad Seibt, "Evacuation of Sicily and Sardinia in August, 1943," Foreign Military Studies *MS # D-091* (Headquarters, U.S. Army Europe, Historical Division).

10. Galland, p. 158.

11. S. W. Roskill, *The War at Sea, 1939–1945* (London: Her Majesty's Stationery Office, 1960), vol. III, part 1, 144 ff. (hereafter cited as Roskill).

12. Normally the heavy guns of a German divisional artillery regiment

were in the IVth Battalion, but this was not the case in the 33rd Motorized Artillery.

13. Morison, *USN,* vol. IX, p. 212.

14. Baldwin, *Battles,* p. 462.

15. Blumenson, *Sicily,* p. 132.

16. Pond, *Sicily,* p. 215.

17. L-boats were armed with one heavy machine gun and had a maximum speed of nine knots. Their use by German army engineers was standard practice in World War II.

18. Bauer, *MS # R-146.*

19. Molony, vol. V, p. 166.

20. D'Este, *Bitter Victory,* pp. 495–6.

21. Blumenson, *Sicily,* p. 96.

22. Nicholson, *Canadians,* vol. II, p. 174, citing von Bonin, pp. 16–7. Morison, *USN,* vol. IX, chap. X.

23. Morison, *USN,* vol. IX, pp. 212–3.

24. Pond, *Sicily,* p. 7; D'Este, *Bitter Victory,* pp. 541–3; Roskill, vol. III, part 1, pp. 149–52; Morison, *USN,* vol. IX, p. 213.

25. Garland and Smyth, p. 376.

26. Walter Warlimont, *Inside Hitler's Headquarters* (New York: Praeger, 1964) p. 379. For the sake of their own operations, Rommel and Doenitz did not want the island evacuated yet.

27. Nicholson, *Canadians,* vol. II, p. 173, citing the war diary of the LXXVIth Panzer Corps, 13 Aug. 43.

28. Max Ulich and Colonel Joachim von Schoen-Angerer, "Special Experience Gained in Marches of Motorized Formations and Units in Sicily," Foreign Military Studies *MS # D-063* (Headquarters, U.S. Army Europe: Historical Division).

29. Linklater, *Italy,* p. 45.

30. Nicholson, *Canadians,* vol. II, p. 173.

31. Molony, vol. V, p. 182.

32. Poeppel, p. 144.

33. Garland and Smyth, p. 416.

34. D'Este, *Bitter Victory,* p. 520.

35. Bauer, *MS # R-145.*

36. Garland and Smyth, p. 417; Wallace, *Italian Campaign,* p. 33; Breuer, *DZ Sicily,* p. 201.

37. Bauer, *MS # R-145.*

38. Winston S. Churchill, *Closing the Ring* (Boston: Little, Brown, 1951), p. 40.

39. USAAF, vol. II, p. 485.

40. Morison, *USN,* vol. IX, p. 59.

41. Ibid.

42. Hart, *Second World War,* vol. II, p. 441.

43. Nicholson, *Canadians,* vol. II, p. 119.

44. Ibid. This figure includes aircraft claimed by both aviation and flak units.

45. Matthew Cooper, *The German Air Force, 1933–1945* (London: Jane's, 1981), p. 485.

46. Bauer, *MS # R-145.*

47. Ibid.

48. Ibid.

49. Molony, vol. V, p. 168.

50. Bauer, *MS # R-145.*

51. Heinrich von Vietinghoff, "Die Kaempfe der 10. Armme in Sued- und Mittelitalien," in Siegfried Westphal et al., "Feldzug in Italien," Foreign Military Studies *MS # T-1a* (hereafter cited as Vietinghoff, "10. Armee").

52. Giuseppe Castellano was born in Prato on September 12, 1893. Commissioned in the artillery, he served in World War I and in 1935 became deputy chief of staff to General Ambrosio, who was then a corps commander. He remained associated with Ambrosio in various staff positions throughout the war.

53. Baldwin, *Battles,* p. 188.

54. Ibid., p. 193.

55. Blumenson, *Sicily,* p. 156.

56. Seaton, *Fortress Europe,* p. 77.

57. John Grigg, *1943: The Victory That Never Was* (New York: Hill & Wang, 1980), p. 97.

58. Higgins, *Soft Underbelly,* p. 89, citing Michael Foot, *Aneurin Bevan* (London: Macgibbon and Kee, 1962), vol. I, p. 432.

59. Baldwin, *Battles,* p. 460, citing Franco Maugeri, *From the Ashes of Disgrace* (New York: Reynal and Hitchcock, 1948), pp. 193–4.

60. Harry C. Butcher, *My Three Years with Eisenhower* (New York: Simon & Schuster, 1946), entry of August 17, 1943.

61. Mavrogordato, *Command Decisions,* p. 312; also see Vietinghoff, "10. Armee."

62. Baldwin, *Battles,* p. 460; Vietinghoff, *MS # D-116.*

63. Albert Kesselring and Siegfried Westphal, "German Strategy During the Italian Campaign," Foreign Military Studies *MS # B-270* (Headquarters, U.S. Army Europe: Historical Division).

64. Hart, *Second World War,* vol. II, p. 446.

65. Seaton, *Fortress Europe,* p. 72.

66. Ibid., pp. 70–1.

EPILOGUE

1. Higgins, *Soft Underbelly,* citing Francois Genoud, ed., *The Testament of Adolf Hitler: The Hitler-Bormann Documents, February–April 1945* (London: 1959), p. 69.

2. Ferdinand and Stefan von Senger, "Senger," p. 392.

3. See the bibliography in this book.

4. Friedrich Ruge, *Rommel in Normandy: Reminiscences by Friedrich Ruge* (San Rafael, Calif., and London: Presidio, 1979).

BIBLIOGRAPHY

Absolon, Rudolf, comp. *Rangeliste der Generale der Deutschen Luftwaffe nach den Stand vom 20. April 1945.* Friedberg: Podzun-Pallas-Verlag, 1984.

Allied Forces Headquarters. Office of the Assistant Chief of Staff, G-2. "German Personality List for Sicily." 17 August 1943. On file, Air University Archives, Maxwell Air Force Base, Ala.

Badoglio, Pietro. *Italy in the Second World War.* London: Oxford University Press, 1948. Reprint ed.: Westport, Conn.: Greenwood Press, 1976.

Baldwin, Hanson W. *Battles Won and Lost.* New York: Harper & Row, 1966.

Barrett, Correlli, ed. *Hitler's Generals.* London: Weidenfeld and Nicolson, 1989.

Bauer, Magna E. "Axis Tactical Operations in Sicily, July–August, 1943." Foreign Military Studies *MS # R-114* through *MS # 146.* Washington, D.C.: Office of the Chief of Military History, 1958–1959.

Bender, R. James, and Petersen, George. *"Hermann Goering": From Regiment to Fallschirmpanzerkorps.* San Jose, Calif.: R. James Bender, 1975.

Bergengruen, Hellmut. "Kampf der Panzer Division 'Hermann Goering' auf Sizilien vom 10.–14.7.1943." Foreign Military Studies *MS # C-087.* Headquarters, U.S. Army Europe: Historical Division.

Blumenson, Martin. *Sicily: Whose Victory?* New York: Ballantine, 1968.

———. *The Patton Papers.* Boston: Houghton Mifflin 1972–1974. 2 volumes.

Boehmler, Rudolf, and Haupt, Werner. *Fallschirmjaeger.* Dorheim: Verlag Hans-Henning Podzun, 1971.

Bonin, Bogislaw von. "Consideratons on the Italian Campaign, 1943–44." Ottawa: Canadian Army Historical Section, 1947.

Bradley, Omar N. *A Soldier's Story.* Chicago: Rand McNally, 1951.

Brett-Smith, Richard. *Hitler's Generals.* Novato, Calif.: Presidio, 1977.

Breuer, William B. *Drop Zone Sicily: Allied Airborne Strike, July 1943.* Novato, Calif.: Presidio, 1983.

———. *Operation Torch: The Allied Gamble to Invade North Africa.* New York: St. Martin's, 1985.

Cooper, Matthew. *The German Air Force, 1933–1945.* London: Jane's 1981.

Davis, Melton S. *Who Defends Rome? The Forty-five Days, July 25–September 8, 1943.* London: Allen & Unwin, 1972.

D'Este, Carlo. "Where Devils Collide." *World War II,* vol. III, no. 2 (July 1988): pp. 26–33.

———. *Bitter Victory: The Battle of Sicily, 1943.* New York: Dutton, 1988.

Dierich, Wolfgang. *Die Verbaende der Luftwaffe, 1935–1945: Gliederungen und Kurzchronikeneine Dokumentation.* Stuttgart: Motorbuch Verlag, 1976.

Eisenhower, Dwight D. *Crusade in Europe.* Garden City, N.Y.: Doubleday, 1949.

Farago, Ladislas. *Patton: Ordeal and Triumph.* New York: Faracorn, 1963. Reprint ed.: New York: Dell, 1970.

Finley, I. M., Smith, Dennis Mack, and Dugger, Christopher. *A History of Sicily.* New York: Viking Penguin, 1987.

Fries, Walter. "The Battle for Sicily." Foreign Military Studies *MS # T-2.* Headquarters, U.S. Army Europe: Historical Division.

"Fuehrer Conferences on Naval Affairs." In *Brassey's Naval Annual 1948,* ed. Rear Admiral H. G. Thursfield. New York: Macmillan, 1948.

Galland, Adolf. *The First and the Last.* New York: Henry Holt, 1954. Reprint ed.: New York: Ballantine, 1969.

Garland, Albert N., and Smyth, Howard McG. *Sicily and the Surrender of Italy.* United States Army in World War II, Mediterranean Theater of Operations. Washington, D.C.: U.S. Government Printing Office, 1965.

Gavin, James M. *Airborne Warfare.* Washington, D.C.: Infantry Journal Press, 1947.

"General Officers of the German Air Force." Unpublished document. Maxwell Air Force Base, Ala.: Air University Archives. Declassified 22 Sept. 1972.

Genoud, Francois, ed. *The Testament of Adolf Hitler: The Hitler-Bormann Documents, February–April 1945.* London: Cassell, 1959.

Gilbert, Felix, ed. and trans. *Hitler Directs His War.* New York: Award, 1960.

Goodspeed, D. J. *The German Wars, 1914–1945.* Boston: Houghton Mifflin, 1977. Reprint ed.: New York: Bonanza, 1985.

Grigg, John. *1943: The Victory That Never Was.* New York: Hill & Wang, 1980.

Guingand, Sir Francis de. *Operation Victory.* New York: Charles Scribner's Sons, 1947.

Hamilton, Nigel. *Master of the Battlefield: Monty's War Years, 1942–44.* New York: McGraw-Hill, 1983.

Hart, B. H. Liddell. *History of the Second World War.* New York: Putnam, 1972. 2 volumes.

Haupt, Werner. *Kriegschauplatz Italien, 1943–45.* Munich: Mortorbuch Verlag, 1977.

Held, Walter. *Verbaende und Truppen der deutschen Wehrmacht und Waffen-SS im Zweiten Weltkrieg.* Osnabrueck: Biblio Verlag, 1978.

Higgins, Trumbull. *Soft Underbelly.* New York: Macmillan, 1968.

Houston, Donald E. *Hell on Wheels: The 2nd Armored Division.* Novato, Calif.: Presidio, 1977.

Irving, David. *Hitler's War.* New York: Viking, 1977. 2 volumes.

———. *The Trail of the Fox.* New York: Dutton, 1977. Reprint ed.: New York: "Night Fighting in the Mediterranean." Foreign Military Studies *MS # D-162.* Headquarters, U.S. Army Europe: Historical Division.

Katz, Robert. *The Fall.* New York: Morrow, 1989.

Keilig, Wolf. *Die Generale des Heeres.* Friedberg: Podzun-Pallas-Verlag, 1983.

Kesselring, Albert. *Kesselring: A Soldier's Record.* New York: Morrow, 1954.

———. "Special Report on the Events in Italy Between 25 July and 8 September 1943." Foreign Military Studies *MS # C-013.* Headquarters, U.S. Army Europe: Historical Division.

———, and Westphal, Siegfried. "German Strategy During the Italian Campaign." Foreign Military Studies *MS # B-270.* Headquarters, U.S. Army Europe: Historical Division.

Kriegstagebuch des Oberkommando des Wehrmacht. Frankfurt-am-Main: Bernard und Graefe Verlag fuer Wehrwesen, 1961. 8 volumes.

Kurowski, Franz. *Das Tor zur Festung Europa.* Neckargemuend: Kurt Vowinckel Verlag, 1966.

Law, Richard D., and Luther, Craig W. H. *Rommel: A Narrative and Pictorial History.* San Jose, Calif.: R. James Bender, 1980.

Lemelsen, Joachim. *29. Division.* Bad Nauheim: Podzun, 1955.

Linklater, Eric. *The Campaign in Italy.* London: His Majesty's Stationery Office, 1951.

Macksey, Kenneth. *Kesselring: The Making of the Luftwaffe.* New York: David McKay, 1978.

Majdalany, Fred. *The Fall of Fortress Europe.* Garden City, N.Y.: Doubleday, 1968. Reprint ed.: New York: Modern Literary Editions, 1968.

Maugeri, Franco. *From the Ashes of Disgrace.* New York: Reynal and Hitchcock, 1948.

Mavrogordato, Ralph S. "Hitler's Decision on the Defense of Italy." In *Command Decisions,* prepared by the Office of the Chief of Military History, United States Department of the Army. New York: Harcourt, Brace, 1959: pp. 224–43.

Molony, C. J. C., et al. *The Mediterranean and Middle East.* vol. V: *The Campaign in Sicily, 1943, and the Campaign in Italy, 3rd September 1943 to 31st March 1944.* London: Her Majesty's Stationery Office, 1973.

Morison, Samuel Eliot. *History of the United States Naval Operations in World War II.* vol. IX: *Sicily-Salerno-Anzio.* Boston: Little, Brown, 1962.

Mosley, Leonard. *Marshall: Hero for Our Times.* New York: Hearst, 1982.

Mueller-Hillebrant, Burkhart. *Germany and Its Allies: A Record of Axis Collaboration Problems.* Frederick, Md.: University Publications of America, 1980.

Murray, Williamson. *Strategy for Defeat: The Luftwaffe, 1933–1945.* Maxwell Air Force Base, Ala.: Air University Press, 1983.

Musciano, Walter A. *Messerschmitt Aces.* New York: Arco, 1982.

New York Times, April 16, 1965, Guzzoni obituary.

Nicholson, G. W. L. *The Official History of the Canadian Army in the Second World War: The Canadians in Italy.* Ottawa: Clouter, 1956. 2 volumes.

Nogueres, Henri. *Munich,* trans. Patrick O'Brien. New York: McGraw-Hill, 1965.

Office of the Chief of Military History, United States Department of the Army. *Command Decisions.* New York: Harcourt Brace, 1959.

Pack, S. W. C. *Operation "Husky."* New York: Hippocrene, 1977.

Patton, George S. *War As I Knew It.* Boston: Houghton Mifflin, 1947. Reprint ed.: New York: Pyramid, 1966.

Poeppel, Martin. *Heaven and Hell: The War Diary of a German Paratrooper*, trans. Dr. Louise Willmot. Tunbridge Wells, U.K.: Spellmount, 1988.

Pond, Hugh. *Sicily*. London: William Kimber, 1962.

Quarrie, Bruce. *Fallschirmpanzerdivision "Hermann Goering."* Vanguard 4. London: Osprey, 1978. Reprint ed.: Warren, Mich.: Squadron/Signal, 1978.

Rodt, Eberhard, et al. "Studie ueber den Feldzug in Sizilien bei der 15. Panzer Grenadier Division, Mai–August 1943." Foreign Military Studies *MS # C-077*. Headquarters, U.S. Army Europe: Historical Division.

Rommel, Erwin. *The Rommel Papers*, ed. B. H. Liddell Hart. New York: Harcourt, Brace, 1953.

Roskill, S. W. *The War at Sea, 1939–1945*. London: Her Majesty's Stationery Office, 1960. 3 volumes.

Royal Air Force Historical Branch. *The Rise and Fall of the German Air Force, 1933–1945*, ed. Cyril March. London: Her Majesty's Stationery Office, 1948. Reprint ed.: New York: St. Martin's, 1983.

Ruge, Friedrich. *Rommel in Normandy: Reminiscences by Friedrich Ruge*. San Rafael, Calif., and London: Presidio, 1979.

Scheibert, Horst. *Die Traeger des Deutschen Kreuzes in Gold: das Heer*. Friedberg: Podzun-Pallas-Verlag, n.d.

Seaton, Albert. *The Fall of Fortress Europe, 1943–1945*. New York: Holmes & Meier, 1981.

Seibt, Conrad. "Stockpiling Supplies for Sardinia and Sicily (May–June, 1943)." Foreign Military Studies *MS # D-090*. Headquarters, U.S. Army Europe: Historical Division.

———. "Evacuation of Sicily and Sardinia in August, 1943." Foreign Military Studies *MS # D-091*. Headquarters, U.S. Army Europe: Historical Division.

Senger und Etterlin, Ferdinand von, and von Senger und Etterlin, Stefan. "Senger." In *Hitler's Generals*, ed. Correlli Barrett. London: Weidenfeld and Nicolson, 1989: pp. 375–9.

Senger und Etterlin, Fridolin von. "Liaison Activities with Italian 6th Army." Foreign Military Studies *MS # C-095*. Headquarters, U.S. Army Europe: Historical Division.

———. "War Diary of the Italian Campaign: Sardinia and Corsica." Foreign Military Studies *MS # C-095a*. Headquarters, U.S. Army Europe: Historical Division.

———. *Neither Fear nor Hope*. New York: Dutton, 1964.

Shine, Alexander P. *Stepchildren: The Rangers of World War II*. Cambridge, Mass.: Harvard University Press, 1970.

Shores, Christopher. *Luftwaffe Fighter Units: Mediterranean, 1941–44.* London: Osprey, 1978.

Steinhoff, Johannes. *The Straits of Messina: Diary of a Fighter Commander.* London: Andre Deutsch, 1971.

Stoves, Rolf. *Die Gepanzerten und Motorisierten deutschen Grossverbaende: Divisionen und selbstaendige Brigaden: 1935–1945.* Friedburg: Podzun-Pallas-Verlag, 1986.

Strawson, John. *Hitler's Battles for Europe.* New York: Charles Scribner's Sons, 1971.

"Stellgenbesetsung Hoeherer Kommandeure der Luftwaffe." Unpublished document. Maxwell Air Force Base, Ala.: Air University Archives, n.d.

Taylor, Telford. *Munich.* Garden City, N.Y.: Doubleday, 1979. Reprint ed.: New York: Vintage, 1980.

Tessin, Georg. *Verbaende und Truppen der deutschen Wehrmacht und Waffen-SS im Zweiten Weltkrieg, 1939–1945.* Osnabrueck: Biblio Verlag, 1973. 14 volumes.

Truscott, Lucian K., Jr. *Command Missions.* New York: Dutton, 1954.

Ulich, Max. "15th Panzer Grenadier Regiment (18–23 July 1943)." Foreign Military Studies *MS # D-023.* Headquarters, U.S. Army Europe: Historical Division.

————. "Reconnaissance in the Battle of Sicily." Foreign Military Studies *MS # D-089.* Headquarters, U.S. Army Europe: Historical Division.

————. "Sicilian Campaign: Special Problems and Their Solution (Jul.–Aug., 1943)." Foreign Military Studies *MS # D-004.* Headquarters, U.S. Army Europe: Historical Division.

————. "Special Experience Gained in Marches of Motorized Formations and Units in Sicily." Foreign Military Studies *MS # D-063.* Headquarters, U.S. Army Europe: Historical Division.

————. "29th Panzer Grenadier Division (30 July 1943)." Foreign Military Studies *MS # D-095.* Headquarters, U.S. Army Europe: Historical Division.

————, and von Schoen-Angerer, Joachim. "Special Experience Gained in Marches of Motorized Formations and Units in Sicily." Foreign Military Studies *MS # D-063.* Headquarters, U.S. Army Europe: Historical Division.

United States Air Force Historical Group. *The Army Air Forces in World War II.* vol. II: *Europe: Torch to Pointblank, August 1942 to December 1943,* eds. Wesley Frank Craven and James L. Cate. Chicago: University of Chicago Press, 1949.

United States Army General Staff, Intelligence Section. *Two Hundred and Fifty-one Divisions of the German Army Which Participated in the War (1914–1918)*. Washington, D.C.: U.S. Government Printing Office, 1920.

United States Army Military Intelligence Division. "Italian Order of Battle." Washington, D.C.: War Department, 1943.

Vietinghoff, Heinrich von. "Overall Situation in the Mediterranean." Foreign Military Studies *MS # D-116*. Headquarters, U.S. Army Europe: Historical Division.

———. "Die Kaempfe der 10. Armee in Sued- und Mittelitalien." In Seigfried Westphal et al., Foreign Military Studies *MS # T-1a*. Headquarters, U.S. Army Europe: Historical Division.

Wallace, Robert, and the editors of Time-Life Books. *The Italian Campaign*. Alexandria, Va.: Time-Life, 1981.

Warlimont, Walter. *Inside Hitler's Headquarters*. New York: Praeger, 1964.

Wedemeyer, Albert C. *Wedemeyer Reports!* New York: Henry Holt and Company, 1958.

Westphal, Siegfried. *The German Army in the West*. London: Cassell, 1951.

———, et al. "Der Feldzug in Italien (Apr 1943–11 Mai 1944)." Foreign Military Studies *MS # T-1a*. Headquarters, U.S. Army Europe: Historical Division.

Whiting, Charles. *Hunters from the Sky: The German Parachute Corps, 1940–1945*. London: Leo Cooper, 1974.

Wiskemann, Elizabeth. *The Rome-Berlin Axis*. London: Oxford University Press, 1949.

Young, Desmond. *Rommel: The Desert Fox*. New York: Harper & Row, 1950.

APPENDIXES

A P P E N D I X   1

TABLES OF EQUIVALENT RANK

U.S. Army	German Army	Italian Army
General of the Army	Field Marshal (Generalfeldmarschall)	Marshal (Maresciallo d'Italia)
General	Colonel General (Generaloberst)	General of Army (Generale d'Armata)
Lieutenant General	General (der Infantrie, Panzertruppen, etc.)	General of Corps (Generale di Corpo)
Major General	Lieutenant General (Generalleutnant)	General of Division (Generale di Divisione)
Brigadier General	Major General (Generalmajor)	General of Brigade (Generale di Brigata)
Colonel	Colonel (Oberst)	Colonel (Colonello)
Lieutenant Colonel	Lieutenant Colonel (Oberstleutnant)	Lieutenant Colonel (Tenente Colonello)
Major	Major (Major)	Major (Maggiore)
Captain	Captain (Hauptmann)	Captain (Capitano)
First Lieutenant	First Lieutenant (Oberleutnant)	First Lieutenant (Tenente)
Second Lieutenant	Second Lieutenant (Leutnant)	Second Lieutenant (Scottotenente)
None	Officer-Cadet (Fahnenjunker)	

Royal Air Force	U.S. Navy
Marshal of the Royal Air Force	Admiral of the Fleet
Air Chief Marshal	Admiral
Air Marshal	Vice Admiral
Air Vice Marshal	Rear Admiral
Air Commodore	Commodore
Group Captain	Captain
Wing Commander	Commander
Squadron Leader	Lieutenant Commander
Flight Lieutenant	Lieutenant
Flying Officer	Lieutenant, j.g. (Junior Grade)
Pilot Officer	Ensign

A P P E N D I X   2

EVOLUTION AND TITLES
OF THE HERMANN GOERING PANZER UNIT

February 17–July 17, 1933: Special Purposes Police Detachment Wecke (Polizeiabteilung z.b.V. Wecke)

July 17–December 22, 1933: Special Purposes State Police Group Wecke (Landespolizeigruppe Wecke z.b.V.)

December 22, 1933–April 1, 1935: "General Goering" Flak Regiment (Regiment "General Goering") (as part of Prussian State Police)

September 24, 1935–July 14, 1942: Regiment "General Goering" (as part of the Luftwaffe)

October 15, 1942–May 20, 1943: "Hermann Goering" Division (Division "Herman Goering")

May 21, 1943–January 6, 1944: "Hermann Goering" Panzer Division ("Hermann Goering" Panzerdivision)

January 6–September 30, 1944: "Hermann Goering" Parachute Panzer Division (Fallschirmpanzerdivision "Hermann Goering")

October 1, 1944–May 8, 1945: "Hermann Goering" Parachute Panzer Corps (Fallschirmpanzerdivision "Herman Goering") with 1st Hermann Goering Parachute Panzer Division (Fallschirm-Panzer-Division 1 Hermann Goering), 2nd Hermann Goering Parachute Panzer Grenadier Division (Fallschirm-Panzer-Grenadier-Division 2 Hermann Goering), activated on September 24, 1944, and the Hermann Goering Parachute Panzer Replacement and Training Brigade (Fallschirm-Panzer-Ers. und Ausb. Brigade Hermann Goering), activated in October 1944

SOURCES: Bender and Petersen, *H.G.*, p. 7; Tessin, vol. XIV, pp. 117–8.

A P P E N D I X   3

ORDER OF BATTLE, ITALIAN 6th ARMY, JULY 10, 1943

6th Army: Generale d'Armata Alfredo Guzzoni

XII Corps: Generale di Corpo Mario Arisio[1]
   202nd C.D. Div: Gen.d.Div. Ficalbi
   207th C.D. Div: Gen.d.Brig. Ottorine Schreiber[2]

208th C.D. Div
136th C.D. Regiment
Port Defense "N" (Palermo): Gen.d.Brig. Giuseppe Molinero

15th Panzer Grenadier Div: MG Eberhard Rodt
  104th Panzer Grenadier Rgt
  115th Panzer Grenadier Rgt
  129th Panzer Grenadier Rgt
  33rd Motorized Artillery Rgt
  215th Panzer Bn
  115th Panzer Reconnaissance Bn
  315th Anti-Aircraft Bn

28th (Aosta) Inf Div: Gen.d.Div. Giacomo Romano
  5th Inf Rgt
  6th Inf Rgt
  22nd Artillery Rgt
  Other smaller units (Blackshirt, engineer, support, etc.)

26th (Assietta) Division: Gen.d.Div. Erberto Papini[3]
  29th Inf Rgt
  30th Inf Rgt
  25th Artillery Rgt
  Assorted smaller units

Mobile Group A at Paceco: Lt. Col. Perrone
  HQ, 12th Light Tank Bn
  4th Co., 102nd Tank Bn
  1st Co., 133rd Artillery Bn (Self-Propelled)
  3rd Co., 448th Mobile C.D. Bn
  2nd Bty, 110th Artillery Bn

Mobile Group B at Santa Ninfa: Lt. Col. Mascio
  HQ, 133rd Artillery Bn (SP)
  3rd Co., 133rd Artillery Bn
  6th Co., 102nd Tank Bn (Renault/35's)
  1st and 2nd Cos., 448th Mobile C.D. Bn
  6th Bty, 233rd "Centauro" Artillery Bn (Motorized)

Mobile Group C at Portella Misilbesi (Maj. Finocchi)
  HQ, 102nd Tank Bn (Renault/35's)
  4th Co., 448th Mobile C.D. Bn
  5th Co., 102nd Tank Bn
  10th Bty, 4th Bn, 25th (Assietta) Artillery Rgt

Tactical Group Inchiapparo-Casale
  51st Bsersaglieri Bn
  One artillery battery

Tactical Group Alcamo-Partinico
  171st Fascist Militia (Blackshirt) Bn
  168th Fascist Militia (Blackshirt) Bn

Tactical Group Chiusa-Sclafani
  10th Bersaglieri Rgt (35th, 73rd, and 74th Bn.s)
  Two batteries of artillery
  One group of armored cars

Tactical Group Campobello di Licata-Ravanusa
  17th Fascist Militia (Blackshirt) Bn
  1st Bn, Cavalry Squadron "Palermo"

Other XII Corps Reserves
  19th "Centauro" Artillery Bn
  112th Machine Gun Bn
  12th Artillery Rgt
  7th Anti-Aircraft Bn
  133rd Artillery Bn (Self-Propelled)
  177th Bersaglieri Rgt

XVI Corps: Gen.d.Corpo Carlo Rossi
  206th C.D. Div: Gen.d.Div. Achille d'Havet
  213rd C.D. Div: Gen.d.Div. Carlo Gotti
  18th C.D. Bde: Gen.d.Brig. Orazio Mariscalco
  19th C.D. Bde: Gen.d.Brig. Giovanni Bocchetti
  Port Defense "E" (Catania): Gen.d.Brig. Azzo Passalacqua (434th and
    477th Inf Bn.s)
  54th (Napoli) Inf Div: Gen.d.Div. Count Giulio Cesare Gotti-Porcinari
    75th Inf Rgt
    76th Inf Rgt
    54th (Napoli) Artillery Rgt
    Other smaller units

Hermann Goering Panzer Division: LTG Paul Conrath
  Hermann Goering Panzer Rgt
  1st Hermann Goering Panzer Grenadier Rgt
  Hermann Goering Panzer Artillery Rgt
  Hermann Goering Panzer Reconnaissance Bn
  Hermann Goering Panzer Engineer Bn

Brigade Schmalz z.b.V.
  115th Panzer Grenadier Rgt (of 15th Pz Gren Div)
  IV/33rd Motorized Artillery Rgt (of 15th Pz Gren)
  904th Fortress Bn[4]
  923rd Fortress Bn[4]
  Fortress Bn "Reggio"[4]
  3rd Parachute Rgt[4]
  4th Parachute Rgt[4]
  1st Parachute Engineer Bn[4]
  Other smaller attached units

Mobile Group D at Misterbianco: Lt. Col. d'Andretta
  HQ, 101st Tank Bn
  3rd Co., 101st Tank Bn
  2nd Machine Gun Co. (on motorcycles) (18 guns)
  1st Co., 103rd Anti-Tank Bn (6 tanks w/47-mm guns)
  HQ, IVth Bn, 54th (Napoli) Artillery Rgt
  10th Bty, IV Bn, 54th (Napoli) Artillery Rgt

Mobile Group E at Niscemi (Captain Granieri)
  1st Co., 101st Tank Bn (Renault/35's)
  2nd Co., 102nd Anti-Tank Bn
  4th Co., 501st C.D. Bn
  155th Motorcycle Co.
  9th Bty, III/54th (Napoli) Artillery Rgt

Mobile Group F at Rosolini: Major Argenziano
  2nd Co., 101st Tank Bn (Renault/35's)
  1st Co., 102nd Anti-Tank Bn
  2nd Co., 542nd Coastal Bersaglieri Bn
  3rd Machine Gun Co. (on motorcycles)

Mobile Group G at Comiso: Col. Porcu
  169th Fascist Militia (Blackshirt) Bn
  3rd Co., 102nd Anti-Tank Bn
  1st Platoon, 2nd Co., 101st Tank Bn
  8th (Motorized) Bty, III/54th (Napoli) Artillery Rgt

Mobile Group H at San Pietro–Caltagirone: Lt. Col. Cixi
  3rd Co., 103rd Anti-Tank Bn
  2nd Tank Co. (Flat 3000's)
  Mortar Platoon of the Ist Bn, 76th Inf Rgt
  7th Bty, IV/54th (Napoli) Artillery Rgt

Tactical Group Barcellona
  7th Machine Gun Co. (on motorcycles)

One "Arditi" platoon of the 447th C.D. Bn
2nd Co., 103rd Anti-Tank Bn
12th Bty, IV/54th (Napoli) Artillery Rgt

Tactical Group Linguaglossa
58th Bersaglieri Bn
54th Motorcycle Co.
11th Bty, 54th (Napoli) Artillery Rgt

Tactical Group Carmito
4th Self-Propelled Artillery Bn (Lt. Col. Tropea)
53rd Motorcycle Co.

Tactical Group Comiso-Ispica
Headquarters, 173rd Fascist Militia (Blackshirt) Bn
173rd Fascist Militia Co.
2nd Co., 54th Mortar Bn
One anti-tank platoon
Ist Bn, 54th (Napoli) Artillery Rgt

Other XVI Corps Reserves
40th Artillery Rgt
230th Artillery Bn (Self-Propelled)

6th Army Reserves
4th (Livorno) Assault and Landing Div
33rd Inf Rgt
34th Inf Rgt
28th Artillery Rgt
4th Mortar Bn
4th Anti-Tank Bn (Self-Propelled)
11th Engineer Bn
Other divisional units

2nd Bn, 10th "Arditi" Rgt

10th Artillery Rgt
161st Artillery Bn
162nd Artillery Bn
163rd Artillery Bn

50th Artillery Bn

Naval Fortress Area Messina: Vice Admiral Pietro Barone[5]
Commander of Army Troops: Gen.d.Brig. Ettore Monacci
116th C.D. Rgt (deployed on coast of Calabria)
156th C.D. Bn

502th C.D. Bn
255th Artillery Bn

23rd Dismounted Cavalry Group
95th Fascist Militia (Blackshirt) Rgt
119th C.D. Rgt (deployed on coast of Sicily)
    370th C.D. Bn
    371st C.D. Bn
    503rd C.D. Bn

158th Artillery Bn
Fourteen dual-purpose antinaval and antiaircraft batteries
Thirty-eight antiaircraft batteries

Naval Fortress Area Augusta-Syracuse: Rear Adm Primo Leonardi[5]

Commander of Army Troops: Col. Mario Damiani
    121st C.D. Rgt
        246th C.D. Bn
        385th C.D. Bn
        504th C.D. Bn
        540th C.D. Bn

One battalion of naval personnel
One battalion of air force personnel
Six coastal medium and heavy antinaval batteries
Eleven dual-purpose antinaval and antiaircraft batteries
Six antiaircraft batteries
One armored train of four 120-mm guns

Naval Fortress Area Trapani: Rear Adm Giuseppe Manfredi[5]
    137th C.D. Rgt
        443rd C.D. Bn
        505th C.D. Bn
        844th C.D. Bn

Several antinaval batteries
Nine dual-purpose antinaval and antiaircraft batteries
Four armored trains (120-mm and 76-mm guns)
Several squadrons of motor torpedo boats (Captain Mimbelli)

[1]Replaced by Generale di Corpo Francesco Zingales on July 12.
[2]Succeeded by Colonel Augusto de Laurentiis.
[3]Succeeded by Generale di Divisione Ottorino Schreiber on July 26.
[4]Attached between July 12 and July 18.
[5]Not under the control of the 6th Army.

APPENDIX 4

ORDER OF BATTLE, 15th ARMY GROUP, JULY 10, 1943

15th Army Group: Gen. Sir Harold R. L. G. Alexander
British 8th Army: Gen. Sir Bernard L. Montgomery

XIII Corps: LTG Miles Dempsey
  5th Inf. Div.: MG H. P. M. Berney-Ficklin (replaced by MG G. C. Bucknall on Aug. 3, 1943)

  13th Inf. Bde.
    2nd Cameronians
    2nd Inniskillings
    2nd Wiltshire

  15th Inf. Bde.
    1st Green Howards
    1st King's Own Yorkshire Light Infantry

  17th Inf. Bde.
    2nd Royal Scots Fusiliers
    2nd Northamptonshire
    6th Seaforth Highlanders

  Divisional Troops
    91st Field Regiment, Royal Artillery
    92nd Field Regiment, R.A.
    156th Field Regiment, R.A.
    18th Light Anti-Aircraft Regiment, R.A.
    5th Reconnaissance Regiment
    52nd Anti-Tank Regiment
    Assorted smaller units (MG, engineers, etc.)

  50th (Northumbrian) Inf. Div.: MG Sidney K. Kirkman
  69th Inf Bde
    5th East Yorkshire
    6th Green Howards
    7th Green Howards

  151st Inf. Bde. (Durham Light Infantry Bde)
    6th Durham Light Infantry
    7th Durham Light Infantry
    8th Durham Light Infantry

168th Inf. Bde.
  1st London Irish
  1st London Scottish
  10th Royal Berkshire

Divisional Troops
  74th Field Regiment, R.A.
  90th Field Regiment, R.A.
  124th Field Regiment, R.A.
  25th Light Anti-Aircraft Regiment, R.A.
  102nd Anti-Tank Regiment
  Assorted smaller units (MG, engineers, etc.)

1st British Airborne Div.: MG G. F. Hopkinson
  1st Parachute Brigade
    1st Battalion, the Parachute Regiment
    2nd Battalion, the Parachute Regiment
    3rd Battalion, the Parachute Regiment

  2nd Parachute Brigade
    4th Battalion, the Parachute Regiment
    5th Battalion, the Parachute Regiment
    6th Battalion, the Parachute Regiment

  4th Parachute Brigade
    10th Battalion, the Parachute Regiment
    11th Battalion, the Parachute Regiment
    156th Battalion, the Parachute Regiment

  1st Airlanding Brigade
    1st Battalion, the Border Regiment
    2nd Battalion, South Staffordshire Regiment
    The Glider Pilot Regiment

  Divisional Troops
    1st Airlanding Light Regiment, R.A.
    Smaller units (antiaircraft, antitank, engineers, etc.)

Corps Reserve
  4th Armoured Brigade
  44th Royal Tank Regiment

XXXth Corps: LTG Sir Oliver Leese
  51st (Highland) Inf. Div.: MG Douglas Wimberley
    152nd Inf. Bde.
    5th Queen's Own Cameron Highlanders

2nd Seaforth Highlanders
5th Seaforth Highlanders

153rd Inf. Bde.
5th Black Watch
5th/7th Gordon Highlanders
1st Gordon Highlanders

154th Inf. Bde.
1st Black Watch
7th Black Watch
7th Argyll and Sutherland Highlanders

Divisional Troops
126th Field Regiment, R.A.
127th Field Regiment, R.A.
128th Field Regiment, R.A.
40th Light Anti-Aircraft Regiment
61st Anti-Tank Regiment
Assorted smaller units

1st Canadian Inf. Div.: MG Guy G. Simonds
1st Inf Bde
The Royal Canadian Regiment
The Hastings and Prince Edward Regiment
48th Highlanders

2nd Inf. Bde.
The Loyal Edmonton Regiment
Princess Patricia's Canadian Light Infantry
The Seaforth Highlanders

3rd Inf. Bde.
Royal 22e Regiment
The Carleton and York Regiment
The West Nova Scotia Regiment

Divisional Troops
Three Rivers Regiment (attached from 1st Canadian Armoured
Regiment)
1st Field Regiment, R.C.H.A.
2nd Regiment, R.C.A.
3rd Regiment, R.C.A.
4th Princess Louise Dragoon Guards (4th Recon Regiment)
1st Anti-Tank Regiment
Assorted smaller units

231st (Malta) Inf. Bde.: Brig. Roy E. Urquhart
  1st Battalion, the Dorsetshire Regiment
  1st Battalion, the Hampshire Regiment
  2nd Battalion, the Devonshire Regiment

Corps Reserve:
  1st Canadian Army Tank Brigade: Brig. R. A. Wyman
    The Ontario Regiment
    The Calgary Regiment

  23rd Armoured Brigade: Brig. G. W. Richards
    40th Royal Tank Regiment
    46th Royal Tank Regiment
    50th Royal Tank Regiment

8th Army Reserve
  Number 3 Commando
  Special Service Bde: Brigadier R. E. Laycock
    40th Royal Marine Commando
    41st Royal Marine Commando
  2nd Special Air Service Regiment
  78th Inf. Div.: MG Vivian Evelegh
    11th Inf. Bde.
      2nd Battalion, the Lancashire Fusiliers
      1st Battalion, the East Surrey Regiment
      5th Battalion, the Northamptonshire Regiment
    36th Inf. Bde.
      6th Battalion, The Royal West Kent Regiment
      5th Battalion, The Royal East Kent Regiment (the Buffs)
      8th Battalion, the Argyll and Sutherland Highlanders
    38th (Irish) Inf. Bde.
      6th Battalion, the Royal Inniskilling Fusiliers
      1st Battalion, the Royal Irish Fusiliers
      2nd Battalion, the London Irish Rifles

  Divisional Troops
    17th Field Regiment, R.A.
    132nd Field Regiment, R.A.
    138th Field Regiment, R.A.
    49th Light Anti-Aircraft Regiment
    56th Reconnaissance Regiment
    64th Anti-Tank Regiment
    Assorted smaller units

U.S. 7th Army: LTG George S. Patton, Jr.

IInd Corps: MG Omar N. Bradley

1st Infantry Division: MG Terry Allen (replaced by MG Clarence R. Huebner, August 9, 1943)
    16th Inf. Regiment
    18th Inf. Regiment
    26th Inf. Regiment
    Division Artillery (DIVARTY)
        5th Field Artillery Battalion
        7th Field Artillery Battalion
        32nd Field Artillery Battalion
        33rd Field Artillery Battalion
    1st Engineer Combat Battalion

Attached
    Force X: Colonel Darby
        1st Ranger Battalion
        4th Ranger Battalion
    1st Battalion, 39th Combat Engineer Regiment
    67th Armored Regiment (–)

45th Infantry Division: MG Troy H. Middleton
    157th Inf. Regiment
    179th Inf. Regiment
    180th Inf. Regiment
    Division Artillery (DIVARTY)
        158th Field Artillery Battalion
        160th Field Artillery Battalion
        171st Field Artillery Battalion
        189th Field Artillery Battalion
    120th Engineer Combat Battalion
Attached
    753rd Medium Tank Battalion

82nd Airborne Division: MG Matthew Ridgway
    504th Parachute Inf. Regiment
    505th Parachute Inf. Regiment
    325th Glider Inf. Regiment
    3rd Infantry Division: MG Lucian K. Truscott
        7th Inf. Regiment
        15th Inf. Regiment
        30th Inf. Regiment
        Division Artillery (DIVARTY)
            9th Field Artillery Battalion

10th Field Artillery Battalion
39th Field Artillery Battalion
41st Field Artillery Battalion
10th Engineer Battalion

Attached Units
  36th Combat Engineer Regiment
  3rd Ranger Battalion
  5th Armored Field Artillery Group
  77th Field Artillery Regiment
  2nd Battalion, 36th Field Artillery Regiment
  Combat Command A, 2nd Armored Division:
    66th Armored Regiment (–)
    41st Armored Infantry Regiment (–)
    Elements, 82nd Reconnaissance Squadron
    14th Armored Field Artillery Battalion

7th Army Floating Reserve
  2nd Armored Division
    Combat Command B
      67th Armored Regiment (–)
      82nd Reconnaissance Squadron (–)
      17th Armored Engineer Battalion
      78th Armored Field Artillery Battalion
      92nd Armored Field Artillery Battalion
      1st Battalion, 41st Armored Inf. Regiment
  18th Infantry Regiment (1st Inf Div)

7th Army Nondivisional Units
  540th Engineer Shore Regiment
  Various other units

15th Army Group Floating Reserve
  9th Infantry Division: MG Manton S. Eddy
    39th Inf. Regiment
    47th Inf. Regiment
    60th Inf. Regiment
    Divisional Artillery
      26th Field Artillery Bn.
      34th Field Artillery Bn.
      60th Field Artillery Bn.
      84th Field Artillery Bn.

INDEX